THE SELF:
FROM SOUL TO BRAIN

ANNALS OF THE NEW YORK ACADEMY OF SCIENCES
Volume 1001

THE SELF:
FROM SOUL TO BRAIN

Edited by Joseph LeDoux, Jacek Debiec, and Henry Moss

The New York Academy of Sciences
New York, New York
2003

Library of Congress Cataloging-in-Publication Data

The self: from soul to brain / Joseph LeDoux, Jacek Debiec, and Henry Moss.
　　p. cm. — (Annals of the New York Academy of Sciences ; v. 1001)
　　Includes bibliographical references and indexes.
　　ISBN 1-57331-450-1 (cloth : alk. paper) . — ISBN 1-57331-451-X (pbk. : alk. paper)
　　1. Self—Congresses. I. LeDoux, Joseph. II. Debiec, Jacek. III. Moss, Henry. IV. Series.
Q11.N5 vol. 1001
[BF697]
500 s—dc21
[155　　　　　　　　　　　　　　　　　　　　　　　　　　　　　　　2003018198

GYAT/PCP
Printed in the United States of America
ISBN 1-57331-450-1 (cloth)
ISBN 1-57331-451-X (paper)
ISSN 0077-8923

ANNALS OF THE NEW YORK ACADEMY OF SCIENCES

Volume 1001
October 2003

THE SELF:
FROM SOUL TO BRAIN

Editors
JOSEPH LEDOUX, JACEK DEBIEC, AND HENRY MOSS

Conference Organizers
JOSEPH LEDOUX AND JACEK DEBIEC

Conference Advisors
MICHAEL S. GAZZANIGA AND JEROME KAGAN

This volume is the result of a conference entitled **The Self: From Soul to Brain** held by the New York Academy of Sciences on September 26–28, 2002 in New York, New York.

CONTENTS

Part III. Implicit Selves

Part IV. Biological Basis of the Self

Financial assistance was received from:

Major funder
• **MUSHETT FAMILY FOUNDATION, INC.**

Supporter
• **THE GLICKENHAUS FOUNDATION**

In-kind support
• **FISHBERG RESEARCH CENTER FOR NEUROBIOLOGY OF
THE MOUNT SINAI SCHOOL OF MEDICINE**

Preface

JOSEPH E. LeDOUX AND JACEK DEBIEC

Center for Neural Science, New York University,
New York, New York 10003, USA

"Who am I?" This universal query has inspired theologians, philosophers, poets, and artists throughout history. From their musings, we have inherited notions—such as the soul, spirit, mind, self, and person—that have shaped our view for millennia of who we are as individuals, as members of social groups, and as a species.

Though traditionally the province of the humanities, questions about the self have begun to be tackled by modern science. Within the sciences, there are two broad approaches—one taken by social scientists (including cultural anthropologists, sociologists, and psychologists) and the other by natural scientists (especially neuroscientists and cognitive scientists). To date, the more common approach has come from the social sciences. This approach, which is closely aligned with the traditional view in the humanities, views the self as a distinctly human achievement closely associated with the human capacity for consciousness, and thus, for self-reflection and self-awareness, and, through introspective reflection, enlightenment or therapy, self-improvement. The unconscious mind, by contrast, is typically viewed as a storehouse of bestial impulses and a source of trouble rather than of healthy mental activity.

Cognitive and brain scientists, though generally less interested in questions about the self, have in recent years begun to consider this puzzle. And the view that is emerging—that the self normally involves processes that operate both consciously and unconsciously—is somewhat different from that traditionally espoused in the humanities and social sciences. The unconscious processes viewed as relevant to the self are diverse, and include aspects of normal perceptual, memory, and emotional functions. Particularly important is the fact that these functions are, at least to some extent, evolutionarily conserved across mammalian species, allowing aspects of the self that depend on these functions to be explored through studies of other creatures, regardless of whether those creatures have the capacity for consciousness and self-awareness. Because animal studies are essential to progress in relating mind and behavior to detailed brain mechanisms, this conception of the self in terms of component processes, such as memory and emotion, makes neuroscience research on these processes relevant to the self.

Ann. N.Y. Acad. Sci. 1001: vii–viii (2003). © 2003 New York Academy of Sciences.
doi: 10.1196/annals.1279.019

How, then, do these diverse views and approaches to the self in the humanities, social sciences and cognitive and brain sciences relate? This was the main question that inspired the New York Academy of Sciences conference "The Self: From Soul to Brain," which took place in September 2002 at the Mount Sinai School of Medicine. There were 16 invited speakers—drawn from neuroscience, cognitive science, social and developmental psychology, anthropology, philosophy, and theology—and more than 600 registered audience members. In addition to delivering addresses, the speakers engaged in stimulating discussions among one another, and with members of the audience. Many of the key papers are reproduced in this volume.

As organizers, we would like to thank a number of people who made the conference possible. First, our gratitude goes to all the speakers, some of whom traveled considerable distances to participate. We also want to thank the audience for their attention and participation. In planning the meeting, construction of the final list of speakers was helped tremendously by numerous consultations with Jerome Kagan of Harvard and Mike Gazzaniga of Dartmouth. The NYAS was a wonderful collaborator in all phases of planning and organizing the meeting, as well as in carrying it off and publishing the proceedings. It was a pleasure to work with them. The conference could not have happened without the support of Rashid Shaikh, Director of Science Programs at the NYAS. He immediately saw the value of such a conference and was behind the concept all the way. Henry Moss, in the same office, was tireless in seeking funding and in planning for the meeting as well as a diligent colleague in editing this volume. Rashid and Henry also played important roles in helping us conceptualize the conference and also in helping us limit the scope in a way that was feasible within the format of a three-day meeting. Sherryl Usmani in the NYAS conference office did an outstanding job of coordinating all the details required to make such a complex event run smoothly. And Justine Cullinan of the Academy's *Annals* series assembled, edited, and oversaw the publication of the papers, a huge task that she made seem simple. The Mount Sinai School of Medicine provided a wonderful auditorium for the event. Financial support came from the Mushett Family Foundation and the Glickenhaus Foundation, and in-kind support was provided by the Fishberg Research Center of the Mount Sinai School of Medicine.

The goal of this conference was not to settle the question about what the self is. The aim was instead to highlight some of the variety in the different approaches, and to look for common points of interest, as well as conceptual gaps. We hope that the conference, and this volume, will thus help to advance efforts in this area, especially future attempts to reconcile the diverse perspectives on this complex concept.

Implicit Selves

A Review of the Conference

HENRY MOSS

New York Academy of Sciences, New York, New York 10021, USA

Know Thyself?, or, Know Thy Self? The first implies a personal, first-hand review of who one is, based upon subjective knowledge, self-awareness, and self-consciousness. The second implies a more objective notion, a self that can be studied in its own right and, potentially, by someone other than its owner. Neuroscientist **Joseph LeDoux,** organizer of the conference,[1] suggests starting with the idea that the self of self-awareness is only a part and perhaps only a small part of a broader, objective self that is mostly unconscious or implicit. The idea that there are unconscious aspects of self is not new, of course, having been discussed by cognitive psychology, psychodynamic theory, social psychology, and cognitive anthropology over many decades. Even Socrates, who encouraged us all to know ourselves, maintained that the human mind is born with innate knowledge that is expressed under quite normal circumstances, as when he demonstrates in the *Meno* that an illiterate slave boy could reason perfectly about geometrical forms. What has been less considered, and what LeDoux establishes in his opening presentation, is that the unconscious or implicit aspects of self must be grounded *somewhere*, and that this somewhere must be the brain, and, in particular, its network of synapses:

> Because you are a unique individual, the particular multifaceted aspects of the self that define "you" are present in your brain alone. And in order for you to remain who you are from minute to minute, day to day, and year to year, your brain must somehow retain the essence of who you are over time. In the end, then, the self is essentially a memory, or more accurately, a set of memories.[2]

Of course if our "selves" are our brains, or, more accurately, the synaptic connections and systems that capture our experiences and memories, and express our habits and dispositions, and, if most of this exists unconsciously or implicitly, then we are faced with the eerie prospect of perhaps not knowing

Address for correspondence: Henry Moss, Ph.D., Program Associate, New York Academy of Sciences, 2 East 63rd Street, New York, NY 10021. Voice: 212-838-0230; fax: 212-838-5640.
  hmoss@libi.edu

Ann. N.Y. Acad. Sci. 1001: 1–30 (2003). © 2003 New York Academy of Sciences.
doi: 10.1196/annals.1279.001

precisely who we are at any given moment. LeDoux supposes that some will be unhappy with such a conclusion, thinking that the psychological, social, and spiritual aspects of who we are would be compromised by such objectivity. But he stresses that synapses "are simply the brain's way of receiving, storing, and retrieving our personalities, as determined by all the psychological, cultural, and other factors .... We don't sacrifice the other ways of understanding existence ... [and] a neural understanding of human nature in fact broadens ... our sense of who we are."[3]

The theme of the symposium was thus established by LeDoux: How can an understanding of the neural aspects of our implicit or unconscious selves contribute to a better understanding of ourselves, one consistent with our explicit, psychological, social, and spiritual selves?

FICTIONAL SELVES?

Several of the conference talks focused on social and psychological aspects of the construction and maintenance of implicit selves. One of the obvious characteristics of our explicit or conscious selves is the subjective sense of unity and continuity over time. If our implicit selves are but a collection of memories and dispositions associated with a vast, distributed complex of neurons and neural systems, how do they support this sense of unity and continuity? Some investigations have yielded surprising results.

One of the more well-known sets of results was reviewed by **Michael Gazzaniga** on the basis of decades of work with split-brain patients. Gazzaniga used these patients to figure out how the mind effectively unifies the multiplicity of modules and capacities that make up a human brain and mind. These neural devices emerged in evolution to carry out specialized perceptual and conceptual tasks involved in navigating the world. Gazzaniga hypothesizes that such highly distributed semantic and perceptual processing requires a distinct neural locus for narrative unification, a place that generates a coherent, stable, and continuous sense of self.

To figure out how and where the brain creates a unified self, it is first necessary to show that self-processing in the brain is, at least in part, a special function, and not just an extension of general semantic and cognitive processing. Gazzaniga described recent work by his colleague William Kelley,[4] using event-related fMRI, which demonstrates that self-related semantic processing, in this case the use of trait-related adjectives, shows selective activation for self-judgment in the medial prefrontal cortex. A recent neuropsychological case study by Klein *et al.*[5] supports this conclusion, finding that an elderly patient with impoverished semantic and episodic knowledge still showed high accuracy in self-recognition semantic tasks. Many other studies have demonstrated that the brain is highly tuned to key aspects of the environment, such as family, faces, and other minds. It would hardly be surprising to find a special brain orientation toward self-related conceptual and perceptual processing.

So self-processing is specialized. The problem, however, is that the various self-processing functions, from self-percept recognition to autobiographical memory, appear fairly widely distributed through the cortex, and across both left and right brain. Indeed, it has been shown that each brain can function autonomously to a degree with many self-processing functions intact. Does each have its own self? No, says Gazzaniga. The capacity for self-awareness seems limited to the left brain. Extensive split-brain studies have shown that the right brain will iteratively process what it receives and no more. It will neither generate, nor be interested in, a unified story or continuous self. But then how does this left brain absorb the right brain's capacities into a single continuous and unified self? More generally, how does the brain-mind unify many distinct and distributed mental modules and their contents into a coherent self?

The short answer implied by Gazzaniga's experiments is: the mind just makes it up. It creates a fictional self. "98% of what the brain does is outside of conscious awareness," says Gazzaniga in the chapter "Fictional Self" in his 1998 *The Mind's Past*.[6] What enters consciousness is in the end a highly selective, interpreted, and biased self concept:

> There seems always to be a private narrative taking place inside each of us. It consists partly of the effort to fashion a coherent whole from the thousands of systems we have inherited to cope with challenges.[7]

The split-brain experiments tested this "coherent narrative" and found that indeed the left brain would routinely invent stories to explain what the right brain experienced, even though it had not experienced it itself. If told or shown what the right brain chose to match a picture that the left brain didn't see, the left brain invariably invented a plausible, but totally fictitious, story to make it coherent with what it itself had seen or experienced. The results were similar for memory and reasoning tasks, and robust enough for Gazzaniga to posit the existence of an "interpreter" module in the left brain, whose purpose is to unify the multiplicity of experiences and functions into a single self-constituting narrative.

Why does it do this? Gazzaniga hypothesizes that the interpreter emerged as an adaptive extension of our ability to reason in a predictive mode and in social-collective contexts. For social reasoning to be effective, we must presume its inherent value and its enhancement of personal standing, to declare, at least to ourselves, that we are "good people, that we are in control and mean to do good."[8] "It is the glue that unifies our story and creates our sense of being a whole, rational agent."[9] And this occurs, one supposes, even despite ourselves.

Psychologist **Daniel Wegner** took up this "fictional self," but from a different vantage point, and independent of the neural aspect. He concentrated on the notion of free will and the sense that the conscious self is the author of actions. He suggests that if we set aside the idea that thoughts *cause* actions and instead think about how the mind *attributes* causation of action to itself, we can better understand the significant role of unconscious factors in our otherwise explicit self-characterizations. Through a series of subtle experiments, Wegner and colleagues have shown that if the experience of causation shows semantic consistency, a sense of priority in time, and a sense of exclusivity from other possible sources, then the mind will attribute authorship to itself. It will do this even if it is clearly not, in fact, the author of the action. We can easily trick our minds into thinking they caused an action, and we can see in syndromes like schizophrenia that minds can sometimes dissociate themselves from actions they have in fact caused. It gets worse, though. The mind must simplify substantially, given the huge mass of experiences and actions that engage us minute to minute, selecting only some actions for self-attribution. This necessarily generates a selection bias, a self that can literally ignore whole aspects of experience and memory. Our self-portrait, he suggests, bears only on aspects of experience that interest us in some way:

> Evidence…suggests that this self-portrait may be a humble and misleading caricature of the mind's operation—but one that underlies the feeling of authorship and the acceptance of responsibility for action.[10]

The interesting experiences, then, are those that relate to authorship and acceptance of responsibility. Wegner also goes on to hypothesize that humans evolved mechanisms suitable to working in social collectives, including a way to interpret the motives, goals, and intentions of others, with the further ability to attribute value to them—good or bad. These same evolved mental mechanisms would of necessity reflect back to the self, so that it may relate its own goals and intentions to this collectivity, and to attribute value to them as well. This value-creating inner sense Wegner calls an "authorship emotion," the basis for empathy and moral engagement. The emotion, he suggests, is caused by unconscious pre-experiences or "previews" of intended actions as self-disclosed to the mind in given situations. Separable from the actual physical source of action, this preview–emotion–action pathway, though more a work of art than fact, nonetheless serves us well, providing a coherent explicit self and anchoring our "moral evaluation of self":

> Moral actions…need not be traceable to a mind for the owner of that mind to experience moral emotions. All that is needed is the occurrence of previews, and the subsequent self-attribution of authorship and results…. We become selves by experiencing what we do, and this experience then informs the processes that determine what we will do next.[11]

The self, then, is a kind of flowing self-portrait, created and recreated from salient experiences in a social collective built on moral valuations.

Daniel Schacter's work further elaborates the idea that our minds are engaged in an unconscious process of selection, interpretation, and distortion.

His starting point is the psychology of memory, which LeDoux had already identified as the essence of the self. His research keys in on what he calls the "sins" or flaws in memory systems. Looked at differently, these turn out not to be flaws, but aspects of the normal maintenance of our conscious and unconscious selves. From among the seven "sins" Schacter focused on two that bear directly on the self: misattribution errors and bias errors.

Investigators have shown that our memory of past events involves far more than explicit recall of distinct experiences. This is one reason why it is so difficult to program computers to function like humans. For most of our everyday life we rely only the "gist" of what happens, not the details. If you prep normal subjects with a cluster of related words (e.g. "sugar," "candy," "sour," or "good-tasting"), they will adamantly insist later that they heard or saw a related word, for example, "sweet," even if they hadn't. As Schacter points out in his *Seven Sins of Memory,* gist memory probably makes evolutionary sense, substantially streamlining the learning and recall process to focus on valuable survival needs.[12] Many amnesiacs lose both explicit and gist memory even though, as Schacter, LeDoux and others point out, they generally retain typical implicit memory capacities, including learning new skills and responding to priming and conditioning stimuli. There is a deep relationship, then, between explicit and gist memory, implying that our minds, at best, reconstruct the past approximately, according to a "best guess" strategy. We see, again, that fictionalization is an intimate aspect of the construction of a self.

Schacter makes the same point when examining bias errors. He discusses three types of bias relevant to the self: egocentric bias, consistency bias, and cognitive dissonance.

Egocentric bias is the ubiquitous tendency to interpret the past in self-enhancing ways. Many robust studies have confirmed this bias, and its universality leads Schacter to suppose that it, too, has adaptive value, implying an affective or value factor that reminds us of Wegner's "emotion of authorship" and Gazzaniga's sense of being "in control." Schacter describes imaging studies that locate selective activation for this bias in the medial prefrontal cortex, implying an evolved capacity, and not just a stronger reinforcement of normal memory circuits. This brain system mediates the encoding and retrieval of self-related memories, and, once again, we find it engaged in fictionalization.

Consistency bias also echoes the Wegner and Gazzaniga themes and again demonstrates the tendency for distortion and exaggeration in our self-conceptions. Here the mind attempts to maintain consistency over time, to preserve the sense of a stable self as author of actions and beliefs. Schacter notes studies showing that subjects who report a type of belief, say a political opinion, early on and then, when revisited years later, report obviously changed beliefs will nonetheless recall their past beliefs in a manner consistent with their current beliefs.

If emotions are involved in self-stability and self-enhancement, then it is clear that these "fallacies" run deep in our evolved natures. The third bias defect, cognitive dissonance, reinforces this idea. We engage in this fallacy when confronted with conflicting beliefs, thoughts, and feelings. Our memory system works hard to iron out the dissonance, and its emotional effects, and return the mind to a stable state, even if it means distorting the past in sometimes significant ways.

Schacter's group have performed clever experiments to show that these types of biases occur unconsciously and are part of the implicit memory system. Amnesics, for example, show an intact ability for all bias distortions, even though explicit memory systems are broken, and even gist systems are dysfunctional. So they must run deep within our mental machinery and within our primary cognitive brain systems, further reinforcing the idea that the implicit self is much of what we call the Self, and that much of the implicit self is, well, made up of distortions and half-truths.

Social psychologist **Mahzarin Banaji** and colleagues have uncovered still other aspects of self that show the effect of implicit, unconscious factors and their ability to distort and fictionalize. Going directly to the collective, social context in which salient self-identity emotions and biases are expressed, Banaji demonstrated the special and powerful role of group identity in shaping self-identity. In a manner similar to Schacter's cognitive dissonance "sin," implicit, historical, emotional investments in group identities can find themselves in conflict with explicit self-conceptions that, for various reasons, are needed to navigate social terrain.

Banaji's most well-known experiments in this area relate to hidden or implicit social bias. Using liberal college students who profess no conscious stereotyping, Banaji and colleague Brian Nosek tested for hidden racial, age, national, and gender bias by using rapid association tests, dubbed Implicit Association Tests or IATs. These require responses to visual and linguistic stimuli too quick to allow for rational consideration. The results over many thousands of tests are quite robust, revealing unconscious biases across the board, and leading Banaji to suggest that group identity bias indeed runs deep: "It is a by-product of the ordinary ways we think, feel, and learn. In some senses, to not show these effects is to not be able to think, not be able to perceive the world...."[13]

We have here then an interesting challenge to investigators wrestling with the nature of the self and implicit memory. Is group identity so deeply embedded as to make bias a largely unchangeable fact of life, a conclusion that would have large implications for political life and social policy? Banaji is deeply concerned with this question and feels that one cannot dismiss the science in addressing the implications. Indeed, in a unique collaboration with LeDoux's lab, she had her findings mapped across the neural domain, finding a close correspondence between the social-psychological patterns and activation of emotional centers in the brain, including the amygdala.[14]

In other research, Banaji has associated these implicit biases with aspects of self-evaluation. Starting with the well-documented fact that most people place a positive valence on self when making judgments of all sorts, researchers have been able to demonstrate quite robust extensions of this positive evaluation with first-order linkages. If one thinks positively about oneself and is from New York, tests show a stronger positive evaluation of other New Yorkers, and a striking predisposition to associate oneself with a "New Yorker" in-group, if formed or hypothesized. The same holds for situations involving ownership, surface similarity, and even preference for the letters in one's name. In this fashion, Banaji shows that not only do we have implicit biases concerning outside groups, but that we build our self-concept accordingly, and with it our attitudes, self-esteem, and stereotypes. Remarkably, women who like math form a weaker positive group association for "women-who-like-math" than men of the same order of preference, exposing the deeper linkages that make up the self-conception of these women.

Banaji suggests that the first step forward is to recognize the problem: "These biases may be more pervasive than we thought…they often stand in opposition to our conscious beliefs… [and] this asks with a new urgency, what it is we wish to do in a variety of domains."[15] In this case the contortions exercised by the self to "cure" the cognitive dissonance and override the emotional conflict between the "good" me and the "biased" me do not in fact cure the problem at all, but simply put it into an unconscious dimension:

> All programs promoting equal opportunity seek the removal of external constraints for individual pursuits. Yet, until the internal, mental constraints that link group identity with preference are removed, the patterns of self-imposed segregation may not change.[16]

Identifying and dealing with these internal constraints is precisely what is at stake in the science that addresses the fictionalizing self, and the modes of interaction between implicit and explicit aspects of self. If, as suggested by Banaji and indeed all the presenters, the self has an emotional, even moral, stake in the outcome, then we can perhaps look forward to a widening of the circle of group identity as we become more conscious of our biases. There is reason to think that this has been the historical trend, at least in some parts of the world.

CULTURAL SELVES

The fictionalizing self draws out the powerful connection between how we function in a social collective, and how our brains organize vast arrays of experiences into narratives adequate to this functioning, using emotion-based mechanisms that reinforce positive values. Cognitive anthropologist **Naomi Quinn** is not surprised that neuroscientists like LeDoux and Gazzaniga are finding powerful neural instantiation for implicit selves or that Banaji's hidden prejudices would show up on fMRI screens. "Cultural knowledge," according to Quinn, "…is overwhelmingly implicitly transmitted, and outside conscious self-awareness."[17]

If this account is on the right track, we should see it reflected in the way children are socialized and acquire a sociocultural identity. Child-rearing, the most powerful of identity-shaping processes, should provide a window into the process of implicit self formation. Quinn shows just that, arguing that, although child rearing practices vary widely from culture to culture, there is indeed an underlying similarity in the way identity, emotion, and moral self-perception are incorporated, which, once unpacked, bears resemblance to the neural and psychological accounts of implicit selves. "Recent cross-cultural studies of child development reveal that child rearing…is everywhere designed to make a child's experience of important lessons constant, to link those lessons to emotional arousal, and to connect them to evaluations of the child's goodness and badness."[18]

In her talk, Quinn presented ethnographic snapshots of several diverse cultural child-rearing practices that she and her collaborators have been studying: American, Chinese, German, Gusii (Kenya), Ifaluk (Micronesia), and Inuit (Baffin Island). In every case, she finds constancy, emotional arousal, and moral valuation at work as adults consciously pursue a "proper" socialization of children.

Constancy of experience probably creates embedded neural patterns or "cognitive schemas," suggests Quinn, which form a substratum for the socialization process. It need not be the same kind of constancy from culture to culture, but there must nonetheless be constancy. Gusii mothers, for example, intent on developing "calm" babies, have a repertoire of behaviors that reinforce their preference for calmness, such as refusing to make eye contact with a child acting silly. Slowly the child unconsciously connects certain behaviors with parental or social attitude.

Emotional arousal deepens this patterning and associates the desired behavior pattern with positive and negative feelings. Simple approval or disapproval of behaviors is itself emotionally arousing, but most cultures go deeper, including beating, frightening, teasing, shaming and the like. Quinn believes that LeDoux's emotional conditioning is at work here: "Hormones released during emotional arousal actually strengthen synaptic connections…and [this] coordinates and organizes brain activity."[19] Moreover, these lessons become indelibly associated with the emotional arousal itself, leading the child, according to Quinn, to overtly seek to maximize praise and minimize negative emotion.

Finally, *moral valuation* is at work, bringing the experiential process into some rational perspective as the child comes to learn what is good and bad, usually associated with being loved or unloved. Parents and others in all cultures constantly use expressions of moral valuation in response to specific behaviors, no matter how much these behaviors may vary from culture to culture. Quinn describes how Taiwanese parents use a shaming emotion and its moral associations. Inuits do the same through teasing. And Quinn concludes by having us listen to Chubby Maata, an Inuit child, tossing over and over her own emerging self-evaluation, "I am good; I am not good; I am good; I am not good...." There is a connection here, we suppose, with the kinds social emotions posited by Gazzaniga, Wegner, and Schacter as central for framing a self.

Child rearing, by its nature, is a powerful means of shaping the implicit self and giving it a cultural stamp. **Hazel Rose Markus**, a social psychologist, suggests that we can generalize this point and show how cultural models are at the core of individual identities. If neural patterns, derived from experience and memory reinforcement through the emotional brain, are the basis of our implicit selves, then we should be able to see this process at work, dynamically, throughout the lifetime, and in the building and maintenance of local customs and institutions.

Agreeing with the general idea that socially related emotions are central to the construction of the self and its unity, Markus goes further, and suggests that this process is bounded, and that the local, cultural context is the key determining factor. Socialization is not a mere shaping of individual identity by a social environment. It is rather a context for agency and it is through individual actions and choices that cultures are both realized and maintained. Culturally situated agency is the way implicit selves are expressed and reinforced:

> Humans don't interact with objective worlds "out there," but are constructors of socially shared reality. These sorts of models should not be thought of as sources of bias and selection; instead they are frameworks that hold the worlds that we create together. They are the mortar for our perceptions and the scaffoldings of our actions... [W]e can't feel their press, but they are there.... Models of agency lead a double life: internal and materialized and objectified in our institutions, practices, and artifacts, and played out in our everyday social interactions.[20]

Our implicit cultural selves, then, are not just superficially cultural, but cultural to the core, affecting even the most innocent of choices. In a clever experiment, the investigators in Markus's lab carried out a simple choice task with individuals patterned by distinct cultural models. In one case it compared "individualistic" Euro-Americans and "collectivistic" East Asians, where the task was to choose a "reward" from among five pens, one or two of which were quite distinctive relative to the other pens. Euro-Americans chose the distinctive pen significantly more often than did the Asians. The findings were quite robust, and were found to select between other groups, including high school-educated Americans vs. college-educated Americans, and Korean-Americans in the U.S. vs. those visiting Korea (using, in effect, dual cultural schemas.) Individuals in cultures that emphasized individual initiative and self-expression acted according to their cultural model, and those that emphasized connectedness to family and others acted according to theirs.

In another experiment with Euro-American and East Asian cultural typology, investigators asked children to select the topics of anagrams they were to then complete. Next, an investigator chose the topics for them, and finally the mothers of the children chose them. Euro-Americans performed better on the self-chosen anagrams. East Asians performed better on the mother-chosen ones. This result is consistent with a finding at Berkeley that Euro-Americans chose their own major 93% of the time, while 32% of East Asian students said that "others" chose their major.

Cultural schemas are sustained and modified through the dynamic of agency and choice putting one in contact with one's social context. In this way, says Markus, we construct social reality and, accordingly, our implicit selves.

OF CHIMPS AND CHILDREN:
EMERGENCE OF THE EXPLICIT SELF

There is much going on below consciousness that has an impact on how the self is constructed. As children develop, and as they interact with their social surroundings, the rich interplay of disposition, experience, emotion, and learning provides the substance for building an individual. No doubt neurally instantiated, such implicit selves may be more or less socially constructed, but cannot be put aside through some Cartesian-like transcendence, in order to invent a "metaphysical" self or soul, as a source of moral worth or pure reason. Yet surely we have here a dilemma. How does an explicit self arise from all this? What does it mean to be aware of what we do, or to know what we know, in addition to just doing it or knowing it, to attribute ownership, in effect, to a "me"? An adequate account of the implicit self must allow for the smooth passage to the explicit self, and to the "higher" accounts of self to which we seem inevitably drawn, at least in our philosophical and spiritual moments.

But we must start slowly, and stay within the bounds of experience, memory, and learning and their embodiment. A first approximation to a notion of an explicit self can be made by looking at the borderlands from within which the explicit self emerges. Evolutionarily, this means looking at non-human primates. Developmentally, this means looking at the emergence of self-awareness in children and those rare, but significant cases, where self-awareness fails to emerge, as in autism.

Marc Hauser investigates the borderland between humans and non-human primates, and his recent work has begun to shed some light on the explicit self. He starts with the notion of a *modular macro*, a kind of mental device, in the sense originally suggested by linguist/philosopher Jerry Fodor, responsible for a fast, automatic, unconscious action sequence. "Each macro," according to Hauser, "represents an adaptive solution to a recurrent problem in the organism's environment…immune to counter-evidence, and difficult to break down once it has been created."[21] The adaptive need for rapid action creates a basic dissociation between the macro and other mental functions, between, for example, action and perception, or action and knowledge. Action may proceed, as such, uninhibited. Monkeys and young children exhibit this dissociation through the inability to exercise self-control, that is, control over actions.

Hauser described a series of studies of this phenomenon, involving mental assumptions about objects and other minds. He demonstrates that, in key cases, the subject is able to represent critical knowledge relating to a problem-solving situation, but still be unable to solve the problem. In the area of folk physics, for example, tamarin and rhesus monkeys, as well as human infants to the age three, insist that an object dropped from above will move straight down, and act accordingly, even if there is transparent evidence of a device deflecting the path of the object. When searching boxes for where the object landed, they expect to see it in the box directly below the apparatus. The error occurs again and again. Hauser attributes this to an evolved "macro" governing action in the context of gravitational effects, a crucial type of innate ability involved with survival in many ways. If the experimental device is turned sideways, the error does not occur, proving that the subject "knew" the right answer in the vertical device, but could not act on it. Importantly, Hauser calls this a failure to *inhibit* the dominant action response. In the case of monkeys this is "due to evolutionary immaturity in the sense that the macaque brain…lacks the requisite circuitry for connecting perception and action knowledge in some contexts."[22]

In folk psychology, where we deal with a "theory of mind," one's own and those of others, similar experiments can be run, demonstrating, for example, a persistent failure to properly interpret how another individual will react in a situation. When shown a clear case of a ball moved from a basket to a box, and asked where a person who saw the ball put in the basket, but who left the room, will look for the ball upon return, a two- or three-year-old will persistently point to the box. Until recently, investigators assumed that the child did not have the requisite knowledge of the belief structure of the other mind. But Hauser and colleagues have made a crucial correction to this theory.

When performing the experiment, the investigators tracked the subject child's eyes and found that there was a tacit recognition of the correct answer through a glance at the basket. Yet the child invariably pointed to the box, unable, according to Hauser, to inhibit the pointing "macro." Here again we see that it is a bridge between mental functions that converts a primitive, in-born, theory of mind, into a mental system with elements of self-conscious control. Adult chimps, according to Hauser, exhibit weak, but clear abilities to overcome the gap and inhibit inappropriate responses. Children over five and adult humans, are very good at it. Development of the prefrontal cortex is probably important here.

If we can understand how brain development and experience come together to bridge these action-knowledge gaps, we may get a handle on the development of the explicit self, suggests Hauser. "One challenge confronting the neurosciences is to establish the circuitry underlying these different kinds of knowledge, what some consider to be a distinction between implicit and explicit knowledge."[23] Through these mechanisms, an individual comes to know what it knows, and can therefore plan and control what it does—elements upon which an explicit self is built. It also allows us to predict what others will do, and in doing so, "recognize that in many ways, each of us has a unique view of the world."[24]

Hauser points out that this research can be further confirmed by studying defects involving knowledge of self and other, as in autism. **Francesca Happé** has done this for many years, and it has helped form her own view about what might go into developing an explicit self. According to Happé, there is evidence that even infants are capable of tracking another's intentions. This activity is implicit and automatic, however, and does not yet reach the level of explicit representation of a mental belief or intentional state to the other. Thus, until a certain age, they will fail a false-belief test, that is, they will not attribute a false belief to an actor who is being fooled by an experimental setup. Attributing mental states to others is the hallmark of a theory of mind, and young children pass smoothly from an implicit awareness of the intentions and beliefs to a representational, explicit theory of mind during the course of early development. Like Hauser, Happé suggests that a neuropsychological road of some sort gets built, though there is much debate as to the neural structures involved.

In autism, the bridge does not get built and the individual fails to develop a theory of mind, where beliefs and intentions can be explicitly attributed to others. This "mindblindness" is the signature element in the disorder, which otherwise assumes many forms. It creates a clear lack of social consciousness and others are viewed in roughly the same manner as inanimate objects. The disorder is also characterized by a distinct lack of pretend play, otherwise virtually universal in children.

Happé goes one step further, however, and suggests that failure to understand the beliefs and intentions of others might also bear on the nature of the self:

> A theoretically important question for philosophers and psychologists is whether the same cognitive mechanism required for attributing thoughts and feelings to others is also necessary for attributing mental states to self.[25]

Happé goes on to suggest that the key transition in theory of mind is to distinguish intentional creatures from mere components of the physical world. The new ingredient is the ability to form meta-representations, that is, to distinguish something that exists outside oneself from thoughts, feelings, and beliefs about the same thing, including false beliefs. She goes on to speculate that perhaps the same neuropsychological deficit with respect to others occurs with respect to self. In autism, then, there would be a corresponding failure to develop self-representations of intention and belief. Though counterintuitive (how can we not know our own intentions and feelings?), Happé believes there is experimental evidence that suggests that self-knowledge is not all that direct. She notes, for example, that in normal development there is little evidence to suggest that mental states are attributed to self before others, and she describes research that appears to show the two capacities to be coincident or near coincident in timing.

If theory of mind applies to self, then autism would also be characterized by a failure of self-consciousness, an inability to introspect or to know that or what one knows. "An individual might not know how she is going to act until she has acted, or know why she acted as she did."[26] There would be no "explicit" self.

Happé is hopeful that fMRI studies will help us get a handle on the neural mechanisms underlying these kinds of deficits and thus better understand the path from implicit to explicit self. She further expects that theory of mind with respect to others may very well be the more fundamental functional element. That is, that self-awareness may have arisen as a consequence of the activities relating to human social interaction: "...[S]elf-reflection may be, in one sense, an epiphenomenon—an extraordinary side-effect of the crucial ability to read other minds."[27]

As in Hauser's studies, Happé's work shows that the explicit self is deeply embedded in those aspects that form the implicit self, and that the explicit self arises in relation to other more general neural and mental capacities, in this case over developmental time.

Michael Lewis has worked with infants and children for decades, and some of his most interesting experimental studies add further insight into the road that is built, somewhere in early childhood, leading from implicit, unconscious selfhood to explicit self-awareness. Of particular significance is an apparent strong emotional component to the transition, social emotions of the same general sort described by Gazzaniga, Wegner, and others.

Lewis, like the others, suggests that infants are born with primitive machinery needed for developing a normal implicit self. We are familiar with the "tongue-out" response of newborns, where the infant seems to miraculously "know" where her tongue is as she responds to an adult sticking her own tongue out. It is also easy to construct an experimental apparatus that can create an anger-like emotional expression in one-month-olds. Lewis's lab had infants associate pulling a string with a particular sound event. If the machine is turned off, the string-pulling increases and the infant has a look of consternation. If the sound occurs, but is dissociated from the string-pulling, the infant will stop pulling, but the consternation remains.

But somewhere in the middle of the second year, says Lewis, there emerges an explicit self, "the idea of 'me'." Lewis identifies three key features of this period: the development of self-recognition; the use of the personal pronouns/adjectives, me/my; and the start of pretend play. Lewis notes "a strong developmental coherence in the emergence of these three things," and he "would argue that this is the onset of the explicit self."[28] He notes further, however, and most significantly, that these three developments coincide with the development of socialization, specifically the onset of social emotions, most notably embarrassment.

In describing the three developmental elements, Lewis notes that they occur within a narrow window of age, 15–24 months, but especially between 15 and 18 months. For self-recognition, this is when a child can identify a spot of rouge on her nose, in a mirror, as part of herself. For the use of personal pronouns, there is the coincident tendency to pull objects toward oneself, associating this with "me," "my," or "mine." In the case of pretend play, the child at just this time knows that a toy telephone is not the real thing, or that one can pretend to be someone or something one is not, like an airplane.

But what is the motive force underlying these three coincident developments? What holds them together? And what kind of neural-psychological mechanism is at work? Lewis' most interesting experimental result ties in emotional development, incorporating the amygdala and other emotional systems. It is emotion, suggests Lewis, that provides the physiological-psychological impetus for the emergence of the explicit self. He focuses particularly on embarrassment, the emotion intuitively associated with self-consciousness.

Three things are at work in an emotion like embarrassment, says Lewis: the recognition of social relationships; the attribution of feelings and intentions to others (theory of mind), and the development of emotions of self-consciousness. In embarrassment, the self becomes a true object of consideration by the subject as it becomes an object of consideration by others. There is also the intense shame-like feeling that is involved, elicited vividly, and quite easily, at this age, just by having an adult point at the child and say "ooooh" in a worrisome way. The child perceives that she has failed some sort of standard, and quickly buries her head in her parent's lap.

We come full-circle back, then, to the social emotions associated with the coherence of the implicit self as described by other speakers, and the salience, and valuation, that brings about a feeling of self-control or of being a good person. With Lewis we see that this same emotional context, when self-directed, allows for the emergence of self-awareness or self-consciousness, the hallmark of the explicit self.

Returning to LeDoux's comments, we also see that the explicit self is not a separable entity, but rather a particular configuration of the implicit, unconscious self. That is, it involves the same neural apparatus which, in adapting to an intensively social world, makes the self *itself,* the object of concern.

Lewis leaves it an open question as to whether this transition is driven mostly by experience, in relation to general-purpose brain structures, or by brain maturation and the emergence of specific neurophysiological mechanisms relating to self and other. Lewis finds nothing in the social environment that relates experimentally to the coherent emergence of the explicit self, however. Even stressed and abused children develop the capacity on time, indeed, slightly earlier. Neuroscientists have only just begun to look at the underlying neural basis of self, however.

THE NEURAL BASIS OF SELF

Eric Kandel is convinced that although a full mapping of the mind and behavior onto the brain and nervous system is near impossibly complex, the basic mechanisms are fairly simple: "There is a 'dogma' in biology," he suggested,

> that deep biological processes have a limited set of solutions, and if you understand them in any context, they can be applied broadly…. Reductionist analysis is useful, and it doesn't trivialize study of the mind … [A]s you begin to understand the components … you appreciate how they fit into the whole."[29]

If, as LeDoux, Kandel, and others assert, the self is ultimately a collection of memories, then an understanding of the basic mechanisms of learning and memory should help establish a neural basis of self. Kandel's reductionist analysis takes us straight to neurons and synapses.

True to his declared strategy, Kandel has studied the learning/memory process at its most simplified level for decades. Using the common sea slug, *Aplysia*, he has been able to detail the neurophysiological and neurochemical changes that underlie simple, but general, memory and learning processes, including operant conditioning, classic conditioning, habituation, and sensitization. Working with behavior controlled by fewer than 100 cells, Kandel's lab has ferreted out several crucial elements that make up associative learning, and both short- and long-term memory.

Using a simple sensitization-reflex training process involving tactile stimulation and subsequent gill withdrawal, Kandel has been able to track how stimulus reinforcement, or fear conditioning, generates both short- and long-term memory in the creature. In both cases there is a linear dependence upon the number of trials, with memory lasting longer, through a stereotypical activation of nerve pathways, when the fear reaction is invoked more often. Modulating serotinergic neurons are implicated in the short-term memory process, by strengthening the pre-existing synaptic connections, allowing the conditioning to last longer.

The long-term memory process is most interesting. Here the repeated salient experience creates a response inside the nuclei of involved neurons, causing gene expression resulting in the growth of new synaptic connections. This creates a more permanent and long-term memory, what can be considered true learning. The specificity of this mechanism is further highlighted by the fact that initiating long-term memory storage involves not just gene activation, but the removal of a suppressor. There are "inactive" presynaptic connections that can be activated through removal of an inhibitory factor. This activation is the first step toward long-term memory. The higher threshold, leading to nuclear gene expression and the construction of new synapses, is step two. Total synaptic connections for a single neuron might typically grow from about 1200 to more than 2800. This learning/memory activation process is so neuron-specific that it can be carried out *in vitro* involving a mere three cells—the epitome of a biological "reduction." If we track the larger systems in humans, incorporating the medial temporal lobe, hippocampus, and other areas, linked to the deeper determiners of affective valence, like the amygdala, we find, not surprisingly, the same underlying mechanisms at work. This includes our conscious recall or explicit memory systems.

The point of Kandel's long experimental relationship to *Aplysia* is not to suggest that memory and learning, and therefore our individuality and selfhood, are built up from passive mechanisms. The opposite is true, according to Kandel. The key discovery, he suggests, is that *experience* is what, in fact, activates gene expression and that the "innate" mechanisms of the brain and CNS are but vehicles for the realization of experiential learning, including culture. Moreover, says Kandel, if the brain is modifiable, then education is important, particularly education during the most plastic periods of early development. It is also the basis for effective therapy, which is nothing other than fostering further gene expression to reduce the ill effects of distorted or diminished memory and learning capacities. The active interplay between experience, gene expression, and long-term memory storage is what ultimately builds an individual, the "implicit self" that forms the foundation and basis for the further expression of our self-consciousness. "We are who we are," says Kandel, "in good part by what we learn and remember."[30]

After Kandel's talk, a member of the audience asked whether one could, in fact, build up a meaningful neural "whole" from "parts" as discrete as neurons and synapses. His response was to suggest that this kind of synthesis was indeed the next step for neuroscience, looking at things from the systems level, and that there should be no conflict between the two levels.

Computational neuroscientist **Terrence Sejnowski** agrees that all levels must be pursued, but he opened his talk with a complaint that molecular and cellular research have become too dominant in neuroscience, creating distortions in how we perceive things at the level of neural systems. He notes, for example, that neurons are never at rest, and that they maintain a "background" spontaneous firing, even without a stimulus. This background "noise" is rarely considered when thinking about neurons, but may, in fact, become important when viewed as part of an overall pattern of system signaling. "Your brain is never at rest," says Sejnowski, "even when sleeping... What changes is the pattern of activity. It is in the patterns that we find traces of the self."[31] Our understanding of neuronal function requires a grasp of the interconnectedness within the overall system that is our total neural self. If we try to understand how an individual neuron, for example, links to a "partner" on a different side of the brain from a merely local perspective, the scaling factor creates an impossible situation, given the relatively slow travel of neurochemical signals. Imagine trying to catalogue a thousand trillion individual synaptic pathways. For Sejnowski, this is a waste of time and our priorities must be reversed. Individual neurons find their place and purpose in the coherence of the whole neural system.

Sejnowski's lab looks at global processing in brain activity by developing computational models of neuronal populations. The task is daunting, of course, but the techniques of computational science, he argues, provide us with algorithms that can simplify, and maintain their robustness in the simplification process. Sejnowski starts from the background wave patterns revealed by typical electroencephalographic recordings, such the well-known alpha, beta, and gamma frequency brain waves. His research then asks whether a local neuron or group of neurons on one side of the brain can immediately have an impact on those on another side by shifting the background patterning. By extension, he asks whether the constant "tuning" of these patterns, may, in fact, be the source of continuing local action. The results are promising.

Through a clever research paradigm modeled on independent component analysis in an audio signal-noise system (finding individual voices at a noisy cocktail party, for example), Sejnowski's lab has developed algorithms that can, in fact, identify neuron and neuronal group signals operating within global signal wave patterns. They have identified both temporal and spatial features, providing a coherent framework for action-over-time processing typical of the stimulus-action system governing most human functions.

Although this systems-computational research is in its infancy, Sejnowski thinks it will shed a great deal of light on how individuality is constructed and how experience shapes or "tunes" our neural selves, particularly during development. He provides a taste of this by describing research into "event-related potentials," where wave pattern frequency can be thought of as creating emotional tension, telling the system, in effect, how things are going. Event-related negativity might define a problem, for example, typically one with impact on survival or well-being. By provoking subjects with challenges that can lead to mistakes, Sejnowski was able to study brain wave patterns corresponding to such negative potentials. Answering correctly led to no pattern change. Answering incorrectly led to amplified coherence in patterning, a kind of alert to other parts of the brain. By looking at fMRI patterns in this amplified coherence, we start to see just how whole populations of neurons, say in the anterior cingulate cortex, can quickly create specific responses in other, distant sectors, not by circuitous routing of axonal pathways, but by global signaling through overall brain wave patterns. This communication within the brain is perhaps the foundation of our implicit self.

Antonio Damasio would agree with Sejnowski that we must look at some kind of holistic process to account for our implicit self, but would likely say that computation would be insufficient as the core mechanism. While electro-chemical signaling and patterning are a part of the process, there is another, perhaps more amorphous and subtle, global process that ripples through a biological system dynamically, giving an organism its internal sense of oneness and wholeness. This material or embodied element is an ancient one, according to Damasio, predating articulated neuronal patterns, and more closely associated with the neurochemical baths that, by sweeping whole sections of tissue, can create certain feeling states. He argues that "the neural basis of self is the neural basis for feeling as well."[32]

These feeling states are not simply happenings but are also representations, that is, representations for the organism about its current state of being. This state is what Damasio refers to as "awareness of homeostasis." Since homeostasis is not a static condition, but a continuous balancing and rebalancing of the organism in its shifting relationship to an environment, this representational awareness is necessarily dynamic and changing. "The minimal self," says Damasio, "is implemented as a mental representation dependent on the regular operation of certain biological systems...a stable representation of individual continuity."[33] This minimal self must be individual, singular, stable, continuous across time, and inclusive of the totality of perceptual experiences of the organism, even as the organism experiences change across time. In this sense, all organisms have such a minimal, implicit self, "implemented in biological tissue," and serving as a foundation or precursor for more explicit forms of self as may arise in self-conscious creatures.

Body awareness as a foundation for a sense of self is the intuition driving Damasio's research on consciousness and the feeling of self. It is a tradition within which he places such figures as Spinoza, James, Nietzsche, Husserl, Merleau-Ponty, and Charles Sherrington, but one largely forgotten in the current era of research. In awe of the computational power of the cortical brain, researchers have lost sight of the importance of this persistent underlying sense of bodily state, even for these very same cortical functions. It serves to draw together the emotional and rational aspects of consciousness into a seamless whole.

This minimal self, according to Damasio, is composed of several distinct evolved systems, which come together in what might be called a generalized somatosensory system, an "ongoing composite representation of certain body structures and activities, present in up to a dozen systems, that regulate homeostasis" and that are tuned to a narrow range of homeostatic variance.[34]

Such a somatosensory system must be more than just the five senses and the motor loops. Indeed, the core systems, he suggests, operate independently of the shifting external-perceptual landscape, and include: *kinesthesia*, the internal perception of the musculoskeletal system; *visceral perception*, the state of internal organs; *internal milieu*, the state of temperature, pain, and other broad indicators of internal state; *proprioception*, or sense of internal pressure on musculoskeletal elements during movement; and *introception*, or sense of physical self, or interiority. Such systems are constitutive of a feeling of self, and are based evolutionarily on the primitive chemical sensings that preceded the emergence of the five senses.

These various feelings are mostly created by direct chemical influences, by cascades of chemical events that continuously and perpetually rebalance the organism and resituate it in its environment. They are systems that regulate such things as pH, O_2 and CO_2 pressure, glucose, acids, glutamate, histamine, and serotonin. They give us our senses of mechanical stress, flush, itch, tickle, sensuous touch, genital arousal, and the many other ancient feelings that direct organism survival. They do not require nerve fiber in most cases, and where they do, we find them in old, slow C and A delta fibers associated with the spinal cord, the trigeminal nucleus, and the vagal system.

In advanced animals we find, according to Damasio, connections to a kind of center in the VMPO (ventral medial posterior) nucleus of the thalamus with aspects in the dorsal and anterior insula. Here the actual mapping of the system occurs, giving the higher organism the kind of representation that can serve as the basis for a conscious bodily self-representation, moving us and the higher primates toward a more explicit sense of self, operating through the anterior cingulate cortex, the orbital frontal cortex, and other regions. Through the course of this mapping, such cortical representations converge with emotional outputs from the amygdala and elsewhere, making the mapping dependent on the salience of the total experience. Here the self can become self-aware, a "me" with an autobiography.

Neurophysiologist **Rodolfo Llinás**[35] also sees the self as deeply connected to the body, but places a greater emphasis on the element of movement. The evolution of movement, he suggests, requires the co-evolution of an internal mechanism capable of representing the position of the body in space over the course of the movement. This is how and why brains came into being, he suggests. The sessile *Ascidiacea,* or sea squirt, requires no brain as it sits glued to its position, filtering water for food. When it is ready to reproduce, however, it gives rise to a tadpole with a brain. The tadpole proceeds to explore its environment, seeking a new place to take root. Upon establishing its location, it proceeds to eat its brain and return to the immobile mode, a dramatic bit of evidence for the claim that movement is at the center of brain function. And it is the representational aspect of this function that gives rise to the self.

The essence of the movement function is *prediction*, that is, the ability to estimate the outcome of motor efforts associated with the various motile elements of the organism. This estimation is no easy task in an ever-changing environment. Indeed, the prediction function is continuously in action to redirect movement based upon feedback. This feedback is related not only to the goal, but to the direction and efficacy of all sub-motions. Hands, arms, legs, thorax, head, and eyes must all work in concert through such feedback. "What is the repository of the predictive function?" asks Llinás in his recent *I of the Vortex,*, "I believe the answer lies in what we call the self: self is the centralization of prediction.*"[36] Nearly all survival functions of most organisms are tied in one way or another to this predictive function and it is the dominant function of the brain as a whole, according to Llinás.

"For the nervous system to predict," Llinás continues, "it must perform a rapid comparison of the sensory-referred properties of the external world with a separate internal sensorimotor representation of those properties."[37] Llinás likens this to many computers working in parallel, taking different measurements of an event in the external world, some computing slowly, others quite quickly, depending on the context. The result is the representation of an event ahead of its time of completion. Rapid sequences of discrete representations are somehow collected into a coherent and continuous stream—the essence of the ongoing self.

Llinás has spent years analyzing the physiological seat of this predictive self, and has zeroed in on the thalamocortical system, the brain's relay system, connecting the vestibular nucleus and the cortex. The thalamus is shielded from direct sensory input, so that it can carry out its representational function with its incessant adjustments through sensorimotor feedback and adjusted goal valuations in the form of feelings and emotions. This "predictive organ," as Llinás refers to the system, must of necessity be unitary. An organism with multiple predictive centers would quickly become chaotic. Such a unitary, continuous predictive center is our best candidate for the neural self.

But this is not the "I" per se, the second-order self, that is the basis for self-awareness and self-consciousness. Like the other neuroscientists, Llinás sees the self as largely implicit, built by evolution to give the organism a continuous awareness of its bodily instantiation for the purpose of survival. The "I," suggests Llinás, "is just a convenient word,"[38] representing the centralized "sense" of a global event, but with no true center, ultimately just the thalamocortical system with its massively distributed, parallel apparatus, built slowly over evolutionary time to give motile creatures an advantage.

A SELF WORTH HAVING:
PHILOSOPHICAL AND THEOLOGICAL PERSPECTIVES

Even as neuroscience has put the self squarely within the domain of natural processes, ancient questions are still not put to rest, particularly with respect to humans. Is there something special about the human self that allows it to be a source of personhood, moral worth, and free will? Does the materialization of self diminish the value of the person? Or, as Tom Wolfe famously put it, has modern neuroscience and evolutionary biology cost us our souls? Presenters Churchland, Dennett, Mauron, and Murphy addressed some aspects of these questions.

Philosopher **Patricia Churchland**, strongly physicalist and materialist, has little patience for claims about the self that transcend its fundamentally neural basis. Neuroscience has repeatedly shown how mental life is realized through nervous tissue. But this need not diminish our conception of self, and knowledge gained from a neurological description of selfhood could be used for social good.

Churchland, like Llinás, argued that neural self-representation is the key to the self, and that this representational capacity captures the essence of what Descartes incorrectly thought must be something necessarily disembodied.[39] Churchland suggests that the self is a transient set of overlaid representational capacities reflecting coordinated, multidimensional survival activities. Some of these activities and capacities we share with other animals, including motility and the inner feeling states associated with homeostatic regulation and basic survival, including body position, inner milieu, proprioception, etc., as described by Damasio. With primates and humans, more explicit forms arise relating, for example, to social positioning. With humans alone, the representational capacity is extended to a second order, including autobiographical memory, reading other minds, and planning ahead. The degree of integration of these representational capacities is an open question, suggests Churchland, but she further agrees with Llinás in that coordination of movement, using an "inner" model, based in the brain stem and linked through the thalamus to the cortical regions, may serve as a "platform" upon which other capacities are constructed.

Also like Llinás, Churchland looks at the predictive function of this inner model-building, the anticipation of consequences of planned behaviors, as the driver within the evolutionary processes that built organisms with selves. The organism establishes a goal state, roughs out a plan or model, and then a crucial step occurs: A neural device, a kind of "emulator," projects the plan into the future and initiates a series of rapid, discrete steps, driven by feedback loops, through which environmental context is assessed and re-assessed and the goal state reached. The emulator also receives continuous input of affective valence, which Churchland calls the "relevance" factor, feeling states, linked to pertinent memories, that keep the organism focused on the goal.

The field of neurology has provided ample evidence for the biological instantiation of these capacities and drivers, in the form of pathologies that diminish or eliminate them. Patients who have lost specific functions, like autobiographical memory or the use of the pronoun "I," because of injury or illness, give us a window into the biological systems that carry these capacities. There are individuals who will not accept part of their body as theirs, and even some who lose all sense of will and simply vegetate in a passive state with no apparent interest in acting.

Churchland is interested in the willful aspects of this process and she illustrates the workings of the emulator-prediction system by considering the question of "self-control." When can we say we are "in control"? When are we out of control? By assessing this question neurologically, suggests Churchland, we can avoid the pitfall of Cartesian reasoning and yet arrive at a personally and socially meaningful notion. She suggests beginning with a cluster of pathologies that can be used to approximate what we mean by being out-of-control: obsessive-compulsive disorders; bipolar depression; loss of impulse control (e.g., failure to function socially owing to prefrontal lesions); loss of satiety feelings causing uncontrolled eating; and epileptic seizures. We can even include the non-pathological inability of children to control themselves under certain circumstances, mostly due to an insufficiently developed prefrontal cortex.

In all such cases, we have made great progress identifying specific neural and other biological deficits and can therefore start to identify parameters associated with being-in-control. By creating a multidimensional mapping of these parameters, together with their thresholds and environmental triggers, we can begin to place individuals into sectors of the parameter space. In cases of loss of control, this may give us a handle on prevention or cure. We can, in effect, gain access to our willful behavior through an understanding of the neural basis of our internal predictive apparatus, the essence of the material self.

Churchland referred to an interesting study of self-control undertaken jointly by the University of Wisconsin, Kings College, London, and the University of Otago, New Zealand. Two large cohorts of boys were studied from childhood to the age 26. Those exhibiting reduced production of monoamine oxidase due to a polymorphic gene on the X chromosome were found to have a greater tendency toward aggressive behavior. But this tendency became actual usually only when boys were subject to stressful conditions in childhood, including poverty and physical abuse. The linkage over time betwee aggressive behavior and both genetic and environmental parameters, is precisely what might be mapped using the goal-directed model-building "emulator" theory. With such a mapping we may find ourselves able to help change behavior for some, from out-of-control to in-control, to change, in effect, their selves.

Daniel Dennett, too, made short shrift of the Cartesian divide—"today, materialism has swept dualism and its insoluble mysteries of interaction aside."[40] But, like Churchland and others, he also seeks to preserve a notion of self that is adequate to our deep-seated need to view ourselves as autonomous, free, and moral agents. Dennett takes his cue from Wegner: "Illusory or not, conscious will is the person's guide to his or her own moral responsibility for action."[41] Like Wegner, Dennett views the self as a construct, a way of "summarizing" the workings of a vast, distributed neural system for the purpose of maintaining a basis for emotionally satisfying social interactions. But it is more than just summarizing. Dennett stresses that this vast network, constitutive of the organism, does not necessarily exhibit internal coherence. "We are just not that unified," says Dennett. We are made up of modules with different modes of operation and purposes, creating at best a fragile coalition of competing and often conflicting functions. But then, Dennett asks,"[G]iven the literal chaos brewing in our brains, given the manifest absence of any King Neuron or Boss Nucleus, why and how does it seem to us that we are unified selves…?"[42] Why is such an "artifact" needed? How did it come about?

In answering these questions, Dennett rejects the viewpoint of some neuroscientists to the effect that the artifact is an epiphenomenon, a "mere" illusion. He takes up at length a well-known neurological finding that has given impetus to this notion: Benjamin Libet's experiments suggesting that we act before we consciously will our actions. The Libet experimental apparatus requires a subject to identify the point, related to a clock, when she consciously wills a motor action. In every case, Libet was able to detect the initiation of the electrophysiological neural potential that yielded the action a hundred milliseconds *before* the conscious decision, as determined by the subject's indication that a decision had, in fact, been made. The "machine" acts ahead of the epiphenomenal "mind." While Libet himself tries to "save" free will by suggesting that there is still time for the "mind" to cancel the action or that there may be some hidden new types of causality at work, most materialistically inclined neuroscientists, including Michael Gazzaniga, see the Libet studies as confirming the deep automaticity and unconscious nature of mind and behavior.

But Dennett detects a hidden bias in the studies and their interpretation. They indirectly accept the Cartesian idea that conscious will, if it exists, must be a unique decision-making locus or organ. Dennett reinterprets the Libet findings on the premise that the decision-making process is a distributed system involving different parts of the brain, where a "decision" is the outcome of a process. Looked at as a distributed process, the hundred milliseconds quickly dissolves. "You are not out of the loop," says Dennett, "You *are* the loop." Of course we still need to know how this kind of immediacy translates into a "me" or "self."

Making explicit what was implicit in several other talks, Dennett looks directly to biological evolution for answers, and arrives at notions not unlike those proposed by Damasio, Llinás, Churchland and others, that at some evolutionary point the brain went from dark to light by creating floating inner models or schemas of the organism in space and time in reference to certain goal states and the prediction of results of actions. In most creatures, such "self-monitoring" functions were simply not needed because the behavioral repertoire was not only simpler, but worked best if set within tight restraints. As creatures acquired increasingly more behavioral options, however, "their worlds become cluttered, and the virtue of tidiness [came] to be 'appreciated' by natural selection."[43] Eventually creatures needed to be capable of "considering different courses of action in advance of committing to any one of them, and weighing them on the basis of some projection of the probable outcome of each."

Finally, new environmental complexities arose and creatures found that social interaction was a modality for survival and reproduction. It is here that the predictive function had necessarily to focus on one's "I" insofar as it had to relate to others and to their relation, in turn, to that "I." This added recursivity, building stable, predictive models hierarchically, is what underlies communication. Referencing McFarlane, Dennett tells us: "In a word, communication. It is only once a creature begins to develop the activity of communication, and in particular communications of its actions and plans, that it has to have some capacity for monitoring not just the results of its actions, but its prior evaluations and formations of intentions as well."[44]

The "self" of communication has the job of maintaining a relationship to the past and to future goals, something more than mere illusion. This self-monitoring, or "center of narrative gravity," as Dennett calls it, is of utmost importance and underlies our sense of being in control of actions and of participating freely in an ongoing and stable social and moral community. Thus can a biological artifact, concocted as a mechanism among other evolutionarily concocted mechanisms, be a powerful and necessary source of moral worth and well-being.

Alexandre Mauron attends to still another level of abstraction and wonders whether it is really possible to develop an ethics that is consistent with a deeply biological notion of self. We can't just declare victory for materialism and expect to be able to answer fundamental ethical questions through an evolved moral "sense" or utilitarian consensus—or can we?

The traditional basis for ethics has been religion, and there is something compelling in the search for a morality based on a transcendent human essence. While neuroscience places us on a continuum with the primates and other creatures, the notion of an internal/mental meta-representation of self that can function through language as a basis for interacting with other minds is challenging for reductive materialism, and classical metaphysical and theological notions have certainly not called it a day. Mauron pointed out that the very pinnacle of reductive science, genomics and the articulation of the human genome, has, in fact, given support in many quarters to an essentialist ethics. "…[T]he genome is increasingly thought of as the 'essence' of the human person," says Mauron, further suggesting that there is "a social representation of the genome as the ontological core of an organism, determining both its individuality and its species identity….[O]ne could say that the human genome is what makes us human, and my genome is what makes me *me* and you *you*."[45]

To make the genome a proper basis for an essentialist ethics, however, there must be a sound basis for explaining development and the interaction of the genome with the environment in defining individuality. Here is where the going gets rough, and where Mauron and ethicists like the controversial German philosopher Peter Sloterdijk effectively point to moral ambiguities involved in defining persons and selves. Clearly religion would like to preserve the sacredness of the human essence even if it should accept the genome as its natural basis. Thus, for example, theological views would have us accept the human individual genome as a "gift" from God or a God-like Nature. We are receivers of our being and, as such, one ethical principle should be a resistance to its engineering, manufacture, or manipulation. At no point should our received essence be open to revision through human means. Sloterdijk cleverly points out, however, that our modern biological understanding of development makes it clear that we have no choice but to engineer and manipulate our nature, in this sense. Even cultural development and education is ultimately a process of gene expression and individual biological development as we develop embodied emotional attachments to family, community, traditions, and local values. Even humanistic education, suggests Sloterdijk, is a form of bio-social control. It changes our gene expression, brain, and mind. Why, therefore, should we not engage in direct biological manipulation? Or at least develop ethical codes that are equivalent for both?

Mauron goes on to point out other problems with essentialist ethical approaches that profess to accept modern scientific findings. The notion of the uniqueness of the individual, for example, loses its standing as we watch a zygote—a human individual—suddenly split into two to form monozygotic twins. Identical genomes, no doubt, but hardly identical individuals. Where is the source, then, of the moral standing of a human individual if we can't really articulate its transcendent essence? And, referring to an argument by bioethicist Dan Brock, are we not generally inclined to recognize, love, and respect the sanctity of all human individuals, even if created through *in vitro* fertilization, germ line manipulation, or cloning? "It is the nature of the being, not how it is created, that is the source of its value and makes it worthy of respect," says Brock.[46] Thus does Mauron urge us to consider the individual *qua* individual, and to recognize that man could perhaps have no essence, except for that which he creates for himself. Mauron points out that some philosophers and theologians have thought this way. Pico della Mirandola, for one, was sure that God intended it this way, that is, man as a "co-creator" of himself.[47] For Mauron, Brock, and others, we must accept the moral ambiguity implied by our biological selves and try to build an ethical framework from within this context.

But the problem gets even stickier once we look carefully at the neural basis of the self. The genomic self is to some extent passive, a kind of template or set of constraints for phenotypic development. Genetic manipulation will, of course, be a significant human transforming technology, but not near half as powerful, says Mauron, as techniques aimed at brain/mind manipulation. Now that we know that experience can change gene expression, which affects synapse growth, and so on, we are facing far greater challenges as we start to manipulate our neural selves, whether through words or drugs. "What looks like 'soft' determinism when looked at the gene level, may be equivalent to 'hard' determinism when taking the brain on board,"[48] says Mauron,

> ...[T]he link between genes and personality is rather indirect, unlike the link between the brain and the Self....[C]hanging the human brain is changing destiny...and more attention could be devoted to the troubling implications of willfully shaping the human brain. At that point we may find ourselves in a similar predicament as Sloterdijk: hunting for the hard-to-find moral difference between the technological fine-tuning of brain states ... and the more traditional brain-shaping tools wielded by educators, prophets and politicians. And we may well conclude that moral ambivalence is to be found everywhere.[49]

Religion has been the context within which most thinking about moral values and human nature has occurred over the ages, and it is common to think that religion-based thinking about these issues is of necessity strongly dualistic, where mind, or soul, is not limited by the material brain. **Nancey Murphy**, a theologian, disagrees. She points out that, while the ordinary religious person may nominally profess belief in miracles, afterlives, and immortal souls, there is little in the history, writings, or systematic theology of at least the Judaeo-Christian tradition, that binds one to such a view. "A purely physicalist account of human nature is equally compatible with contemporary science and with Christian thought."[50] In a brief survey of the history of theology, philosophy, and Biblical scholarship, Murphy pointed out that mainstream religious thinking and writing does not conflict with the findings of science and the idea of a fully material mind.

The Hebraic and early Christian period, for example, did not establish a metaphysical doctrine of the person or personal soul at all, and there were a wide range of views about the soul and its relation to the body. It is only with Augustine's Neoplatonism, she argues, that there is put forward an explicit and influential notion that mind and body are of two different causal natures. In Augustinian thought, the mind or soul "uses" the body, as an agent would use a tool, suggesting further that causality relating the two is unidirectional, that is, that body cannot affect mind. Compounding this dualistic rift, is the Augustinian–Platonic notion that appetites or emotions are of a limited, even negative, nature and must be overcome or overruled by the intellect and will.

But Christian theology in later centuries came to be influenced more by the Thomist tradition, which traces back to the moderated dualism of Aristotle and his Muslim interpreters. Aristotelian "hylomorphism," "thought of the soul not as an entity, but more as a life principle—the aspect of the person which provide[s] the powers or attributes characteristic of the human being."[51] On this account even plants and lower animals could have "souls," nutritive and sensitive, respectively. Form and matter, soul and body, were seen as inextricably united.

Thomist theology could then address something Augustine could not, the faculties of perception and emotion, which bridge body and mind or soul, and, suggests Murphy, such thinking accords well with modern neuroscience:

> For example, in addition to the five exterior senses, (Aquinas) recognized four faculties that he designated "interior senses." One of these, what he called the *sensus communis*, is the capacity to collate information derived from the senses in order to recognize that they all pertain to the same object. This is now discussed in neuroscience under the heading of the binding problem. His *vis aestimativa* (estimative power) is the capacity we share with animals to recognize something as harmful or harmless, friendly or unfriendly. This is strikingly similar to what Joseph LeDoux calls "emotional appraisal." LeDoux's distinction between object recognition and emotional appraisal is Thomas's distinction between the *sensus communis* and the *vis aestimativa*.[52]

Murphy also finds a distinctly modern tone in Thomas's account of morality, as he links affect and cognition:

> [Aquinas] describes the will as the ability to be attracted to goods of a nonsensible sort. Morality is a function of attraction to the good combined with rational judgment about what is truly good. Antonio Damasio's account of certain victims of temporal lobe damage who lose their ability to act prudently and morally could be translated into Thomistic terms: their intellect is intact but they have lost the capacity to be attracted to the good.[53]

Thus, as Christian thinking entered the period of the scientific revolution, there was no inherent bias against the findings of science, and indeed, religion and theology have not diminished in their global influence as science has moved forward. Murphy points to recent papal pronouncements on the compatibility of Christian doctrine with the findings of evolutionary science as indicative of the openness of religion to science, and to the emergence of a strong "liberal" tradition within Protestant theology over the past 50 years, in which physicalism, which claims a purely physical basis for human nature, has become the norm. She also notes the relatively limited references in Biblical scholarship and Christian theology to notions like resurrection or immortality, as applied to the otherwise vague idea of the soul, and suggests that we have overinterpreted this aspect of religion. Indeed, the notion of an immortal soul, for many religious thinkers, tends to promote "otherworldliness," a distraction from doing God's work on Earth.

The problem, as Murphy sees it, is with the question of *reductionism*. It is here that religion and theology must part ways with a current mainstream tendency in scientific thinking: causal and atomistic reductionism. Causal reduction suggests that influences flow only upward, from the level of physics, to the more complex living world. Atomistic reduction claims that the only "real" things are physical particles and their interactions, and that everything else is epiphenomenon or illusion. Dismissing atomistic reduction as mere *"attitude,"* since no one really denies the reality of chemicals, organisms, and minds, Murphy pauses at causal reduction, where the real debate is taking place. The Pope may accept evolutionary theory as scientifically valid, but he would argue that there is "more" involved than mere chance on a wing. Liberal theologians may accept neuroscience, but would hardly agree with Francis Crick that we "are nothing but a pack of neurones."[54]

It is here where Murphy feels science must assess its shortcomings with respect to a metaphysics adequate to our deepest sense that the universe contains meanings and influences beyond those of physical particles. She refers to work already under way involving systems theory and holistic approaches, echoing remarks by Sejnowski and Damasio about the need for paradigms beyond the single neuron. She also mentions figures like Donald Campbell and Robert Van Gulick, and other theoretical biologists who are looking at "downward causation" and "whole–part" interaction as emerging new ways of thinking about biological systems. It is through these kinds of approaches that Murphy sees science avoiding the pitfalls of reductionism, and getting closer to modern religious thinkers, like herself, who seem willing to accept the exciting findings of contemporary cognitive neuroscience, including those presented at this conference—*The Self: From Soul to Brain.*

NOTES AND REFERENCES

1. Except where otherwise noted, this review is based on audiotapes and transcripts of presentations at the NYAS conference, *The Self: From Soul to Brain,* which took place on September 26–28, 2002 in New York City.
2. LeDoux, Joseph E. (2003). The self: clues from the brain. *Annals of the New York Academy of Sciences, 1001,* 298 [this volume].
3. Ibid., p. 303.
4. Kelley, W.M. et al. (2002). Finding the self? An event related fMRI study. *Journal of Cognitive Neuroscience, 14* (5), 785–794.
5. Klein, S.B., et al. (2002). A social-cognitive neuroscience analysis of the self. *Social Cognition, 20,* 105–135.
6. Gazzaniga, Michael S. (1998). *The mind's past,* p. 21. Berkeley: University of California Press.
7. Ibid., p. 23.
8. Ibid., p. 27.
9. Ibid., p. 174.
10. Wegner, Daniel M. (2003). The mind's self-portrait. *Annals of the New York Academy of Sciences, 1001,* 212 [this volume].
11. Ibid., p. 222.
12. Schacter, Daniel L. (2001). *The seven sins of memory.* Boston: Houghton-Mifflin.
13. Quoted in Potier, Beth (2002). Prejudice is not only black and white. *Harvard University Gazette,* online archives <http://www.hno.harvard.edu/gazette/2002/04.18/03-banaji.html> 4-18-02.
14. NYU/Yale research team explores neural basis of racial evaluation. *Science Daily* <http://www.sciencedaily.com/releases/2000/09/000913203757.htm> September 18, 2000, adapted from an NYU press release.

15. Quoted in POTIER, BETH (2002). Op cit.
16. BANAJI, M., NOSEK, B. & GREENWALD, A. (2002). Math = male, me = female, therefore math ≠ me. *Journal of Personality and Social Psychology* (pre-publication paper) at <www.briannosek.com/papers/nosek.math.JPSP.2002.pdf>
17. QUINN, NAOMI (2002). Cultural selves. *Annals of the New York Academy of Sciences, 1001,* 146 [this volume].
18. Ibid., p. 145.
19. Ibid., p. 148.
20. References are to a transcript of the NYAS conference presentation by Hazel Rose Markus "Models of Agency: From Soul to Brain and Back Again."
21. HAUSER, MARC D. (2003). Knowing about knowing: Dissociations between perception and action systems over evolution and during development. *Annals of the New York Academy of Sciences, 1001,* 80 [this volume].
22. Ibid., pp. 89.
23. Ibid., p. 98.
24. Ibid., p. 100.
25. HAPPÉ, FRANCESCA (2003). Theory of mind and the self. *Annals of the New York Academy of Sciences, 1001,* 136 [this volume].
26. Ibid., p. 138.
27. Ibid., p. 142.
28. Reference is from transcript of NYAS conference presentation by Michael Lewis, "The Emergence of Consciousness and Its Impact on Children's Development."
29. References are to a transcript of the NYAS conference presentation by Eric Kandel, "Genes, Synapses, and Long-Term Memory: Steps toward a Biological Basis for Individuality."
30. Ibid.
31. References are to a transcript of the NYAS conference presentation by Terrence J. Sejnowski, "Computation of Self."
32. References are to a transcript of the NYAS conference presentation by Antonio R. Damasio, "Feelings and Self."
33. Ibid.
34. Ibid.
35. References are to a transcript of the NYAS conference presentation by Rodolfo R. Llinás, "Cognition as a Pre-motor Event."
36. LLINÁS, RODOLFO R., (2001). *I of the vortex,* p. 23. Cambridge, MA: MIT Press.
37. Ibid., p. 23.
38. Ibid., p. 128.
39. References are to a transcript of the conference presentation by Patricia Churchland, "Philosophy of Brain and Self."
40. DENNETT, DANIEL C., (2003). "The self as a responding—and responsible—artifact. *Annals of the New York Academy of Sciences, 1001,* 39 [this volume].
41. WEGNER, DANIEL (2002). *The illusion of conscious will,* p. 341. Cambridge, MA: MIT Press.
42. DENNETT, op. cit., p. 40.
43. Ibid., p. 45.
44. Ibid., p. 46.
45. MAURON, ALEX. (2003). Renovating the house of being: Genomes, souls, and selves. *Annals of the New York Academy of Sciences, 1001,* 245 [this volume].

46. BROCK, D.W. (2002). Human cloning and our sense of self. *Science, 296,* 314–316.
47. MIRANDOLA, PICO DELLA Oratio de hominis dignitate. Accessible at <http://www.gmu.edu/departments/fld/CLASSICS/mirandola.oration.html.>
48. MAURON, op. cit., p. 250.
49. Ibid., p. 250, 251.
50. MURPHY, NANCEY (2003). Whatever happened to the soul?: Theological perspectives on neuroscience and the self. *Annals of the New York Academy of Sciences, 1001,* 51 [this volume].
51. Ibid., p. 55.
52. Ibid., p. 55, 56.
53. Ibid., p. 56.
54. CRICK, FRANCIS. (1994). *The astonishing hypothesis: The scientific search for the soul.* New York: Simon and Schuster.

Self-Representation in Nervous Systems

PATRICIA S. CHURCHLAND

*Philosophy Department 0119, University of California, San Diego,
La Jolla, California 92093, USA*

ABSTRACT: The brain's earliest self-representational capacities arose as
evolution found neural network solutions for coordinating and regulating
inner-body signals, thereby improving behavioral strategies. Additional
flexibility in organizing coherent behavioral options emerges from neural
models that represent some of the brain's inner states as states of its body,
while representing other signals as perceptions of the external world.
Brains manipulate inner models to predict the distinct consequences in the
external world of distinct behavioral options. The self thus turns out to be
identifiable not with a nonphysical soul, but rather with a set of representational capacities of the physical brain.

KEYWORDS: self-representation; brainstem; Grush emulator; co-evolution
of psychology; neuroscience

WHAT IS "THE SELF"?

Descartes proposed that the self is not identical with one's body, or indeed,
with any physical thing. Instead, he famously concluded that the essential
self—the self one means when one thinks, "I exist"—is a nonphysical, conscious thing. At this stage of scientific development, the Cartesian approach
is unsatisfactory for three reasons: (i) psychological functions generally, including conscious thoughts such as "I exist," are activities of the physical
brain[1,2]; (ii) aspects of self-regulation (e.g., inhibiting sexual inclinations),
and self-cognition (e.g., knowing where I stand in my clan's dominance hierarchy), may be nonconscious[3]; and (iii) as the Scottish philosopher David
Hume (1711–1776) realized, there is in any case no introspective experience
of the "self" as a distinct thing apart from the body.[4] Introspection, Hume
concluded, reveals only a continuously changing flux of visual perceptions,

Reprinted with full permission from *Science* 296: 308–310 (2002) ©2002 American Association for the Advancement of Science. http://www.sciencemag.org
    Address for correspondence: Patricia S. Churchland, Ph.D., Philosophy Department 0119,
University of California, San Diego, La Jolla, CA 92093. Voice: 858-822-1655; fax: 858-534-
8566.
    pschurchland@ucsd.edu

Ann. N.Y. Acad. Sci. 1001: 31–38 (2003). © 2003 New York Academy of Sciences.
doi: 10.1196/annals.1279.002

sounds, smells, emotions, memories, thoughts, feelings of fatigue, and so forth.

To identify the phenomenon that we want explained, it is useful to start with the idea that one's self-concept is a set of organizational tools for "coherencing" the brain's plans, decisions, and perceptions. Thus, if a brick falls on my foot, I know the pain is mine. I know without pausing to figure it out that "this body is my own," and that a decision to fight rather than flee is a decision affecting my body's painful encounter with the body of another. If I scold myself about jaywalking, I know that it is me talking to myself. We know that if we fail to plan for future contingencies, our future selves may suffer, and we care now about that future self. Sometimes we use "myself" to mean "my body," as when we say "I weighed myself." By contrast, when we say "I deceived myself," we are not referring to our physical bodies. We talk of our social and our private selves, of discovering and realizing ourselves, of self-control, self-improvement, and self-denial.[5]

This remarkably diverse range of uses of the self-concept motivates recasting problems about "the self" in terms of self-representational capacities of the brain. Doing so deflates the temptation to think of the self as a singular entity and encourages the idea that self-representing involves a plurality of functions, each having a range of shades, levels, and degrees. Further, it broadens the inquiry beyond humans to other species, suggesting that varying levels of coherencing operate in all nervous systems of any significant complexity. The reformulation also sets the stage for designing experiments to determine more precisely the types of self-representations nervous systems have, how they are connected to one another, and the nature of their neural substrates.[6]

The expectation that the brain and behavioral sciences will eventually understand the nature of self-representational capacities is not universally shared. Traditionalists prefer to hive off the fundamental questions about the self or consciousness as philosophical in the "armchair-only" or "forever-beyond-science" senses of the term.[7] The dominant ideology in academic philosophy, functionalism, acknowledges the relevance of the behavioral sciences, but discounts the neurosciences as largely irrelevant to making progress in understanding the higher functions.[8] The functionalist rationale depends on an allegedly close analogy between psychological processes and running software on a computer. According to the analogy, the brain is only the hardware on which the cognitive software happens to run.[9] The brain is thus deemed a mere implementation of the software. The corollary is that understanding the hardware is therefore unimportant, by and large, in figuring out the software. Though the analogy between cognitive functions and running software is not close but feeble, and though the corollary fails to follow, functionalism retains considerable popularity beyond the borders of neuroscience.[10]

Mysticism and functionalism notwithstanding, questions about self-representation are steadily shifting into the province of the brain and cognitive sciences. This shift is part of a general trend enabled by the scientific advances in the 20th century at all levels of brain organization from synapses to systems. These advances, along with improvements in technology, data analysis, and computational modeling, have meant that virtually all topics concerning the mind are now vigorously explored at the interface of neuroscience, cognitive science, and philosophy. This has been the fortune, for example, of color perception,[11] autobiographical memory,[12,13] the emotions,[3,14–16] decision making,[3,12,14,17,18] sleep and dreaming,[19] and consciousness.[6,12,15,20]

As in any science, some discoveries force a more enlightened articulation of the very questions themselves. For example, the split-brain studies revealed that interrupting information flow between the two hemispheres by surgical section of the cerebral commissures gives rise to striking disconnection effects; that is, the perceptions and decisions of one hemisphere are disconnected from those of its counterpart hemisphere.[21] This implied that the "unity of self," advertised by some philosophers as a "transcendental" necessity, was actually subject to anatomical manipulation. The results implied that such unity and coherence as exist in one's self-conception depend not on transcendental necessity, whatever that might be, but on neuronal organization. A recharacterization of the phenomenon of unity of the self was consequently occasioned by the new empirical data.

A standard principle, illustrated by the split-brain results, is that the definition of the phenomenon to be explained *co-evolves* with experimental discoveries. In the early stages of the scientific attack on any problem, accurate definition of the phenomenon is hampered precisely because not enough is known to permit an accurate definition. A pragmatic strategy is to begin by studying those cases agreed to be obvious examples of the phenomenon. Powered by this agreement, provisional, rough characterizations can leverage the science's first stages, with refinements in the phenomenon's definition emerging as the surrounding facts become clear. From a historical perspective, the interdependence of definition and discovery typifies the transformation of assorted problems of what was originally "pure" philosophy (e.g., the nature of fire, space, matter, life, the cosmos) into problems of the experimental sciences.[2,6]

SELF-REPRESENTATIONAL CAPACITIES

In the brain, some networks are involved in representing things in the external world, such as the face of Groucho Marx or a looming bus. Other networks represent states of the body, such as its posture or its need for water. Some networks operate on other representations, yielding meta-representations such as knowing that my need to flee is more urgent than my need for water, knowing that John dislikes me, or remembering that John hit me. Neural networks engaged in integrating such meta-representations are probably the ones most relevant to questions about self-representation.

Self-representations may be widely distributed across brain structures, coordinated only on an "as-needed" basis, and arranged in a loose and loopy hierarchy. We see the slow emergence and elaboration of self-representational capacities in children,[22] and the tragic fading of these capacities in patients with dementia. Despite large gaps in our knowledge, human as well as animal studies have made it possible to begin to distinguish different types of self-representational functions, and in some instances, to identify, albeit in general terms, their neural dependencies.

Self-representational capacities include representing the internal milieu and viscera via chemical and neural pathways aimed largely at the brainstem and hypothalamus; representing musculoskeletal structures via the somatic sensory system; representing autobiographical events via medial temporal lobe structures; deferring gratification and controlling impulses via prefrontal lobe and limbic structures; and representing the sequence of actions to take next, as well as representing where one is in space-time and the social order.

Studies of human patients reflect the multidimensionality of self-representation by showing that particular functions can be spared when others are impaired. For example, a subclass of amnesic subjects with bilateral lesions in the hippocampal and associated cortical structures are unable to acquire new knowledge and have lost essentially all autobiographical information. For example, the patient R.B. lives essentially within a moving 40-s time bin.[3] Although R.B. does suffer diminished self-understanding, he nevertheless retains many elements of normal self capacities, including self-control in social situations and the fluent and correct use of "I." He also knows his current body configuration and status, and he can engage in self-imagery, identify feelings such as happiness, and show sympathy with the distress of others. The existence of such amnesics is a counterexample to the seemingly obvious hypothesis that one's self is constituted by personal narrative.[9]

Schizophrenia, known to involve decreased prefrontal activity and increased striatal activity[23] presents a different dimension of self-dysfunction. During a florid episode, a schizophrenic may have good autobiographical memory, but suffer deep confusion about self/nonself boundaries, for example, responding to a tactile stimulus by claiming that the sensation belongs to someone else or that it exists somewhere outside of him. Auditory hallucinations, often considered diagnostic of schizophrenia, exemplify integrative failure. The "voices" appear to be the patients' own thoughts or inner speech, but they are not represented, and thus not recognized, as such.[24,25] The anesthetic ketamine and drugs such as LSD can trigger similar phenomena.

A patient with lesions in the right parietal cortex, resulting in loss of sensation and movement on the left side of the body, may firmly deny that her left limbs are in fact hers. On occasion, a patient with limb denial will use the normal right arm to try to throw the paralyzed left leg out of the bed, insisting it is alien. Despite suffering compromised body-representation, the patients may nevertheless have normal autobiographical memory as well as other self-representational functions such as knowing whether they feel bored or hungry. Patients with lesions in the anterior cingulate region may exhibit alien hand syndrome. In these cases, the contralesional hand will sometimes behave as though it is independently controlled. Patients with alien hand syndrome sometimes control their embarrassing alien hand with verbal commands.

Self-regulating functions can also be selectively impaired. Lesions in the prefrontal cortex, especially in the ventromedial region, have been followed by significant changes in self-control, and particularly in the capacity to inhibit unwise impulses, despite normal functioning of many other self-representational capacities. Personality changes commonly occur with prefrontal damage. Hitherto quiet and self-controlled, a person with lesions in the ventromedial region of frontal cortex is apt to be more reckless in decision making, impaired in impulse control, and socially insensitive.[3,17,18]

EVOLUTION OF SELF-REPRESENTATIONAL CAPACITIES

The most fundamental of the self-representational capacities probably arose as evolution stumbled on solutions for coordinating innerbody signals to generate survival-appropriate inner regulation. The basic coordination problems for all animals derive from the problem of what to do next. Pain signals should be coordinated with withdrawal, not with approach. Thirst signals should be coordinated with water-seeking, not with fleeing, unless a present threat takes higher priority. Homeostatic functions and the ability to switch between the different internal configuration for fight and flight from that needed for rest and digest require coordinated control of heart, lungs, viscera, liver, and adrenal medulla. Body-state signals have to be integrated, options evaluated, and choices made, since the organism needs to act as a coherent whole, not as a group of independent systems with competing interests.

THE NEURAL PLATFORM

The most basic level of inner coordination and regulation occurs in the brainstem, anchoring what Damasio refers to as "the proto self."[12] In vertebrates, the brainstem-hypothalamic axis is the site of convergence of signals from the viscera, internal milieu, and the somatic sensory system. Also located in the brainstem are nuclei that regulate vital functions, sleep-wakefulness cycles, arousal, attention, and the emotions. This level of integration, shared across many species, is the nonconscious neurobiological platform for higher levels of self-representation.

Other, more complicated and flexible aspects of the self demand greater computational resources. Wolpert[26] and Grush[27] have proposed that increased accuracy in planning and execution of movement in space-time is achieved by cortical models of the body in relation to its environment. Roughly, a somewhat sloppy inverse model is connected to an error-predicting forward model, and the two converge on a good answer to the problem of how to move a many-limbed body in just the right way at just the right time.

If, for example, the goal is to reach a plum, the inverse model gives a first-pass answer to this question: What motor command should be issued to get my arm to contact the plum? Taking the command-proposal, the forward model calculates the error by running the command on a neuronal emulator, and the inverse model responds to the error signal with an upgraded command. Emulation is faster and safer than real-world feedback. Assuming the forward and inverse models are also capable of learning, this organization can be very efficient in acquiring a wide range of sensorimotor skills. With sufficient access to background knowledge, goal priorities, and current sensory information, emulators can compute accurate solutions to complex motor problems.

Rudimentary neuronal emulators, grounded in the basic coordinating and self-regulating functions, can in turn be upgraded to yield fancier inner models of planning. Emulators can facilitate making an appropriate movement after the target has become invisible, perhaps because the prey is in a cavity or the predator is sneaking up on the prey. More generally, with appropriate connectivity, an emulator could run off-line to plan for the long-term future, thus deploying extended body-image manipulation. Additional modification permits off-line emulation of cognitive states. For example, when planning the details of a raid, one may imagine oneself feeling anxiety while stalking the enemy camp, assessing the attentiveness of the camp guards, formulating specific intentions to outfox wary guards, and so on. Like body-image manipulation used in planning a climb, this is mind-image manipulation used in planning a complex, extended me-them encounter.[27]

CONSCIOUSNESS AND SELF-REPRESENTATION

An appealing hypothesis defended by Damasio[12] is that the self/nonself distinction, though originally designed to support coherencing, is ultimately responsible for consciousness. According to this view, a brain whose wiring enables it to distinguish between inner-world representations and outer-world representations and to build a metarepresentational model of the relation between outer and inner entities is a brain enjoying some degree of consciousness. Thus, such a system could represent the relation between the thistle and itself as "that (outer) thing causes me (inner) pain." Conceivably, as wiring modifications enable increasingly sophisticated simulation and deliberation, the self-representational apparatus becomes correspondingly more elaborate, and therewith the self/not-self apparatus. On this hypothesis, the degrees or levels of conscious awareness are upgraded in tandem with the self-representational upgrades. Thus, chimpanzees, but not frogs, know whether they can be seen by a subordinate female but not the dominant male. Infant human development studies and nonhuman primate studies support these hypotheses.[28,29]

Whether neuroscience can build on these foundations to discover full and detailed explanations of all self-representational phenomena remains to be seen. Still, unpredictability obscures the destiny of essentially all neurobiological puzzles, including noncognitive functions such as thermoregulation. An abiding challenge in neuroscience is to discover the basic principles governing the integration of information at various levels of brain organization and at various time scales. This challenge is not confined to the neuroscience of self-representation, but confronts neuroscience generally.

ACKNOWLEDGMENTS

Special thanks are extended to P.M. Churchland, M. Churchland, A. Churchland, J. Cohen, F. Crick, A. Damasio, D. Eagleman, and R. Grush.

REFERENCES AND NOTES

1. CHURCHLAND, P.M. (1988). *Matter and consciousness,* 2nd ed. Cambridge, MA: MIT Press.
2. CHURCHLAND, P.S. (1986). *Neurophilosophy.* Cambridge, MA: MIT Press).
3. DAMASIO, A.R. (1994). *Descartes' error.* New York: Grossett/Putnam.
4. HUME, D. (1739; 1888, modern edition). *A treatise of human nature.* L.A. Selby-Bigge (Ed.) Oxford: Clarendon Press.
5. LAKOFF, G. & JOHNSON, M. (1999). *Philosophy in the flesh.* New York: Basic Books.
6. CHURCHLAND, P.S. (in press). *Brain-wise: Studies in neurophilosophy.* Cambridge, MA: MIT Press.

 7. See the essays by Z. Vendler and by C. McGinn, in *The mind-body problem:* A
    Guide to the Current Debate. R. Warner, T. Szubka (Eds.) Oxford: Blackwell.
 8. FODOR, J.A., *Synthese 28,* 97 (1974). For criticism of this view, see P. S.
    Churchland & T.J. Sejnowski (1992) *The computational brain.* Cambridge,
    MA: MIT Press.
 9. DENNETT, D.C. (1991). *Consciousness explained.* Boston: Little, Brown.
10. PINKER, S. (1997). *How the mind works.* New York: Norton.
11. PALMER, S.E. (1999).*Vision science.* Cambridge, MA: MIT Press.
12. DAMASIO, A.R. (1999). *The feeling of what happens.* New York: Harcourt
    Brace.
13. SQUIRE, L.R. & KANDEL, E.R. (1999). *Memory: From mind to molecules.* New
    York: Freeman.
14. LEDOUX, J. (1996). *The emotional brain.* New York: Simon & Schuster.
15. LLINAS, R.R. (2001). *I of the vortex.* Cambridge, MA: MIT Press.
16. PANKSEPP, J. (1998). *Affective neuroscience.* New York: Oxford University
    Press.
17. ANDERSON, S.W. *et al.* (1999). *Nature Neuroscience, 2,* 1032.
18. BECHARA, A. *et al., Science , 275,* 1293.
19. HOBSON, A.R. (1989). *Sleep,* New York: Freeman.
20. CRICK, F. & KOCH, C. (in press) In *Problems in systems neuroscience.* J.L. van
    Hemmen & T.J. Sejnowski (Eds.) Oxford: Oxford University Press.
21. SPERRY, R.W. (1982). *Science, 217,* 1223.
22. HARTER, S. (1999). *The construction of the self:* A *developmental perspective.*
    New York: Guilford.
23. MEYER-LINDENBERG, A. *et al.* (2002). *Nature Neuroscience, 5,* 267.
24. FRITH, C.D. (1992). *The cognitive neuroscience of schizophrenia.* Hillsdale,
    NJ: Erlbaum.
25. STEPHENS, G.L. & GRAHAM, G. (2000). *When self-consciousness breaks.* Cam-
    bridge, MA: MIT Press.
26. WOLPERT, D.M. *et al.* (1995). *Science, 269,* 1880.
27. GRUSH, R. (1997). *Philosophy and Psychology, 10,* 5.
28. SCHORE, A.N. (1994). *Affect regulation and the origin of the self.* Hillsdale, NJ:
    Erlbaum.
29. TOMASELLO, M. & CALL, J. (1997). *Primate cognition.* New York: Oxford Uni-
    versity Press.

The Self as a Responding—and Responsible—Artifact

DANIEL C. DENNETT

Center for Cognitive Studies, Tufts University,
Medford, Massachusetts 02155, USA

ABSTRACT: The powerful illusion of a unified, Cartesian self responsible for intentional action is contrasted with the biologically sounder model of competitive processes that yield an only partially coherent agency, and the existence of the illusion of self is explained as an evolved feature of communicating agents, capable of responding to requests and queries about their own decisions and actions.

KEYWORDS: self; consciousness; agency; free will; timing of voluntary actions

It *seems* to us as if each of us *is* a self, a unified, rational agent, in control of a body. I am in charge of my body and you are in charge of your body. Descartes, in the 17th century, famously called this agent-in-charge a *res cogitans*, a thinking thing, and deduced to his own satisfaction that it could not be a physical, mechanical thing, but rather an immaterial thing, which he could conveniently identify with his immortal soul. (It was convenient, given his Roman Catholicism.) Today, materialism has swept dualism and its insoluble mysteries of interaction aside, so this is no longer regarded as a convenient, or even tenable, hypothesis.

Efforts to identify the self—a mortal and material soul, you might say—with a particular subsystem in the brain run into snags at every turn. I call this the fallacy of the Cartesian Theater, the place in the brain where it all comes together for conscious appreciation and decision. This just cannot be right. All the work done by the imagined homunculus in the Cartesian Theater must be distributed around to various lesser agencies in the brain. But some people just hate this idea. They think, mistakenly, that unless there is a Cartesian

Address for correspondence: Daniel C. Dennett, Center for Cognitive Studies, Tufts University, Medford, MA 02155-3952. Voice: 617-627-3297; fax: 617-627-3952.
ddennett@tufts.edu

Ann. N.Y. Acad. Sci. 1001: 39–50 (2003). © 2003 New York Academy of Sciences.
doi: 10.1196/annals.1279.003

Theater, there is no consciousness. They are wrong for many reasons, not least of which is that the *specs* for such a organ or faculty of the body turn out to be, shall we say, optimistic. We are just not that unified. The late, lamented evolutionary biologist William Hamilton, reflecting on his own uneasiness with his recognition of this fact, put the issue particularly well:

> In life, what was it I really wanted? My own conscious and seemingly indivisible self was turning out far from what I had imagined and I need not be so ashamed of my self-pity! I was an ambassador ordered abroad by some fragile coalition, a bearer of conflicting orders, from the uneasy masters of a divided empire.... As I write these words, even so as to be able to write them, I am pretending to a unity that, deep inside myself, I now know does not exist. (Hamilton, 1996, p. 134)

Such coherence as we manage in our lives is the dynamic and shifting resultant of competitions between all manner of structures, some of them deeply rooted in our genes (and with our paternally and maternally inherited genes in something of a permanent tug-of-war) and some of them temporary *ad hoc* coalitions of "interests" engaged in "intertemporal bargaining" (in the terms of George Ainslie, 2001), a recursive and self-referential process on a hair-trigger.

> Philosophers and psychologists are used to speaking about an organ of unification called the "self" that can variously "be" autonomous, divided, individuated, fragile, well-bounded, and so on, but this organ doesn't have to exist as such. (Ainslie, 2001, p. 43)

Given the literal chaos brewing in our brains, given the manifest absence of any King Neuron or Boss Nucleus, why and how does it *seem* to us that we are unified selves, and, come to think of it, who is this *us* that it so seems to in the first place?

It is almost impossible to talk about human cognition without invoking this "I" or "we" that is the witness and appreciator of the cognitive products, doer of the cognitive deeds. In his recent, and excellent, book, *The Illusion of Conscious Will*, Daniel Wegner lets himself put it this way: "We can't possibly know (let alone keep track of) the tremendous number of mechanical influences on our behavior because we inhabit an extraordinarily complicated machine" (Wegner, 2002, p. 27). These machines "we inhabit" simplify things for *our* benefit. Who or what is this "we" that inhabits the brain? If Hamilton is to be believed, it is a commentator and interpreter with limited access to the actual machinery, more along the lines of an ambassador or press secretary than a president or boss. And this imagery leads straight to Benjamin Libet's vision of "conscious will" as being almost out of the loop. I will briefly describe Libet's experiment, exposing the misinterpretations and explaining its significance for human responsibility. As I put it in *Consciousness Explained,*

> We are not quite "out of the loop" (as they say in the White House), but since our access to information is thus delayed, the most we can do is intervene with

last-moment "vetoes" or "triggers." Downstream from (unconscious) Command Headquarters, I take no real initiative, am never in on the birth of a project, but do exercise a modicum of executive modulation of the formulated policies streaming through my office. (Dennett, 1991, p. 164)

But I was expressing this view in order to demonstrate its falsehood. I went on to say: "This picture is compelling but incoherent." Others, however, don't see this incoherence. As the sophisticated neuroscientist Michael Gazzaniga has put it: "Libet determined that brain potentials are firing three hundred and fifty milliseconds before you have the conscious intention to act. So before you are aware that you're thinking about moving your arm, your brain is at work preparing to make that movement!" (Gazzaniga, 1998, p.73)

William Calvin, another fine neuroscientist puts it this way:

> My fellow neurophysiologist, Ben Libet has, to everyone's consternation, shown that the brain activity associated with the preparation for movement (something called the "readiness potential")....starts a quarter of a second before you report having decided to move. You just weren't yet conscious of your decision to move, but it was indeed under way.... (Calvin, 1990, p. 80–81)

and Libet himself has recently summarized his own interpretation of the phenomenon thus:

> The initiation of the freely voluntary act appears to begin in the brain unconsciously, well before the person consciously knows he wants to act! Is there, then, any role for conscious will in the performance of a voluntary act? (see Libet, 1985) To answer this it must be recognized that conscious will (W) does appear about 150 msec before the muscle is activated, even though it follows the onset of the RP [readiness potential]. An interval of 150 msec would allow enough time in which the conscious function might affect the final outcome of the volitional process. (Actually, only 100 msec is available for any such effect. The final 50 msec before the muscle is activated is the time for the primary motor cortex to activate the spinal motor nerve cells. During this time the act goes to completion with no possibility of stopping it by the rest of the cerebral cortex.) (Libet, 1999, p. 49)

Only a tenth of a second—100 msec—in which to issue presidential vetoes. As the astute neuroscientist Vilayanur Ramachandran once quipped, "This suggests that our conscious minds may not have free will, but rather 'free won't'!" (Ramachandran, 1998, p. 35) I hate to look a gift horse in the mouth, but I certainly want more free will than that. Can we find any flaws in the reasoning that has led this distinguished group of neuroscientists to this dire conclusion?

My suggestion builds on what I have come to regard as the most important sentence in my 1984 book, *Elbow Room* (p. 143): "(If you make yourself really small, you can externalize virtually everything.)" Stupidly, I made the mistake of putting this sentence in parentheses! Here is what I mean by it. Consider Libet's experiment more closely. When do *you* consciously decide?

Libet needs to hear from you, and he gives you a clock to watch. The experiment depends, in effect, on plotting the intersection of two trajectories:

the visual perception of the clockface and the rising-to-consciousness of the intention or decision or desire to flick the wrist. Putting his two sources of data—your subsequent report and his timed clock positions and EEG tracings—together, he gets an ominous result, but one that depends on his interpretation of the situation, which is only one of several possibilities. Consider three of these alternatives:

A. You are busy making your free decision in the *faculty of practical reasoning* (where all free decisions are made), and you have to wait there for visual contents to be sent over from the *vision center*. How long does this take? If time-pressure is not critical, perhaps the visual content is sent very slowly and is seriously out of date by the time it arrives, like yesterday's newspaper.

B. You are busy watching the clock in the *vision center*, and have to wait for the *faculty of practical reasoning* to send you the results of its latest decision-making. How long does this take? This might be another dawdling transmission, mightn't it?

C. You are sitting where you always sit: in *command headquarters* (otherwise known as the Cartesian Theater), and have to wait for both the *vision center* and the *faculty of practical reasoning* to send their respective outputs to this place, where everything comes together and consciousness happens. If one of these outposts is farther away, or transmits at a slower rate, you will be subject to illusions of simultaneity—if you judge simultaneity by actual arrival time at command headquarters, instead of relying on something like postmarks or time stamps.

Putting the matter this baldly helps, I hope, to see the problems with Libet's picture. What is the presumed implication of these different hypotheses? What would it mean for you to be in one of these places rather than the other? The governing idea is presumably that you can only *act* where you *are*, so if you are not *in* the faculty of practical reasoning when a decision is made there, *you* didn't make it. At best you delegated it. ("I want to be *in* the faculty of practical reasoning. After all, if I'm not *there* when decisions are made, the decisions won't be mine. They will be *its!*") But when you are there, you may get so engrossed in making your decision that "your eyes glaze over" and the vision center's good work goes unattended, never getting to you at all. So, perhaps, you should move back and forth between the faculty of practical reasoning and the vision center. But if that is what you do then it is quite possible that you were in fact conscious of the decision to flick *at the very moment you made it*, but it then took you more than 300 milliseconds to move to the vision center and pick up an image of the clock face showing the position of the moving millisecond mark, so you misjudged the simultaneity because you lost track of how long it took you to get from place to place. Whew! This is one hypothesis, call it *Strolling You*, that could save free will, by showing that the gap was an illusion, after all. According to this hypothesis, you *consciously* decided to flick when that part of your brain decided to flick (hey, you were *there, at the time,* riding the readiness potential as it was created), but you later misjudged the objective clock time of that decision because of the time it took you to get to the vision center and pick up the latest clockface position.

If you don't like that hypothesis, here is another one that could do the trick, based on alternative C, in which both the vision center and the faculty of practical reasoning are moved out of command headquarters. Call it *Out-of-touch You*. You have outsourced all these tasks, as today's business world would put it, delegating them to subcontractors, but you do keep limited control of their activities from your seat in command headquarters by sending them orders and getting results from them, in a continuous cycle of commands and responses. If asked to think of a reason not to dine out tonight, you send out to your faculty of practical reasoning for a reason, and pretty quick it sends two back: *I'm too tired* and *there's food in the fridge that will spoil if we don't eat it tonight.* How did the faculty come up with these? Why in this order? What operations did it execute to generate them? You haven't a clue—you just know what you sent out for, and recognize that what arrived back is a satisfactory fulfillment of your request. If asked what time it is, you send the appropriate command to the vision center, and it sends back the latest view of the watch on your wrist, with a little help from the *wrist-motion-control center,* but you have no insight into how that collaborative effort was achieved either. Given the problem of variable time delays, you institute a time-stamp system, which works well for most purposes, but you misuse it in Libet's rather unnatural setting. When asked, from your *underprivileged* position in command headquarters to judge just when, exactly, your faculty of practical reasoning issued its flick order (a judgment you are to render in terms of the time-stamps you discern on the streams of reports coming in from both the faculty of practical reasoning and the vision center), you match up the wrong reports. Since you're relying on second-hand information (reports from the two outlying subcontractors), you can easily just be wrong about which event happened first, or whether any two were simultaneous. If you don't like that hypothesis, there are others that could be considered, including, of course, all manner of hypotheses that *don't* "save free will" because they tend to confirm Libet's view of the matter: that in the normal course of moral decision-making, *you* in fact have at most 100 milliseconds in which to veto or otherwise adjust decisions made earlier (and elsewhere) unconsciously. Can't we just dismiss the whole sorry lot of them, on the grounds that these hypotheses are wildly unrealistic oversimplifications of what is known about how decision-making works in the brain? Yes indeed, we could, and we should. But when we do that, we don't just dismiss all these fanciful hypotheses that could "save free will" in the face of Libet's data; we must also dismiss Libet's own hypothesis and all the others that purport to show we only have "free won't." His hypothesis, just as much as those I've just sketched, depends on taking seriously the idea that *you* are restricted to the materials you can get access to from a particular subregion of the brain. How so? Consider his idea of a strictly limited window of opportunity to veto. Libet tacitly presupposes that *you* can't start thinking seriously about whether to veto something until you're conscious of what it is that you might want to veto, and you have to wait 300 milliseconds or more for this, which gives you only 100 milliseconds in which to "act": "This provides a period during which the conscious function could potentially determine whether the volitional process will go on to completion." (Libet, 1993 p. 134.) The "conscious function" waits, in the Cartesian Theater, until the information arrives, and only then *for the first time* has access to it, and can start thinking about what to do about it, whether to veto it, etc. But why couldn't *you* have been thinking ("unconsciously") about whether to veto *Flick!* ever since *you* decided ("unconsciously") to flick, half a second ago? Libet must be assuming that the brain is talented enough to work out the details of implementation on how to flick over that period of time, but only a "conscious function" is talented enough to work on the pros and cons of a veto decision.

In fact, at one point Libet sees this problem and addresses it candidly: "The possibility is not excluded that factors, on which the decision to veto (control) is *based*, do develop by unconscious processes that precede the veto." (1999, p. 51). But if that possibility is not excluded, then the conclusion Libet and others should draw is that the 300-millisecond "gap" has *not* been demonstrated at all. After all, we know that in normal circumstances the brain begins its discriminative and evaluative work as soon as stimuli are received, and works on many concurrent projects at once, enabling us to respond intelligently just in time for many deadlines, without having to stack them up in a queue waiting to get through the turnstile of consciousness before evaluation begins. Libet's 100-millisecond veto window is an artifact of the Cartesian Theater.

When you distribute the work in time and space, you distribute the responsibility in time and space. You are not out of the loop. You *are* the loop.

But why, then, does Libet's Cartesian vision *seem so compelling*? I think we can understand the illusion better if we think about the phenomenon from an evolutionary perspective. For Descartes, the mind was perfectly transparent to itself, with nothing happening out of view, and it has taken more than a century of psychological theorizing and experimentation to erode this ideal of perfect introspectability, which we can now see gets the situation almost backwards. Consciousness of the springs of action is the exception, not the rule, and it requires some rather remarkable circumstances to have evolved at all.

In most of the species that have ever lived, "mental" causation has no need for, and hence does not evolve, any elaborate capacity for self-monitoring. In general, causes work just fine in the dark, without needing to be observed by anybody, and that is as true of causes in animals' brains as anywhere else. So however "cognitive" an animal's faculties of discrimination might be, the capacity of their outputs to cause the selection of appropriate behavior does not need to be experienced *by anything or anybody*. A bundle of situation-action links of indefinite sophistication can reside in the nervous system of a simple creature and serve its many needs without any further supervision. Its individual actions may need to be guided by a certain amount of internal self-monitoring (specific to the action), in order to make sure, for example, that each predatory swipe snags its target, or to get the berries into the mouth, or to guide the delicate docking with the sexual parts of a conspecific of the opposite sex, but these feedback loops can be as isolated, as local, as the controls that spur the immune system into action when infection looms, or adjust the heart rate and breathing during exercise. (This is the truth behind the deeply misleading intuition that invertebrates, if not "higher, warm-blooded" animals, might be "robots" or "zombies" altogether lacking minds.)

As creatures acquire more and more such behavioral options, however, their worlds become cluttered, and the virtue of tidiness can come to be "appreciated" by natural selection. Many creatures have evolved simple instinctual behaviors for what might be called home improvement, preparing paths, lookouts, hideouts, and other features of their neighborhoods, generally making the local environment easier to get around in, easier to understand. Similarly, when the need arises, creatures evolve instincts for sprucing up their most intimate environments: their own brains, creating paths and landmarks for later use.

The goal unconsciously followed in these preparations is for the creature to come to know its way around itself, and how much of this internal home improvement is accomplished by individual self-manipulation and how much is incorporated genetically is an open empirical question. Along one of these paths, or many of them, lie the innovations that lead to creatures capable of considering different courses of action in advance of committing to any one of them, and weighing them on the basis of some projection of the probable outcome of each.

In the quest by brains to produce a useful future, this is a major improvement over the risky business of *blind* trial and error, since, as Karl Popper once put it, it permits some of your hypotheses to die in your stead. Such Popperian creatures, as I have called them, get to test some of their hunches in informed simulations, rather than risking them in the real world, but they needn't understand the rationale of this improvement in order to reap the benefits. The appreciation of the likely effects of particular actions is built into any such assessment, but the appreciation of the effects of the contemplation itself is a still higher, even more optional, level of self-monitoring. You don't have to know you're a Popperian creature to be one. After all, any chess playing computer considers and discards thousands or millions of possible moves on the basis of their probable outcomes, and it is manifestly not a conscious or self-conscious agent. (Not yet—the future may hold conscious and even self-conscious robots, which are certainly not impossible.)

What was it that arose in the world to encourage the evolution of a *less unwitting* implementation of Popperian behavioral control? What new environmental complexity favored the innovations in control structure that made this possible? In a word, communication. It is only once a creature begins to develop the activity of communication, and in particular the communication of its actions and plans, that it has to have some capacity for monitoring not just the results of its actions, but of its prior evaluations and formation of intentions as well (McFarland, 1989). At that point, it needs a level of self-monitoring that keeps track of which situation–action schemes are in the queue for execution, or in current competition for execution, and which candidates are under consideration in the faculty of practical reasoning, if that is not too grand a term for the arena in which the competition ensues. How could this new talent arise? We can tell a Just So Story that highlights the key features.

Compare the situation confronting our ancestors (and Mother Nature) to the situation confronting the software engineers who wanted to make computers more user-friendly. Computers are fiendishly complex machines, most of the details of which are nauseatingly convoluted and, for most purposes, beneath notice. Computer-users don't need information on the states of all the flip-flops, the actual location of their data on the disk, and so forth, so software designers created a series of simplifications—even benign distortions in many cases—of the messy truth, cunningly crafted to mesh with, and enhance, the users' pre-existing powers of perception and action. Click and drag, sound effects, icons on desktops, are the most obvious and famous of these, but anybody who cares to dig deeper will find a bounty of further metaphors that help make sense of what is going on inside, but always paying the cost of simplification. As people interacted more and more with computers, they devised a host of new tricks, projects, goals, ways of using and abusing the competences designed for them by the engineers, who thereupon went back to the drawing board to devise further refinements and improvements, which were then used and abused in turn, a co-evolutionary process that continues apace today. The user interface we interact with today was unimagined when computers first appeared, and it is the tip of an iceberg in several senses: not only are the details of what goes on inside your computer hidden; but so are the details of the history of R & D, the false starts, the bad ideas that fizzled before ever reaching the public (as well as the notorious ones that did, and failed to catch on).

A similar process of R & D created the user interface between talking people and other talking people, and it uncovered similar design principles and (free-floating) rationales. It too was co-evolutionary, with people's behaviors, attitudes and purposes evolving in response to the new powers they discovered. Now people could *do things with words* that they could never do before, and the beauty of the whole development was that it *tended* to make those features of their complicated neighbors that they were most interested in adjusting readily accessible to adjustment from outside—even by somebody who knew nothing about the internal control system, the brain. These ancestors of ours discovered whole generative classes of behaviors for adjusting the behavior of others, and for monitoring and modulating (and if need be, resisting) the reciprocal adjustment of their own behavioral controls by those others.

The centerpiece metaphor of this co-evolved human user-illusion is the Self, which appears to reside in a place in the brain, the Cartesian Theater, providing a limited, metaphorical outlook on what's going on in our brains. It provides this outlook to others, *and to ourselves*. In fact, we wouldn't exist, as Selves "inhabiting complicated machinery" as Wegner vividly puts it, if it weren't for the evolution of social interactions requiring each human animal to create within itself a subsystem designed for interacting with others. Once created, it could also interact with itself at different times. Until we human beings came along, no agent on the planet enjoyed the curious *non*-obliviousness we have to the causal links that emerged as salient once we human beings began to talk about what we were up to.[a] As Wegner puts it, "People become what they think they are, or what they find that others think they are, in a process of negotiation that snowballs constantly." (p. 314)

When psychologists and neuroscientists devise a new experimental setup or paradigm in which to test nonhuman subjects such as rats or cats or monkeys or dolphins, they often have to devote dozens or even hundreds of hours to training each subject on the new tasks. A monkey, for instance, can be trained to look to the left if it sees a grating moving up and look to the right if it sees a grating moving down. A dolphin can be trained to retrieve an object that looks like (or *sounds* like, to its echolocating system) an object displayed to it by a trainer. All this training takes time and patience, on the part of both trainer and subject. Human subjects in such experiments, however, can usually just be told what is desired of them. After a brief question-and-answer session and a few minutes of practice, we human subjects will typically be as competent in the new environment as any agent ever could be. Of course, we do have to *understand* the representations presented to us in these briefings, and what is asked of us has to be composed of action-parts that fall within the range of things we can do. That is what Wegner means when he identifies voluntary actions as things we can do when asked. If asked to lower your blood pressure or adjust your heartbeat or wiggle your ears, you will not be so ready to comply, though with training not unlike that given to laboratory animals, you may eventually be able to add such feats to your repertoire of voluntary actions.

When language came into existence, it brought into existence the kind of mind that can transform itself on a moment's notice into a somewhat different virtual machine, taking on new projects, following new rules, adopting new

---

[a]Philosophers may want to compare my Just So Story to Wilfrid Sellars' (1963) myth of "our Rylean ancestors," and Jones, the inventor of "thoughts." My debt to Sellars should be clear to them.

policies. We are transformers. That's what a mind is, as contrasted with a mere brain: the control system of a chameleonic transformer. A virtual machine for making more virtual machines. Non-human animals can engage in voluntary action of sorts. The bird that flies wherever it wants is voluntarily wheeling this way and that, voluntarily moving its wings, and it does this without benefit of language. The distinction embodied in anatomy between what it can do voluntarily (by moving its striated muscles) and what happens autonomically, moved by smooth muscle and controlled by the autonomic nervous system, is not at issue. We have added a layer on top of the bird's (and the ape's and the dolphin's) capacity to decide what to do next. It is not an anatomical layer in the brain, but a functional layer, a virtual layer composed somehow in the micro-details of the brain's anatomy: We can ask each other to do things, and we can ask ourselves to do things. And at least sometimes we readily comply with these requests. Yes, your dog can be "asked" to do a variety of voluntary things, but it can't ask why you make these requests. A male baboon can "ask" a nearby female for some grooming, but neither of them can discuss the likely outcome of compliance with this request, which might have serious consequences for both of them, especially if the male is not the alpha male of the troop. We human beings not only can do things when requested to do them; we can answer inquiries about what we are doing and why. We can engage in the practice of asking, and giving, reasons.

It is this kind of asking, which we can also direct to ourselves, that creates the special category of voluntary actions that sets us apart. Other, simpler intentional systems act in ways that are crisply predictable on the basis of the beliefs and desires we attribute to them based on our surveys of their needs and their history, their perceptual and behavioral talents, but some of our actions are different, in a *morally relevant* way: they result from decisions we make in the course of trying to make sense of ourselves and our own lives (Coleman, 2001).

Once we begin talking about what we're doing, we need to keep track of what we're doing so we can have ready answers to these inquiries. Language requires us to keep track, but also helps us keep track, by helping us categorize and (over)simplify our *agendas*. We cannot help but become amateur auto-psychologists. Nicholas Humphrey and others have spoken of apes and other highly social species as *natural psychologists*, because of the manifest skill and attention they devote to interpreting each other's behavior, but since, unlike academic psychologists—and other human beings—apes never get to compare notes, to argue about attributions of motives and beliefs, their competence as psychologists never obliges them to use explicit representations. With us, it is different. We need to have something to say when asked what the heck we think we're doing. And when we answer, our authority is problematic, as Hamilton noted.

Wegner is right, then, to identify the Self that emerges in his and Libet's experiments as a sort of public-relations agent, a spokesperson instead of a boss, but these are extreme cases set up to isolate factors that are normally integrated, and we need not identify *ourselves* so closely with such a temporarily isolated self. ("If you make yourself really small, you can externalize virtually everything." (Dennett, 1984, p. 143) Wegner draws our attention to the times—not infrequent among those of us who are "absent-minded"—when we find ourselves with a perfectly conscious thought that just baffles us; it is, as he wonderfully puts it, *conscious but not accessible* (p. 163). (Now why am I standing in the kitchen in front of the cupboard? I know I'm in the place I meant to be, but what did I come in here to get?) At such a moment, *I* have lost track of the context, and hence the *raison d'être*, of this very thought, this conscious experience, and so its meaning (and that's what is most important) is temporarily no more accessible to *me*—the larger me that does the policy-making—than it would be to any third party, any "outside" observer who came upon it. In fact some onlooker might well be able to re-mind me of what it was I was up to. My capacity to be reminded (re-minded) is crucial, since it is only this that could convince me that this onlooker was right, that this was something *I* was doing. If the thought or project is any-one's, it is mine—it belongs to the me who set it in motion and provided the context in which this thought makes sense; it is just that the part of me that is baffled is temporarily unable to gain access to the other part of me that is the author of this thought.

I might say, in apology, that I was *not myself* when I made that mistake, or forgot what I was about, but this is not the severe disruption of self-control that is observed in schizophrenia, in which the patient's own thoughts are in-terpreted as alien voices. This is just the fleeting loss of contact that can dis-rupt a perfectly good plan. A lot of what *you* are, a lot of what you are doing and know about, springs from structures down there in the engine room, caus-ing the action to happen. If a thought of yours is *only* conscious, but not also accessible *to that machinery* (to some of it, to the machinery that needs it), then *you* can't do anything with it, and are left just silently mouthing the damn phrase to yourself, your isolated self, over and over. Isolated conscious-ness can indeed do nothing much on its own. Nor can it be responsible.

As Wegner notes, "If people will often forget tasks for the simple reason that the tasks have been completed, this signals a *loss of contact* [emphasis added–DCD] with their initial intentions once actions are over—and thus a susceptibility to revised intentions." (p. 167) A loss of contact between what and what? Between a Cartesian Self that "does nothing" and a brain that makes all the decisions? No. A loss of contact between the you that was in charge then and the you that is in charge now. A *person* has to be able to keep in contact with past and anticipated intentions, and one of the main roles of the brain's user-illusion of itself, which I call the self as a center of narrative gravity, is to provide *me* with a means of interfacing with myself at other times. As Wegner puts it, "Conscious will is particularly useful, then, as a guide to ourselves."(p. 328) The perspectival trick we need in order to escape the clutches of the Cartesian Theater is coming to see that *I*, the larger, temporally and spatially extended self, can control, to some degree, what goes on inside of the simplification barrier, where the decision-making happens, and that is why, as Wegner says, "Illusory or not, conscious will is the person's guide to his or her own moral responsibility for action." (p. 341)

ACKNOWLEDGMENTS

This essay is adapted from a chapter in my forthcoming book, *Freedom Evolves* (Viking Penguin, 2003). It also draws on material in my Nicod Lectures and Daewoo Lectures, forthcoming from MIT Press.

REFERENCES

AINSLIE, GEORGE (2001). *The breakdown of will.* Cambridge: Cambridge University Press.

CALVIN, WILLIAM (1990). *The cerebral symphony: Seashore reflections on the structure of consciousness.* New York: Bantam.

COLEMAN, MARY (2001). *Decisions in action: Reasons, motivation, and the connection between them.* Ph.D. dissertation, Philosophy Department, Harvard University.

DENNETT, DANIEL C. (1984). *Elbow room: The varieties of free will worth wanting.* Cambridge, MA: Bradford Books/MIT Press and Oxford University Press

DENNETT, DANIEL C. (1991). *Consciousness explained.* Boston: Little, Brown

GAZZANIGA, MICHAEL. (1998) *The mind's past.* Berkeley and Los Angeles: University of California Press.

HAMILTON, WILLIAM D. (1996). *Narrow roads of gene land: Vol 1: Evolution of social behaviour.* Oxford: Freeman.

LIBET, BENJAMIN, *et al.* (1983). Time of conscious intention to act in relation to onset of cerebral activities (readiness potential): The unconscious initiation of a freely voluntary act. *Brain, 106,* 623–642.

LIBET, BENJAMIN (1999). Do we have free will? in Benjamin Libet, Anthony Freeman, and Keith Sutherland (Eds.), *vide infra,* pp. 45–55.

LIBET, BENJAMIN, FREEMAN, ANTHONY & SUTHERLAND, KEITH (1999). *The volitional brain: Towards a neuroscience of free will.* Thorverton, UK: Imprint Academic.

RAMACHANDRAN, V. Quoted in *New Scientist*, 5 September 1998, p. 35.

SELLARS, WILFRID (1963). Empiricism and the philosophy of mind, in Sellars, *Science, perception and reality.* London: Routledge & Kegan Paul, pp. 127–196.

WEGNER, DANIEL (2002). *The illusion of conscious will.* Cambridge, MA: Bradford Books/MIT Press.

Whatever Happened to the Soul?

Theological Perspectives on Neuroscience and the Self

NANCEY MURPHY

Fuller Theological Seminary, Pasadena, California 91182, USA

ABSTRACT: Traditional religious teachings about the nature of the person, especially body–soul dualism, influence majority views of the self. Following a historical overview, it is argued that a purely physicalist account of human nature is equally compatible with contemporary science and with Christian thought. However, an account that reduces higher human capacities to neurobiology is unacceptable from a theological perspective.

KEYWORDS: dualism; physicalism; reductionism; science and religion; self; soul

INTRODUCTION

The statement of purpose for the conference for which this essay was written includes the following: "It is particularly important that neuroscientific research on the self be adequate to our broader understanding, as reflected through philosophical, theological, and social-scientific perspectives." What should neuroscientists know about religious views of the self in order to pursue this goal? In this essay I shall first offer a very rough, anecdotal overview of what assorted segments of our society believe about the nature of the person. Second, I shall argue that there is no necessary conflict between *normative* Christian views and current scientific views. In particular, Christian scholarship rejected body–soul dualism at least 50 years ago, leaving the way open for agreement with science on the purely physical makeup of humans. (Unfortunately I shall not be able to speak for other religious bodies. I believe that what I say about Christians is closely paralleled by Jewish thought. Regarding other religions I simply cannot say.) Third, I suggest that if there is a

Address for correspondence: Nancey Murphy, Fuller Theological Seminary, 135 N. Oakland Avenue, Pasadena, CA 91182. Voice: 626-584-5253; fax: 626-584-5251.
nmurphy@fuller.edu

Ann. N.Y. Acad. Sci. 1001: 51–64 (2003). © 2003 New York Academy of Sciences.
doi: 10.1196/annals.1279.004

point of contention between science and Christian scholarship it is more philosophical then theological; it regards the issue of reductionism.

A SKETCHY OVERVIEW OF IDEAS OF THE SELF

A remarkable thing about our culture is the fact that we have no shared concept of the nature of the self. Even more remarkable is the fact that up until quite recently, no one seemed to recognize the unspoken divisions among us. On the issue that we might call the "metaphysical makeup" of the person there are at least four types of theories: First, there is the view that humans are composed of three parts, generally labeled as body, soul, and spirit; this is called trichotomism. The second view is that humans are composed of two parts, body and soul *or* body and mind; this is dualism. Third is the view that humans are purely physical beings; this is most often called physicalism. Finally, there is another sort of monism that has been important in earlier philosophical systems and now is espoused by some New Age thinkers: the view that humans are purely spiritual beings and that their apparent physicality is an illusion; I'll call this idealist monism.

Because this issue has not been much discussed in public forums it is difficult to know how large a following each of these theories has. Here are some rough generalizations about the general population based on polling my audiences when I lecture on this subject. The majority (I was surprised to discover) are trichotomists, many are dualists of one sort or another, and very few are physicalists. I do not know the prevalence of idealist monism. (Idealism is a philosophical system according to which all reality is fundamentally mental in nature.)

Among those with theological education there is a split between conservative and liberal Protestants. Conservatives are much more likely to be dualists. Liberals, while perhaps not describing themselves as physicalists, tend to take for granted the mid-20th-century critique of body–soul dualism as a Hellenistic addition to or distortion of biblical teaching. I shall come back to this below.

Since the 1950s the number of physicalists in philosophy has been increasing. The success of the neurosciences in addressing mental capacities, combined with a general agreement that we all want to be post- or anti-Cartesian, has quite recently made for a near consensus on physicalism. Nearly all of the remaining dualists have religious commitments which I take to motivate their positions.

Again, based on anecdotal information, it seems that scientists tend to divide according to disciplines. Biologists and neuroscientists are overwhelmingly physicalists, but physicists and chemists are unpredictable. The issue of reductionism is crucial here. Does physicalism necessarily involve a reductionist view of human life? If it does, then despite a host of problems with dualism, dualism might appear to be the better option. Physicists are more likely than biologists to be reductionists, and thus more likely to be dualists.

A NORMATIVE VIEW

The neat typology of views of the self that I have offered belies a great deal of individual diversity: If one asks individuals what is meant by terms such as "soul" or "spirit" or even "physical," one gets all sorts of answers, so in effect there are almost as many accounts of human nature as there are people! It will be helpful to consider a brief historical sketch in order to see where some of these various views have originated. The history will also provide grounds for my argument in favor of a Christian physicalist account. My focus will be on the Christian tradition, but there are important parallels with Judaism, and to a lesser extent with Islam. Interactions among theology, philosophy, and science have been crucial.

I have failed to discover any comprehensive history of the issue with which I'm concerned here—the metaphysical makeup of the human person. One aspect that needs to be included is the history of *oversimplifications* of earlier history, to which I am sure to be contributing, given the brevity of this essay!

There were a variety of theories of human nature available to the writers of the New Testament, with correlative expectations regarding what happens after death. It is widely agreed among current Christian and Jewish scholars that early Hebraic accounts of the person were holistic and physicalist, and there was no well-developed account of life after death. By Jesus' day, however, there was a lively debate as to whether or not the dead would rise at the end of time. The Hellenization of the region had begun several centuries earlier and some Jews had adopted a dualistic view of body and soul, along with a conception of the soul's survival of death. Early Gentile Christians probably held an even wider variety of views. The important fact to note is that there is no explicit teaching on the metaphysical composition of the person.

As Christianity spread throughout the Mediterranean world, its theology was developed in conversation with a variety of philosophical and religious systems. Tertullian (160–220) followed the Stoics in teaching that the human soul is corporeal and is generated with the body. Origen (185–254) followed Plato in teaching that the soul is incorporeal and eternal, pre-existing the body. Plato (427?–348 BCE) described the person as an immortal soul imprisoned in a mortal body. The soul is tripartite and hierarchically organized. There is an analogy between the harmonious functioning of the soul and that of the ideal state. The appetitive or impulsive element of the soul is analogous to the lowest class in society, the consumers. Reason is the highest element, and corresponds to the ruling class. In between is an element corresponding to the soldier–police. The name for this element, *thumos,* may be translated "spirit" (in the sense in which a horse has spirit). The proper coordination of these three elements or faculties constitutes human well-being.

Plato's concept of the soul was related to his "other-worldly" view of reality. During much of his career he held the doctrine of the *Forms* or *Ideas*— the view that concepts have a real existence and are eternal. He argued that, since people possess knowledge of these concepts or Forms without being taught them, they must have come to know them by acquaintance before birth. Thus, the rational part of the soul pre-exists the body, dwelling in the transcendent realm of the Forms, and returns there at death.

Augustine (354–430) has been the most influential teacher on these matters because of his legacy in both Protestant and Catholic theology and because of his importance in the development of Christian spirituality. Augustine's conception of the person is a modified Platonic view: a human being is an immortal (not eternal) soul using (not imprisoned in) a mortal body. The soul is tripartite and hierarchically ordered. However, the "parts" are slightly different from those recognized by Plato. Our modern conception of the will is an Augustinian notion, and for Augustine the will is superior to the intellect.

Foreshadowed in Augustine's thought is the modern problem of causal interaction. If the soul is to the body as an agent to a tool, then it is inconsistent to say that the body affects the soul. Consequently Augustine was never able to give a satisfactory account of sensory knowledge. Augustine's notion that one knows one's own soul directly will have striking repercussions in modern epistemology.

There are interesting points of contact between Augustine's thought and current controversies. Descartes has become the philosopher everyone loves to criticize: see, for example, Antonio Damasio on "Descartes's error"[1] and Daniel Dennett's critique of the "Cartesian theater" in consciousness studies.[2] Damasio criticizes Descartes for developing the idea that we are most rational and moral when we are least emotional. But it is really Augustine whom we should blame for importing from Platonic thought the idea that the emotions or appetites need to be overruled by the intellect and will. Augustine was much influenced by the Neoplatonists, who had incorporated Platonic philosophy into religious systems emphasizing the care and development of the soul as the means of salvation. Augustine and other early theologians so influenced bequeathed this emphasis on the soul to subsequent spiritual writers. It is by cultivating the higher faculties of the soul (and often by repressing the lower faculties and the body) that one develops the capacity for knowledge of and relation to God.

Augustine was also the inventor of the peculiar metaphor that is now anachronistically called the Cartesian theater.[3] He spoke (in his *Confessions*) of entering into the roomy chambers of his memory, wherein he could examine the deliverances of the senses, mathematical ideas, and all of the other contents of consciousness. This metaphor was not preserved in the philosophical tradition, but came down to Descartes through the Christian spiritual tradition.

A major turning point in Christian history came as a result of borrowing from Muslim scholarship. The Muslims had preserved and commented on Aristotle's philosophy and through their work brought about an Aristotelian revival in Europe during the later Middle Ages. In his mature position, Aristotle (384–322 BCE) thought of the soul not as an entity, but more as a life principle—that aspect of the person which provides the powers or attributes characteristic of the human being. Plants and animals have souls as well, nutritive and sensitive souls, which give them the powers to grow and reproduce and to move and perceive, respectively. Human souls are organized hierarchically and incorporate the nutritive and sensitive powers, but in addition provide rational powers. Aristotle illustrates the relation of soul to body with an analogy: if the eye were a complete animal, sight would be its soul. Because the soul is a principle of the functioning of the body, it would follow that the soul dies with the body. However, a vestige of Aristotle's earlier, Platonic dualism remains in his speculation that perhaps one aspect of rationality (*Nous*) survives death. But even if this is the case, this does not amount to personal immortality, since *Nous* is an impersonal rational faculty.

Aristotle's conception of the soul and body fits well into his general "hylomorphic" conception of reality. All material things are composed of matter and form. Form is an immanent principle that gives things their essential characteristics and powers. The soul is but one type of form. Although Aristotle uses the same term ("form") as Plato, it is important to stress the differences between their views. Aristotle's forms are not pre-existent, transcendent entities, as for Plato. Since for Aristotle the soul is a form, this difference matters a great deal in his concept of the person, and makes it questionable whether Aristotle's view should be considered an instance of body–soul dualism at all.

In the writings of Thomas Aquinas (1225–1274) we have the most systematic development of an Aristotelian alternative to the largely Platonic account developed by Augustine. Thomas took up both Aristotelian hylomorphic metaphysics and Aristotle's thesis that the soul is the form of the body. This position might be described as a modified rather than radical dualism, and it is still held by many Catholic theologians.

Thomas (inheriting a great deal from Muslim scholars) had an elaborate account of the hierarchically ordered faculties or powers of the soul, which is in some ways surprisingly perceptive when compared with contemporary cognitive and neurosciences. For example, in addition to the five exterior senses, he recognized four faculties that he designated "interior senses." One of these, what he called the *sensus communis,* is the capacity to collate information derived from the senses in order to recognize that they all pertain to the same object. This is now discussed in neuroscience under the heading of the binding problem. His *vis aestimativa* (estimative power) is the capacity we share with animals to recognize something as harmful or harmless, friendly or unfriendly. This is strikingly similar to what Joseph LeDoux calls "emotional appraisal." LeDoux's distinction between object recognition and emotional appraisal is Thomas's distinction between the *sensus communis* and the *vis aestimativa*. LeDoux writes:

> When a certain region of the brain is damaged [the temporal lobe], animals or humans lose the capacity to appraise the emotional significance of certain stimuli without any loss in the capacity to perceive the stimuli as objects. The perceptual representation of an object and the evaluation of the significance of an object are separately processed in the brain. [In fact] the emotional meaning of a stimulus can begin to be appraised before the perceptual systems have fully processed the stimulus. It is, indeed, possible for your brain to know that something is good or bad before it knows exactly what it is.[4]

Another interesting point of contact concerns Thomas's account of morality. He describes the will as the ability to be attracted to goods of a non-sensible sort. Morality is a function of attraction to the good combined with rational judgment about what is truly good. Antonio Damasio's account of certain victims of temporal lobe damage who lose their ability to act prudently and morally could be translated into Thomistic terms: their intellect is intact but they have lost the capacity to be attracted to the good.[5]

Two factors at the dawn of modernity challenged the Aristotelian/Thomistic account of human nature. One was the Protestant Reformation's tendency to associate Aristotelianism with Catholicism and to reject it in favor of the more Platonic elements in Augustine's thought. The other was the demise of Aristotelian metaphysics as a whole due to the rise of modern science—the substitution of atomism for hylomorphism.

Galileo (1564–1642) is famous for his role in the Copernican revolution. However, he played a comparable role in a development that has had equally revolutionary consequences: the substitution of a corpuscular or atomist conception of matter for ancient and medieval hylomorphism. The revolution in astronomy called for adjustments in physics and chemistry, and even in theology, ethics, and political theory. Atomism in metaphysics and physics eventually affected chemistry, psychology, the social sciences, and, indirectly, theology. The animosity toward any sort of teleology that one still encounters in contemporary philosophy of biology seems to be residual heat from the explosive collision of these two worldviews.

No less were there consequences in philosophy. René Descartes (1596–1650) is considered the originator of modern philosophy. We can see why he would turn away from the (still official) Catholic account of the soul as the substantial *form* of the body and propose a radical substance dualism more akin to Platonism when we recall that Descartes was also involved in the atomist revolution in physics. Descartes distinguished two basic kinds of realities, extended substance (*res extensa*) and thinking substance (*res cogitans*); the latter included angels and human minds.

Notice the shift from "souls" to "minds." The two terms could be used interchangeably in Descartes's writings. In addition to its new metaphysical status as substance independent of matter, Descartes's notion of soul differed from his predecessors' in rejecting the Aristotelian notion of degrees or orders of soul. For Aristotle and his followers the vegetative or nutritive soul was that which animated the body, the sensitive or animal soul accounted for perception and emotion, and the rational soul accounted for intellect and will. Descartes saw no need for soul to animate the body—it is a machine that works on its own. Both emotions and sensations were caused by the body, but consciousness of them was an aspect of cognition. So whereas earlier the mind had been one part or function of the soul, now mind, cognition, consciousness (thus expanded to include consciousness of sensation and emotion) became the soul's sole function.

Only in recent years have the connotations of "mind" and "soul" so diverged that "soul" is used exclusively in religious contexts. It is interesting to note that where earlier translators of Descartes's *anima* (Lat.) or *l'âme* (Fr.) used "soul," more recent translations substitute "mind."

It has become common to project something like Cartesian dualism back onto ancient philosophers, but this is an oversimplification: First, as we have already seen, the philosophers of Greece and Rome were not at all united on these issues. Second, it is difficult to think our way back to these ancient sources; we have a fairly precise concept of the material, which allows for a sharp distinction between the material and the nonmaterial. However, one of the contentious issues in ancient philosophy was the nature of matter itself. For many Greek thinkers reality was conceived of as a hierarchy of beings exhibiting varying degrees of materiality. One important conflict in ancient philosophy concerned the question of whether or not the soul belonged to this gradation of material realities. Epicureans provided an atomist–materialist account of the soul; the Stoics regarded the human soul as but an aspect of an all-pervading cosmic logos.

The shift from hylomorphism to atomism and substance dualism created what is now seen by many to be an insoluble problem: mind–body interaction. Whereas for Aristotle and his followers the mind/soul was but one instance of form, in modern thought the mind becomes something of an anomaly in an otherwise purely material world of nature. Furthermore, the very conception of matter has changed. Before, matter and form had been correlative concepts—matter was that which had the potential to be activated by form. Matter (at least as unformed, prime matter) was entirely passive. For early moderns, matter is also passive, inert. But now, instead of being moved by immanent forms, it is moved by external forces—physical forces. Now there is a dilemma: hold on to the immateriality of mind, and there is then no way to account for its supposed ability to move the body; interpret it as a quasi-physical force and its effects ought to be measurable and quantifiable as is any other force in nature. But nothing of the latter enters into modern physics.

Throughout the modern period dualism, idealism (e.g., George Berkeley [1685–1753]), and physicalism (e.g., Thomas Hobbes [1588–1679]) have been options in philosophy. Cartesian dualism and idealism have by turns had considerable impact on theological conceptions of the self.

For all of its repercussions elsewhere in theology, the Reformation seems not to have brought the issue of human nature to the forefront. Controversies regarding purgatory led to disputes about the "intermediate state" between death and the final resurrection. Martin Luther and some of the radical reformers argued that the soul either dies with the body or "sleeps" until the general resurrection; Calvin wrote a treatise titled *Psychopannychia* (1542) to contest such views. Yet even those who argued for the death of the soul were obviously presupposing a dualistic conception of the person.

Some interesting twists in this story are the result of critical church history and historical-critical biblical scholarship, beginning especially in the nineteenth century. At that time many scholars called into question the authenticity of miracle accounts in the Bible, and especially the chief miracle, the resurrection of Jesus. This led to an emphasis in theological circles on an immortal soul as the only basis for Christian hope for life after death. Immanuel Kant's (1724–1804) transcendental argument for the immortality of the soul played a complementary role.

At the same time, though, critical scholarship made it possible to ask whether current doctrines (including doctrines regarding the soul) were in fact original Christian (and Hebraic) teaching or whether they were the result of later doctrinal developments *read back* into the biblical texts. It became common during the twentieth century to make a sharp distinction between original Hebraic conceptions and later Greek accretions such as body–soul dualism, and to favor the former as authentic Christian teaching. In addition, both theologians and biblical scholars in the past 50 years have rediscovered the centrality of the resurrection of the *body* (or better, the resurrection of the whole person) in primitive Christian proclamation.

Given these many shifting views of normative Christian teaching, reference works dealing with concepts such as *body, soul, resurrection, immortality,* and others are likely to tell one more about the assumptions of the era in which they were written than they do about original or authentic Christian teaching. For example, in *The Encyclopedia of Religion and Ethics* (1909–1921) there is a lengthy article on "soul" and no entry for "resurrection." In *The Anchor Bible Dictionary* (1992) there is no entry for "soul" and a very long set of entries on "resurrection."

Science has affected these debates at three major points. First, as already mentioned, the atomist revolution in physics represented the replacement of Aristotelian hylomorphism, so not only did it become impossible to understand the soul as the *form* of the body, but the very conception of *matter* involved in speaking of the body changed radically.

Second, evolutionary biology pushed many in the direction of physicalist accounts of human nature: if animals have no souls (as moderns, beginning with Descartes, assumed), then humans must not have them either. Many theologians (including Pope Pius XII) evaded this materialist conclusion by granting that the human body is a product of biological evolution, but maintaining that God creates a soul for each individual at conception. This intellectual maneuver runs into difficulties, however, when we ask when the *human* species appeared. Contemporary biologists now offer a very complex account of human origins in which there is no clear distinction between animals and humans. Were our first hominid ancestors human, or are only modern humans truly human, or did the change take place somewhere in between? What about hominid species that are not in the direct line of descent to modern humans? To claim that humans alone have the gift of a soul seems to force an arbitrary distinction where there is much evidence for continuity.

Pope John Paul II issued a statement recently that bears on these issues. The purpose of the address to the plenary session of the Pontifical Academy of Sciences in October of 1996 was to reaffirm the teaching of Pius XII regarding the compatibility of evolutionary biology with Catholic teaching, so long as certain qualifications are borne in mind. One of these qualifications concerns human origins. John Paul quoted Pius XII's statement that "if the human body takes its origin from pre-existent living matter, the spiritual soul is immediately created by God."[6]

Pius's teaching affirms a dualist account of the human person and uses this account to delimit the scope of science's investigation of human origins. Many readers take the current Pope to affirm the same dualist anthropology and the same limits to the scientific study of humankind. However, as George Coyne (Director of the Vatican Observatory) points out, after the quotation from Pius XII, the word "soul" does not reappear in the document.[7] Rather than speaking of the moment when the soul is created, John Paul II speaks of "the moment of transition to the spiritual." This transition is not scientifically observable; science can discover valuable signs indicating what is specific to the human being, but only theology can explain the ultimate meaning of these distinctively human features.

So the current Pope recognizes limits to the scientific study of human nature, yet without a compartmentalization based on dualistic anthropology. His chief concern is reductionism. He says that "theories of evolution which, in accordance with the philosophies inspiring them, consider the mind as emerging from the forces of living matter, or as a mere epiphenomenon of this matter, are incompatible with the truth about man."

The most significant scientific development having a bearing on this long history of debates, of course, is now occurring in the cognitive neurosciences.

So what does all this mean for a normative view; that is, what *ought* Christians to believe about the nature of the person? I want to make two points: First, most of the dualism that has *appeared* to be biblical teaching has been a result of poor translations. The original Aramaic and Hebrew terms were first translated into Greek, and later taken to mean what Greek philosophers would mean by them. These meanings come down to us in older English translations. After the translations have been fixed, it is hard to find any clear *teaching* on the metaphysical make-up of the person—this is simply not a question the biblical authors were interested in. They apparently assumed a variety of extant views and then used them for their own purposes. So, insofar as the Bible is normative for Christians, it appears that they are free to adopt either physicalism or dualism. However, the very popular trichotomist view (humans composed of body, soul, and spirit) has no textual warrant.

Second, despite lack of clarity on this issue in the Bible, it is in fact the case that most Christians throughout most of their history have been dualists of one sort or another. However, the fact that this has been largely due to cultural influences should free contemporary Christians to formulate accounts of human nature that are in keeping with current cultural developments such as science. And as already noted, this has in fact been happening throughout the twentieth century, primarily among the more liberal scholars.

One might ask, though, if scholars have been thinking along these lines for so long, why is it still the case that the general population has not. Part of the explanation is simply the time that it always takes for changes in scholarly opinion to become widely disseminated. Part is due to theological conservatism (and there are theological sticking points that I am passing over here). Finally, and now I am speculating, part is due to the arrival on the intellectual scene of the handy word "self," which is the focus of this publication. At some point in modernity philosophers and essayists began to speak of "self," first speaking about self-reflection, self-mastery, self-exploration, and then about *the self* itself.[8] This neologism made it possible for dualists, idealists, and physicalists all to use the same language, and so metaphysical differences became cloaked under agreement about phenomenological descriptions of human experience.

Scientists need to keep in mind the wide gap between scholars and laity on this issue. It underlies longstanding disputes about issues such as abortion, as well as current debates about cloning and stem-cell research. And here it may not be scholarly opinion that matters so much as numbers of votes.

WHAT THEOLOGY NEEDS FROM SCIENCE

The question with which I began was this: what does neuroscience need to take into account in order to be adequate to a theological perspective on the self? So far I have emphasized instead the possibility of accommodating theology to current science. I would go further and say that this accommodation is good for Christianity: body–soul dualism has been linked for centuries to Platonic other-worldliness, which has given Christians something to distract them from the hard business of seeking God's reign *on earth*. It has also allowed for an inflated self-image: the fact that someone in nearly every audience I address takes the denial of the existence of the human soul to be equivalent to the denial of God's existence shows the extent to which Christian dualists have thought of their souls as little gods!

What I take to be the most significant point at which science needs to take account of other perspectives on the self is with regard to the issue of reductionism. I refer here to what Malcolm Jeeves[9] calls "nothing buttery"—the tendency of some scientists to make pronouncements such as: "you are nothing but a pack of neurones" (Crick [10]), or "religious experience is nothing but an artifact of temporal lobe function" (Persinger [11]). Just as neuroscience provides a legitimate level of description that cannot (ordinarily) be reduced to chemistry or, especially, to physics, so too there are psychological, social-scientific, ethical, and religious levels of description that have their own validity, and that cannot be supplanted by a neurobiological account.

It is easy enough to avoid talking in a reductionist manner: one can discuss the neural and cognitive functions that *enable* or *subserve* higher human capacities such as emotion, intelligence, morality, and religious awareness without saying that these higher capacities are nothing but brain functions. However, a technical account of what is wrong with reductionism is difficult to produce.

First it is necessary to make distinctions among various meanings of "reductionism." I distinguish as follows:

1. Methodological reductionism: a research strategy of analyzing the thing to be studied into its parts.

2. Epistemological reductionism: the view that laws or theories pertaining to the higher levels of the hierarchy of the sciences can (and should) be shown to follow from lower-level laws, and ultimately from the laws of physics.

3. Logical or definitional reductionism: the view that words and sentences referring to one type of entity can be translated without residue into language about another type of entity.

4. Causal reductionism: the view that the behavior of the parts of a system (ultimately, the parts studied by subatomic physics) is determinative of the behavior of all higher-level entities. Thus, this is the thesis that all causation in the hierarchy is "bottom-up."

5. Ontological reductionism: the view that higher-level entities are nothing but the sum of their parts. However, this thesis is ambiguous; we need names here for two distinct positions:

   5a. One is the view that as one goes up the hierarchy of levels, no new kinds of metaphysical "ingredients" need to be added to produce higher-level entities from lower. No "vital force" or "entelechy" must be added to get living beings from non-living materials; no immaterial mind or soul needed to get consciousness; no *Zeitgeist* to form individuals into a society.

5*b*. A much stronger thesis is that only the entities at the lowest level are *really* real; higher-level entities—molecules, cells, organisms—are only composite structures made of atoms. This is the assumption, mentioned above, that the atoms have ontological priority over the things they constitute. I shall designate this position "atomist reductionism" to distinguish it from 5*a,* for which I shall retain the designation of "ontological reductionism." It is possible to hold a physicalist ontology without subscribing to atomist reductionism. Thus, one might want to say that higher-level entities are real—as real as the entities that compose them—and at the same time reject all sorts of vitalism and dualism.

I conclude that causal reductionism is the form of reductionism that raises the most significant issues. Ontological reductionism is entirely unobjectionable. In fact, this is simply what "physicalism" means as applied to the human person. Atomist reductionism expresses more of an attitude than a philosophical thesis: it is difficult to state it without employing, as I have done, the nonsense phrase "really real," and so it is not clear what it could mean to refute it.

Both logical and epistemological reduction are now seen to be impossible in many cases even if causal and atomist reductionism are true. Finally, while methodological reductionism is a useful strategy for scientific research, it is now widely recognized that in practice it needs to be complemented by systems approaches. In short, even if causal reductionism is true, there are a variety of reasons why methodological, epistemological, and logical reduction might still fail. Thus, showing that these three forms of reductionism fail tells us about the limitations of our knowledge, but not about what really makes things happen.

The significant issue, then, is causal reductionism, which is the assumption that the behavior of any complex entity or system is *entirely* determined by the behavior of its parts—the qualifier "entirely" is very important. From a commonsense perspective it is clearly false that a person's thoughts and behavior are *entirely* determined by neurobiology: this leaves out environmental influences. But philosophers of science have so far failed to produce a compelling explanation of *how* the denial of causal reductionism avoids violation of the causal closure of the lower level. There are some philosophical resources available.

Most helpful, I believe, is the concept of downward or top-down causation, as some philosophers have explicated it. Donald Campbell [12] seems to have been the first to introduce the concept. To put it briefly: downward causation happens wherever something outside a given system selects from among a variety of possible states or processes internal to the system. The physicalist assumption is that everything that happens in the universe is realized by some physical process—there are no forces beyond physical forces—but the process that occurs often does so because it has been selected from among a number of possible physical processes on the basis of how it subserves a larger causal system.

Robert Van Gulick states:

> A given physical constituent may have many causal powers, but only some subsets of them will be active in a given situation. The larger context (i.e., the pattern) of which it is a part may affect which of its causal powers get activated....Thus the whole is not any simple function of its parts, since the whole at least partially determines what contributions are made by its parts.[13]

The concept of emergence may be another useful resource. Emergence was much talked about in early twentieth-century philosophy of biology, but the concepts employed then were quite vague. However, some recent accounts (which involve downward causation) may turn out to be quite valuable.[14] Nonetheless we still seem to be fumbling for adequate terminology to express what I believe neuroscientists are coming more and more to recognize: that complexity, levels of organization, and holistic features matter.

What a theological perspective brings to the table, then, is the insistence that neurobiological determinism not supplant traditional concepts of rationality, self-determination, morality, and at least minimal accounts of free will.[15]

REFERENCES

1. DAMASIO, A.R. (1994). *Descartes' error: Emotion, reason, and the human brain.* New York: G.P. Putnam's Sons.
2. DENNETT, D.C. (1991). *Consciousness explained.* New York: Little, Brown.
3. CARY, P. (2000). *Augustine's invention of the inner self: The legacy of a Christian Platonist.* Oxford: Oxford University Press.
4. LEDOUX, J. (1998). *The emotional brain: The mysterious underpinnings of emotional life.* New York: Simon and Schuster.
5. In DAMASIO.[1]
6. POPE JOHN PAUL II. (1996.) Message to the Pontifical Academy of Sciences, *L'Osservatore Romano.*
7. COYNE, J.V. (1998). Evolution and the human person: The pope in dialogue. In R.J. Russell et al. (Eds.) *Evolutionary and molecular biology: Scientific perspectives on divine action,* pp. 11–17. Vatican City State: Vatican Observatory.
8. TAYLOR, C. (1989). *Sources of the self: The making of the modern identity.* Cambridge, MA: Harvard University Press.
9. JEEVES, M. (1998). Mind, brain, and behavior. In W. S. Brown et al. (Eds.) *Whatever happened to the soul?: Scientific and theological portraits of human nature,* pp. 73–98. Minneapolis, MN: Fortress Press.

10. CRICK, F.H. (1994). *The astonishing hypothesis: The scientific search for the soul.* New York: Simon and Schuster.
11. PERSINGER, A. (1983). Religious and mystical experiences as artifacts of temporal lobe function: A general hypothesis. *Perceptual and Motor Skills, 557,* 1225–1262.
12. CAMPBELL, D.T. (1974). Downward causation in hierarchically organised biological systems. In F.J. Ayala & T. Dobzhansky (Eds.) *Studies in the philosophy of biology,* pp. 179–186. Berkeley and Los Angeles: University of California Press.
13. VAN GULICK, R. (1995). Whose in charge here? And who's doing all the work? In J. Heil and A. Mele (Eds.) *Mental causation,* pp. 233–256. Oxofrd: Clarendon Press.
14. DAVIES, P. & CLAYTON, P. (Eds.) (in press). *The re-emergence of emergence.*
15. As in DENNETT, DANIEL. (1984). *Elbow room: Varieties of free will worth wanting.* Cambridge, MA: MIT Press.

Out of Contact, Out of Mind

The Distributed Nature of the Self

DAVID J. TURK, TODD F. HEATHERTON, C. NEIL MACRAE,
WILLIAM M. KELLEY, AND MICHAEL S. GAZZANIGA

*Center for Cognitive Neuroscience, and the Department of Psychological and
Brain Sciences, Dartmouth College, Hanover, New Hampshire 03755, USA*

ABSTRACT: A truly remarkable aspect of human existence is the unitary
sense of self that exists across time and place. Understanding the nature of
self—what it is and what it does—has challenged scholars since antiquity.
How can empirical research measure what it is to have a sense of self? We
propose that the sense of self may emerge from the functions of a left hemisphere "interpreter" (Gazzaniga, 2000). First, we examine evidence for the
existence of self-processing mechanisms in the intact brain, from behavioral and functional neuroimaging research. The available evidence suggests
that the sense of self is widely distributed throughout the brain. Second, we
discuss these findings in relation to what is known about higher cognitive
functions in humans who have undergone a surgical procedure to sever the
connection between the two cerebral hemispheres. Split-brain research has
facilitated an understanding of the way in which each cerebral hemisphere
independently processes information. Research in this area has shown that
each cerebral hemisphere features distinct information-processing capabilities. This cognitive asymmetry is reflected in the notion of a left hemisphere *interpreter* module which, we have argued, generates a unitary
sense of consciousness even in the disconnected brain. This chapter describes how this *interpreter* may also give rise to a unified sense of self.

KEYWORDS: callostomy; split-brain; self; interpreter; left hemisphere;
recognition; lateralized; face recognition

WHAT IS THE SELF?

Although the term *self* is widely used in everyday speech, and most people
have an intuitive sense of what the term means, formal definitions have
proved more elusive. Kihlstrom and Klein (1997) offered a conceptual defi-

Address for correspondence: David J. Turk, Center for Cognitive Neuroscience, 6162 Moore
Hall, Dartmouth College, Hanover, NH 03755. Voice: 603-646-9322; fax: 603-646-1181.
david.j.turk@dartmouth.edu

Ann. N.Y. Acad. Sci. 1001: 65–78 (2003). © 2003 New York Academy of Sciences.
doi: 10.1196/annals.1279.005

nition of the self as being a representation of what we know about ourselves. This knowledge, they argued, can be broadly categorized against four types:

(1) a concept comprising a fuzzy set of context-specific selves;

(2) a set of narratives that address our past, present, and future;

(3) an image- or percept-based representation containing face, body, and gesture represinformation; and

(4) an associative network that contains information about personality traits, autobiographical memories, thoughts, and behaviors separated on the basis of episodic and semantic self-knowledge.

These definitions suggest that any notion of a cognitive self may be implemented across a distributed network of cortical representation. However, such a model does not directly specify or confer any special status to the representation of the self from other forms of episodic and semantic knowledge. Indeed, it has been argued that the apparent special status of self-referential processing can be accommodated by semantic processing accounts. However, we will argue that the representation of self is special, and is subserved by a unique cortical network that differs from brain regions involved in other forms of semantic processing.

SELF-KNOWLEDGE AS DISTINCT FROM OTHER REPRESENTATIONS OF KNOWLEDGE

With respect to memory function, knowledge about the self is often remembered better than other types of semantic knowledge (Rogers et al., 1977; for review see Symons & Johnson, 1997). Why does this memory advantage occur? One possibility is that distinct brain regions are engaged during self-referential processing that enhance memory for this material. Recent evidence that the cortical representation of the self is distinct from other forms of semantic knowledge is provided from two different strands of cognitive neuroscience. In an event-related fMRI study, Kelley et al. (2002) recorded brain activation while participants made judgments about trait adjectives under three conditions: whether the adjective was self-descriptive, whether the adjective described U.S. President George W. Bush, or whether the word was presented in uppercase font. Compared to case judgments, judgments about the self and a familiar other (President Bush) were characterized by increased activation in the left inferior frontal cortex, a region that has been implicated in a wide range of semantic appraisal tasks. Of interest, activity in this area did not differ between self judgments and judgments about a familiar other, even though self-judgments led to better memory on a surprise recognition test. When the self-reference judgments were compared directly to judgments about a familiar other, however, self-referential processing selectively activated regions of the medial pre-frontal cortex (MPFC).

In subsequent work, the level of activity in MPFC was shown to predict, on average, whether a word judged in reference to the self would later be remembered or forgotten (Macrae et al., submitted for publication). Collectively, these findings demonstrate that self-referential processing is functionally dissociable from other forms of semantic processing.

Klein et al (2002) provided further evidence for a distinct self-processing network. They report the case of patient D.B., a 78 year-old man who, as a result of cardiac arrest with presumed anoxia, was left with a dense anterograde and retrograde amnesia. Although D.B. was unable to recall information from autobiographical or from more general semantic memory, he was able to accurately identify trait adjectives that best described his personality. Thus, even with the most impoverished episodic and semantic memory, he is able to accurately reflect on personal attributes. This provides further support for the existence of a distinct cortical network specific to self-knowledge that remained intact in this individual.

NEUROPSYCHOLOGICAL INVESTIGATIONS OF THE CORTICAL LOCUS OF SELF-REPRESENTATION

While the first two tenets of Kihlstrom and Klein's (1997) categorization of self-knowledge do not lend themselves easily to empirical investigation using standard cognitive neuropsychological methodologies, the concept of the self as being percept-based, or a collection of semantic and episodic knowledge, has received a great deal of recent attention.

THE SELF AS A PERCEPT

The ability to recognize oneself from a photograph or from a mirror image seems to develop in humans around the middle of the second year. This ability can be seen to play a pivotal role in the development of other higher-order cognitive capacities, including a theory of mind (Keenan et al., 2000). However, a definitive anatomical substrate of self-recognition remains elusive.

Neuroimaging and neuropsychology have identified regions of the right cerebral hemisphere as being central to the ability to process information about familiar faces, and damage to these cortical areas impairs our ability to recognize others (De Renzi, 1994; Gazzaniga & Smylie, 1983). It is not surprising therefore that recent imaging (and behavioral) studies have identified regions in the right cerebral hemisphere as being specialized for self-recognition. Keenan et al. (1999) presented participants with photographs of themselves, familiar others (co-workers), and strangers. They reported that identification of self-images was faster when participants responded with the left hand. As each hand is predominantly controlled by the contralateral cerebral hemisphere, this indicated the importance of right cerebral hemisphere in self-recognition.

Keenan et al. (2001) tested self-recognition in individuals who underwent a sodium amytal (Wada) procedure and showed a right-hemisphere superiority for self-recognition. At encoding, a morphed facial photograph (generated by combining the patient's face with a famous face) was presented while a portion of one hemisphere was anesthetized. When patients had recovered from the effects of the anesthesia they were shown two photographs (self and a famous other) and asked to report which one they had seen before (although note, in fact, that they had seen neither face, only a morph of the two). A bias towards perception of the morph as "self" occurred when it was presented to the right- rather than the left hemisphere, whereas the left hemisphere appeared better at recognizing famous faces. It is unclear, however, the extent to which this is a memory effect or an indication of right hemispheric specialization in self-recognition.

Keenan et al. (2000) showed movie sequences comprising the transition from a self-image to a famous-other image (or familiar-other to famousother). They demonstrated that left hand (and consequently right hemisphere) responses to self were faster than for a movie sequence that involved a familiar other-to-famous face, providing additional support for the notion of structures in the right hemisphere mediating self-recognition.

However, imaging studies of self-recognition undertaken by Kircher and colleagues (Kircher et al., 2001; Kircher et al., 2000) have shown a different pattern of results. Participants were shown morphed self or familiar-other images. Self-recognition was characterized by increased activity in the right hemisphere limbic system and the left pre-frontal cortex. These studies demonstrate that while it is possible to study a percept-based model of the self, the resulting anatomical locus of this process from studies of the normal brain remains elusive.

THE SELF AS AN ASSOCIATIVE NETWORK

The study by Kelley et al. (2002) described earlier demonstrated regions of the medial frontal lobes associated with making trait judgments relevant to the self. However, this region could not easily be lateralized to a single cerebral hemisphere. Furthermore, the neurological profile of the patient reported by Klein et al. (2002) is not well documented and does not permit any clear insight into the lateralization of any self-trait processing.

The distributed nature of the self is further characterized by recent imaging studies on autobiographical memory. It has been argued that autobiographical memories are strongly related to the concept of self. Indeed, it has been suggested that it is the intrinsic self-referential nature of autobiographical memories that dissociates them from other forms of long-term knowledge (Brewer, 1986). Others have suggested that autobiographical memory is actually a component of the self (Conway & Taachi, 1996; Robinson, 1986). So is autobiographical memory lateralized to one cerebral hemisphere?

Conway and Pleydell-Pearce (2000) proposed that autobiographical memories were constructed in what they referred to as a self-memory system (SMS). This system contains a knowledge base and a set of control processes that mediate access to that knowledge. Contained within the knowledge base are layers of autobiographical knowledge that are arranged from conceptual and abstract, through to highly specific details of single events. Access to this knowledge is mediated by the active goals set by the control process (or what they referred to as the "working self"). The role of generating goals and evaluating responses to those goals for autobiographical memory retrieval would seem to fit the characteristics of the *interpreter* module in left hemisphere (Gazzaniga, 2000). Moreover, several imaging studies identified regions of the left pre-frontal cortex as the locus for the retrieval process in autobiographical memory (Conway et al., 1999; Conway et al., 2001; Nolde et al., 1998; see also Maguire, 2001, for a review).

This then would seem to imply a left hemisphere–lateralized autobiographical memory system. However, Markowitsch and colleagues (Fink et al., 1996; Markowitsch, 1998; Markowitsch, 1995) have demonstrated greater right hemisphere activation during the retrieval of autobiographical memories. It may be possible to explain the differences in cortical activity associated with retrieval from autobiographical memory in terms of the methodological differences across these studies (for a review see Conway et al., 2002). It is also conceivable that one hemisphere sets retrieval goals while the other reconstructs the resultant episode. The latter process is more likely to include imagery and emotional constituents that would trigger activation in the right hemisphere, but does not preclude a left hemisphere goal-directed approach to the retrieval of that information. This hypothesis necessitates temporal differences in brain activation for retrieval and reconstruction that can not easily be dissociated in the PET or fMRI studies cited earlier. To address this issue, Conway and Pleydell-Pearce (2000) utilized temporally superior EEG techniques to measure regions of the brain associated with autobiographical retrieval and reconstruction. They demonstrated that the early retrieval processes in autobiographical memory are indeed mediated by frontal regions in the left hemisphere.

In summary, it is clear that the self appears to be a measurable construct both behaviorally and cortically, and that aspects of self-knowledge are distributed throughout the cortex. While there is some evidence that frontal regions of the left hemisphere may play a pivotal role at least in setting the goals for the retrieval and reconstruction of autobiographical knowledge (Conway et al., 2002; Conway et al., 2001), the issue of hemispheric laterality remains equivocal.

THE LEFT HEMISPHERE INTERPRETER

Split-brain research has identified different cognitive processing styles for the two cerebral hemispheres. The right hemisphere appears to process what it receives and no more, while the left hemisphere appears to make elaborations, associations and searches for logical patterns in the material, even when none are present. In lateralized memory experiments, for example, the right hemisphere retains a veridical representation of each to-be-remembered item and tends to accurately recognize previously viewed items and correctly reject new items, even when they are similar to the target material. The left hemisphere tends to elaborate and make inferences about the material presented, often at the expense of veracity (Metcalfe et al., 1995; Phelps & Gazzaniga, 1992).

In addition to elaboration of information, the left hemisphere also attempts to assign a coherent explanation to events or behavior, even when in reality none is present. Wolford et al. (2000) tested a split-brain patient on a probability-guessing paradigm. In this procedure there are two events (e.g., the presentation of either a red or green circle) that each have a different probability of occurring (e.g., 75% red & 25% green). However, the assignment of these events is stochastic. The two main strategies employed for making responses are *matching* and *maximizing*. The matching strategy takes account of the ratio of occurrences of each event type. Therefore, red stimuli appear 75% of the time, so 75% of responses made are for red. It is possible to get a maximum of 100% correct responses using this strategy if all responses are correctly aligned with the different trial types. However, it is also possible with incorrect predictions to fall as low as 50% accuracy on this task. This is because every incorrect prediction made essentially represents two errors. An incorrect prediction for one trial type must be mirrored by a subsequent prediction error on the other trial type. Thus while this matching strategy would seem to follow a logical vein and carries with it the highest potential gain, it also results in the highest potential loss to the individual. The second strategy, maximizing, involves choosing the response associated with the highest frequency event on every trial (in this case, red). This strategy results in only 25% errors and thus maximizes the number of correct responses. It is noteworthy that human participants tend to use the matching strategy whereas animals like the rat or goldfish tend to maximize. In the split-brain, the right hemisphere tends to maximize responses whereas the left hemisphere tends to look for order and match responses.

The left hemisphere of the split-brain patient also attempts to explain the behaviors elicited from the disconnected right hemisphere. In a classic study (see Gazzaniga & LeDoux, 1978) using the simultaneous concept test, a split-brain patient was presented with two pictures (one to each cerebral hemisphere), and asked to select an associated picture from an array placed in front of him or her. When a picture of a chicken claw was presented to the left hemisphere and a snow scene presented to the right hemisphere, subject P.S. responded by selecting a picture of a shovel with the left hand and a picture of a chicken with the right hand. These choices would seem to be logical since a shovel might be used to clear snow and the chicken claw obviously goes with the chicken. However, when asked to explain why he selected these items, P.S. responded "Oh that's simple. The chicken claw goes with the chicken, and you need a shovel to clean out the chicken shed." Thus the left hemisphere explains the response of the disconnected the right hemisphere (left hand) in terms of its own experience, which does not include information about the snow scene (perceived only by the right hemisphere). In fact, this same interpretive process can also be demonstrated in participants with an intact connection between the two hemispheres (Schachter & Singer, 1962).

A further example of this type of biased interpretation of events or behavior by the left hemisphere is evident from studies of patients with various delusional disorders (see Cooney & Gazzaniga [2003] for a review). One such disorder, anosognosia for hemiplegia (Prigatano & Schacter, 1991; see also Ramachandran, 1995) resulting from damage to the right parietal cortex, renders patients unable to maintain a representation of the left side of the body. However, when confronted with resulting paralysis the patient generates a plausible excuse. For example, patient B.M. was asked to explain her inability to use her left hand to point to a student in the room. "Because I didn't want to" she replied (Ramachandran, 1995, p. 24). The same patient then goes on to identify her left hand as belonging to her son. The absence of sensory input to the left hemisphere *interpreter* from the right parietal system essentially means that for her subjective experience the limb does not exist as a part of her anatomy and as a result she engages in elaborate confabulations to explain its presence. The left hemisphere's drive to interpret and explain its world, no matter how bizarrely, is also evident in Capgras' syndrome (Doran, 1990). Here the visual representation of a familiar loved one is divorced from the accompanying emotional feelings for that person. Therefore when meeting a spouse, for example, the patient recognizes the individual physically, but not on an emotional level. As a result, the patient's interpretation is that the person is an imposter. Thus, the "interpreter' attempts to make sense of its input both from the external environment and from its own body. Where the information it receives is nonsensical or even absent, it constructs a plausible reality, such that in the case of delusional syndromes "bizarre information yields bizarre results" (Cooney & Gazzaniga, 2003).

What is the advantage of hemispheric asymmetry in processing the world? The left hemisphere strives to provide an understanding of not only the event, but also the underlying cause of that event. In this way, one can develop a mechanism to cope with future occurrences of that (or a related) event. However, this strategy carries a cost in terms of the accuracy with which specific perceptual inputs can be matched and with which other information can be recalled from memory. The right hemisphere does not engage in interpretive processing of information and maintains a veridical representation of its input. In the normal brain, these two cognitive styles complement each other and facilitate elaborative information processing (and by definition comprehension of the world) without the associated cost to immediate memory. Thus novel events can be accommodated within the existing knowledge base, but concomitant access to an episodic record of the specific incident in question is also available. Gazzaniga (2000) has argued that this difference in processing style between the two hemispheres might be seen as adaptive and represents an underlying role for the left hemisphere in the generation of a unified consciousness experience. More specifically:

> Insertion of an interpreter into an otherwise functioning brain creates many byproducts. A device that begins by asking how one thing relates to another, a device that asks about an infinite number of things, in fact, and that can get productive answers to its questions cannot help but give birth to the concept of self" (Gazzaniga, 2000, p. 1320).

There are evident parallels between the notion of conscious experience and a self-construct. Kihlstrom (1995) states that conscious experience necessitates a specific connection between a mental representation of a current or past event and of the "self" as the agent of that event. Any notion of a conscious left hemisphere must also include the notion of a similarly lateralized concept of the self. While the self appears to be constructed from information located throughout the brain, even in the most extreme cases, such as the callosotomized brain, a unified self-construct is still possible. This unified experience of self is the result of the actions of the left hemisphere "interpreter" (Gazzaniga, 1985 and 1989; Gazzaniga & LeDoux, 1978), which integrates all of the available information to form a coherent explanation of the world. Where some of the information is either missing or inaccessible, the interpreter creates an explanation of reality based upon what it does know, no matter how bizarre.

THE INTERPRETER AND SELF-RECOGNITION

Neuropsychological disorders, such as anosognosia for hemiplegia and Capgras delusions described earlier, provide an insight into the way the left hemisphere interpreter creates its own virtual reality from information received via intact neural pathways, even when this reality is or appears implausible. However, studies of the normal brain have not yielded any definitive insight into a laterally biased representation of self-referential information processing (although Conway et al. reported evidence for early-onset left hemisphere processing of autobiographical memory retrieval). This may in part be seen as the result of the employment of differing empirical methods and the variety of self-processing investigated via such methods. In addition, there appears to be an inherent difficulty in investigating some processes in the normal brain, what Martin (2000) refers to as the "contamination problem." Despite attempts to invoke a particular process, complete isolation of that process appears to be problematic in the intact brain.

In order to assess the contribution of a specific cerebral hemisphere to any given self-referential task, and to reduce the risk of "contamination" from the opposite hemisphere, one can readdress these questions in persons with a callosotomized brain. Such individuals are unable to transfer information between the two cerebral hemispheres and as a result are only able to process information within the hemisphere to which it was encoded. However, owing to the asymmetry of inter-hemispheric cognitive aptitudes in the split brain (language mediated by the left cerebral hemisphere and attentional processing mediated by the right), verbal responses load unevenly on the language-dominant hemisphere. As a result, the paradigms utilized for self-knowledge and autobiographical memory-retrieval tasks reported earlier do not lend themselves easily to split-brain research. The most appropriate methodology for identifying the lateral locus of the self in the disconnected brain would appear to be self-face recognition.

Turk et al. (2002) assessed person-recognition (self and familiar-other person) in a split-brain patient. This provided an excellent test of hemispheric differences in person-recognition as information (i.e., photographs of self or familiar others) can be independently presented to a single hemisphere in isolation. We tested J.W., a 48 year-old right-handed male who, at the age of 25, underwent two-stage callosal surgery with sparing of the anterior commissure. The surgery was undertaken as a treatment for pharmacologically intractable epilepsy. In this experiment, J.W. viewed a series of morphed facial photographs that ranged from 0% to 100% self-images. The 0% self-image was a photograph of Dr. Michael Gazzaniga (M.G.), (i.e., a familiar other). The remaining nine images were generated using computer morphing software with each image representing a 10% incremental shift from J.W. to M.G. (FIG. 1).

The images were laterally presented in a random order to each cerebral hemisphere for 250 ms. In the self-recognition condition, J.W. was asked to indicate whether the presented image was himself; in the familiar other condition, he was asked to indicate whether the image was of Dr. Gazzaniga. The same morphed images were used for each judgment task. The only difference across the two conditions was the judgment that was required ("Is it me?" vs. "Is it Mike?"). Data were collected across six separate sessions. In each session, the 11 images (i.e., self or Mike plus 9 intermediate morphs) were presented four times to each cerebral hemisphere. The results revealed a double dissociation in J.W.'s face-recognition performance. J.W.'s right hemisphere was biased towards recognizing the morphed faces as a familiar other, whereas his left hemisphere was biased in favor of self-recognition.

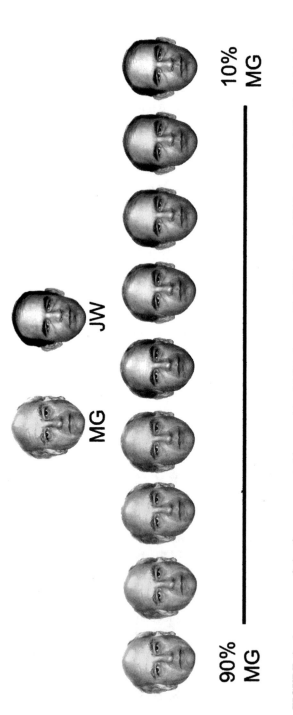

FIGURE 1. A sequence of nine faces was created by morphing M.G.'s image with J.W.'s face in 10% incremental shifts. The initial image contained 10% of J.W. and 90% M.G. and the end image was the reverse. These images, together with the two original photographs of M.G. and J.W., were randomly presented to each hemisphere. In one condition J.W. was asked to determine whether the image was self, while in the other condition J.W. was asked to determine whether the image was M.G.

To ensure that this dissociation was not dependent on the identity of the familiar other (M.G.), we repeated the entire procedure (again across six testing sessions) using three additional targets (Dr. Paul Corballis, a personally known individual; current U.S. President George W. Bush; and former U.S. President, Bill Clinton). The same double dissociation was observed across all four targets. This demonstrated that while both hemispheres were capable of recognizing faces, J.W.'s left hemisphere displayed a recognition bias for self and his right hemisphere displayed a recognition bias for others.

The results presented here support the viewpoint that, although both hemispheres are capable of self-recognition (Gazzaniga, 1998), cortical networks in the left hemisphere play a significant role in this process (Kircher et al., 2000; Kircher et al., 2001; Kircher et al., 2002). The observed double dissociation in J.W.'s person-recognition performance is theoretically important since it provides further evidence that that self-recognition is functionally dissociable from general face processing, which itself has important implications for contemporary models of social cognition.

The objectives set by the self-memory system (SMS) guide behavior in a deliberate and meaningful manner (Conway & Pleydell-Pearce, 2000). Distributed across a discrete cortical network, the SMS comprises autobiographical knowledge, personal beliefs, currently active goal states, and conceptions of self (Conway et al., 1999; Conway & Pleydell-Pearce, 2000; Conway et al., 2002). Through its enhanced ability to recognize and reconstruct aspects of self, the left hemisphere may play an important role in the functioning of the SMS. In the case of self-recognition, the left hemisphere appears to think that it sees itself, even when the image contains as much information about a familiar other as it does about the self. Thus even in the disconnected brain, the self appears to be a unified construct. This unified self-construct is underpinned by the "interpreter" within the left cerebral hemisphere.

The left hemisphere also shows a bias towards the self in experiments on spatial frames of reference conducted on the split-brain. Funnell, Johnson and Gazzaniga (2001) reported different patterns of hemispheric lateralization associated with mental rotation. The left hemisphere was shown to be superior when mental rotation was undertaken with an egocentric (internal) frame of reference. In contrast, the right hemisphere showed an advantage on tasks that demand representing spatial information relative to an external (allocentric) frame. Results from an fMRI study on neurologically intact participants indicates that the right superior parietal lobule may play a key role in representing spatial information in allocentric coordinates, while left parietal areas may be involved in the formation of egocentric representations. Interestingly, brain regions involved in motor planning and preparation are activated during egocentric mental rotation but not during allocentric rotation. These parietal-frontal circuits in the motor-dominant left hemisphere appear to be specialized for spatial transformations within a frame of reference centered on one's own body.

SUMMARY

This paper addresses the question of whether the self is unique from other forms of semantic and episodic representation, and whether there is a specific role for a left hemisphere "interpreter" in the generation of a unified sense of self. The evidence available in the literature so far suggests that self-referential trait processing is somehow special, not simply an extension of other forms of semantic information processing, and is subserved by a unique cortical network. However, until now the cortical locus of critical components of this self-processing network was equivocal. Imaging studies of autobiographical memory retrieval and of self-face recognition had not elicited clear laterality effects for these self-referential processes, although there is some compelling evidence that left hemisphere frontal systems mediate the retrieval of autobiographical information. To further investigate the laterality of self-processing, Turk et. al (2002) examined person-recognition processes (self vs. familiar other) in a split-brain patient. This work revealed a left hemisphere bias toward recognizing the self, whereas the right hemisphere was biased to recognize the faces of familiar other people.

We argue that the findings from our split-brain study, together with data from other self-referential processing studies, reflect a critical role for the left hemisphere *interpreter* in self-recognition. This interpretive function of the left hemisphere takes available information from a distributed self-processing network and creates a unified sense of self from this input. When information from the entire network is available, a realistic interpretation can be made, but when portions of the network are disconnected, the interpretation verges on fantasy. However, in all cases, this left hemisphere interpretation results in a unified sense of self, even in the disconnected brain. Thus, even when there appear to be two brains, there is still only one self.

REFERENCES

BREWER, W.F. (1986). What is autobiographical memory? In D.C. Rubin (Ed.), *Autobiographical memory* (pp. 25–49). Cambridge, England: Cambridge University Press.

CONWAY, M.A., TURK, D.J., MILLER, S.L., LOGAN, J., NEBES, R.D., MELTZER, C. C. & BECKER, J.T. (1999). A positron emission tomography (PET) study of autobiographical memory retrieval. *Memory, 7 (5/6),* 679–702.

CONWAY, M.A. PLEYDELL-PEARCE, C.W. & WHITECROSS, S. (2001). The neuroanatomy of autobiographical memory: A slow cortical potential study (SCP) of autobiographical memory retrieval. *Journal of Memory and Language, 45,* 493–524.

CONWAY, M.A., PLEYDELL-PEARCE, C.W., WHITECROSS, S. & SHARPE, H. (2002). Brain imaging autobiographical memory. *Psychology of Learning and Motivation, 4,* 229–263.

CONWAY, M.A. & PLEYDELL-PEARCE, C.W. (2000). The construction of autobiographical memories in the self-memory system. *Psychological Review, 107 (2)*, 261–288.

CONWAY, M.A. & TAACHI, P.C. (1996). Motivated confabulation. *Neurocase, 2,* 325–339.

COONEY, J.W. & GAZZANIGA, M.S. (2003). Neurologic disorders and the structure of human consciousness. *Trends in Cognitive Sciences, 7(4),* 161–165.

DE RENZI, E. (1994). Prosopagnosia in two patients with CT scan evidence of damage confined to the right hemisphere. *Neuropsychologia, 24,* 385–389

DORAN, J.M. (1990). The Capgras syndrome: Neurological/neuropsychological perspectives. *Neuropsychology, 4 (1),* 29–42.

FINK, G.R., MARKOWITSCH, H.J., REINKEMEIER, M., BRUCKBAUER, T., KESSLER, J. & HESS, W. (1996). Cerebral representation of one's own past: Neural networks involved in autobiographical memory. *Journal of Neuroscience, 18 (13),* 4275–4282.

FUNNELL, M.G., JOHNSON, S.H. & GAZZANIGA, M.S. (2001). Hemispheric differences in egocentric and allocentric mental rotation: Evidence from fMRI and a split-brain patient. Presented at the 8th Annual Meeting of the Cognitive Neuroscience Society, New York.

GAZZANIGA, M. S. (1985). *The social brain.* New York: Basic Books.

GAZZANIGA, M. S. (1989). Organization of the human brain. *Science, 245,* 947–952.

GAZZANIGA, M.S. (1998). The split-brain revisited. *Scientific American, 279,* 50–55.

GAZZANIGA, M.S. (2000) Cerebral specialization and interhemispheric communication: Does the corpus callosum enable the human condition? *Brain, 123,* 1293–1326.

GAZZANIGA M.S. & LEDOUX J.E. (1978). *The integrated mind.* New York: Plenum Press.

GAZZANIGA, M.S. & SMYLIE, C.S. (1983). Facial recognition and brain asymmetries: Clues to underlying mechanisms. *Annals of Neurology, 13,* 536–540.

KEENAN, J.P., MCCUTCHEONN, B., FREUND, S., GALLUP, G.G. JR., SANDERS, G. & PASCUAL-LEONE, A. (1999). Left hand advantage in a self-face recognition task. *Neuropsychologia, 37,* 1421–1425.

KEENAN, J.P., FREUND, S. HAMILTON, R.H., GANIS, G., & PASCUALE-LEONE, A. (2000). Hand response differences in a self-face identification task. *Neuropsychologia, 38,* 1047–1053

KEENAN, J.P., NELSON, A., O'CONNOR, M. & PASCUALE-LEONE, A. (2001). Self-recognition and the right hemisphere. *Nature, 409,* 305.

KELLEY, W.M., MACRAE, C.N., WYLAND, C.L., CAGLAR, S., INATI, S., & HEATHERTON, T.F. (2002). Finding the self? An event related fMRI study. *Journal of Cognitive Neuroscience, 14 (5),* 785–794.

KIHLSTROM, J.F. (1995). Consciousness and me-ness. In J. Cohen & J. Schooler (Eds.), *Scientific approaches to the question of consciousness.* Hillsdale, NJ: Erlbaum.

KIHLSTROM, J.F. & KLEIN, S.B. (1997). Self-knowledge and self-awareness. In J.G. Snodgrass & R.L. Thompson (Eds.), *The self across psychology: Self-recognition, self-awareness and the self concept.* Annals of the New York Academy of Sciences, Vol. 818.

KIRCHER, T.T.J., SENIOR, C., PHILLIPS, M.L., BENSON, P.J., BULLMORE, E.T., BRAMMER, M., SIMMONS, A., WILLIAMS, S.C.R., BARTELS, M. & DAVID,

A. S. (2000). Towards a functional neuroanatomy of self processing: Effects of faces and words. *Cognitive Brain Research, 10,* 133–144

KIRCHER, T.T.J., SENIOR, C., PHILLIPS, M.L., RABE-HESKETH, S., BENSON, P.J., BULLMORE, E.T., BRAMMER, M., SIMMONS, A., BARTELS, M. & DAVID, A S. (2001). Recognizing one's own face. *Cognition, 78 (1),* B1–B15.

KIRCHER, T.T.J., BRAMMER, M., BULLMORE, E., SIMMONS, A., BARTELS, M. & DAVID, A.S. (2002). The neural correlates of intentional and incidental self processing. *Neuropsychologia, 40,* 683–692.

KLEIN, S.B., ROZENDAL, K. & COSMIDES, L. (2002). A social-cognitive neuroscience analysis of the self. *Social Cognition, 20,* 105–135

MACRAE, C.N., MORAN, J.M., HEATHERTON, T.F., BANFIELD, J.F. & KELLEY, W.M. (submitted for publication). Medial prefrontal activity predicts memory for self.

MAGUIRE, E.A. (2001) Neuroimaging studies of autobiographical event memory. *Philosophical Transactions of the Royal Society of London, 356,* 1409-1419.

MARKOWITSCH, H.J. (1995). Which brain regions are critically involved in the retrieval of old episodic memory? *Brain Research Reviews, 21,* 117–127.

MARKOWITSCH, H.J. (1998). Cognitive neuroscience of memory. *Neurocase, 4,* 429–435.

MARTIN, R.C. (2000). Contributions from the neuropsychology of language and memory to the development of cognitive theory. *Journal of Memory & Language, 43,* 149–156.

METCALFE, J., FUNNELL, M.K., & GAZZANIGA, M.S. (1995). Right hemisphere memory superiority: studies of a split-brain patient. *Psychological Science, 6 (3),* 157–164.

NOLDE, S.F., JOHNSON, M.K. & RAYE, C.L. (1998) The role of prefrontal cortex during tests of episodic memory. *Trends in Cognitive Sciences, 2,* 399–406.

PHELPS, E.A. & GAZZANIGA, M.S. (1992) Hemispheric differences in mnemonic processing: the effects of left hemisphere interpretation. *Neuropsychologia, 30,* 293–297.

PRIGATANO, G.P. & SCHACTER, D.L. (1991) Awareness of deficit after brain injury. New York: Oxford University Press.

RAMACHANDRAN, V.S. (1995). Anosognosia in parietal lobe syndrome. *Consciousness & Cognition, 4,* 22–51.

ROBINSON, J.A. (1986). Autobiographical memory: A historical prologue? In D. C. Rubin (Ed.), *Autobiographical memory* (pp. 19–24). Cambridge, England: Cambridge University Press.

ROGERS, T.B., KUIPER, N.A. & KIRKER, W.S. (1977). Self-reference and the encoding of personal information. *Journal of Personality and Social Psychology, 35,* 677–688.

SCHACHTER, S. & SINGER, J.E. (1962). Cognitive, social and physiological determinants of emotional state. *Psychological Review, 69,* 379–399.

SYMONS, C.S. & JOHNSON, B.T. (1997). The self-reference effect in memory: A meta-analysis. *Psychological Bulletin, 121 (3),* 371–394

TURK, D.J., HEATHERTON, T., KELLEY, W.M., FUNNELL, M.G., GAZZANIGA, M.S. & MACRAE, C.N. (2002). Mike or Me? Self recognition in a split-brain patient. *Nature Neuroscience, 5 (9):* 841–842

WOLFORD, G., MILLER, M.B., & GAZZANIGA, M.S. (2000). The left hemisphere's role in hypothesis formation. *Journal of Neuroscience, 20,* RC64.

Knowing about Knowing

Dissociations between Perception and Action Systems over Evolution and during Development

MARC D. HAUSER

Department of Psychology and Program in Neurosciences, Harvard University, Cambridge, Massachusetts 02138, USA

ABSTRACT: Studies of human patients reveal dissociations between perception and action; some patients have implicit knowledge for a given domain, but can't access this knowledge for action. Studies of human infant development reveal a similar dissociation, suggesting that the neural systems connecting action with perception are not formed until the early preschool years, perhaps later. These connections are fundamental to our knowledge, to what we know about what we know. In this chapter I discuss the evolution of this knowledge, and argue that the dissociations seen in patients and in infant development are also seen in normal adult nonhuman primates, especially in the domain of folk physics. This suggests that for some domains of knowledge, animals don't know what they know. The disconnect between perception and action leads, in some cases, to perseverative errors. These errors, in turn, provide the signature of a highly encapsulated, modular system.

KEYWORDS: knowledge; perception; self-awareness; neural dissociations; primates; evolution; development; action

How does it know? This is not a question that we ask about inanimate objects, unless we are speaking metaphorically. When we ask about how or what "it" knows, we are referring to animate objects or living things. But even here, we must be careful. We don't usually ask about what a plant knows, even though botanists may talk about the behavior of plants, their capacity to dupe pollinators or avoid the jaws of herbivores. We usually ask about what

Address for correespondence: Marc D. Hauser, Department of Psychology, Harvard University, 33 Kirkland Street, Room 980, Cambridge, MA 02138. Voice and fax: 617-496-7077.
mdhauser@wjh.harvard.edu

Ann. N.Y. Acad. Sci. 1001: 79–103 (2003). © 2003 New York Academy of Sciences.
doi: 10.1196/annals.1279.006

animals know. Here, however, is where the controversy begins. Some would claim that animals not only have knowledge of the world, but know what they know. Others would deny this claim for *some* animals, while acknowledging the possibility that perhaps chimpanzees know what they know. Yet others would deny this claim for *all* animals, and extend it further to many humans, including infants and adults with certain kinds of brain damage.

I will address two problems in this essay, the first conceptual and the second practical. Conceptually, what does it mean to know? What does it mean to know how a tool works or what someone else believes? Methodologically, how can we know what non-linguistic organisms know? This is a question that hinges on the competence–performance distinction, and I will show how we must tread cautiously in interpreting data from different kinds of experimental procedures. I address both questions by focusing on non-linguistic animals, pre-linguistic infants, and young children, with brief mention of patients with brain deficits. In Part I, the bulk of the chapter, I focus on folk physics, on what organisms know about the physical world. In Part II, I briefly turn to folk psychology, exploring what organisms know about themselves and others.

In a nutshell, the argument I will attempt to defend runs as follows. First, appropriate action depends on appropriate knowledge of the world. When an organism knows what it knows, its actions are different from an organism that is locked out of its library of knowledge. Individuals who are locked out may act appropriately in some contexts, but when things go wrong, they will often lack the capacity to break with tradition. Actions win, beliefs lose. Second, recent studies of nonhuman primates and human infants implicate a dissociation between knowledge that is revealed through perception and knowledge revealed through action, a phenomenon paralleling work on brain-damaged patients (Goodale et al., 1991) and especially, human infants (Baillargeon, 1995; Hood et al., 2000; Munakata et al., 1997; Spelke, 1994; Spelke et al., 1995). Whereas the primate's perceptual system appears to interpret events in the world appropriately, generating the correct expectations, their action system often fails, leading to perseverative errors—a signature of an improperly functioning inhibitory mechanism. I suggest, on the basis of this dissociation, that both nonhuman primates and young human children are vulnerable to creating habitual action sequences (Graybiel, 1998), or what I refer to as *modular macros* (Hauser, in preparation). In the sense of Fodor's (1983) original position regarding perceptual modules, I argue that there are parallel action modules, systems that operate in an encapsulated manner, immune to counter-evidence (for somewhat similar views, especially in terms of procedural knowledge, see Dienes and Perner [1999]). More specifically, modular macros are fast, automatic, unconscious, action sequences. Each macro represents an adaptive solution to a recurrent problem in the organism's environment. Because of their structure and adaptive significance, they are immune to counter-evidence and difficult to break down once they have been created.

If a macro misfires, creating an error, a different system must evaluate the error and correct the problematic subroutine. Animals and young children generally lack the capacity to reorganize their macros. Consequently, although they may know, at some level, that they are making an error, they may not know why, or have the resources to fix things. Although much of the evidence in favor of a dissociation comes from studies of folk physics, work in folk psychology suggests parallel processes, especially among human children. I conclude with a few remarks on how a dissection of what organisms know represents a first, albeit critical step in understanding how a sense of self evolved, and how the legacies from our past have shaped our unique individual life histories.

I. FOLK PHYSICS

Piaget (1954) proposed that children construct an understanding of the world by acting upon it. Action underlies much of the child's developing knowledge of the world. This view of development emerged from an extraordinary range of studies. All of Piaget's studies, however, had one thing in common: every task involved reaching for and acting on an object. Consider a classic experiment. Show a 6-month-old child a novel toy and she will reach for and play with it. Present the same toy, but now place an opaque screen between her and the toy. The game stops. No more reaching. Out of sight is out of mind. This result led Piaget to conclude that the capacity to keep an object in mind—object permanence—emerges some time around the child's first birthday, largely as a result of her sensorimotor experiences with objects. Between the ages of 1 and 2 years, when children will reach for a hidden object, you can play a different game with them. Show a child two opaque screens, A and B, and hide the toy behind A. Once she successfully and repeatedly retrieves the toy behind A, switch sides and hide it behind screen B. Although the hiding game is the same, and although she appears to understand object permanence, she searches behind A, not B. This search error reoccurs over many tries. This error occurs in all infants, independent of socioeconomic background or culture. It is an error that reveals a signature of the developing mind. For 40 years, developmental psychologists have been battling over the cause of this signature (Baillargeon and DeVos, 1991; Baillargeon et al., 1990; Baillargeon et al., 1985; Diamond et al., 1994; Harris, 1986; Marcovitch and Zelazo, 1999; Smith et al., 1999; Wellman et al., 1986; Zelazo et al., 1998).

When the field of developmental psychology works well, it is like the science of anatomy or medicine. It dissects a problem into its component parts, and then attempts to extract the broken bits. Descriptively, the child's error is to repetitively search at the previously rewarded location, screen A. What components are broken? A fragile memory, one that fails to encode the new location until it has been hidden in the same place over many trials? A disconnect between the system that guides reaching and the system that stores the knowledge of the object's location? A deficit in following a simple rule such as "search behind the screen where the object was last seen"? An inability to take risks, searching in a location that has never been reinforced (B) as opposed to an area that has consistently been reinforced (A)? This kind of anatomical dissection is important because it helps isolate the locus of control, and the component or components that must develop for the child to gain control.

If repeatedly searching behind A builds up a strong association between screen A and the reward, then this problem reduces to the case of an arbitrary, but overlearned response—a learned habit. If this explanation is correct, then the more trials a child has with A before switching to B, the harder it will be for her to make the switch. This is correct, but with an interesting twist. If an experimenter repeatedly hides and then reveals the object behind A, but doesn't allow the child to search until the switch trial to B, the child shows no deficit, searching right away at B. This shows that actively searching is crucial; simply observing, passively, is not. To show whether the child's control problem stems from difficulties inhibiting a reaching response or from difficulties associated with representing—keeping in mind—one location and not the other, several researchers have presented three or more hiding locations. If the child can't inhibit either the response to A or the representation of the object at A, then when she fails to find the object at A, she should next search at random behind the other hiding locations. In contrast, if the error arises because of a reaching bias (targeted at A), then when she fails to find the object at A, she should only look at the correct location next. Results show that after failing at location A, children look behind B next. The locus of control is the reaching system. When infants and children fail to switch, it is because the reaching response to A dominates. No matter how loudly the representational system is yelling "Behind B," it is effectively silenced by the reaching system that yells louder, and first "Reach for A." Infants at this age reach ballistically. They appear to be guided by a modular macro for action that is immune to counter-evidence.

During his studies of the A-not-B problem, Piaget made an intriguing observation that has been reported by other developmentalists. Sometimes, a child will look toward the B screen while reaching toward the A screen. It's as if the child's visual system says one thing while her action or reaching system says something completely different. When infants look at B but reach behind A, it appears that their eyes know where the toy is but their hands don't. These observations led to the suggestion that the Piagetian framework of child cognitive development was flawed. Since Piaget derived all of his insights from watching children act on the world, he was measuring the development of the action system and how it is guided by what the child knows.

What he failed to provide was a full account of the child's knowledge, independently of her ability to act on this knowledge. There are many things that we all know, but that we fail to use in action; often, when we use it to act, we do so incompetently, at least when contrasted with the depth of our knowledge. Similarly, there are many things that we act upon with supreme competence, but lack almost complete access to the knowledge that drives such actions. All professional baseball players can catch a fly ball, but most likely none can explain how they coordinate their catching hand with the physics of a flying ball. Upon considering the possibility that a child might know more about the physical world than her actions reveal, developmentalists turned to a different approach, one targeted at the child's eyes and attentional system. The logic of this approach—the expectancy violation looking time technique—parallels the logic of a magic show: when we perceive something that violates our understanding of the physical world, such as levitation or knives moving through human flesh without causing injury, we stare. Our attentional systems attempt to uncover the violation. The amount of time spent looking therefore becomes a measure of whether a violation has been detected.

Baillargeon (Baillargeon and DeVos, 1991; Baillargeon et al., 1990; Baillargeon et al., 1985) was one of the first to take on the possible dissociation between reaching and looking in the context of the child's developing understanding of object permanence. Starting with 4- to 5-month-old infants—individuals who, by Piagetian standards, are months away from grasping object permanence—she first allowed subjects to play with a ball and then showed them a rotating panel. Next, she placed the ball on one side of the rotating panel and then concealed the ball and part of the panel with an opaque screen; now, when the experimenter rotated the panel, the child only saw its tip. In one test condition, the experimenter rotated the panel 120 degrees, giving the correct impression that the panel had stopped at the apex of the concealed ball. In a second test condition, the experimenter rotated the panel 180 degrees, giving the impression that the panel had rotated (magically) through the ball. Infants looked longer in the second condition. Although the ball was out of sight, the infants continued to represent the ball's spatial location. This must be the case given differences in looking. To detect the violation—the magic—children must remember that the ball lies in the path of the rotating panel and must block its path upon rotation. When the panel apparently rotates through the ball, this represents a violation of solidity, one of the core principles of object-hood (Spelke, 1994). Although some details of this experiment have been criticized (Bogartz et al., 1997), leading to a healthy exchange of new experiments and controls (Baillargeon, 1995), the general finding, replicated in other labs, holds: infants are equipped with an understanding of object permanence well before they can act upon such knowledge.

The distinction between looking and reaching emerges elsewhere in development. Spelke and colleagues (Spelke et al., 1992) showed that 6-month-old infants look longer at a ball that drops behind a screen and then appears, magically, below a solid table, than at the same ball falling and landing on top of the table. However, when the same kind of task is run almost two years later, but with active searching substituted for looking, these toddlers fail to appreciate that a solid ball can't pass through a solid table (Hood et al., 2000). An experimenter shows a toddler a table with one cup on top and one below. The experimenter sets up a screen, hiding the table and cups, drops a ball, removes the screen, and asks the child to search. Repeatedly, the child searches in the cup that is under the table, and repeatedly, the child never finds the ball. How can a mere 6-month-old baby know that a solid ball can't travel through a solid table, while a 2-year-old thinks that this kind of physical event is not only possible, but the way the world works? Why doesn't the toddler's search error kick in, guiding her to look in the cup on top of the table? Like the A-not-B error, the toddler's action system has kicked in, ballistically, immune to counter-evidence. The toddler has developed a modular macro.

Much of the work on the infant's developing knowledge of the physical world finds direct parallels with nonhuman primates, a field that owes much to the work of Adele Diamond (Diamond, 1988, 1990; Diamond and Goldman-Rakic, 1989). For example, like young infants, many nonhuman primate species show the A-not-B-error, and in other contexts, commonly fail to solve problems due to inhibitory difficulties. For example, Diamond ran a comparative study of developing rhesus monkeys and human children, as well as an exploration of the underlying neurobiology by using a lesion technique. The task involved showing subjects an object (food for monkeys, toys for infants), and then placing it inside a transparent box with only a single open side on any given trial. The subject's task was to find the opening and reach inside to retrieve the object. Infant rhesus monkeys, 2- to 4-months old, reach straight ahead on every trial; this action works when the front face is open, but fails on all other trials. Older rhesus monkeys find the opening first, and then reach in to grab the food. Adult rhesus monkeys with lesions in dorsolateral prefrontal cortex are like infants, reaching straight ahead on every trial. These data suggest that a mature prefrontal cortex is essential. Diamond's parallel studies with human infants revealed that prior to 7–9 months, subjects repeatedly reach straight ahead; older infants find the opening and then reach in to grab the toy. Young rhesus and human infants are incapable of controlling the straight-ahead reach even though they never obtain the object inside the box. This can't be a memory problem. The toy is always in view. It can't be a motivational problem: these young infants reach straight ahead dozens of times, with no success. Again, the modular macro has fired. These two primate infants are on autopilot. These perseverative errors have parallels in other tasks with primates and, importantly, also show the signature of a dissociation. I first describe two tasks that reveal striking errors of action, and then turn to matched experiments that show success using perception, but no action.

In collaboration with Hood (Hood et al., 1999), who first ran these experiments with children (see below), we presented cotton-top tamarin monkeys (*Saguinus oedipus*) with a vertical frame, open in the middle, and with three short pipes (A, B, and C) on top and three boxes (1, 2, and 3) lined up below. While subjects watched, the experimenter attached an opaque S-shaped tube from pipe-C to box-1 and dropped a piece of food down the C-pipe. On their first try, the tamarins looked in box 3, the box directly beneath the release point. No food. Since there was no connection between pipe-C and box-3, and since the tamarins never saw food drop into this open space, nothing about their perceptual experiences would give them this result. After they opened box-3 and found nothing, they then opened box-2 and finally box-1, where they found the food. When the experimenter ran another trial, keeping the tube in the same C-1 configuration, the tamarins typically repeated the same error, searching first in box-3, then 2, then 1. Some individuals repeated this error 20–30 times. Eventually, some tamarins picked box-1 on the first try. At this point, the experimenter moved the tube from pipe-B to box-3. The tamarins searched in box-2, the box beneath the release point. The tamarins repeated this error over and over again. In fact, when the experimenter replaced the opaque tube with a transparent one, allowing the tamarins to see the food fall, they searched in the correct box, and did so consistently. But when the experimenter put the opaque tube back in, placing it in the same position as the transparent tube on the previous trial, the tamarins bounced back to their original error, searching in the box beneath the release point.

The tamarins appear to have a remarkable gravity bias, one that causes search error after search error. It is puzzling that they don't use their failed attempts to find food beneath the release point to try some other strategy. It is even more puzzling that they don't try the most obvious solution to this problem and pick the box *associated* with the tube. Without even looking at the food's release point, the correct response on every trial is always the box associated with the tube. Since we know that animals as evolutionarily distant as worms and humans use associations to solve problems in the world, why don't the tamarins fall back on this simple strategy? Perhaps tamarins, unlike their distant relatives the worms, are too smart for their own good. Instead of using the simplest strategy for finding food, they are overthinking the problem. Or perhaps this kind of gravity bias pays off most of the time, falling victim to the exceptional cases when a warped experimental mind sets up something equivalent to a Rube Goldberg contraption.

To show that there is not just something odd about the tubes apparatus, or about tamarins, consider two additional experiments. If gravity is really the problem, as opposed to some other factor such as that there are no tubes in the real world, then removing gravity should change the patterns of search. An experimenter presented the tamarins with the same apparatus, but set it up horizontally as opposed to vertically (Hauser et al., 2001). When the experimenter rolled the food down the tube, the tamarins showed a marked improvement in their search patterns, and most importantly, did not show the equivalent of the gravity bias. This shows that when there is no effect of gravity, tamarins can find a piece of food that has been invisibly displaced within a tube. Tubes are not the problem. But since the same tamarins were run on the horizontal test after they were run on the vertical test, perhaps this experience helped them. We can't distinguish between tamarins learning about tubes and tamarins learning about objects that move out of view. To explore these possibilities, an experimenter tested the tamarins on a vertical setup that was identical to the original experiment, but replaced the tube with a hidden ramp, a flat piece of plastic concealed by an opaque screen. Although these animals had hundreds of trials with the vertical tubes apparatus, and many trials with the horizontal tubes, they once again failed on the vertical ramps, and with the same repetitive errors. They first picked the box beneath the release point, then the middle, and then the correct box. And then they started all over again on consecutive trials. Like infants committing the A-not-B-error, the tamarins' response bias is the result of a modular macro. Unlike the A-not-B error, however, this response bias is not the result of an arbitrarily learned action sequence. Rather, reaching for the location beneath the release point appears to be the result of a long evolutionary history, one dominated by the physics of life on earth. Gravity dominates. Things that fall typically do fall straight down. The mind of a tamarin has been designed with this knowledge. Although we can't say for sure whether they have an innate expectation about falling objects, it is a reasonable starting assumption, one that could potentially be tested by rearing tamarins in a gravity-free environment, or perhaps less technologically challenging, in an environment where they never saw objects fall.

A second experiment shows that tamarins are not the only species to form such expectations about falling objects. Following up on the table experiments described above with infants and toddlers, I (Hauser, 2001) ran a comparable series of experiments with free-ranging rhesus monkeys, the same species used by Diamond in her box experiments. An experimenter showed a rhesus monkey a table, and then placed one box on top and one box directly below. The experimenter then hid the boxes and table from view with a screen, dropped an apple over the two aligned boxes so that it fell out of view, removed the screen and allowed the subject to approach. Consistently, the rhesus monkeys searched in the box below the table, and consistently, of course, they failed to find the apple. How could rhesus monkeys, who have survived for approximately 20–30-million years on earth, not *know* this? They can't really think that if you jump off a branch from the top of a tree that you will just effortlessly drop *through* the branches to the spot directly below on the ground. They can't. But the results are strikingly consistent. In parallel with the tamarin results, if the experimenter now turns the problem on its side, removing gravity, and then rolling an apple toward two concealed boxes placed in a straight line, rhesus always pick the near box. Here, they seem to *know* that when you roll an apple towards two boxes, that the closest box will stop or contain the apple. Rhesus know that an apple can't roll *through* a box. But they somehow think that an apple can drop through a box and then a table and into a box below.

Tamarins, rhesus and many other animals have some understanding of physical principles. The fact that they fail when searching for invisibly displaced falling objects is actually more, rather than less evidence for what they know or understand. What is striking about their error with falling objects is how consistent it is. Their search patterns reveal an immunity to counter-evidence. This kind of immunity is precisely what one would predict if the animal's expectations are based on theory-like principles. This proposal is similar to what Carey (Carey, 1985) and Keil (Keil, 1994) have proposed for conceptual change in child development (see also Gopnik and Meltzoff, [1997]), an argument that mirrors Kuhnian (Kuhn, 1970) views of scientific change. Like scientists with a pet theory, both tamarins and rhesus appear to hold a theory of falling objects, one that they adhere to even in the face of evidence that the theory is wrong and requires modification. We can say that it is a theory about falling objects rather than objects or moving objects in general, because both tamarins and rhesus have the right theory when it comes to making predictions about objects that move along the horizontal plane. And what gives this story even greater support is the fact that the searching pattern for tamarins and rhesus are similar even though each species lives in a different environment and has been designed to solve somewhat different ecological and social problems. Importantly, tamarins are highly arboreal animals, spending most of their time high up in the canopy. Rhesus, in contrast, are largely terrestrial, spending most of their time on the ground. Tamarins have therefore had little experience watching objects roll on a flat surface, and although they have presumably seen objects such as fruit falling, they are unlikely to track and search for such objects on the ground. Rhesus have presumably seen numerous objects moving on the ground and falling from trees, and most likely have searched for falling objects since they spend more time on the ground than do tamarins. Nonetheless, both species show a strong gravity bias.

Although tamarins and rhesus may be like children and scientists in terms of holding a theory about falling objects, they differ in one critical way: most children and scientists eventually give in, acknowledging at some level that their own theory no longer accounts for the data, and that a new theory is necessary. They engage in conceptual change. It is possible, of course, that if an experimenter had tested the tamarins or rhesus over thousands of trials that, eventually, they would select the correct box. But then it would be necessary to distinguish between theory change and mere training or shaping. The main point here is that for many animals, the action system spontaneously dominates, thereby blocking the kind of conceptual change that is required for deepening one's knowledge of the physical world. Such rigidity may be especially common when the expectations or theories that underlie their behavior represent statistical regularities of the world. Gravity is one such regularity.

Humans up to the age of three years are no different from adult tamarins with respect to performance on the tubes task (Hood, 1995). Over dozens of trials, these relatively old children searched for the ball in the gravity box, the box directly below the release point. Is their error due to a problem of memory, inattention, motivation, or sheer puzzlement over the nature of tubes? We can easily rule out the first three. The memory requirements are slim: from release to search is only a few seconds, well within the child's capacity for recall. On every trial, the child is deeply focused on the task, attending to the experimenter dropping the ball and then immediately running over to search. And the child is highly motivated, moving to find the ball, looking in the gravity box, then the middle box and finally, the correct one, only to start the same steps all over again on the tenth, twentieth, and thirtieth trial. Moreover, even if the child does have problems of memory, attention, and motivation, these three factors can't explain the systematic and biased pattern of search to the gravity box. To explore the possibility that children are just flummoxed by the tube, possibly ignoring it and just assuming that things fall straight down, Hood (1998) re-ran the experiment, but with an interesting twist. The experimenter presented the tubes apparatus on a video monitor, dropped the ball down the tube, and then asked the child to point to the box with the ball. As in the original experiment, children pointed to the gravity box and did so over dozens of trials. In a second condition, the experimenter inverted the apparatus, with the tube's opening on the bottom and boxes above. Due to a concealed suction pump above, when the experimenter let go of the ball, it was sucked up into the tube. No gravity. No error. Children point to the correct box, the one attached to the tube. Children have no problem with tubes. They have problems with gravity. What gets in the way is their modular macro, their tendency to assume that when things fall, they fall straight down. The action system then takes this assumption as true, and causes the child to reach, ballistically, for the gravity box.

One might have assumed, initially at least, that the tamarin's gravity bias was due to sheer stupidity. Such stupidity should have been replaced over evolution by the acquisition of language and other useful mental capacities. However, this same stupid, primitive system rears itself in child development, even in children who can speak and comment on their failed attempts to retrieve the ball.

What these studies show about our species is that we start life as folk physicists, individuals endowed with a core set of principles for understanding the physical world. This folk physics effectively guides perceiving in all children, independent of their culture. Sometimes it does the right thing, and sometimes it doesn't. Because children lack the resources to change this initial system, it takes years for them to develop an understanding of the physical world that is sufficiently rich and accurate that it can guide adaptive actions.

Back to the argument against Piaget, and his focus on action as a measure of knowledge. Recall that both the table and tubes tasks are action tasks. To succeed, and provide evidence that they know about invisible displacements as well as the core principles of object knowledge, subjects must retrieve the object from the appropriate location. In an attempt to explore whether the action system's dominance might cover up knowledge at another level, Santos and I (Santos and Hauser, 2002) re-ran the table task with free-ranging rhesus monkeys, this time using the violation of expectancy looking time method. Show rhesus monkeys the table and box set up as before. Hide the display, show them an apple, and then drop it behind the screen. Remove the screen and show them the contents of the boxes. In one trial, the apple appears in the top box and the bottom box is empty (the correct outcome), while in a second trial the apple appears in the bottom box and the top box is empty (the incorrect outcome); we create this low-tech magic by pre-loading the boxes before we set up, and then dropping the apple into a hidden pouch behind the screen. On the basis of results from the searching experiments, rhesus should expect the apple to land in the bottom boxæthis is where they search. Consequently, for a rhesus monkey watching this show, the violation arises when the apple appears in the top box. Rhesus should therefore look longer in trial one than in trial two. In fact, they do the opposite. When the apple appears in the bottom box, rhesus monkeys look longer than when the apple appears in the top box. What these results suggest is that rhesus monkeys know that the apple can't travel through the top box, and then through the table, into the bottom box. This is a violation of the solidity principle, *sensu* Spelke (1994), and it draws their attention. But what rhesus know as revealed by their eyes is inconsistent with what they know as revealed by their reaching behavior. Perceptual know-how appears to be different from action know-how. This distinction is not due to an immature brain as we only tested adult animals. It may, however, be due to *evolutionary* immaturity in the sense that the macaque brain, in contrast to the human brain, lacks the requisite circuitry for connecting perception and action know-how in some contexts.

To date, my students and I have run a variety of experiments on rhesus monkeys and tamarins, using both reaching and looking tasks. In some contexts, perhaps especially situations involving contact mechanics (Santos, in preparation), we find a dissociation between perception and action, with looking measures suggesting accurate knowledge of the physical world, while action measures suggest inaccurate or incomplete knowledge of the physical world. For example, while tamarins tested on the vertical tubes task search in the incorrect location for an invisibly displaced object, they correctly predict the object's location on the basis of looking-time data (Hauser, in preparation). In contrast, studies of numerical representation using looking time and search measures converge on the same limits or capacities (Hauser and Carey, in press; Hauser et al., 2000; Hauser et al., 1996). Thus, rather than a domain-general dissociation between perception and action, there appears to be a domain-specific dissociation. Fleshing out the details of these dissociations is am important goal for future research.

The fact that some animals may have perceptual know-how without action know-how raises a puzzle: individuals may perceive a situation correctly without being able to correctly act on the same situation. Neither tamarins nor rhesus appear capable of reaching into the library of knowledge that guides looking in order to use it to guide reaching, at least with respect to certain aspects of their folk physics. Based on their behavior, the information appears to be sealed off in a section of the brain. This kind of inaccessibility is directly relevant to Fodor's modularity thesis. As Fodor originally postulated, modules are automatic, fast, effortless, susceptible to breakdown from damage, task or content-specific, and, critically, informationally *encapsulated* from other parts of the brain. Thus, when we perceive a visual illusion such as the Mueller-Lyer line illusion, we can't turn them off even when we convince ourselves by measuring the lengths of the lines. The information tucked away in our visual systemsæthe parts responsible for seeing the lengths as equalæis encapsulated. No matter how sure we are about the dimensions of these lines, we can't convince our visual systems to change their opinion. The action system seems to be constructed in a similar fashion. When there are statistical regularities that map onto habitual motor responses, the brain constructs modular macros, designed to implement adaptive responses. Due to their long evolutionary history, such responses are immune to counter-evidence. For animals, such immunity blocks conceptual change, blocking access to knowledge that is available to perception and prediction, but not action. For human infants, such immunity represents one barrier that must be overcome in order to engage in conceptual change. As the inhibitory veil is lifted in the young child, knowledge of the world is enriched.

II. FOLK PSYCHOLOGY

In the previous section I alluded to the fact that the dissociation between perception and action is domain-specific. What about the domain of folk psychology? Although far less empirical work on animals has targeted this question, there is a general sense in which inhibitory problems play an equally powerful role in constraining conceptual change in the domain of folk psychology as they do in the domain of folk physics. The bulk of this work stems from studies of normally developing children and contrasting patterns among autistics, with only a smattering of evidence from nonhuman primates. The goal of this section is therefore to build the argument from studies of human children, and then show how the conceptual and methodological conclusions from this work bear on studies of nonhuman primates.

A telltale sign that the child has grasped the richness of other minds is that he or she appreciates the logical possibility of false beliefs, that a person can believe something that is false because they missed a key event or because another person told them something incorrect. To test young children's understanding of false beliefs, developmental psychologists have used what is now famously referred to as the "Sally–Ann" task, named after the two puppets that appeared in Wimmer and Perner's (1983) original experiments. Though there are literally hundreds of variants of this task, each designed to pick apart why children either fail or succeed, the core narrative runs as follows. A child watches as Sally and Ann play with a ball. Sally then puts the ball in a basket and leaves the room. While Sally is away, Ann takes the ball out of the basket and places it in a box. Sally then returns to the room. The experimenter now asks the child "Where will Sally look for the ball?" The classic result is that 3-year-olds point and say the box, while 4- to 5-year olds point and say the basket. The older children understand that Sally has a false belief. She must believe that her ball is in the basket because this is where she left it and she didn't see Ann move it to the box. Since she didn't see Ann move the ball, she can't know or believe that it is in the box. In the absence of a critical perceptual event—seeing—Sally lacks a critical mental state: knowing or believing. From their third to their fifth birthdays, children undergo a conceptual revolution. Faced with the fact that Sally searches in the basket and not the box, 3-year-olds are handed a piece of counter-evidence. They predicted that Sally would look in the box. Their prediction was wrong. Over a period of one year, their conceptual system changes, as they grasp a critical fact about human minds: sometimes we believe things that others don't. This was the party line until the mid-1990s.

In the last section I mentioned the idea that what children or nonhuman primates appear to know as revealed by their eyes may well be different from what they know as revealed by their actions. Now reconsider the Sally–Ann test. In the classic version, the experimenter asks the child to point or say where Sally will look for the ball. These are actions. What are her eyes doing before or during her actions? To address this question, Clements and Perner (1994) ran a Sally-Ann test with 3- and 4-year olds, but in addition to asking them to point and say where Sally would look, they also filmed their eyes. Like Piaget's child who looked to the B-screen but reached behind the A-screen in the A-not-B task, 3-year-olds looked to the basket and then pointed or said "the box"; 4-year-olds, predictably, looked and pointed/said "the basket." Three-year-olds appear to have knowledge of what others know or believe, but they can't access it, consciously. It's as if they have a hunch, but lack sufficient confidence to bet on it. In fact, in a follow-up study by Ruffman and colleagues (Ruffman et al., 2001), when children were asked to bet on where Sally will search, the amount they bet matched their pointing and verbal responses, but not the direction of their looks. Three-year-olds have implicit knowledge of others' beliefs. They lack explicit knowledge (Dienes and Perner, 1999). They don't really know what they know. What blocks access to this knowledge?

In the A-not-B error, I suggested that action dominates perception and perhaps even beliefs; reaching wins over thinking about the object's location. The infant might know that the object is hidden behind B. But since she has been reaching with success behind A, the action system pulls its trump card. Perhaps the same explanation holds for the Sally–Ann test. Though the children tested have never seen the puppet show before, and the experimenter only tests them a single time, the task itself involves a common, one might even say habitual, response: pointing. When we point, we point to where something is. But to demonstrate an understanding of Sally's false belief, the child must point to the basket. She must point to where the ball is not. To succeed, she must inhibit the natural, habitual tendency to point to where something is (the box), pointing instead to where something is not. In a series of experiments, Carlson, Moses and their colleagues (Carlson and Moses, 2001; Carlson et al., 1998) ran 3-year-olds on the classic Sally–Ann test, but instead of pointing, asked them to place a sticker on the relevant container. They succeeded, putting the sticker on the box. Unlike pointing, sticker-ing is not a habitual response. We can place stickers wherever we like.

What these simple and clever experiments show is that young children may understand false beliefs, but the original task prevented them from displaying their abilities. The classic Sally–Ann test is insensitive to the child's developing control problems. Unlike older children, 3-year-olds are more vulnerable to inhibitory problems (Carlson and Moses, 2001; Carlson et al., 1998; Leslie, 2000; Leslie and Polizzi, 1998; Russell, 1997; Russell et al., 1994; Zelazo and Frye, 1997). Like reaching for the ball behind screen A or searching for a dropped ball in the cup below the table, young children lack the level of control needed to reveal their conceptual understanding of Sally's false beliefs.

Some humans never acquire an understanding of other minds. As Baron-Cohen (Baron-Cohen, 1995) has put it, they have mindblindness. Unlike certain kinds of neurological deficits that can be repaired through therapy or by the natural compensatory abilities of the brain, these individuals are locked into a surreal social world, one in which others' beliefs are terra incognito. These individuals are autistic. This clinical label is itself somewhat controversial in that the syndrome is characterized by a highly variable etiology, ranging from severely retarded to high-functioning individuals. What appears to be characteristic of all autistics is that they have poor social, communicative, and imaginative abilities, as well as difficulties with planning. Given these descriptions, the critical question is whether the deficit is domain-specific, restricted to the individual's folk psychology, or whether it is domain-general, a reflection of general intelligence and control, the province of the frontal lobes?

Consider the following statistics (Baron-Cohen, 2000). First, autism is highly heritable. Second, autism is much more common in males than in females; the ratios run from as low as 4:1 to as high as 40:1. Third, high-functioning autistics often have brilliant careers in the physical and mathematical sciences, but never in the humanities or social sciences. Fourth, the non-autistic parents of autistic children are disproportionately represented in jobs that involve little to no social interactions, including engineering and mathematics. Fifth, autistics are not vulnerable to visual illusions such as the Ebbinghaus-Titchner illusion: when shown two identically sized circles, one surrounded by larger circles and the other by smaller circles, normal individuals perceive a difference in size between the two inner circles while autistics do not (Happe, 1996). One explanation for this effect is that autistics tend to perceive the world at a local level, ignoring contextual or global information; non-autistics see things in context, looking at the relationship between objects in a scene. Thus, when asked to describe a scene involving two or more characters, autistics tend to overlook the relationship between the characters and how one individual's actions might influence what the other does; rather, they focus on each individual or object in the scene. They are blind to relationships. Taken together, these observations raise an intriguing idea, one developed by Baron-Cohen: if autistics have a genetic deficit that leads to a selective impairment of their folk psychology, might they have not only a selective sparing of their folk physics, but a selective enhancement?

A first step into the problems raised by the statistics summarized above is to explore how autistics fare on classic theory of mind tests. In contrast to normal children of the same age, autistic children tend to look away when someone looks at them, tend not to look where someone is looking, do not understand that seeing is a proxy for knowing, and do poorly when asked about the emotions expressed in someone's eyes (Baron-Cohen, 2000; Frith, 1989, 1991; Happe and Frith, 1996). Two simple tasks reveal this deficit. Show an autistic child a picture of two girls standing in front of an open box, with one girl looking in and the other looking straight ahead. When asked "Which girl knows what is in the box?," autistics are as likely to say the girl looking in the box as the girl looking straight ahead. In a second task, an experimenter shows a picture of a cartoon character whose eyes are looking up and to the left, in the direction of a Hershey candy bar; in the other corners are different candy bars, labeled by name. When asked "Which candy bar does Johnny want?," autistics are as likely to say "Hershey bar" as they are to say the names of the other three candies. However, when asked "Which candy bar is Johnny looking at?," they answer "Hershey bar." What this study shows is that perception is spared in autistics, while folk psychology is impaired. "Looking" refers to Johnny's perception, "want" to his beliefs and desires.

Two further contrasts help make the case that autistics have a selective impairment in their folk psychology. If general intelligence is necessary for understanding what others believe, then children with Down syndrome, who suffer from extreme mental retardation and low IQs, should perform as poorly on the Sally–Ann test as do autistics. They don't. Down syndrome children correctly attribute false beliefs, while autistics do not. Are autistics like normal 3-year-olds who also fail false belief tasks? Not quite. Recall that normal 3-year-olds seem to have some understanding of false beliefs as revealed by their eyes, as opposed to their pointing or verbal responses. Thus far, the looking version of the Sally–Ann test has not been explored in autistics. What Leslie and his colleagues have run, however, is a simplified Sally–Ann test that 3-year-olds pass (Leslie, 2000; Leslie and Polizzi, 1998). Instead of asking children "Where will Sally look for the ball?," an experimenter asks "Where will Sally look first for the ball?" Simply inserting "first" into the sentence causes 3-year-olds to answer "the basket." Perhaps this extra word causes the child to think about where Sally placed the ball first, as opposed to considering what Sally believes. To control for this possibility, Leslie and colleagues ran the same experiment, but this time, Sally stayed in the room while watching Ann move the ball to the box. When the experimenter asked three year olds "Where will Sally look first for the ball?", they answered "the box." Though this change helped 3-year-olds understand Sally's beliefs, it did not help autistic children. Leslie argues that the simplified Sally–Ann test reduces some of the inhibitory burden for 3-year-olds, thereby allowing their folk psychology to surface. For autistics, in contrast, lifting the inhibitory burden is irrelevant, because the difficulty lies in their folk psychology, the fact that they just don't have an understanding of others' beliefs; see, however, Zelazo and colleagues (2002).

I previously mentioned that autistics often have brilliant careers in the physical and mathematical sciences, and often have non-autistic parents who have similar professions. Baron-Cohen (1999) used these observations to ask whether the selective deficit in folk psychology might not be paired with a selective sparing or even an enhancement of folk physics. In one study, he tested three high-functioning autistics on three tasks, one for folk physics, one for folk psychology, and one for planning and inhibitory control. Of the three subjects, one was a professor of mathematics who had won the Field medal, equivalent in prestige to the Nobel prize; the other two were accomplished university students in physics and computer science, respectively. To test for their folk psychology, Baron-Cohen presented a "Reading the Mind in the Eyes" task. Subjects looked at a picture of a person's eyes and picked one of four adjectives to describe the person's emotional state. All three autistics scored well below normal adults. The folk physics test involved questions about the functioning of mechanical/physical devices. For example, the experimenter first showed a picture of a balanced scale, with one small box on one side and two larger boxes on the other, and then asked "Which box is the heaviest?" All three autistics scored well above normal adults. For the planning and inhibitory control task, Baron-Cohen presented the Tower of

Hanoi. In this task, an experimenter sets up a stack of rings around a center peg, ordered from largest to smallest; next to this peg are two others, both empty. The experimenter asks the subject to place the rings in the same order (large to small) on the empty far peg by making the fewest moves to the center peg. Here too, the three autistics far surpassed normal adults, completing the task in lightening speed. These results show that there can be a significant impairment in folk psychology without a corresponding impairment in other domains, or in other forms of reasoning, planning or control. The bottom line appears to be that autism looks like a highly selective deficit of folk psychology.

Studies of autism also bear on another aspect of inhibitory control. Many autistics appear to be uninhibited copy cats, parroting precisely what others say and do, as if it were a reflex. They have what clinicians refer to as echolalia. Autistics are also prone to repetitive rocking, in addition to obsessional thoughts and actions. But autistics are not alone in this deficit, as evidenced by patients with obsessive-compulsive disorder. Is the inhibitory problem the same, however, in these two clinical populations? More specifically, is the inhibitory problem domain-specific or domain-general? To address this question, Baron-Cohen and colleagues (Baron-Cohen and Wheelwright, 1999) explored the content of obsessions in high-functioning autistics. Given the impairment in folk psychology, autistics should have few if any thoughts in this domain. Further, given that autistics seem to escape from the challenges that the social world presents by focusing on the physical world, they should have most of their thoughts focused on folk physics. If the inhibitory problem is domain-specific, then autistics should have obsessional thoughts about the physical world. To test this logic, Baron-Cohen used parental reports of obsessions in autistic children, as well as children with Tourette's syndrome, a disorder associated with facial or body tics—an apparent failure of inhibition at the motor level. In contrast to the children with Tourette's, whose obsessions focused largely on motor and sensory events (touching, smelling objects), autistics' obsessions focused on folk physics, with almost no observations in the domain of folk psychology. These studies show that the problem of inhibitory control is domain-specific.

In parallel with the child's conceptual revolutions in the domain of folk physics, the child undergoes comparable changes in the domain of folk psychology. Each child is endowed with core building blocks in each of these domains, naïve theories that help them make roughly correct predictions of the world. From birth to at least 6 or 7 years old, these initial theories are refined, and in some cases, radically transformed. During the reorganization period, the child is vulnerable to significant errors. The child's theory runs like a macro, immune to counter-evidence. No matter how much experience, and how much painstaking teaching she receives, the child will simply not learn. Learning, or more accurately, conceptual change, arises when the counter-evidence is so significant that a new theory is required. It is at this tipping point that critical experiences move the child to a new level of under-standing. In the domain of folk psychology, there is a transformation at around 4 to 5 years. For the first time, what others believe, intend, desire, and want is transparent or at least, translucent. With this knowledge, children can not only understand how their own actions will influence what others believe and how they feel, but can think about how they would feel if someone did something to them. Their folk psychological expertise enables them to model the world, running mini-simulations of how their actions influence their own lives and those with whom they interact. For the autistic child, this world is a deep mystery.

How might we characterize the folk psychology of different nonhuman primates? Since many of the insights into the child's developing theory of mind come from tasks that use language, we can not use the same sorts of approaches with animals. The pioneering work in this area was Premack and Woodruff's (Premack and Woodruff, 1978) classic experiment on chimpanzees, research that led to the birth of the term "theory of mind." In the original task, a chimpanzee saw food placed in one of two boxes. In one condition, a cooperative trainer entered the room and if the chimpanzee indicated the box with food, the trainer opened it and shared the food. In a second condition, a non-cooperative trainer entered the room and if the chimpanzee indicated the box with food, the trainer opened it and took all the food for himself. The prediction was that if chimpanzees have a theory of mind, recognizing that only they know where the food is because the other trainers did not see the food placement, then they should indicate the food box to the cooperative trainer but not to the non-cooperative trainer. Results suggested that chimpanzees could make this distinction, using their knowledge of what each trainer knows and believes to guide their own behavior, pointing to the food box with the cooperative trainer and the non-food box with the non-cooperative trainer. This, together with a suite of other studies, led Premack (Premack, 1986; Premack and Premack, 2002) to conclude that the chimpanzee has a theory of mind, albeit not as well developed as in humans.

Since Premack's pioneering work, there have been an increasing number of studies exploring mental state attribution in primates. Unfortunately, the field is in a state of complete chaos (Cheney and Seyfarth, 1990; Hauser, 2000; Heyes, 1998; Tomasello and Call, 1997). Starting with Premack's original work, some have argued that these data fail to provide evidence for a theory of mind because the chimpanzees' ability to discriminate between trainers only emerged after dozens of trials, suggesting that they learned a discrimination based on behavior as opposed to beliefs. More recent work with chimpanzees (Call and Tomasello, 1999; Povinelli and Eddy, 1996) reveals a suite of failures, using a variety of tasks and subjects, as well as targeting different building blocks to a theory of mind, such as an understanding of the seeing–knowing distinction. All of these studies, however, share two potential problems in common: they ask whether chimpanzees have a theory of human minds as opposed to other chimpanzee minds, and they require inhibitory control, a capacity that is weak even among chimpanzees (Boysen et al., 1996; Boysen et al., 1999). For example, in Premack and Woodruff's original experiment, the chimpanzee must inhibit pointing to the box where the food is in order to deceive the non-cooperative trainer, pointing instead to the box without food. In Povinelli's experiments, where chimpanzees are required to beg for food from one of two trainers, they must inhibit begging from one individual on each trial. In the initial training, chimpanzees were required to beg from a trainer who was sitting facing and looking forward. In subsequent conditions, two trainers are present, each positioned in a slightly different way, designed to assess whether the chimpanzees are using the seeing–knowing proxy or some physical feature, perhaps linked to the original training condition. This design therefore creates an inhibitory problem as the chimpanzee must inhibit begging from a trainer who might be seated in such a way that it appears like the original condition (e.g., torso facing the chimpanzee, but eyes closed or head averted backwards), but in fact is inappropriate because this trainer is looking away.

The most recent work in this area appears to solve both problems raised above. Hare and colleagues (2000; 2001) asked whether chimpanzees know about other chimpanzees' beliefs, using a competitive task that requires some level of inhibitory control, but perhaps less than the others because of the absence of training. In the first experiment, an experimenter placed a subordinate chimpanzee on one side of a center arena and a dominant on the opposite side; the center arena included two opaque screens with two bananas located in view of the chimpanzees, in between the screens. When the chimpanzees' doors were opened, allowing them access to the center arena, the dominant marched out and grabbed the bananas. The subordinate didn't move, even when he was given a head start. Subordinates clearly know that they can't compete for food with a dominant; they exert some level of inhibitory control by staying put as opposed to rushing out. In the second condition, an experimenter placed one banana in between the screens and the other banana behind one screen, in view of the subordinate but not the dominant. If the subordinate recognizes what the dominant can see, and therefore understands what the dominant knows, then when the doors open, the subordinate should make a bee-line for the concealed banana. This is precisely what happens: the subordinate grabs the concealed banana while the dominant grabs the center banana. In a final condition, an experimenter concealed one banana on the dominant's side and placed the other centrally between the screens. Here, the dominant can see both bananas while the subordinate can only see the center banana. Each animal does the right thing: the subordinate stays put while the dominant first grabs the banana in view, and then grabs the concealed banana. This makes sense because there is no contest over the concealed banana. The subordinate can't know about this piece. These results, together with several other experiments involving critical controls, has led Hare and colleagues to conclude that chimpanzees know what other chimpanzees know. Comparable experiments with monkeys have all failed to provide evidence for mental state attribution, suggesting a phylogenetic difference in the evolution of this capacity.

At present it is difficult to say with confidence whether chimpanzees are endowed with a folk psychology that is as well developed as in humans, and if so, whether we are referring to an adult human or a child of age three, four or five years. The studies by Hare and colleagues are encouraging, especially since the design of their experiment bypasses some of the inhibitory problems inherent in the earlier approaches; given the results on children, avoiding problems of inhibitory control is crucial. What we also lack thus far are tests that explore whether chimpanzees, or other animals, have knowledge of others that is implicit as opposed to explicit, or more descriptively, knowledge that is available to perception but not action. Given the success of looking-time methods in studies of folk physics, it is time to implement such approaches in the domain of folk psychology (Hauser, 1998).

III. WHEN "I" KNOWS

Over the last twenty or so years, there have been an increasing number of cases reported where a patient exhibits a dissociation between perception and action. Such dissociations suggest that the knowledge that mediates perception may in fact be different from the kind of knowledge mediating action. Consequently, one challenge confronting the neurosciences is to establish the circuitry underlying these different kinds of knowledge, what some consider to be a distinction between implicit and explicit knowledge. The study by Goodale and colleagues (1991) provides a useful starting point. The patient studies showed preserved capacities with respect to action, with deficits in perception. In the classic test, the patient is presented with a slot (resembling a slot in a mail box) positioned at different angles. In the action task, the patient's task is to take a letter-sized piece of paper and place it into the slot. The patient performs at the level of normal subjects. In the perception task, the patient must hold the letter with an orientation that matches the orientation of the slot (i.e., the orientation that would be appropriate should the patient be required to put the letter in the slot). Here, and on several other variants of the task, the patient fails. The patient suffers from a deficit that causes a decoupling between the knowledge mediating action and the knowledge mediating perceptual judgments. In contrast, work by Damasio and colleagues (Damasio et al., 1982; Tranel and Damasio, 1985, 1993) on patients with prosopagnosia suggests that these individuals may have some implicit or covert level of knowledge about facial identity, but no explicit or overt knowledge. Evidence for implicit/covert knowledge comes from skin-conductance data (showing differentiating of familiar and unfamiliar faces), as well as experiments where prosopagnosic patients are introduced to nurses associated with different emotional valences (e.g., one is very pleasant and never tests the patient, one is neutral, and one is negative, always running tests, never allowing breaks, and so on) and subsequently show differentiated responses to each without any explicit recognition. Cases such as these, together with others including work on blindsight (Weiskrantz, 1986), and patients with prefrontal damage (Bechara et al., 1997), suggest that brain damage can cause a disconnect between different systems of knowledge.

What I have argued in this essay is that normal animals and developing human children show similar kinds of dissociations. In the case of children, the dissociation appears to reflect the immaturity of the brain, while in animals, a different explanation must be invoked. In particular, because all of the studies conducted on this topic have thus far been run with adult animals, it is not possible to invoke the standard arguments used thus far with infants and young children (Diamond et al., 1994; Diamond and Goldman-Rakic, 1989; Munakata et al., 1997). Rather, what seems to account for the primate data is that within particular domains of knowledge, circuitry connecting up perception and action systems are either weak or not there at all. Although we know relatively little about such circuitry, I believe the data speak to an additional factor. In parallel with developmental studies, it appears that for many if not most animals, the action system largely dominates the perception system. More specifically, whenever animals are confronted with statistical regularities, such that selection favors fast, automatic, and unconscious responses, animals will create what I have called modular macros. These action sequences are immune to counter-evidence. More particularly, they are immune to perceptual evidence that might, if allowed to surface, cause the animal to change what it believes about the world. This conclusion has both conceptual and practical implications. Conceptually, these results suggest that future work in the neurosciences might profitably look for circuitry connecting between perception and action systems, not in a domain-general sense, but in a domain-specific sense. I reiterate this point here because in some domains, the perceptual and action tasks reveal comparable underlying knowledge; number is one such domain. Given convergence in some domains and divergence in others, it should be possible to isolate why these differences emerge both in evolution (comparisons across species) and within development (e.g., perhaps some individuals acquire certain habits early in development that set the stage for a dominant action system)

Methodologically, work on animals must follow the lead of those working in infant cognitive development, recognizing the fact that inhibitory problems may get in the way of revealing conceptual knowledge. Said more starkly, what an animal does may not capture what it knows. This is an old problem, but one that must be reemphasized today given our increasing understanding of the psychology and neurobiology of control.

In conclusion, what makes each individual unique is his or her knowledge, what he or she knows and how he or she experiences it. As a species, we evolved a perhaps unique sense of self, one that allows us to reflect upon what we know, to use such knowledge to generate expectations about others who are similar to and different from us, and to recognize that in many ways, each of us has a unique view of the world. That said, many of the ways in which we view the world is derived from an ancient stock, innate knowledge that we share with our primate ancestors because we evolved in the face of comparable social and ecological pressures, problems that have reoccurred over and over again.

REFERENCES

BAILLARGEON, R. (1995). Physical reasoning in infancy. In M. Gazzaniga (Ed.), *The cognitive neurosciences* (pp. 181–204). Cambridge: MIT Press.

BAILLARGEON, R. & DEVOS, J. (1991). Object permanence in young infants: Further evidence. *Child Development, 62*, 1227–1246.

BAILLARGEON, R., GRABER, M., DEVOS, M.J. & BLACK, J. (1990). Why do young infants fail to search for hidden objects? *Cognition, 36*, 255–284.

BAILLARGEON, R., SPELKE, E. & WASSERMAN, S. (1985). Object permanence in five month old infants. *Cognition, 20*, 191–208.

BARON-COHEN, S. (1995). *Mindblindness.* Cambridge, MA: MIT Press.

BARON-COHEN, S. (2000). The cognitive neuroscience of autism: Evolutionary approaches. In M. Gazzaniga (Ed.) *The new cognitive neurosciences* (pp. 1249–1257). Cambridge: MIT Press.

BARON-COHEN, S. & WHEELWRIGHT, S. (1999). "Obsessions" in children with autism or Asperger syndrome. *British Journal of Psychiatry, 175*, 484–490.

BARON-COHEN, S., WHEELWRIGHT, S., STONE, V.E. & RUTHERFORD, M. (1999). A mathematician, a physicist and a computer scientist with Asperger syndrome: Performance on folk psychology and folk physics tests.q. *Neurocase, 5*, 475–483.

BECHARA, A., DAMASIO, H., TRANEL, D. & DAMASIO, A.R. (1997). Deciding advantageously before knowing the advantageous strategy. *Science,. 275*, 1293–1294.

BOGARTZ, R.S., SHINSKEY, J.L. & SPEAKER, C. (1997). Interpreting infant looking. *Developmental Psychology, 33*, 408–422.

BOYSEN, S.T., BERNTSON, G.G., HANNAN, M.B. & CACIOPPO, J.T. (1996). Quantity-based inference and symbolic representations in chimpanzees (*Pan troglodytes*). *Journal of Experimental Psychology: Animal Behavior Processes, 22*, 76–86.

BOYSEN, S.T., MUKOBI, K. & BERNTSON, G.G. (1999). Overcoming response bias using symbolic representations of number by chimpanzees (*Pan troglodytes*). *Animal Learning and Behavior, 27*, 229–235.

CALL, J. & TOMASELLO, M. (1999). A nonverbal theory of mind test: The performance of children and apes. *Child Development, 70*, 381–395.

CAREY, S. (1985). *Conceptual change in childhood.* Cambridge: MIT Press.

CARLSON, S.M. & MOSES, L.J. (2001). Individual differences in inhibitory control and children's theory of mind. *Child Development, 72,* 1032–1053.

CARLSON, S.M., MOSES, L.J. & HIX, H.R. (1998). The role of inhibitory processes in young children's difficulties with deception and false belief. *Child Development, 69(3),* 672–691.

CHENEY, D.L. & SEYFARTH, R.M. (1990). *How monkeys see the world: Inside the mind of another species.* Chicago: University of Chicago Press.

CLEMENTS, W.A. & PERNER, J. (1994). Implicit understanding of belief. *Cognitive Development, 9,* 377–395.

DAMASIO, A., DAMASIO, H. & VAN HOESEN, G. (1982). Prosopagnosia: Anatomic basis and behavioral mechanisms. *Neurology, 32,* 331–342.

DIAMOND, A. (1988). Differences between adult and infant cognition: Is the crucial variable presence or absence of language? In L. Weiskrantz (Ed.) *Thought without language* (pp. 337–370). Oxford: Clarendon Press.

DIAMOND, A. (1990). Developmental time course in human infants and infant monkeys, and the neural bases of higher cognitive functions. *Annals of the New York Academy of Sciences, 608,* 637–676.

DIAMOND, A., CRUTTENDEN, L. & NEIDERMAN, D. (1994). AB with multiple wells: 1. Why are multiple wells sometimes easier than two wells? 2. Memory or memory + inhibition? *Developmental Psychology, 30,* p. 192–205.

DIAMOND, A. & GOLDMAN-RAKIC, P.S. (1989). Comparison of human infants and infant rhesus monkeys on Piaget's AB task: Evidence for dependence on dorsolateral prefrontal cortex. *Experimental Brain Research, 74,* 24–40.

DIENES, Z. & PERNER, J. (1999). A theory of implicit and explicit knowledge. *Behavioral and Brain Research, 22,* 735–755.

FODOR, J.A. (1983). *The modularity of mind.* Cambridge, MA: MIT Press.

FRITH, U. (1989). *Autism: Explaining the enigma.* Oxford: Blackwell Scientific Publications.

FRITH, U. (1991). *Autism and Asperger syndrome.* Cambridge: Cambridge University Press.

GOODALE, M.A., MILNER, A.D., JAKOBSON, L.S. & CAREY, D.P. (1991). A neurological dissociation between perceiving objects and grasping them. *Nature, 349,* p. 154–156.

GOPNIK, A. & MELTZOFF, A. (1997). *Words, thoughts, and theories.* Cambridge, MA: MIT Press.

GRAYBIEL, A.M. (1998). The basal ganglia and chunking of repertoires. *Neurobiology of Learning and Memory, 70,* 119–138.

HAPPÉ, F. (1996). Studying weak coherence at low levels: Children with autism do not succumb to visual illusions. *Psychology and Psychiatry, 37,* 873–877.

HAPPÉ, F. & FRITH, U. (1996). The neuropsychology of autism. *Brain, 119,* 377–400.

HARE, B., CALL, AGNETTA, J.B. & TOMASELLO, M. (2000). Chimpanzees know what conspecifics do and do not see. *Animal Behaviour, 59,* 771–785.

HARE, B., CALL, J. & TOMASELLO, M. (2001). Do chimpanzees know what conspecifics know? *Animal Behaviour, 61,* 139–151.

HARRIS, P.L. (1986). Bringing order to the A-not-B error. *Monographs of the Society for Research in Child Development, 51,* 52–61.

HAUSER, M.D. (1998). Expectations about object motion and destination: Experiments with a nonhuman primate. *Developmental Science, v. 1,* 31–38.

HAUSER, M.D. (2000). *Wild minds: what animals really think.* New York: Henry Holt.

HAUSER, M.D. (2001). Searching for food in the wild: A nonhuman primate's expectations about invisible displacement. *Developmental Science, 4,* 84–93.

HAUSER, M.D. (in preparation). *The anatomy of temptation: How problems of control led to the birth of a moral grammar.* New York: Henry Holt.

HAUSER, M.D. & CAREY, S. (in press). Spontaneous representations of small numbers of objects by rhesus macaques: Examinations of content and format. *Cognitive Psychology.*

HAUSER, M.D., CAREY, S. & HAUSER, L.B. (2000). Spontaneous number representation in semi-free-ranging rhesus monkeys. *Proceedings of the Royal Society, London, 267,* 829–833.

HAUSER, M.D., MACNEILAGE, P. & WARE, M. (1996). Numerical representations in primates. *Proceedings of the National Academy of Sciences, 93,* 1514–1517.

HAUSER, M.H., WILLIAMS, T., KRALIK, J. & MOSKOVITZ, D. (2001). What guides a search for food that has disappeared? Experiments on cotton-top tamarins (*Saguinus oedipus*). *Journal of Comparative Psychology, 115,* 140–151.

HEYES, C.M. (1998). Theory of mind in nonhuman primates. *Behavioral and Brain Sciences, 21,* 101–114.

HOOD, B. (1995). Gravity rules for 2-4 year olds? *Cognitive Development, 10,* 577–598.

HOOD, B.M. (1998). Gravity does rule for falling objects. *Developmental Science, 1,* 59–64.

HOOD, B.M., CAREY, S. & PRASADA, S. (2000). Predicting the outcomes of physical events. *Child Development, 71,* 1540–1554.

HOOD, B.M., M.D. HAUSER, L. ANDERSON & L. SANTOS. 1999, Gravity biases in a nonhuman primate? *Developmental Science, 2,* 35–41.

Keil, F.C. (1994). The birth and nurturance of concepts by domains: The origins of concepts of living things. In L.A. Hirschfield & S.A. Gelman (Eds.), *Mapping the mind: Domain specificity in cognition and culture* (pp. 234–254). Cambridge: Cambridge University Press.

KUHN, T. (1970). *The structure of scientific revolutions.* Chicago: University of Chicago Press.

LESLIE, A.M. (2000). Theory of mind as a mechanism of selective attention. In M. Gazzaniga (Ed.), *The new cognitive neurosciences* (pp. 1235–1247). Cambridge: MIT Press.

LESLIE, A.M. & POLIZZI, P. (1998). Inhibitory processing in the false belief task: Two conjectures. *Developmental Science, 1,* 247–253.

MARCOVITCH, S. & ZELAZO, P.D. (1999). The A-not-B error: results from a logistic meta-analysis. *Child Development, 70,* 1297–1313.

MUNAKATA, Y., MCCLELLAND, J.L., JOHNSON, M.H. & SIEGLER, R.S. (1997). Rethinking infant knowledge: Toward an adapative processing account of successes and failures in object permanence tasks. *Psychological Review, 104,* 686–713.

PIAGET, J. (1954). *The construction of reality in the child.* New York, Basic Books.

POVINELLI, D.J. & EDDY, T.J. (1996). What young chimpanzees know about seeing. *Monographs of the Society for Research in Child Development, 247.*

PREMACK, D. (1986). *Gavagai!* Cambridge: MIT Press.

PREMACK, D. & A. PREMACK. (2002). *Original Intelligence.* New York: McGraw Hill.

PREMACK, D. & WOODRUFF, G. (1978). Does the chimpanzee have a theory of mind? *Behavioral and Brain Sciences, 4,* 515–526.

RUFFMAN, T., GARNHAM, W. IMPORT, A. & CONNOLLY, D. (2001). Does eye gaze indicate implicit knowledge of false belief? Charting transitions in knowledge. *Journal of Experimental Child Psychology, 80,* 201–224.

RUSSELL, J. (1997). How executive disorders can bring about an inadequate "theory of mind." In J. Russell (Ed.) *Autism as an executive disorder* (pp. 256–304). Oxford: Oxford University Press.

RUSSELL, J., JARROLD, C. & POTEL, D. (1994). What makes strategic deception difficult for children—the deception or the strategy? *British Journal of Developmental Developmental Psychology, 12,* 301–314.

SANTOS, L.R. & HAUSER, M.D. (2002). A nonhuman primate's understanding of solidity: Dissociations between seeing and acting. *Developmental Science, 5,* F1–F7.

SMITH, L.B., THELEN, E., TITZER, R. & McLIN, D. (1999). Knowing in the context of acting: The task dynamics of the A-not-B error. *Psychological Review, 106,* 235–260.

SPELKE, E.S. (1994). Initial knowledge: six suggestions. *Cognition, 50,* 431–445.

SPELKE, E.S., K. BREILINGER, J. MACOMBER & K. JACOBSEN. (1992). Origins of knowledge. *Psychological Review, 99,* 605–632.

SPELKE, E.S., VISHTON, P. & VON HOFSTEN, C. (1995). Object perception, object-directed action, and physical knowledge in infancy. In M. Gazzaniga (Ed.) *The cognitive neurosciences* (pp. 165–179). Cambridge, MA: MIT Press.

TOMASELLO, M. & J. CALL (1997). *Primate cognition.* Oxford: Oxford University Press.

TRANEL, D. & DAMASIO, A.R. (1985). Knowledge without awareness: An autonomic index of recognition of prosapagnosics. *Science, 228,* 1453–1454.

TRANEL, D. & DAMASIO, A.R. (1993). The covert learning of affective valence does not require structures in hippocampal system of amydala. *Journal of Cognitive Neuroscience, 5,* 79–88.

WEISKRANTZ, L. (1986). *Blindsight: A case study and implications.* Oxford: Clarendon Press.

WELLMAN, H.M., CROSS, D. & BARTSCH, K. (1986). Infant search and object permanence: a meta-analysis of the A-not-B error. *Monographs of the Society for Research in Child Development, 51,* 1–51; 62–67.

WIMMER, H. & PERNER, J. (1983). Beliefs about beliefs: Representation and constraining function of wrong beliefs in young children's understanding of deception. *Cognition, 13,* 103–128.

ZELAZO, P. D. & D. FRYE. (1997). Cognitive complexity and control: A theory of the development of deliberate reasoning and intentional action. In M. Stamenov (Ed.) *Language structure, discourse, and the access to consciousness* (pp. 113–153). Amsterdam: John Benjamins.

ZELAZO, P.D., JACQUES, S., BURACK, J.A. & FRYE, D. (2002). The relation between theory of mind and rule use: Evidence from persons with autism-spectrum disorders. *Infant and Child Development, 11,* 171–195.

ZELAZO, P.D., REZNICK, J.S. & SPINAZZOLA, J. (1998). Representational flexibility and response control in a multistep multilocation search task. *Developmental Psychology, 34,* 201–214.

The Emergence of Consciousness and Its Role in Human Development

MICHAEL LEWIS

Institute for the Study of Child Development, Robert Wood Johnson Medical School, New Brunswick, New Jersey 08903, USA

ABSTRACT: In this paper, I talk about several issues in regard to self and consciousness. I do so from a developmental perspective, since such a perspective may provide a framework to help understand consciousness as seen in the adult human. Briefly, the two processes I will call the *machinery of the self* and the mental state of the *idea of me* develop over the first two years of the child's life. Moreover, and perhaps of equal importance is the fact that the development of consciousness (the *idea of me*) provides the scaffolding for the development of the child's social and emotional development and is the first step in the child's development of other mental states, which provide the underpinning of a theory of mind. I will first explore what a self is and what it is not; then I will present a developmental model that provides a way of measuring early the *idea of me* or consciousness. Having shown how to measure this mental state, I will show how it has an impact on the development of a theory of mind, as well as on the child's emotional and social life. Finally, I will turn to the emergence of explicit and implicit consciousness.

KEYWORDS: self-recognition; development; consciousness

This paper discusses several issues in regard to consciousness and development. The study of the emergence of consciousness in the human child provides a framework for understanding consciousness as seen in the adult human. Briefly, what exists in the adult, what has been called implicit and explicit consciousness, has as its precursor first what I have called the *machinery of the self*, and subsequently the mental state of the *idea of me*. FIGURE 1 presents this model. From birth, the infant has, for example, the capacity to differentiate self from other or the capacity to receive and trans-

Address for correspondence: Dr. Michael Lewis, Institute for the Study of Child Development, Robert Wood Johnson Medical School, 97 Paterson Street, New Brunswick, NJ 08903. Voice: 732-235-7901; fax: 732-235-6189.

lewis@umdnj.edu

Ann. N.Y. Acad. Sci. 1001: 104–133 (2003). © 2003 New York Academy of Sciences.
doi: 10.1196/annals.1279.007

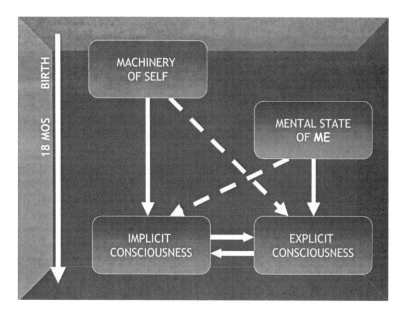

FIGURE 1. The development of implicit and explicit consciousness.

mit information within the system. These capacities are innate and part of the apparatus of all living systems. They do not require nor do they utilize mental states. At around the middle of the second year of life, mental states, in particular the mental state of the *idea of me,* emerge. At this point in development, it is possible to talk about consciousness as emerging in the human child. Implicit and explicit consciousness emerge from these two basic processes. As we shall argue, both forms of consciousness are derived from both the *machinery of the self* and from the mental state of the *idea of me.* Moreover, implicit consciousness can become explicit; as well, explicit consciousness can become implicit.

From a developmental point of view, what is important first is to understand the emergence of the mental state of the *idea of me,* and second to show how this emerging mental state provides the scaffolding for the development of the child's social and emotional development and how it constitutes the first step in the child's development of other mental states which provide the underpinning of a theory of mind. In this paper, I will first explore what a self is and what it is not; then present a developmental model which provides a way of measuring early the *idea of me* or consciousness. Having shown how to measure this mental state, I will show how it has an impact on the development of a theory of mind, as well as on the child's emotional and social life. Finally, I will turn to the emergence of explicit and implicit consciousness.

WHAT A SELF IS

As I sit here in my study looking out at the garden, the late afternoon sun blinds my sight. The taste of my coffee in my mouth lingers as I think about the paper I am writing. I have no trouble recognizing myself. I know where I am and why I am here. I feel my arm and hand move as I write. When I answer my wife's calls, my voice sounds like me. Sitting here, I can think about myself. I can wonder whether I will go to New York tonight. I wonder about my appearance. Do I need to wear a tie and jacket? Is my hair combed properly? As I get up to leave the room, I pass a mirror; there I see myself, the reflected surface of my being. "Yes, that is me," I say, fixing my hair.

I know a great deal about me. One of the things I know is how I look; for example, there is a scar in my left eyebrow. I look familiar to myself, even though I have changed considerably with age. Pictures taken of me 30 years ago look like me. Nevertheless, I know when I look at myself in the mirror I will not look as I did then; my hair and beard are now white, not the brown they were then. My face will be less smooth and I will have to tuck in my belly in order to look like anything I wish to be.

I know many people might argue that the concept of self is merely an idea. I would agree, and argue that this idea of self is a particularly powerful one; it is an idea with which I cannot part. It is one around which a good portion of the network of many of my ideas center. This is not to say that what I know explicitly about myself is all I know. In fact, this idea of myself is only one part of myself; there are many other parts of which I do not know. These have been called implicit knowledge. There are the activities of my body; the joints moving, the blood surging, the action potentials of my muscle movements as well as the calcium exchange along the axons. There are many other things that are part of me which are implicit. I have no knowledge of a large number of my motives—organized, coherent thoughts and ideas that have been called unconscious—that control large segments of my life. I have no explicit knowledge of how my thoughts occur. Nevertheless, I know that I think and feel even without this knowledge. This is my explicit consciousness.

Although it might be true that I could explicitly know more of some parts of my implicit self if I chose to, it is nonetheless the case that what is known by my self-system is greater than what I can state I know. If such facts are true, then, it is fair to suggest a metaphor of myself. I imagine myself to be a biological machine that is an evolutionarily fit complex of processes: doing, feeling, thinking, planning, and learning. One aspect of this machine is explicit; it is the *idea of me*. This idea or mental state knows itself and knows it does not know all of itself! My self, then, is greater than the me, the explicit me being only a small portion of myself. The difference between myself and me also can be understood from an epistemological point of view. The idea that *I know* is not the same as the idea that *I know I know*. The explicit aspect of the self that I refer to is that which knows it knows.

In the adult, we can refer to the *machinery of self* as implicit consciousness while the *idea of me,* explicit consciousness. From this perspective, we can say that for the adult human, these two aspects of consciousness both exist. One implicit aspect of the self is the *machinery of the body* or implicit consciousness; another is implicit consciousness that has been explicit. The other is the *idea of me* or explicit consciousness. While implicit consciousness as well as the *machinery of self* can learn and have memories, and while it is likely to be functioning even in sleep, explicit consciousness is transient; that is to say it can be explicit some of the time as well as implicit, much like Hilgard's idea of divided attention (Hilgard, 1977). From a developmental perspective, the *machinery of self* exists at birth and the mental state of the *idea of me* develops in the first two years in the child's life.

Consciousness: The Machinery of Self and the Mental State of Me

In order to deal with the problem of how to understand the development of the mental state of the *idea of me,* we need first to address the issue of the meaning of a behavior. It is a problem in development with a long history (Werner, 1961). The equivalence of a behavior across age is the problem. One can often observe that a very young infant can perform some action that, when performed at an older age, would be considered to represent some complex mental state. Take, for example, the problem of imitation. Imitation is particularly important, since the establishment of a true imitative response heralds the development of a child's understanding of itself (Baldwin, 1973).

However, the newborn infant will imitate certain body movements. For example, a tongue protrusion by an adult will produce a tongue protrusion in the infant (Meltzoff & Moore, 1977). Other forms of imitative behavior have been reported (Field, Woodson, Greenberg & Cohen, 1982). Although there may be some question as to the reliability of this behavior (Anisfeld et al., 2001), such actions have been called "imitation." "Imitation" has a particular meaning, usually implying some intention on the part of the imitator (Piaget, 1954). The finding that matching behavior exists in the newborn constitutes a challenge for developmental theory. We could claim that intentional behavior exists in the newborn, and therefore that imitation takes place. However, this is a nativistic explanation, implying that there is no development in the process of intention or in imitation.

Alternatively, the same behavior can be said to have different meanings. We can say that the behavior at Time 1 is called X, whereas at Time 2 it is called Y. This solution has the effect of saying that Y, the more mature behavior, does not exist until Time 2. Thus, for example, imitation in the newborn can be called "matching behavior," whereas in the 8-month-old it can be called "imitation" (Jacobson, 1979). It is much like stage theory, since X at Time 1 is not Y, nor is it Y-like.

Another way of handling this problem of the meaning of behavior is to consider that X and Y are functionally similar, but that they represent different levels of the same meaning. In this case, X and Y could be called the same behavior, but it would be acknowledged that X represents a lower level of the behavior than Y. In the imitation example, we may call both behaviors "imitation," but we recognize that newborn "imitation" is an earlier level of imitation than is 8-month-old "imitation." This position requires us to consider that a particular ability may have multiple levels. These levels are ordered and may be controlled by different processes. Moreover, the level of the ability may be found as both a phylogenetic and an ontogenetic function. From a phylogenetic perspective, a nonhuman animal (e.g., a rat) may imitate, but this imitation is controlled by different processes than that of a one-year-old child. Likewise, from an ontogenetic perspective, a newborn human may imitate, but this imitation is controlled by implicit consciousness while the imitation of a two-year-old is explicit. Whether the levels found phylogenetically match those found ontogenetically is unknown, although there is every reason to assume that they might.

The problem of equivalence is especially relevant to the understanding of self and consciousness. In our theory of the development of explicit consciousness, we see that the same behavior at two ages may be a function of different processes, one having to do with the *machinery of the self,* what will become part of implicit consciousness, the other, the mental state of the *idea of me,* which will become explicit consciousness. For me, implicit consciousness of the *machinery of self* precedes the *idea of me* or explicit consciousness, with each dependent upon different processes and different brain structures.

Two early features of the self that can be relegated to the machinery of the systems are well known and have been given considerable attention: These are self–other differentiation and the conservation of self across time and place (Rochat & Striano, 2002). By three months, and most likely from birth, the infant can differentiate itself from other. Self–other differentiation also has associated with it a type of recognition. This type of recognition—the self–other differentiation—is part of the machinery of any living complex system. This differentiation does not contain, nor is it analogous to, explicit consciousness. For example, T cells can recognize and differentiate themselves from foreign protein. The rat does not run into a wall but knows to run around it. The newborn infant recognizes intersensory information. These examples indicate that both simple and complex organisms possess the ability to differentiate self from other. We should not expect this aspect of self to be a differentiating feature when we compare widely different organisms since all organisms have this capacity. The single T cell must organize the information needed to distinguish self from other in a less complex manner than the multicell creature having a central nervous system. Nevertheless, in both cases, self–other differentiation exists in order for the organism to survive.

This is built into the biological machinery and is not predicated on any mental state or explicit consciousness.

Another aspect of the machinery of the system has to do with the idea of conservation of the self across time and place. What formal aspects imply conservation? It could entail responding the same way to similar occurrences, or it could mean adapting to them, as in habituation. The ability to maintain conservation appears in all creatures. For example, the ability to reach for an object requires some implicit consciousness, as it requires one to act as if there is something other than the self in space–time. This relationship to the other in space–time has consistency. Habituation, if used as a measure of conservation, also suggests its general appearance. Very simple organisms are able to habituate to redundant information. This suggests that in almost all organisms, from one-cell organisms on, biological machinery exists that is capable of maintaining information and utilizing that information in making a response. There is also self-conservation in the process we call identity: "This is me regardless of how I look." This type of conservation, unlike the former, requires explicit consciousness or the mental state(s) which involves the *idea of me*.

These two features–self–other and self-conservation—appear relatively early in the child's life. They are based on the biological machinery of the self and are a part of implicit consciousness; they are simple aspects of the functioning of a complex process. All complex creatures, by definition, contain many elements (Von Bertalanffy, 1967). These elements must be in communication with one another. Moreover, in order for the elements to work, they need to be interacting with each other and with the environment. In order to be in interaction with the environment, they need to be able to differentiate self from other. The processes that allow this to occur are multidetermined, but do not require explicit consciousness.

The ontogenetic and phylogenetic coherences found to date support the idea that in order to understand the concept of self, we need to disentangle the common term, self, into at least these two aspects; the *machinery of the self* which is a part of implicit consciousness, and explicit consciousness or the mental state of the *idea of me*. They have been referred to by other terms, for example, as objective self-awareness, which reflects the idea of "me"; and subjective self-awareness, which reflects the machinery of self (Lewis, 1990a, 1991, 1992a). The same objective–subjective distinctions have been considered by Duval and Wicklund (1972). In any consideration of the concept of self, especially in regard to adult humans, it is important to keep in mind that both biological aspects exist. There is, unbeknownst to us most of the time, an elaborate complex of machinery that controls much of our behavior, learns from experience, has states and affects, and affects our bodies, most likely including what and how we think. The implicit processes are, for the most part, unavailable to us. What is available is explicit consciousness.

Both the *machinery of the self,* as part of implicit consciousness, and explicit consciousness or the mental state involving the *idea of me* appear to be the consequences of different biological processes and perhaps different brain structures. LeDoux's work (1990) suggests that specific brain regions may be responsible for different kinds of self-processes. LeDoux's findings indicate that the production of a fear state can be mediated by subcortical regions, the thalamic–amygdala sensory pathways. Similar findings have been reported in humans, which suggests that implicit emotional states can exist without one part of the self explicitly experiencing them (Bechara et al., 1995). Weiskrantz (1986), among others, has reported on a phenomena called "blindsightedness." Patients have been found who lack the visual cortex, at least in one hemisphere. When they were asked if they could see an object placed in their blind spot, they report that they cannot see it—that is, they do not have the experience of the visual event. They have no explicit consciousness. When they are asked to reach for it, they show that they can reach for it. Thus, they can see the event, implicit consciousness, but cannot experience their sight, explicit consciousness. These findings, as well as Gazzaniga's work (1988) on split-brain patients, suggest that separate brain regions are responsible for the production and maintenance of both the implicit and explicit consciousness. A similar analysis involving memory has been suggested by Tulving (1985). Karmeloff-Smith (1986), from a developmental–cognitive perspective, has also taken up this type of distinction, arguing as we do, that early in the developmental process, knowledge is part of the system and therefore implicit, whereas later knowledge became explicit (see also Dienes & Perner, 1999).

The difference between implicit and explicit consciousness is easily seen as we observe our emotional lives. I have tried, in the past, to distinguish between emotional states and experiences, and have argued that adults can have emotional states and yet may have no experience of them (Lewis, 1990b; Lewis & Michalson, 1983). Thus, if I say "I am happy," it can be assumed that I mean by the statement that I am in an emotional state of happiness *and* I can experience that state. Emotional states, therefore, refer to implicit consciousness. Implicit consciousness can have goals, can learn and profit from experience, can control functions, and can react to events, including people. The experiences of our emotional states refer to implicit consciousness. An interesting example of this distinction in emotional life is given by Pribram (1984), who describes a patient in whom the medial part of the temporal lobe, including the amygdala, had been bilaterally removed:

> I once had the opportunity to examine some patients in whom the medial part of the temporal lobe—including the amygdala—had been removed bilaterally. These patients, just as their monkey counterparts, typically ate considerably more than normal and gained up to 100 pounds in weight. At last I could *ask* the subject how it felt to be so hungry. But much to my surprise, the expected answer was not forthcoming. One patient who had gained more than 100 pounds in the several years since surgery was examined at lunchtime. "Was she hungry?" She answered, "No." "Would she like a piece of rare, juicy steak?"

"No." "Would she like a piece of chocolate candy?" She answered, "um-hum," but when no candy was offered she did not pursue the matter. A few minutes later when the examination was completed, the doors to the common room were opened, and she saw the other patients already seated at a long table eating lunch. She rushed to the table, pushed the others aside, and began to stuff food into her mouth with both hands. She was immediately recalled to the examining room, and questions about food were repeated. The same negative answers were obtained again, even after they were pointedly contrasted with her recent behavior at the table. Somehow the lesion had impaired the patient's *feelings* of hunger and satiety, and this impairment was accompanied by excessive eating! (Pribram, 1984)

Here, Pribram's reference to feelings refers to the patient's explicit consciousness as she lacked explicit knowledge of her state of hunger, although there might have been an implicit consciousness that controlled her eating.

A DEVELOPMENTAL MODEL AND THE MEASUREMENT OF EXPLICIT CONSCIOUSNESS

Measurement follows from the constructs we make; so if we are interested in the development of explicit consciousness, then we need to measure explicit rather than implicit consciousness. Since early imitation, intersensory integration, and coordination between infant and mother all are likely to reflect the *machinery of self* as part of implicit consciousness, they are not adequate measures of explicit consciousness.

The study of the *idea of me* or explicit consciousness requires, for the most part, language capacity. If the emergence of this mental state occurs before two years of age, using language as a measure of this mental state is difficult. In an adult or older child we can ask, "Who are you?" or "Tell me something about yourself," or "Tell me something that you know that others don't know." Alternatively, following R. D. Laing (1970), we can see whether the child understands statements such as "I know, you know, that I know, where you put your teddy bear." As is readily understood, all of these questions imply some *idea about me* or explicit consciousness.

Without language, however, the child cannot through language explain this idea to us. One alternative is to require, without using language, that the child do certain tasks and see whether he or she can do them. If the child understands the task given, it is possible to demonstrate that the child has the idea, even though he does not have language. Thus, for example, in the work on deception (Lewis, Stanger & Sullivan, 1989), and in the research on theories of mind, Wellman (1990) and others (Moses & Chandler, 1992) have been able to show that the child can intentionally deceive and, as well, place itself in the role of another. In each of these types of studies there is an implicit theory of mind (TOM) that includes the mental state or explicit consciousness.

Unfortunately, even these studies require that children understand complex language although they do not have to produce it. Thus, for example, in the deception studies, children have to understand the experimenters' instructions and therefore cannot be much less than three years old. By this age, it seems clear that children have explicit consciousness. The question, then, is whether explicit consciousness emerges earlier, and if so, how might it be measured. We could still focus on language and argue that explicit consciousness can be measured by whether children have acquired their names; after all, we are what we are called. The risk of accepting this as proof is that the child may have been taught to use its name by associating it with a visual array, a photograph of itself, without explicit consciousness being present (see Putnam [1981] for a discussion of this type of problem).

Another language measure, a bit less suspect, is that of personal pronoun usage. Because parents do not use the label "me" or "mine" when referring to the child or teaching it to recognize its pictures, the use of these terms by the child is likely to be a reasonable measure of explicit consciousness. This appears even more the case when we observe children's use of the terms and how they behave when using them. One can observe a child saying "mine" as he or she pulls the object away from another child and toward him- or herself. Because moving the object toward oneself does not move the object as far away from the other as possible, the placement of the object next to the body, together with the use of the term "me" or "mine," appears to reference explicit consciousness. Children begin to use personal pronouns including "me" and "mine" by the latter part of the second year of life, which can provide a linguistic demonstration of the emerging mental state (Harter, 1983; Hobson, 1990).

Another procedure that can be used to measure explicit consciousness is self-recognition. We have studied self-recognition in infants and young children in detail (Lewis, 2003; Lewis & Brooks-Gunn, 1979b; Lewis & Ramsay, 1997). The procedure is simple. Unknown to the child, its nose is marked with rouge and then the child is placed in front of a mirror, where it is possible to observe whether the child, looking in the mirror, touches its marked nose or whether it touches the image in the mirror. The data from a variety of studies indicate that infants even as young as two months, when placed in front of mirrors, will show interest and respond to the mirror image. Children will smile, coo, and try to attract the attention of the child in the mirror, although they do not behave as if they recognize that it is they in the mirror. At older ages, when locomotion appears, on occasion infants have been observed going behind the mirror in order to see if they can find the child in the mirror. In addition, they often strike the mirror as if they are trying to touch the other. Somewhere around 15–18 months, they appear to know that the image is themselves, since they touch their noses or comment about their noses when looking in the mirror. The mental state of the *idea of me* or explicit consciousness is captured by the children's use of self-directed referential behavior.

The touching of their noses when they look in the mirror seems to reveal that they know that it is "me" there.

The ability to use the mirror to reference themselves has been mistaken for the child's understanding of the reflective property of mirrors. There is ample evidence that although children are able to produce self-referential behavior through the use of the mirror–mark technique, they do not know many of the properties of reflected surfaces; for example, they cannot use the mirror to find an object reflected in its surface (Butterworth, 1990). What is important about the self-referential behaviors in the mirror is that they need not be a marker of general knowledge about reflected surfaces, but rather a marker for the child's knowledge about itself. They are the equivalent of the phrase, "that's me." This recognition, if put into words, says, "That is me over there, this is me, here."

Measuring other aspects of explicit consciousness is possible, pretend play in particular. From a variety of theoretical perspectives (Huttenlocher & Higgins, 1978; Leslie, 1987; McCune-Nicolich, 1981; Piaget, 1962), it is apparent that pretense is an early manifestation of the ability to understand mental states including one's own and others'. Pretense involves double knowledge or dual representation of the literal and pretend situation. The dissociable relation between the two allows the child to distinguish between appearance and reality. Research by Piaget (1962) and subsequent investigators (Fein, 1975; Lowe, 1975; McCune, 1995; Nicolich, 1977) indicates that pretense emerges in children by the middle to latter part of the second year of life. The capacity for pretense not only marks explicit consciousness, but also the beginning of a theory of mind, the process that leads to the 3- to 4-year switch when children know that what they know is not necessarily what another knows (Flavell, 1988; Perner, 1991; Rosen, Schwebel, & Singer, 1997; Taylor & Carlson, 1997; Wellman, 1990; Wimmer & Perner, 1983). The *mental state of me* seen in pretense distinguishes children's early explicit consciousness from abilities likely to reflect implicit rather than explicit consciousness seen earlier in development such as joint attention, social referencing, and preverbal communication abilities (Bretherton, 1991; Carpenter, Nagel & Tomasello, 1999).

There have been several studies which have examined the relation between verbal measures of self-recognition (including the use of the personal pronoun "me" and one's name) and the mark-directed behavior (Bertenthal & Fischer, 1978; Pipp, Fischer & Jennings, 1987). These studies have generally found that verbal measures appear after the mark-directed behavior (Harter, 1983). Surprisingly, while it is apparent that self-awareness and pretense emerge at approximately the same point in development, no research has assessed whether self-awareness is necessary for pretend play. A mental state of the *idea of me* (or explicit consciousness) is taken for granted in Leslie's (1987) model on the relation between pretend play and theory of mind. That pretend play emerges as soon as the onset of self-recognition would support the belief that both reflect the emergence of explicit consciousness as well as a source for a theory of mind.

In a recent study, Lewis and Ramsay (1999) have looked at the relation between these three measures of explicit consciousness. There appears to be a relatively strong association between them, supporting our belief that they can be used to measure the onset of explicit consciousness. Moreover, there is a developmental sequence in the acquisition of these behaviors in the following order: self-recognition, personal pronoun use, and pretend play. Self-recognition by itself or along with personal pronoun use and/or pretend play was most likely to emerge first in development.

Self-recognition, personal pronoun use, and pretend play all indicate explicit consciousness. FIGURE 2 presents the relation between personal pronoun use and pretend play as it relates to self-recognition in a group of children varying in age from 15–21 months. It is apparent that with development, self-representation increasingly becomes a more complex and multi-faceted phenomenon that progressively includes other cognitive and evaluative aspects of self-knowledge (Lewis & Brooks-Gunn, 1979a,b). Nonetheless, the results suggest that in terms of emergent time, self-recognition is earliest in the formation of a complex self-representation. Of the three self abilities assessed, self-recognition was the one most likely to emerge first in development, suggesting that physical self-recognition may provide the core aspect of self-representation that continues to develop beyond the second year of life.

Consistent with the present findings is work that indicates children's emerging understanding of a theory of mind by the middle of the second year

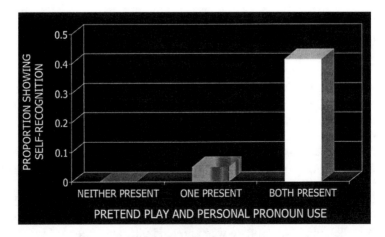

FIGURE 2. Relation between self-recognition, pretend play, and personal pronoun use.

of life. Meltzoff (1995) reports that 18-month-old toddlers have the ability to understand the intentions of others. After observing adult models demonstrate the intention to act in a certain way by starting, but not completing, a given activity, the toddlers, when given the opportunity, performed the complete acts the adult intended. Similarly, Asendorph and colleagues (Asendorph & Baudonniere, 1993; Asendorph, Warkentin & Baudonniere, 1996) found increases in imitative play linked to the presence of self-recognition in 20-month-old infants.

The degree of correspondence between self-recognition, pretend play, language self-referents and object permanence suggests the emergence of explicit consciousness (measured in a multitude of ways) and with it the organizing role of self-knowledge in cognitive development (Lewis, 1992b; Lewis & Brooks-Gunn, 1979b; Lewis & Michalson, 1983; Mounoud & Vinter, 1981).

THE ROLE OF EXPLICIT CONSCIOUSNESS IN DEVELOPMENT

The problem in studying development or, for that matter, adult behavior is that our studies usually divide the organism's cognitive, social, and emotional life into separate domains. Lost in this epistemological division is the idea of the organism itself. In terms of infants and young children, different studies provide information, but with little attempt at unifying these separate domains. Thus, while we shall separate out the role of explicit consciousness in cognitive, social, and emotional development, it should be understood that these domains are connected with each other through the child's developing mental state of itself. The organization of development follows from the assumption that social, emotional, and cognitive knowledge are interrelated and interdependent since all are aspects of the same unified development of the individual's explicit consciousness. Individuals develop social, emotional, and cognitive knowledge in interaction with each other. Moreover, we see development as a gradual differentiation among the various domains. The change from a unified system of knowledge based on the emergence of consciousness to one which is differentiated and specialized occurs as a function of development. The system is like a tree, the trunk representing the unified and integrated system generated by consciousness, while the branches represent the separate areas of knowledge, some of which are interrelated whereas others are independent. This model allows for both the integration of knowledge from a developmental perspective and the functional independence of the end product. *Thus, as a central premise, the development of explicit consciousness provides the scaffolding for the development, integration, and separation of the various other behaviors of the child.*

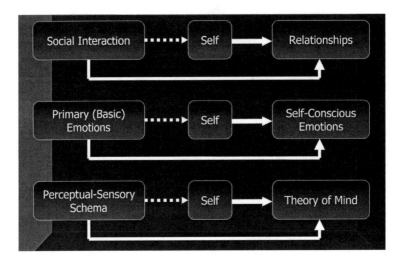

FIGURE 3. The role of consciousness in the development of social relationships, self-conscious emotions, and a theory of mind.

FIGURE 3 presents in schematic form the proposed relations. As can be seen, each of the early classes of behavior are transformed by the emergence of explicit consciousness. Thus, perceptual–sensory become a theory of mind, social interactions become social relationships, and the early or basic emotions become the self-conscious emotions. Each is considered below.

Social Cognition, Theory of Mind, and Explicit Consciousness

The work on social cognition predates and provides the logical basis for the newer work called, "Theory of Mind." We address both from the need to include explicit consciousness as the basis of this development.

When we use the term *social cognition*, we imply that there is a role of the self in knowing. To the degree that the self as knower is part of the process of knowing is the degree to which the cognition is social (Lewis, 1993, 1997). So, for example, I may know about a sunset over the Chianti hills of Tuscany by watching it, or I may know of it by reading a guidebook. In both cases, I have knowledge, but in one, that knowledge is gained through the self's experience of the phenomenon whereas in the other, it is through the self's knowledge of words.

Another example has to do with knowledge that involves the self. This is best captured by the sentence, "I know that you know that I know your name." Such sentences and their meaning cannot be independent of explicit consciousness since the self knows something about what another self knows about itself. The meaningfulness of such a sentence is dependent upon the knowledge of myself and knowledge of another self's knowledge of myself. While some of this may become implicit, at least it has in its origins, explicit consciousness.[a] This aspect of explicit consciousness has been studied under the heading of a theory of mind; something which we will consider later.

The epistemological issue of the relation between the knower and the known has been widely recognized for 50 years (Merleau-Ponty, 1964; Piaget, 1960; Polyani, 1958). Explicit consciousness involves the interaction of the knower with objects, events, or people. Social cognition depends on just such a connection. Following the work of Mead (1934) and Cooley (1902), explicit knowledge of the self and knowledge of others are dependent on one another: "I cannot know another unless I have knowledge of myself." Furthermore, a child's knowledge of self and others is developed through interactions with these others, social interaction and consciousness being the basic unit out of which social cognition derives. Many who subscribe to an interactionist position agree that knowledge of others (and the world in general) is derived through interaction: "To understand that a person is... involves understanding what sorts of relationships can exist between mere things and between people and things" (Hamlyn, 1974).

Because what a child knows of the other through interaction (usually nonsocial "other," characterized by physical properties such as weight, length, etc.) has been the major focus of researchers, the fact that knowledge of other, gained through interaction, must provide information about oneself has been ignored. If I find one object hard and the other soft by holding them, then not only do I know something about objects (in this case, hardness), but I know something about myself (how hard the object feels to me). As Merleau-Ponty (1964) has stated, "If I am a consciousness turned toward things, I can meet in things the actions of another and find in them a meaning, because they are themes of possible activity for my own body" (p. 113).

Although it may be possible to separate explicit from implicit consciousness for some forms of knowledge, in even the most abstract knowledge, the known interacts with the knower. For instance, Bower and Gilligan (1979) some time ago demonstrated that whom one identifies with in a story will affect and change the person's interpretation of the story. There also is evidence in memory research to indicate that the older memory is facilitated if what is to be remembered is made relevant to the self (Hyde & Jenkins, 1969; Kuiper & Rogers, 1979; Rogers, Kuiper & Kirker, 1977).

---

[a]The question of whether explicit can become implicit and whether implicit can become explicit we save for another time. However, it does seem possible that explicit can become implicit. Evidence in the area of physical skills supports such an assumption. For example, Kohler's demonstration of skiing with glass prisms on and the learning to ski when the visual field is reversed suggests that the explicit can become implicit consciousness.

A "theory of mind," like social cognition, involves explicit knowledge of one's own and others' mental states (Gallup, 1991; Leslie, 1987; Povinelli & Eddy, 1996; Premack & Woodruff, 1978). The origins of a theory of mind can be found in the early work of psychologists, such as Shantz (1975) and Youniss (1975). From the broad social cognition perspective, children's per-spective-taking or role-taking ability, their ability to "put themselves in the place of the other," or their "theory of mind," has been examined in various situations including those that assess children's capacity for the expression of empathy. It has long been recognized that taking the point of view of an-other presupposes explicit knowledge of one's own self (Leslie, 1987; McCune, 1995).

With this in mind, especially given our work on the development of explicit consciousness, let me suggest a brief outline in the development of a theory of mind. There are at least three or four levels: (1) I know; (2) I know I know; (3) I know you know; (4) I know you know I know.

Level 1 is called *knowing* (or *I know*). This level prevails from birth until the middle of the second year of life and is likely to be driven by basic processes common to other animals. It is based on implicit consciousness, and involves little or no language; it is not supported by the mental state of the *idea of me* or explicit consciousness. Many organisms can share in this kind of knowl-edge. For example, when an object in the visual field rapidly expands, chil-dren, as well as adults and animals, show surprise and discomfort. This response is simply built into the machinery of perceptual-motor knowledge.

Level 2 is *I know I know*. This level involves explicit consciousness and self-referential behavior. It is based on the mental state of me and allows for the capacity to reflect on one's self and to reflect on what one knows. This mental state is a meta-representation. It is similar to a memory of a memory. Whereas a child at the first level may have a memory, it is at the second level that meta-memory is possible. Here the child remembers that he or she remembers. As we have seen, this capacity emerges somewhere in the middle of the second year of life (Lewis, 1990a,b).

Level 3 is *I know you know*. This form of knowing takes into account the mental state that not only do I know something, but I believe others know it as well; it is the ability and basis of shared meaning. This representation, that you know what I know, does not need to be accurate. Adults know more than children know; thus the child may not really know what the adult knows. The child is likely to make errors, something called egocentric errors; that is, he or she assumes that what they know is what the other knows. At this level children know, they know they know, and they also know you know. What they cannot yet do is to place themselves in opposition to what they know. This level, in combination with the earlier ones, accounts in part for the early ability to deceive. A 2½-year-old child who deceives knows that he knows and he knows that you know; thus deception is possible. It is also the reason why children are likely to make the traditional false belief error.

Before going on to the fourth level, it is worth mentioning that the third level may not be distinct from the one before it in which children know they know. It is possible that the mental state of the *idea of me* and what I know may emerge at the same time as the mental state of what I know about what others know. In other words, it is not possible that what I know about me is not part of what I know about the other. If this indeed is the case, then a separate level might not be called for.

Level 4 is the adult-like level. It addresses the interactive and recursive nature of cognition. It is characterized as *I know you know I know*. At this level, not only are there two actors, as at Level 3, but each actor has a perspective. These perspectives can be different. It is when there are two perspectives that one has the ability to recognize false belief. Only when one has reached the level of knowing that "they know I know" that your knowledge about what *they know* can be corrected, since you can check their knowledge of what they know about you against what you know. That is, once a child knows that he or she can be the subject and also the object of the knowledge of another, the child is capable of recognizing the difference in perspectives between individuals. It is at this final level of perspective-taking that mature meta-knowledge can emerge.

As these levels of knowing are reached and mastered, there is at the same time an increase in general cognitive competence, in particular language usage. Language ability is laid down on the general cognitive scaffolding that allows the language to reflect increasingly the available cognitive ability. Our problem in studying children's early development is that language ability may not precede this general cognitive capacity but may follow it. Thus, children's observed social behavior and cognition may reflect a level higher than their verbal capacities.

Social Relationships and Explicit Consciousness

When I think about relationships, by definition they involve me; and when I think about relationships, one of the things that I may think about is what the other thinks of me. Recursive cognitions can become quite complex, as, for example, when I think of what others think that I think of them. In his discussion of interpersonal relationships, Asch (1952) made a similar point: "The paramount fact about human interactions is that they are happenings that are psychologically represented in each of the participants. In our relationship to an object, perceiving, thinking, and feeling take place on one side, whereas in relations between persons, these processes take place on both sides and are dependent upon one another."

Knowledge about self and other, whether they occur sequentially or at the same time, eventually become a part of the duality of knowledge. For example, Bannister and Agnew (1977) note, "The ways in which we elaborate our construing of self must be essentially those ways in which we elaborate our construing of others. For we have not a concept of self, but a bipolar construct of self-not self, or self-other" (p. 101). The definition of social knowledge involves the relationship between the knower and the known, rather than characteristics of people as objects. By utilizing the self in knowing, we can differentiate when we are treating people as objects from when we are treating them as people. If the self is not involved, then the people are being treated as objects; when the self is involved, people are being treated as people.

Interactions versus Relationships

The developmental issue in social relationships is quite complex, especially given the wide acceptance of attachment theory and the argument that children form relationships with their mothers by one year of age. If, however, we believe that social relationships require explicit consciousness, then children cannot form relationships that early, although adults can and do. For example, Hinde (1976, 1979) articulated six dimensions that can be used to characterize relationships. These are (1) goal structures, (2) diversity of interactions, (3) degree of reciprocity, (4) meshing of interactions, (5) frequency, and (6) patterning and multidimensional qualities of interactions.

These six features of interaction define lower levels of relationships that are likely supported by the machinery of the system or implicit consciousness, at least on the part of the infant. Their mothers, however, can form relationships. Thus the nature of the infant–mother relationship is complex, but not the same as one where both child and mother can form adult relationships. Adult relationships require explicit consciousness of both parties to the relationship. In this regard, Hinde's two additional features that define a relationship, supported by explicit consciousness, are relevant. These features include: (7) cognitive factors, or those mental processes that allow members of an interaction to think of the other member as well as of themselves, and (8) something which Hinde (1979) calls penetration, which I would interpret as something having to do with ego boundaries, which also has to do with the explicit consciousness of the two participants in the relationship.

If interactions alone (features 1–6) are insufficient to describe a higher-level human relationship, then a rather asymmetrical pattern exists between the very young infant and its mother; this pattern is likely to be supported by the *machinery of the self* in the case of the infant and by explicit consciousness for the mother. Because of this, it needs to be distinguished from adult relationships since two explicit consciousnesses are needed (Lewis, 1987). Such a view was suggested by Sullivan (1953). For him, a relationship is by necessity the negotiation of at least two selves. Higher-level abilities are vital for a relationship since without two selves (one has only an I–it, not an I–thou), there can be no relationship (Buber, 1958). Emde (1988) makes reference to the "we" feature of relationships, and in support of the timetable of consciousness (self-awareness) points to the second half of the second year of life for its appearance.

Our model of mature human relationships requires that we consider different levels in the development of a relationship over time, rather than seeing it exist in adult form from the first. Uniquely mature human relationships may arise from interactions only after the development of explicit consciousness and the ability to represent self and other on the part of the child. From this point of view, the achievement of adult human relationships for the child has a developmental progression. This progression involves, first, interactions that may utilize implicit consciousness and which may be similar to those shown by all social creatures and, second, cognitive structures or mental states, in particular, explicit consciousness and with it such skills as empathy and the ability to place the self in the role of other (Lewis, 1987). The relationships of one-year-olds do not contain these cognitive structures and, therefore, may not be that of adults. By two years most children have explicit consciousness and the beginning of such skills as empathy (Borke, 1971; Zahn-Waxler & Radke-Yarrow, 1981). Their relationships now approximate more closely those of the adult level. Mahler's concept of individuation is relevant here, for as she has pointed out, only when the child is able to individuate, can it be said that a more mature relationship exists (Mahler, Pine & Bergman, 1975).

Such an analysis raises the question of the nature of the child's relationships prior to the emergence of explicit consciousness. For me, relationships not built on mental states are complex social species-patterned processes, which are imposed by the caregiver's consciousness and which, through adaptive processes, may be wired in the human infant. This imposed (or socialized) complex patterned system—a lower level relationship based on the mother's explicit and the infant's implicit consciousness—gives way to a mature relationship in which the child joins the socialization process. The nature of the higher-level relationship is dependent on many factors. These include the nature of the socialization practices (the initial interactions imposed on the infant), mental states related to the *idea of me* or implicit consciousness, and the cognitions about the interactions of self and other; that is, the meaning given to them by the selves involved (Bowlby, 1980).

Main and colleagues (Main, Kaplan & Cassidy, 1985) and Bretherton (1987) consider a more cognitive view of attachment, as suggested by Bowlby (1980), that of a "working model." By a working model, these authors suggest a schema concerning the mother as a secure base. By focusing attention on the child's cognitive construction rather than on just the interactive patterns of the dyad, the theory of attachment and relationships moves toward a greater realization that an attachment relationship involves the self and the mental states involved in self and other. For example, Bowlby (1973) states, "The model of the attachment figure and the model of the self are likely to develop so as to be complementary and mutually nonconforming. Thus, an unwanted child is likely not only to feel unwanted by his parents, but to *believe that he is essentially unwanted*" (emphasis added, p. 208).

Such a view of relationships is much more similar to the one that we posit but assumes a more adult-like form in early infancy. The level of representation of relationship, including the self, is far different from relationships formed by simple interactions. Notice that in Bowlby's quote, children believe that they—their selves—are unwanted. Such a representation must involve a child capable of the mental state of the *idea of me* or explicit consciousness.

As soon as we come to consider relationships in terms of mental states or representations, we need to return to the child's capacity for explicit consciousness. This, we believe, occurs after the first year of life, somewhere toward the middle of the second. If this is so, then our observation of the attachment relationship at one year reflects (1) the interactions based on socialization patterns that the child will subsequently use to form a working model of the relationship, and (2) the adult caregivers' relationship, which includes the adults' explicit consciousness as well as the working model of their attachment relationship with their parents.

Emotions and Explicit Consciousness

I have spent considerable time studying the relation between emotion and consciousness and thus here I will only briefly comment on it (Lewis, 1992a, 1997, 2000, 2001; Lewis & Michalson, 1983). Briefly, I have proposed a model of emotional development where explicit consciousness gives rise to two sets of self-conscious emotions, those I refer to as self-conscious exposed emotions and self-conscious evaluative emotions (Lewis, 1992a, 2002). All of these self-conscious emotions require explicit consciousness, although, as in the case of the evaluative emotions, more is required.

While the emotions that appear early—such as joy, sadness, fear, and anger—have received considerable attention, the set of later-appearing emotions that I wish to consider has received relatively little attention. There are likely to be many reasons for this; one reason is that these self-conscious emotions cannot be described solely by examining a particular set of facial movements, necessitating the observation of bodily action as well as facial cues. A second reason for the neglect of study of these later emotions is the realization that there are no clear specific elicitors of these particular emotions.

While happiness can be elicited by seeing a significant other, and fear can be elicited by the approach of a stranger, there are few specific situations that will elicit shame, pride, guilt, or embarrassment. These self-conscious emotions are likely to require classes of events that only can be identified by the individuals themselves.

The elicitation of self-conscious emotions involves elaborate cognitive processes that have, at their heart, mental states about the self or explicit consciousness. While some theories, such as psychoanalysis (Erikson, 1950; Freud, 1963; Tomkins, 1963), have argued for some universal elicitors of self-conscious emotions, such as failure at toilet training or exposure of the backside, the idea of an automatic non-cognitive elicitor of these emotions does not make much sense. Cognitive processes must be the elicitors of these complex emotions (Lewis, 1992b). It is the way we think or what we think about that becomes the elicitor of these emotions. There may be a one-to-one correspondence between thinking certain thoughts and the occurrence of a particular emotion; however, in the case of this class of emotions, the elicitor is a cognitive event. This does not mean that the earlier emotions, those called primary or basic, are elicited by non-cognitive events. Cognitive factors may play a role in the elicitation of any emotion; however, the nature of cognitive events are much less articulated and differentiated in the earlier ones (Plutchik, 1980).

The need for cognitive elicitors having to do with the self was known to Darwin (1969). He suggested that these emotions were a consequence of our thoughts about other's thoughts of us, there being therefore no clear or universal elicitors. Darwin saw these latter emotions as involving the self, although he was not able to distinguish among the various types (see also Tomkins, 1963 and Izard, 1977 for similar problems). His observation in regard to blushing indicates his concern with the issue of appearance and the issue of explicit consciousness. He repeatedly makes the point that these emotions depend on sensitivity to the opinion of others, whether good or bad.

We have attempted to clarify those specific aspects of self that are involved in self-conscious emotions. First let us consider self-conscious exposed emotions. The self-conscious exposed emotions have been differentiated from the self-conscious evaluative emotions since the latter require fairly elaborate family cognitions around standards, rules, and goals and around attributions relevant to the self (Lewis, 1992a; Lewis & Michalson, 1983). These evaluative emotions will be considered later. The exposed emotions consist, at least, of embarrassment, empathy, and jealousy. While some work has been done looking at empathy (Bischof-Kohler, 1991), most of the work has been conducted on embarrassment (Lewis, 1995). I have tried to distinguish between two different types of embarrassment—one related to exposure and one related to evaluation, which has much in common with shame.

Exposure embarrassment emerges once self-recognition (explicit consciousness) can be shown, around 15–24 months, while evaluative embarrassment does not emerge until 2½ years. An example of exposure embarrassment is the embarrassment that occurs when one is complimented. Praise rather than a negative evaluation is the source of this type of embarrassment. Another example of this type of embarrassment can be seen in our reactions to public display. When people observe someone looking at them, they are apt to become self-conscious, look away, and touch or adjust their bodies. In few cases do the observed people look sad. If anything, they appear pleased by the attention. This combination—gaze turned away briefly, no frown, and nervous touching—is exposure embarrassment.

Another example of embarrassment as exposure can be seen in the following example. When I wish to demonstrate that embarrassment can be elicited just by exposure, I announce that I am going to point randomly to a student. I repeatedly mention that my pointing is random and that it does not reflect a judgment about the person. I close my eyes and point. My pointing invariably elicits embarrassment in the student pointed to. When we experimentally point to a child and call his or her name, it invariably leads to exposure embarrassment. In a series of studies, we have demonstrated the effectiveness of complimenting, pointing to the child, and asking him/her to perform—dance to music—in front of us as three different elicitors of exposure embarrassment (Lewis et al., 1989; Lewis, Stanger, Sullivan & Barone, 1991).

The relation between self-recognition measuring explicit consciousness and exposure embarrassment has been explored (Lewis et al., 1989) and the findings are quite clear. Exposure embarrassment is significantly more likely to be seen once the child shows self-recognition. However, the earlier, more basic emotions, such as wariness or fearfulness, are unaffected by the child's emerging explicit consciousness (Lewis et al., 1989). Thus, while the basic emotions such as joy, sadness, fearfulness, disgust, anger, and interest all emerge prior to self-recognition and explicit consciousness, the exposed self-conscious emotions require its emergence. Looking at another nonevaluative self-conscious emotion, empathy, finds a similar result (Bischof-Kohler, 1991). This should not be surprising given that adult empathic responses require that one be able to place one's self in the role of the other, an ability that obviously requires explicit consciousness.

Self-conscious evaluative emotions not only require explicit consciousness but also require an elaborate set of other cognitive capacities. Because of this, these emotions do not emerge until 2½ to 3 years (Lewis, 1992a). They all require explicit consciousness, since they require knowledge about standards, rules, or goals. These standards are inventions of the culture which are transmitted to the child and involve the child's learning of and willingness to consider these as their own. This process of incorporating the standards has been discussed by Stipek, Recchia, and McClintic (1992). What is apparent from this work is that learning starts quite early in life. Standards, rules, and goals imply self-evaluation, and therefore explicit consciousness, for it would make little sense if we had standards but no evaluation of our action *vis à vis* them.

Having self-evaluative capacity allows for two distinct outcomes; we can evaluate our behavior and hold ourselves responsible for the action that is being evaluated, or we can hold ourselves not responsible. In the attribution literature, this distinction has been called either an internal or an external attribution (Weiner, 1986). If we conclude that we are not responsible, then evaluation of our behavior ceases. However, if we evaluate ourselves as responsible, then we can evaluate our behavior as successful or unsuccessful *vis à vis* the standard. Finally, *global self-attributions* refer to the whole self, while *specific self-attributions* refer to specific features or actions of the self

(Dweck & Leggett, 1988; Weiner, 1986). These are sometimes referred to as performance vs. task orientation (Dweck, 1996). In every one of these processes, the mental state of the *idea of me* needs to be considered.

The terms *global* and *specific* are used to specify the tendency of individuals to make specific evaluations about themselves (Beck, 1967, 1979; Seligman, 1975). *Global* evaluations about themselves refers to an individual's focus on the total self and on his or her performance. Thus, for any particular behavior violation, an individual can focus on the totality of the self; and then use such self-evaluative phrases as, "Because I did this, I am bad [or good]." Janoff-Bulman's (1979) distinction is particularly relevant here. In global attributions, the focus is upon the self and performance. The self becomes embroiled in the self. The focus is not upon the self's behavior as in task focus, but upon the self. There is little wonder that in using such global attribution one can think of nothing else, and one becomes confused and speechless (H. B. Lewis, 1971). We turn to focus upon ourselves, not upon our actions. Because of this, we are unable to act and are driven from the field of action into hiding or disappearing.

Specific, in contrast, refers to the individual's propensity to focus on specific actions of the self and on the task. It is not the total self that has done something wrong or good, it is specific *behaviors* in context that are judged. Individuals use such evaluative phrases as, my behavior was wrong, I mustn't do it again." Notice that the individual's focus is on the task in a specific context, not on the totality of the self. These cognitions, which focus on the self, give rise to the self-conscious evaluative emotions. Our research indicates that these emotions do not emerge until after the onset of explicit consciousness (in the middle of the second year of life) and not until the child is capable of the complex cognitions associated with standards. By 2½ to 3 years, these cognitive capacities are present and so is the emergence of these self-conscious evaluative emotions (Lewis, 1992a).

We can see, therefore, that the role of explicit consciousness in both classes of emotion is quite elaborate, involving: (a) explicit consciousness; (b) knowledge of standards, rules, and goals; (c) evaluation of one's behavior *vis à vis* the standards; (d) distribution of the blame to oneself or to others; and (e) attribution focus, either global or performance focus or specific and task focus. In each one of these processes, mental structures around the *idea of me,* therefore, rest on the emergence of explicit consciousness.

SOME WORDS ON THE IMPLICIT–EXPLICIT PREDICAMENT

We have used a variety of terms, including the *idea of me*, mental structures, meta-representations, and explicit consciousness in talking about issues of epistemology and the development of emotions, cognitions, and social behavior.

It is clear that while explicit consciousness is needed, it often seems that much of what we do, think, and feel seems automatic; that is, with the minimum of attention directed at ourselves. Indeed, this provides the basis in adults to posit implicit consciousness. It also seems that when too much attention is paid to the self (too much explicit consciousness), psychopathology is often the consequence. Thus, explicit consciousness, while necessary, also is potentially disruptive. Moreover, explicit consciousness can become implicit consciousness. So, for example, we know that early learning of complex motor acts (like skiing) requires explicit consciousness, but that becoming well-learned, the acts become implicit. Likewise, it is possible that implicit consciousness can become explicit. In this regard, it appears that Eastern traditions, such as Yoga, urge us to get in touch with processes usually not open to explicit consciousness. Thus, it may be possible to make explicit, implicit consciousness.

From a developmental perspective we have argued that the machinery of the system is the first example of implicit consciousness and is part of the primitives that infants are born with. In the middle of the second year of life explicit consciousness emerges and provides the scaffolding for all other development. Thus, the human child, by the middle of the second year, has both implicit and explicit consciousness. After the development of explicit consciousness, the young child as the adult can move between implicit and explicit consciousness, although much of implicit consciousness in the machinery of the system is not open to explicit consciousness. For example, I may never know directly what my amygdala knows. In order to address this problem in the adult, we need to consider that adults have the capacity to direct their attention inward toward themselves or outward toward the world. Even without directing their attention inward toward themselves (e.g., their actions and emotional states), they are capable of performing highly complex and demanding tasks. In fact, the example of solving complex mental problems without focusing on them explicitly is well known. Solutions to mental problems often "come to us" as if someone inside our heads has been working on it while we go about attending to other problems.

The term consciousness is used in talking about attention directed inward toward the self as well as outward to the world. In order to understand this, we may wish to consider Hilgard (1977) and, before him, Janet (1929), who talked about divided consciousness, while others have talked about subconsciousness or unconsciousness and consciousness (Freud, 1960). Modularity of brain function has demonstrated that areas of the brain are quite capable of carrying out complex tasks or learning complex problems without other areas having explicit knowledge of them (Bechara et al., 1995; Gazzaniga, 1985;

LeDoux, 1990). They have demonstrated that both perceptual processes as well as complex learning can take place in the amygdala and hippocampus without cortical involvement or without explicit knowledge of that learning.

Such findings lend support to the idea of modularity of brain function—that is, for the involvement of some brain areas without the involvement of others—as well as the idea that complex operations can take place without the subject's own knowledge or self-attention (what we call explicit consciousness) of these operations, although they could. These new findings of brain function fit with our own well-known experiences of sudden insight or spontaneous solution to complex mental problems, as well as a set of common phenomena which require intra-psychic differentiation and even conflict. I list, in no particular order, some of these well-known phenomena: hypnotism, perceptual defenses, self-deception, active forgetting, loss of will or akraxia, and multiple personality. These processes, although receiving some attention, have not been given the study they need. Hilgard (1977), for one, has called the underlying processes involved in each of them "disassociation," a term once in favor but now not used. This is because Freud (1960) argued for an active process of repression rather than splitting off of consciousness, a concept more favored by Charcot (1889) and Janet (1929). Each of these phenomena appears to rest on a process involving the idea of divided consciousness, or as we now call it, implicit and explicit consciousness, which may be supported by the modularity of brain functions.

The ability to direct attention both toward ourselves (explicit) and toward the outer world is an adaptive strategy. Divided consciousness's adaptive significance is that it allows us to check on our own internal responses in addition to our behavior in the world and quite separately to act in the world. It is obvious from observations of animals, or even cells, that it is possible to behave in a highly complex fashion in the world as a function of internally generated plans and programs. This action-in-the-world does not require that we pay attention by thinking about our actions. Thus, when I want to cross a busy street, it is probably adaptive not to be thinking about how well I am doing, but rather coordinating action in context. On the other hand, if I have almost had an accident, then thinking about myself and my fear at being almost hit allows me to modify my plans for the future. Both directions of consciousness are important.

From a developmental perspective, this distinction may mean that attention focused outward is reflected by the *machinery of the self*, a process which is likely to be hard-wired into the nervous system. It is only after development of mental states, in particular the mental state about the *idea of me,* that the human child becomes capable of looking inward; that is, to have explicit consciousness. Thus, for the adult human, divided attention is the consequence of the development of explicit consciousness in addition to the given primitives or *machinery of the self.*

REFERENCES

ANISFELD, M., TURKEWITZ, G., ROSE, S.A., ROSENBERG, F.R., SHEIBER, F.J., COU-
TURIER-FAGAN, D.A., GER, J.S. & SOMMER, I. (2001). No compelling evidence that newborns imitate oral gestures. *Infancy, 2*, 111–122.
ASCH, S.E. (1952). *Social psychology.* Englewood Cliffs, NJ: Prentice-Hall.
ASENDORPH, J.B. & BAUDONNIERE, P.M. (1993). Self-awareness and other-aware-
ness: Mirror self-recognition and synchronic imitation among unfamiliar
peers. *Developmental Psychology, 29*(1), 88–95.
ASENDORPH, J.B., WARKENTIN, V. & BAUDONNIERE, P.M. (1996). Self-awareness
and other-awareness II: Mirror self-recognition, social contingency aware-
ness, and synchronic imitation. *Developmental Psychology, 32*(2), 313–321.
BALDWIN, J.M. (1973). *Social and ethical interpretations in mental development.*
New York: Arno [original work published 1899).
BANNISTER, D. & AGNEW, J. (1977). The child's construing of self. In J. Cole (Ed.),
Nebraska Symposium on Motivation, Vol. 25. Lincoln, NE: University of
Nebraska Press.
BECK, A.T. (1967). *Depression: Clinical, experimental, and theoretical aspects.*
New York: Harper & Row.
BECK, A.T. (1979). *Cognitive therapy and emotional disorders.* New York: Times
Mirror.
BECHARA, A., TRANEL, D., DAMASIO, H., ADOLPHS, R., ROCKLAND, C. & DAMASIO,
A.R. (1995). Double dissociation of conditioning and declarative knowledge
relative to the amygdala and hippocampus in humans. *Science, 269*, 1115–
1118.
BERTENTHAL B.I., & FISCHER, K.W. (1978). Development of self-recognition in the
infant. *Developmental Psychology, 14*, 44–50.
BISCHOF-KOHLER, A. (1991). The development of empathy in infants. In M. E.
Lamb & H. Keller (Eds.), *Development: Perspectives from German-speaking
countries* (pp. 245–273). Hillsdale, NJ: Lawrence Erlbaum.
BORKE, H. (1971). Interpersonal perception of young children: Egocentricism or
empathy. *Developmental Psychology, 5*, 263–269.
BOWER, G.H. & GILLIGAN, S.G. (1979). Remembering information related to one-
self. *Journal of Research on Personality, 113*, 404–419.
BOWLBY, J. (1973). *Attachment and loss, Vol. 2: Separation: Anxiety and anger.*
London: Hogarth Press.
BOWLBY, J. (1980). *Attachment and loss, Vol. 3: Loss, sadness, and depression.*
New York: Basic Books.
BRETHERTON, I. (1987). New perspectives on attachment relations: Security, com-
munication, and internal working models. In J.D. Osofsky (Ed.), *Handbook of
infant development, 2nd ed* (pp. 1061–1100). New York: John Wiley & Sons.
BRETHERTON, I. (1991). *Intentional communication and the development of an
understanding of mind.* Hillsdale, NJ: Erlbaum Associates.
BUBER, M. (1958). *I & thou* (2nd ed.). Ronald Gregor Smith (Trans.). New York:
Scribner.
BUTTERWORTH, G. (1990). Origins of self-perception in infancy. In D. Ciccheti &
M. Beeghly (Eds.), *The self in transition: Infancy to childhood* (pp. 119–137).
Chicago: University of Chicago Press.

CARPENTER, M., NAGEL, K. & TOMASELLO, M. (1999). Social cognition, joint attention, and communicative competence from 9 to 15 months of age. *Monographs of the Society for Research in Child Development, 63*, 1–212.

CHARCOT, J.M. (1889). Clinical lectures on diseases on nervous system. London: New Sydenham Society.

COOLEY, C.H. (1902). *Human nature and the social order.* New York: Scribner's.

DARWIN, C. (1969). *The expression of the emotions in man and animals.* Chicago: University of Chicago Press [original work published 1872].

DIENES, Z. & PERNER, J. (1999). A theory of implicit and explicit knowledge. *Behavioral and Brain Sciences, 22*, 735–808.

DUVAL, S. & WICKLUND, R.A. (1972). *A theory of objective self-awareness.* New York: Academic Press.

DWECK, C.S. (1996). Social motivation: Goals and social-cognitive processes. In J. Juvonen & K. R. Wentzel (Eds.), *Social motivation: Understanding children's school adjustment* (pp. 181–195). New York: Cambridge University Press.

DWECK, C.S. & LEGGETT, E.L. (1988). A social-cognitive approach to motivation and personality. *Psychological Review, 95*, 256–273.

EMDE, R.N. (1988). Development terminable and interminable II: Recent psychoanalytic theory and therapeutic considerations. *International Journal of Psychoanalysis, 69*, 283–296.

ERIKSON, E. (1950). *Childhood and society.* New York: Norton.

FEIN, G.G. (1975). A transformational analysis of pretending. *Developmental Psychology, 11*, 291–296.

FIELD, T., WOODSON, R., GREENBERG, R. & COHEN, O. (1982). Discrimination and imitation of facial expression by neonates. *Science, 218*, 179–181.

FLAVELL, J. H. (1988). The development of children's knowledge about the mind: From cognitive connections to mental representations. In J.W. Astington, P.L. Harris & D.R. Olson (Eds.), *Developing theories of mind* (pp. 244–267). Cambridge, England: Cambridge University Press.

FREUD, S. (1963). *The problem of anxiety.* (H.A. Bunker, trans.). New York: Norton [original work published in 1936].

FREUD, S. (1960). *The psychopathology of everyday life.* (A. Tyson, trans.). New York: Norton.

GALLUP, G.G., Jr. (1991). Toward a comparative psychology of self-awareness: Species limitations and cognitive consequences. In G.R. Goethals & J. Strauss (Eds.), *The self: An interdisciplinary approach* (pp. 121–135). New York: Springer-Verlag.

GAZZANIGA, M.S. (1985). *The social brain: Discovering the networks of the mind.* New York: Basic Books.

GAZZANIGA, M.S. (1988). Brain modularity: Towards a philosophy of consciousness experience. In A.J. Marcel & E. Besearch (Eds.), *Consciousness in contemporary science* (pp. 218–256). Oxford: Clarendon.

HAMLYN, D.W. (1974). Person-perception and our understanding of others. In T. Mischel (Ed.), *Understanding other persons.* Totowa, NJ: Rowman & Littlefield

HARTER, S. (1983). Developmental perspectives on the self-system. In E.M. Hetherington (Ed.), *Handbook of child psychology. Socialization, personality, and social development* (Vol. IV, pp. 275–385). New York: Wiley.

HILGARD, E.R. (1977). *Divided consciousness: Multiple controls in human thought and action.* New York: Wiley.

HINDE, R.N. (1976). Interactions, relationships, and social structure. *Man, 11*, 1–17.

HINDE, R.N. (1979). *Towards understanding relationships*. London: Academic Press.

HOBSON, R.P. (1990). On the origins of self and the case of autism. *Development and Psychopathology, 2*, 163–181.

HUTTENLOCHER, J. & HIGGINS, E.T. (1978). Issues in the study of symbolic development. In W. Collins (Ed.), *Minnesota Symposia on Child Psychology* (Vol. 11., pp. 98–140). Hillsdale, NJ: Erlbaum.

HYDE, T.S. & JENKINS, J.J. (1969). The differential effects of incidental tasks on the organization of recall of a list of highly associated words. *Journal of Experimental Psychology, 82*, 472–481.

IZARD, C.E. (1977). *Human emotions*. New York: Plenum Press.

JACOBSON, S.W. (1979). Matching behavior in young infants. *Child Development, 50*, 425–430.

JANET, P. (1929). *Major symptoms of hysteria*. New York: Hafner.

JANOFF-BULMAN, R. (1979). Characterological versus behavioral self-blame: Inquiries into depression and rape. *Journal of Personality and Social Psychology, 37*, 1798–1809.

KARMELOFF-SMITH, A. (1986). From eta-processes to conscious access: evidence from children's metalinguistic and repair data. *Cognition, 23*, 95–147.

KUIPER, N.A. & ROGERS, T.B. (1979). Encoding of personal information: Self-other differences. *Journal of Personality and Social Psychology, 37*(4), 499–514.

LAING, R.D. (1970). *Knots*. New York: Pantheon.

LEDOUX, J. (1990). Cognitive and emotional interactions in the brain. *Cognition and Emotions, 3*(4), 265–289.

LESLIE, A.M. (1987). Pretense and representation: The origin of "Theory of Mind." *Psychological Review, 94*, 412–426.

LEWIS, H.B. (1971). *Shame and guilt in neurosis*. New York: International Universities Press.

LEWIS, M. (1987). Social development in infancy and early childhood. In J. Osofsky (Ed.), *Handbook of infant development*, 2nd ed. (pp. 419-493). New York: Wiley.

LEWIS, M. (1990a). Social knowledge and social development. *Merrill-Palmer Quarterly, 36*(1), 93–116.

LEWIS, M. (1990b). Thinking and feeling—The elephant's tail. In C.A. Maher, M. Schwebel & N.S. Fagley (Eds.), *Thinking and problem solving in the developmental process: international perspectives (the WORK)* (pp. 89–110). Hillsdale, NJ: Lawrence Erlbaum.

LEWIS, M. (1991). Ways of knowing: Objective self-awareness or consciousness. *Developmental Review, 11*, 231–243.

LEWIS, M. (1992a). Shame, the exposed self. *Zero to Three, 7*(4), 6–10.

LEWIS, M. (1992b). *Shame, The exposed self*. New York: The Free Press.

LEWIS, M. (1993). Commentary. (C.C. Raver & B.J. Leadbeater). The problem of the other in research on theory of mind and social development. *Human Development, 36*, 350–362.

LEWIS, M. (1995). Embarrassment: The emotion of self exposure and evaluation. In J.P. Tangney & K.W. Fischer (Eds.), *Self-conscious emotions: The psychology of shame, guilt, embarrassment, and pride* (pp. 198–218). New York: Guilford Press.

LEWIS, M. (1997). *Altering fate: Why the past does not predict the future.* New York: Guilford Press.

LEWIS, M. (2000). The emergence of human emotions. In M. Lewis & J. Haviland-Jones (Eds.), *Handbook of emotions,* 2nd ed. (pp. 265–280). New York: Guilford Press.

LEWIS, M. (2001). The origins of the self-conscious child. In R. Crozier & L.E. Alden (Eds.), *International handbook of social anxiety: Concepts, research, and interventions relating to the self and shyness* (pp. 101–118). Sussex, England: John Wiley & Sons, Ltd.

LEWIS, M. (2002). Early emotional development. In A. Slater & M. Lewis (Eds.), *Introduction to Infant Development* (pp. 192–209). England: Oxford University Press.

LEWIS, M. (2003). The development of self-consciousness. In J. Roessler & N. Eilan (Eds.), *Agency and self-awareness: Issues in philosophy and psychology* (pp. 275–295). New York: Oxford University Press.

LEWIS, M. & BROOKS-GUNN, J. (1979a). The search for the origins of self: Implications for social behavior and intervention. Paper presented at Symposium on the Ecology of Care and Education of Children under Three, Berlin, West Germany, February 23-26, 1977. Also in L. Montada (Ed.), *Brennpunkte der Entwicklungspsycholgie* (pp. 157–172). Stuttgart: W. Kohlhammer, GmbH.

LEWIS, M. & BROOKS-GUNN, J. (1979b). Toward a theory of social cognition: The development of self. In I. Uzgiris (Ed.), *New directions in child development: Social interaction and communication during infancy* (pp. 1–20). San Francisco, CA: Jossey-Bass.

LEWIS, M. & MICHALSON, L. (1983). *Children's emotions and moods: Developmental theory and measurement.* New York: Plenum.

LEWIS, M. & RAMSAY, D.S. (1997). Stress reactivity and self-recognition. *Child Development, 68,* 621–629.

LEWIS, M. & RAMSAY, D. (1999). Intentions, consciousness, and pretend play. In P.D. Zelazo, J.W. Astington & D.R. Olson (Eds.), *Developing theories of intention* (pp. 77–94). Mahwah, NJ: Lawrence Erlbaum Associates.

LEWIS, M., STANGER, C. & SULLIVAN, M.W. (1989). Deception in three-year-olds. *Developmental Psychology, 25(3),* 439–443.

LEWIS, M., STANGER, C., SULLIVAN, M.W. & BARONE, P. (1991). Changes in embarrassment as a function of age, sex and situation. *British Journal of Developmental Psychology, 9,* 485–492.

LOWE, M. (1975). Trends in the development of representational play in infants from one to three year—an observational study. *Journal of Child Psychology and Psychiatry, 16,* 33–47.

MAHLER, M.S., PINE, F. & BERGMAN, A. (1975). *The psychological birth of the infant.* New York: Basic Books.

MAIN, M., KAPLAN, N. & CASSIDY, J. (1985). Security in infancy, childhood, and adulthood: A move to the level of representation. In I. Bretherton & E. Waters (Eds.), Growing points of attachment theory and research. *Monographs of the Society for Research in Child Development, 50* (1–2, Serial No. 209), 66–104.

MCCUNE, L. (1995). A normative study of representational play at the transition to language. *Developmental Psychology, 31,* 198–206.

MCCUNE-NICOLICH, L. (1981). Toward symbolic functioning: Structure of early pretend games and potential parallels with language. *Child Development, 52*(3), 785–797.

MEAD, G.H. (1934). *Mind, self, and society: From the standpoint of a social behaviorist*. Chicago: University of Chicago Press.

MELTZOFF, A.N. (1995). Understanding the intentions of others: Re-enactment of intended acts by 18-month-old children. *Developmental Psychology, 31*, 838–850.

MELTZOFF, A.N., & MOORE, M.K. (1977). Imitation of facial and manual gestures by human neonates. *Science, 198*, 75–78.

MERLEAU-PONTY, M. (1964). *Primacy of perception*. (J. Eddie, Ed.; W. Cobb, Trans.). Evanston, IL: Northwestern University Press.

MOSES, J. & CHANDLER, M.J. (1992). Traveler's guide to children's theories of mind. *Psychological Inquiry, 3*, 285–301.

MOUNOUD, P., & VINTER, A. (Eds.)(1981). *La reconnaissance de son image chez l'enfant et l'animal*. Paris: Delachaux et Niestle.

NICOLICH, L. (1977). Beyond sensorimotor intelligence: Assessment of symbolic maturity through analysis of pretend play. *Merrill-Palmer Quarterly, 23*, 89–102.

PERNER, J. (1991). *Understanding the representational mind*. Cambridge, MA: MIT Press.

PIAGET, J. (1954). *Construction of reality in the child*. Paterson, NJ: Littlefield, Adams.

PIAGET, J. (1960). *The psychology of intelligence*. New York: Littlefield Adams.

PIAGET, J. (1962). *Play, dreams and imitation in childhood* (C. Gattegno and F. M. Hodgson, Trans.). New York: Norton. (Original French edition, 1951).

PIPP, S., FISCHER, K.W. & JENNINGS, S. (1987). Acquisition of self- and mother knowledge in infancy. *Developmental Psychology, 23*, 86–96.

PLUTCHIK, R. (1980). A general psychoevolutionary theory of emotion. In R. Plutchik & H. Kellerman (Eds.), *Emotion: Theory, research, and experience, Vol. 1* (pp. 3–33). New York: Academic Press.

POLYANI, M. (1958). Personal language: Toward a post-critical philosophy. London: Routledge

POVINELLI, D.J. & EDDY, T.J. (1996). What young chimpanzees know about seeing. *Monographs of the Society for Research in Child Development* (Serial No. 247, Vol. 61, No. 3).

PREMACK, D. & WOODRUFF, G. (1978). Does the chimpanzee have a theory of mind? *The Brain and Behavioral Sciences, 4*, 515–526.

PRIBRAM, K.H. (1984). Emotion: A neurobehavioral analysis. In K. R. Scherer & P. Ekman (Eds.), *Approaches to emotion* (pp. 13–38). Hillsdale, NJ: Erlbaum.

PUTNAM, H. (1981). *Reason, truth, and history*. Cambridge University Press.

ROCHAT, P. & STRIANO, T. (2002). Who's in the mirror? Self-other discrimination in specular images by four- and nine-month-old infants. *Child Development, 73*(1), 35–46.

ROGERS, T.B., KUIPER, N.A. & KIRKER, W.S. (1977). Self-reference and the encoding of personal information. *Journal of Personality and Social Psychology, 35*, 677–688.

ROSEN, C.S., SCHWEBEL, D.C. & SINGER, J.L. (1997). Preschoolers' attributions of mental states in pretense. *Child Development, 68*, 1133–1142.

SELIGMAN, M.E.P. (1975). *Helplessness: On depression, development and death*. San Francisco: Freeman.

SHANTZ, C.U. (1975). *The development of social cognition*. Chicago: University of Chicago Press.

STIPEK, D., RECCHIA, S. & MCCLINTIC, S. (1992). Self-evaluation in young children. *Monographs of the Society for Research in Child Development, 57,* serial no. 226.

SULLIVAN, H.B. (1953). *The interpersonal theory of psychiatry.* New York: Norton.

TAYLOR, M. & CARLSON, S. M. (1997). The relation between individual differences in fantasy and theory of mind. *Child Development, 68,* 436–455.

TOMKINS, S.S. (1963). *Affect, imagery, and consciousness: Vol. 2. The negative affects.* New York, NY: Springer.

TULVING, E. (1985). How many emotion systems are there? *American Psychologist, 40,* 385–398.

VON BERTALANFFY, L. (1967). *Robots, men, and mind.* New York: Braziller.

WEINER, B. (1986). An attributional theory of motivation and emotion. New York: Springer-Verlag.

WEISKRANTZ, L. (1986). *Blindsight: A case study and implications.* Oxford: Oxford University Press.

WELLMAN, H. M. (1990). *The child's theory of mind.* Cambridge, MA: MIT Press.

WERNER, H. (1961). *Comparative psychology of mental development.* New York: Science Editions.

WIMMER, H. & PERNER, J. (1983). Beliefs about beliefs: Representation and constraining function of wrong beliefs in young children's understanding of deception. *Cognition, 13,* 103–128.

YOUNISS, J. (1975). Another perspective on social cognition. In A.D. Pick (Ed.), *Minnesota Symposium on Child Psychology, Vol. 9.* Minneapolis: University of Minnesota Press.

ZAHN-WAXLER, C. & RADKE-YARROW, M. (1981). The development of prosocial behavior: Alternative research strategies. In N. Eisenberg-Berg (Ed.), *The development of prosocial behavior* (pp. 109–138). New York: Academic Press.

Theory of Mind and the Self

FRANCESCA HAPPÉ

Social, Genetic and Developmental Psychiatry Research Centre,
Institute of Psychiatry, King's College, London, United Kingdom

ABSTRACT: This paper will discuss one aspect of the self, the ability to reflect on one's own inner states, in relation to recent work on the cognitive and neural basis of "theory of mind." Are the same representational resources required for "reading" one's own and other minds? Relevant literature from the study of normal development of theory of mind will be reviewed, along with research on a developmental disorder characterized by an apparent inability to think about thoughts: autism. Functional neuroimaging studies of theory of mind will be discussed as will studies that may tap the neural basis of self-reflection. From these different strands of evidence the speculative suggestion will be made that reflecting on one's own thoughts is not a privileged process, but rather relies on—and may have evolved from—the same cognitive and neural functions used for attributing thoughts to others.

KEYWORDS: theory of mind; autism; self-awareness; development; neuroimaging; brain

THEORY OF MIND AND THE SELF

"Theory of mind" refers to the everyday ability to attribute independent mental states to self and others in order to predict and explain behavior (Premack & Woodruff, 1978). This ability appears to be a prerequisite for normal social interaction: In everyday life we make sense of each other's behavior by appeal to a belief–desire psychology. For instance, it is trivially easy to explain why John will carry his umbrella with him: it is because he *believes* it will rain and he *wants* to stay dry. Attribution of mental states is vital for everyday social interaction (e.g., cooperation, lying, keeping secrets).

The cognitive processes that underlie the development of Theory of Mind (ToM) are still a matter of debate. The practitioners in the field can be divided

Address for correspondence: Dr. Francesca Happé, Institute of Psychiatry, Box P080, De Crespigny Park, Denmark Hill, London SE5 8AF, UK. Voice: +44 (0)20 7848 0928; fax: +44 (0)20 7848 0866.

f.happe@iop.kcl.ac.uk

Ann. N.Y. Acad. Sci. 1001: 134–144 (2003). © 2003 New York Academy of Sciences.
doi: 10.1196/annals.1279.008

into those who favor a more general explanation for ToM (e.g., simulation, general theory building) and those who argue for the necessity of a dedicated cognitive mechanism (for debate see, for example, chapters in Carruthers & Smith, 1996). Evidence in favor of a dedicated, innately specified cognitive mechanism underlying ToM includes the relative lack of normal individual difference or cross-cultural variation, the rapidity of acquisition in early childhood, and the case of autism, a biologically based disorder characterized by selective ToM impairment (see below). Of course, even with an innate predisposition underlying ToM, triggering input will be required, including experience of social interactions.

Despite the sometimes tortuous debate concerning the nature of ToM, paradigms for testing ToM are extremely simple. The litmus test for ToM has been the ability to attribute *false beliefs*, where prediction and explanation of action cannot be based simply on own convictions or the state of the world. In other words, in order to pass the test, the particular beliefs held by another must be considered and held separate from own knowledge. Because of its relatively high verbal and executive task demands, this test can only be given to children from age 3 or 4 onwards. This is not to say that below that age children are not implicitly aware of others' mental states. There are plenty of signs that even in infancy the young child is capable of tracking another's intention (e.g., Gergely et al, 1995).

The two most frequently used false-belief tasks, both developed by Wimmer and Perner (1983), are location change and content change tasks. In the *Sally–Anne task*, a location-change task, Sally has a box and Anne has a basket. Sally puts her marble into her box, then goes out for a walk. While she is out, naughty Anne takes the marble from the box and puts it into her own basket. Now Sally comes back and wants to play with her marble. Where will she look for the marble—where does she think the marble is? The answer that seems obvious to a 4-year-old child is: Sally will look inside her box, where she *thinks* the marble is. Younger children have some difficulty with this task and often point to the basket, indicating that Sally will look where the marble really is.

In the *Smarties task* (Hogrefe, Wimmer & Perner, 1986), a content-change task, the experimenter shows a well-known sweet container, a tube, to the child and asks: What is in here? The child answers "Smarties," or sweets. The experimenter reveals that the tube contains a small pencil, and closes the tube again. Now the experimenter says: "Your friend John is going to come in now. He hasn't seen this tube. When John comes in, I'll show him this tube just like this and ask: 'What's in here?' What will John say?" The average 4-year-old will answer that John will say "Smarties." Younger children have trouble with this task and claim that John will say "a pencil." Furthermore, when asked what they themselves at first thought was in the tube, children under four will typically assert: "a pencil."

THEORY OF OWN MIND AND THEORY OF OTHER MINDS

A theoretically important question for philosophers and psychologists is whether the same cognitive mechanism required for attributing thoughts and feelings to others is also necessary for attribution of mental states to self. At first glance the two attributions seem entirely different: own mental states do not have to be inferred through observation, and might be expected to be more accurate. However, even though the input channels by which the relevant information is received may well be different, a crucial part of the process is to distinguish mental states, be they first person or other people's, from representations of the physical world. For example, it is necessary to distinguish the representation of the reality, that "there is a pencil in the tube," from the representation of the belief, I *thought* "there are sweets in the tube," and John *thinks* "there are sweets in the tube." It seems plausible that the mechanism that keeps separate representations of mental states from representations of physical states is the same whether the mental states in question are ascribed to self or others.

Leslie (1987) provided the first and most explicit description of the computational underpinnings required for ToM. He suggested that understanding of pretense in infancy demonstrates the availability of a special form of representation for mental states as mental states. Second-order or meta- representations are kept separate from first-order or primary representations of real states of affairs. Hence, the child observing his mother playfully using a banana as a telephone does not get confused about the normal use of phones and bananas. A meta-representation represents the attitude an agent takes to a description of a particular aspect of reality. In contrast, a primary representation describes a particular aspect of reality. Leslie postulates that meta-representation is necessary for attribution of any mental state, including (false) beliefs, and is necessary equally for self and other attribution.

Whether or not Leslie's general theory of ToM is accepted, it seems clear that underlying our social understanding must be representations that capture who is thinking what and in what sense they are thinking it. Are they believing it, desiring it, hoping it, fearing it? Without in some way tagging a representation with an agent marker, own and other's beliefs would be confused. Without marking an attitude, beliefs, desires, and pretense would be confused.

Despite the intuition that we know our own minds better than the minds of others, there is little evidence from the developmental literature to suggest that mental states are attributed to self before they are attributed to others. For instance, children do not systematically pass the self-question in the Smarties test ("What did *you* think was in the tube?") before passing the other's belief question ("What will John think...?"). Relevant studies are summarized by Gopnik and Meltzoff (1994), who conclude that when children are able to report their own mental states they are also able to report the mental states of others. Conversely, when they cannot report and understand the psychological states of others, they do not report those states of themselves. Lang and Perner (2002), too, found a strong relation between performance on standard (other) false-belief tasks and a test requiring insight into own reflexive (knee-jerk) versus intentional action—with the two tasks being of about equal difficulty for young children. If there is a common representational mechanism for attributing mental states to self and to others, then these findings make sense.

AUTISM—A DISORDER OF "THEORY OF MIND"

It is arguable whether we would ever have thought of such a thing as a neurologically specified theory of mind (ToM) mechanism, let alone a circumscribed brain system underlying this mechanism, were it not for the fact that individuals with autism appear to lack the ability to attribute mental states. Autism is a developmental disorder with a genetic basis and a prevalence of 0.1 to 0.6 %. It is diagnosed on the basis of early emerging qualitative abnormalities in social interaction, communication, and imagination (with restricted interests and activities). One striking feature of young children with autism is the lack of pretend play. It was this observation that originally suggested that, on Leslie's account, meta-representation and hence ToM might be impaired in autism. From this observation it was predicted that false-belief attribution might also be impaired, despite sufficient verbal and nonverbal ability to follow the Sally–Anne task (Baron-Cohen, Leslie & Frith, 1985).

There now exists ample experimental evidence that individuals with autism have difficulty in conceptualizing mental states, and thus fail to attribute (false) beliefs to others (Baron-Cohen, Tager-Flusberg & Cohen, 1993). This failure is extremely specific and cannot be reduced to a failure in more general cognitive processes. This is seen in a number of contrasts between assets and deficits in otherwise very similar behavior, distinguished only by the necessity to attribute mental states (for review see, e.g., Frith & Happé, 1994).

While it has been easy for many people to accept that the devastating social and communicative handicaps of autism may result from a failure to attribute mental states to others, the notion that this mind-blindness might also apply to the child's own mind has scarcely been acknowledged (but see Carruthers, 1996). However, if the mechanism that underlies the computation of mental states is dysfunctional, then it is possible that the ability to reflect on own mental states will also be impaired. The logical extension of the ToM deficit account of autism is that individuals with autism may know as little about their own minds as about the minds of other people. This is not to say that these individuals lack mental states, but that in an important sense they are unable to reflect on their mental states. Simply put, they may lack the cognitive machinery to represent their thoughts and feelings *as* thoughts and feelings.

What would a mind without introspective awareness be like? One important consequence of impaired self-consciousness might be impaired understanding of one's own actions. In other words, without self-awareness, an individual might not know how she is going to act until she acted, nor why she acted as she did. This is different from the usual experience of actions, where we take access to our own imagined or true motivations for granted. It is easy to believe that we know what we are going to do before we do it. A person who lacks self-consciousness, however, may be unable to distinguish her own willed and involuntary actions (c.f., Lang & Perner, 2002).

While the (in)ability to attribute mental states to others has been studied extensively in children with autism, there is little work on the ability to attribute mental states to self. However, some evidence is available to indicate that the latter may be just as impaired as the former. For instance, Perner et al. (1989) asked children with autism about what they knew and what the experimenter knew concerning the contents of a box, depending on whether they had been allowed to look inside. On some occasions only the child was allowed to look inside, and on other occasions only the experimenter. While it may seem obvious that only the person who has looked inside the box will know what it contains, this was not at all obvious to children with autism. Many failed this task of self-reflection, and there was no sign of better performance on the "self" versus "other" questions. A similar finding is reported by Kazak, Collis, and Lewis (1997), who asked young people with autism whether they/the experimenter knew or only guessed what was in a box, having on some trials seen inside. Again, the results showed no superiority in judging own knowledge versus judging other's knowledge, in any of the experimental groups (autism, Down Syndrome, typical development).

Other evidence suggesting deficits in self-reflection in autism includes relative difficulty in reporting back own past thoughts (despite verbal IQ in the normal range; Fisher, unpublished Ph.D. thesis), and inability to keep track of own prior intention, in the face of conflicting outcome information (in a rigged target-shooting game [Phillips et al., 1999]). Contrary evidence, however, has been reported recently by Russell and Hill (2001), who found no autism-specific impairment in three intention-tracking tasks. It may be worth noting that intention is, in some ways, an interesting mental attitude that appears to hover between a simple (nonpropositional) desire (akin to a tropism; e.g., intending to get the cake) and a fully-fledged propositional attitude (intending that I have the cake). People with autism appear to have a basic understanding of their own and other people's desires (Tan & Harris, 1991).

The often-observed executive function deficits in autism (problems in planning and monitoring goal-directed action [Pennington & Ozonoff, 1996]) may be indirect signs of an inability to reflect on own mental states. Carruthers (1996) and Perner (1998) have each argued that these impairments may result from an inability to represent one's own intended and imagined future behaviors. For example, planning ahead in a task such as the Tower of Hanoi, may require meta-representation of possible (not actual) moves and of the desired (but not yet realized) end goal state. In the normal case, monitoring of performance and correction of errors can occur even in the absence of external feedback, because of access to own action intentions—access which may be impaired in autism. It has also been argued, however, that executive function deficits may be the primary cause of impaired theory of mind (Russell, 1996).

FUNCTIONAL IMAGING STUDIES OF ToM AND SELF-REFLECTION

Functional brain imaging studies are attempting to identify brain pathways sufficient to support mental state attribution (i.e., ToM) in healthy volunteers. Studies to date are summarized in TABLE 1 (see also Siegal & Varley, 2002). All have identified regions of the frontal lobes, among others, as showing increased regional cerebral blood flow (rCBF) during ToM tasks. Seven of the eight studies published to date (using different modalities and types of tasks) implicate medial frontal regions in ToM, along with different regions of the temporal lobes. Our current hypothesis is that this region is a key part of a neural system also including temporo-parietal cortex (STS) and the temporal poles/amygdala complex (Castelli et al., 2000; Frith & Frith, 1999).

The key paracingulate region (BA 8/9) found to be specifically activated in normal subjects engaged in ToM tasks was not activated by individuals with Asperger syndrome (a form of high-functioning autism) during these tasks (Happé et al., 1996). This region shows decreased grey matter volume in adults with autism (Abell et al., 1999), and an association has been found between rCBF in this region and socio-communicative symptom scores in 23 children with autism (Ohnishi et al., 2000).

A number of imaging studies using tasks that might be considered to tap self-reflection suggest that medial frontal and cingulate regions are also activated when subjects reflect on their *own* inner states. Tasks include monitoring one's own intended speech (McGuire et al., 1996), reflecting on one's emotional reaction to stimuli (Lane et al., 1997; Gusnard et al., 2001), and judging whether trait adjectives apply to self (Kelly et al., 2002). Thus online monitoring of own mental states may engage the anterior cingulate cortex and neighboring medial frontal regions, regardless of the specific source of information.

Only one study to date has asked, specifically, whether self-reflection and ToM applied to reading other minds activate any distinct brain regions or pathways. Vogeley et al. (2001) asked volunteers to read short vignettes

TABLE 1. Functional neuroimaging studies of theory of mind

Authors	Task (technique)	Results (ToM-related activation)
Baron-Cohen et al. (1994)	Identify mind words (PET regions of interest)	R. orbito-frontal cortex
Fletcher et al. (1995)	Infer mental states in stories (PET)	L. medial frontal (BA 8/9), inferior temporal
Goel et al. (1995)	Infer other's knowledge of object uses (PET)	L. medial frontal, L. middle temporal lobe
Happé et al. (1996)	Asperger volunteers, Fletcher '95 task (PET)	Asperger Ss do not activate BA 8/9
Baron-Cohen et al. (1994)	Identify mind words (PET regions of interest)	R. orbito-frontal cortex
Baron-Cohen et al. (1999)	Infer inner state from photo of eye region (fMRI) normal and Asperger participants	L. medial frontal, L. dorsolateral, L. amygdala, bilateral temporo-parietal; Asperger Ss do not activate amygdala, activate frontal regions less than controls
Brunet et al. (2000)	Choose final scene for picture sequence (PET)	R. medial frontal, R. inferior prefrontal, R. inferior temporal gyrus, L. STG, bilateral anterior cingulate, middle temporal gyri
Gallagher et al. (2000)	Infer mental state in single-frame cartoons and in stories (fMRI)	Medial frontal, temporal poles, temporo-parietal junction
Castelli et al. (2000	Infer mental state in silent animation (geometric shapes) (PET)	Medial frontal, temporal poles, temporo-parietal junction

which either did or did not include self as a protagonist. In the ToM vignettes the test question was about a character's thoughts, while in the Self vignettes the question was about your own likely behavior or attitudes in the imagined situation. The Self condition activated a network of brain regions highlighted in other ToM imaging studies. However, on the basis of an interaction of conditions, the authors interpret their findings as suggesting non-overlapping neural circuits for self and other mind-reading. Given that studies of ToM using different materials do not lead to exactly the same activation patterns, it is also possible to interpret the very tiny region emerging in this interaction (in the right prefrontal cortex) as suggestive of strikingly overlapping brain substrates for reading own and other minds.

Recently, Raichle and colleagues have suggested that the relative increase in blood flow in portions of the medial prefrontal (MPF) cortex during resting baseline conditions indicates a default state of self-referential mental activity in this region. Judging images for pleasantness (versus whether they were indoor or outdoor scenes) was associated with increased activation in dorsal MPF cortex, whereas both tasks resulted in decreased activation in ventral MPF cortex compared with baseline (Gusnard et al., 2001; Lane et al., 1997). These findings appear compatible with the above results on ToM activity in proximal regions, along with other data, including studies showing a relation between number of "stimulus-independent thoughts" and level of activity in medial prefrontal cortex (BA 8, 9, and 10 [McGuire et al., 1996]). It may be that when our minds are not attending to external stimuli they naturally turn in upon themselves, reflecting upon internal states.

CONCLUSIONS AND SPECULATIONS

Data from typical development give little evidence, to date, of better performance on tasks requiring reflection on own mental states (as mental states) and attribution of mental states to another person. People with autism, who show striking deficits in ToM, may show parallel impairments in knowing their own minds, although this has as yet received little research attention. Finally, neuroimaging findings to date, appear to suggest a network of regions involved in attribution of mental states to others, which largely overlaps with areas of activity in self-reflection tasks. On the basis of this work, systematic investigations of the effects of acquired brain lesions on self- and other-mind-reading would seem warranted. While devising tasks to tap consciousness is a notoriously knotty problem, a first step would be investigation of insight in relation to social cognition. Is it possible to find individuals who can no longer judge what others may be thinking, but can reflect on and report without problem their own mental states? More intriguingly, is it possible that some patients might lose the ability to self-reflect while still being able to attribute mental states accurately to other people?

If reflection on own mental states uses the same cognitive and neural "machinery" as representing others' mental states, emerges no earlier in development, and is lost or impaired in conditions of ToM deficit, an intriguing possibility presents itself. The evolutionary function of self-reflection, or more broadly self-consciousness, has remained uncertain, despite much discussion. On the other hand, the fitness advantages of anticipating the thoughts of competitors (so called Machiavellian intelligence) or cooperators (collaboration and communication) are clear. Might, then, the ability to read others' minds have evolved first, with the turning inward of the meta-representational spotlight upon our own inner states developing only later?

If so, self-reflection may be, in one sense, an epiphenomenon—an extraordinary side-effect of the crucial ability to read other minds.

REFERENCES

ABELL, F., KRAMS, M., ASHBURNER, J., PASSINGHAM, R., FRISTON, K., FRACKOWIAK, R., HAPPÉ, F., FRITH, C. & FRITH, U. (1999). The neuroanatomy of autism: A voxel based whole brain analysis of structural scans. *NeuroReport, 10,* 1647–1651.

BARON-COHEN, S., LESLIE, A.M. & FRITH, U. (1985). Does the autistic child have a "theory of mind?" *Cognition, 21,* 37–46.

BARON-COHEN, S., RING, H., MORIARTY, J., SCHMITZ, B., COSTA, D. & ELL, P. (1994). The brain basis of theory of mind: the role of the orbitofrontal region. *British Journal of Psychiatry, 165,* 640–649.

BARON-COHEN, S., RING, H., WHEELWRIGHT, S., BULLMORE, E.T., BRAMMER, M.J., SIMMONS, A. & WILLIAMS, S.C.R. (1999). Social intelligence in the normal and autistic brain: An fMRI study. *European Journal of Neuroscience, 11,* 1891–1898. .

BARON-COHEN, S., TAGER-FLUSBERG, H. & COHEN, D. J. (Eds) 2000. *Understanding other minds: Perspectives from autism,* 2nd edit. Oxford: Oxford University Press.

BRUNET, E., SARFATI, Y., HARDY-BAYLE, M-C. & DECETY, J. (2000). A PET investigation of the attribution of intentions with a nonverbal task. *NeuroImage, 11,* 157–166.

CARRUTHERS, P. (1996). Simulation and self-knowledge: a defence of theory-theory. In P. Carruthers & P.K. Smith (Eds.) *Theories of theories of mind,* pp.22–38. Cambridge: Cambridge University Press.

CARRUTHERS, P. & SMITH, P.K. (Eds.) (1996). *Theories of theories of mind.* Cambridge: Cambridge University Press.

CASTELLI, F., HAPPÉ, F., FRITH, U & FRITH, C. (2000). Movement and mind: A functional imaging study of perception and interpretation of complex intentional movement patterns. *NeuroImage, 12,* 314–325.

FLETCHER, P.C., HAPPÉ, F., FRITH, U., BAKER, S.C., DOLAN, R.J., FRACKOWIAK, R.S.J. & FRITH, C.D. (1995). Other minds in the brain: a functional imaging study of "theory of mind" in story comprehension. *Cognition, 57,* 109–128.

FISHER, N.C. (2002). Unpublished Ph.D. thesis, University of London.

FRITH, U. & FRITH, C. (2001). The biological basis of social interaction. *Current Directions in Psychological Science, 10(5),* 151–155.

FRITH, U. & HAPPÉ, F. (1999). Theory of mind and self-consciousness: What is it like to be autistic? *Mind & Language, 14(1),* 1–22.

GALLAGHER, H.L., HAPPÉ, F., BRUNSWICK, N., FLETCHER, P.C., FRITH, U. & FRITH, C.D. (2000). Reading the mind in cartoons and stories: an fMRI study of Theory of Mind in verbal and nonverbal tasks. *Neuropsychologia, 38,* 11–21.

GERGELY, G., NADASDY, Z., CSIBRA, G. & BIRO, S. (1995) Taking the intentional stance at 12 months of age. *Cognition, 56,* 165–193.

GOEL, V., GRAFMAN, J., TAJIK, J., GANA, S. & DANTO, D. (1998). Modelling other minds. *Brain, 120,* 1805–1822.

GUSNARD, D.A., AKBUDAK, E., SHULMAN, G.L. & RAICHLE, M.E. (2001). Medial prefrontal cortex and self-referential mental activity: relation to a default mode of brain function. *Proceedings of the National Academy of Sciences of the United States of America, 98(7),* 4259–4264.

HAPPÉ, F., EHLERS, S., FLETCHER, P., FRITH, U., JOHANSSON, M., GILLBERG, C., DOLAN, R., FRACKOWIAK, R. & FRITH, C. (1996) "Theory of mind" in the brain: Evidence from a PET scan study of Asperger syndrome. *NeuroReport, 8,* 197–201.

HOGREFE, G-J., WIMMER, H. & PERNER, J. (1986). Ignorance versus false belief: a developmental lag in attribution of epistemic states. *Child Development, 57,* 567–582.

KAZAK, S., COLLIS, G.M. & LEWIS, V. (1997). Can young people with autism refer to knowledge states? Evidence from their understanding of "know" and "guess." *Journal of Child Psychology and Psychiatry, 38,* 1001–1009.

LESLIE, A.M. (1987) Pretence and representation: The origins of "Theory of Mind." *Psychological Review, 94,* 412–426.

LANE, R.D., FINK, G.R., CHAU, P.M. & DOLAN, R.J. (1997). Neural activation during selective attention to subjective emotional responses. *Neuroreport, 8,* 3969–3972.

LANG, B. & PERNER, J. (2002). Understanding of intention and false belief and the development of self-control. *British Journal of Developmental Psychology. 20(1),* 67–76.

MCGUIRE, P.K., SILBERSWEIG, D.A. & FRITH, C.D. (1996a). Functional neuroanatomy of verbal self-monitoring. *Brain, 119,* 907–17.

MCGUIRE, P.K., PAULESU, E., FRACKOWIAK, R.S. & FRITH, C.D. (1996b). Brain activity during stimulus independent thought. *Neuroreport, 7,* 2095–9.

OHNISHI, T., MATSUDA, H., HASHIMOTO, T., KUNIHIRO, T., NISHIKAWA, M., UEMA, T. & SASAKI, M. (2000). Abnormal regional cerebral blood flow in childhood autism. *Brain, 123,* 1838–1844.

PENNINGTON, B.F. & OZONOFF, S. (1996). Executive function and developmental psychopathology. *Journal of Child Psychology and Psychiatry, 37,* 51–87.

PERNER, J. (1998). The meta-intentional nature of executive functions and theory of mind. In P. Carruthers & J. Boucher (Eds.) *Language and Thought* (pp. 270–283). Cambridge: Cambridge University Press.

PERNER, J., FRITH, U., LESLIE, A.M. & LEEKAM, S.R. (1989). Exploration of the autistic child's theory of mind: Knowledge, belief, and communication. Child Development, *60,* 689–700.

PERNER, J. & WIMMER, H. (1985). 'John thinks that Mary thinks that....": Attribution of second-order beliefs by 5–10 year old children. *Journal of Experimental Child Psychology, 39,* 437–471.

PHILLIPS, W., BARON-COHEN, S. & RUTTER, M. (1998). Understanding intention in normal development and in autism. *British Journal of Developmental Psychology, 16,* 337–346.

PREMACK, D. & WOODRUFF, G. (1978). Does the chimpanzee have a theory of mind? *Behavioural and Brain Sciences, 4,* 515–526.

RUSSELL, J. (Ed.) (1997). *Autism as an executive disorder.* New York: Oxford University Press.

RUSSELL, J. & HILL, E.L. (2002). Action-monitoring and intention reporting in children with autism. *Journal of Child Psychology & Psychiatry & Allied Disciplines. 42(3),* 317–328.

SIEGAL, M. & VARLEY, R. (2002). Neural systems involved in "theory of mind." *Nature Reviews Neuroscience. 3(6),* 463–71.

TAN, J. & HARRIS, P.L. (1991). Autistic children understand seeing and wanting. *Development and Psychopathology, 3,* 163–174.

VOGELEY, K., BUSSFELD, P., NEWEN, A., HERRMANN, S., HAPPÉ, F., FALKAI, P., MAIER, W., SHAH, N.J., FINK, G.R. & ZILLES, K. (2001). Mind reading: neural mechanisms of theory of mind and self-perspective. *Neuroimage, 14,* 170–181.

WIMMER, H. & PERNER, J. (1983). Beliefs about beliefs: Representation and the constraining function of wrong beliefs in young children's understanding of deception. *Cognition, 13,* 103–128.

Cultural Selves

NAOMI QUINN

*Department of Cultural Anthropology, Duke University,
Durham, North Carolina 27708, USA*

ABSTRACT: Recent cross-cultural studies of child development reveal that
child rearing, while strikingly culturally variable, is everywhere designed
to make the child's experience of important lessons constant, to link those
lessons to emotional arousal, and to connect them to evaluations of the
child's goodness and badness. These claims are illustrated from research
on Americans, Chinese, Germans, Gusii (Kenya), Ifaluk (Micronesia), and
Inuit (Baffin Island). These three universal features of child rearing
accomplish what is a highly specialized task. Constancy of experience
alters synaptic connections to grant the pattern of their firing especially
high-resolution, so that the lessons to be learned are unmistakable ones.
Accompanied by emotional arousal, these lessons are especially motivating
and unforgettable. Brought home with evaluations of the learner's goodness and badness, these lessons are even more motivating and unforgettable. Children get the point of the lesson, enact it once they get it, and
remember to enact it on subsequent occasions. Cultural models of child
rearing, thus, exploit the neural capacities of the children so reared, to
achieve a result, human adulthood, that could not be accomplished by the
human brain alone. From exposure to these practices result distinctive cultural selves. These selves are partly implicit, based on the largely unmarked practices designed to make children's experience of important
lessons constant and these lessons arousing, and partly explicit, based on
the labeling and other marking that connects these lessons to evaluations
of children's goodness and badness. The conscious, self-reflective self that
emerges from such explicit evaluation lays the basis for identity—everywhere profoundly culturally shaped, infused with powerful evaluative
meanings, and itself highly motivating.

KEYWORDS: cultural models; child rearing; cultural task solutions; cultural selves

By Joseph LeDoux's account, in the final chapter of his recent book *Synaptic
Self* (2002), self is the upshot of the ways the brain remembers, synchroniz-
es, connects, communicates among, and integrates the input and output of

Address for correspondence: Dr. Naomi Quinn, Department of Cultural Anthropology, Duke
University, Durham, NC 27708-0091. Voice: 919-684-2810; fax: 919-681-8483.
naomi.quinn@duke.edu

Ann. N.Y. Acad. Sci. 1001: 145–176 (2003). © 2003 New York Academy of Sciences.
doi: 10.1196/annals.1279.010

different neural systems. As he (2002: 17) puts it, "You are your synapses. They are who you are." Who you are is not circumscribed by the brain, however; there is an additional, and critical, piece to the story. Synaptic connections are more or less durably altered by experience. This is possible owing to the plasticity of neurons—a phenomenon now much better understood than when Donald Hebb first called attention to it (LeDoux, 2002: 80). The shape of experience governs the pattern of neuronal connections strengthened in this way and the shape of the resulting pattern of synaptic firing.[1]

A profound source of the patterning of experience is the culture in which we find ourselves. Thus, to LeDoux's picture of how neural processes engage multiple neural systems to endow each person with a self, must be added a description of how a very different set of processes, those that enter the cultural patterning of experience, shape and enhance that self. Cognitive anthropologists have used the terms *cultural models* or *cultural schemas* to describe the neural patterns resulting from the way culture organizes experience (Strauss & Quinn, 1997). The cultural patterning of the world we live in is so far-reaching and so all-encompassing that it cannot help but pattern our synaptic connections. While the cultural models any person has internalized in this way are multitudinous, I will argue that one component of culture in particular, cultural models for child rearing, has the greatest cultural influence of all on who we are.

Paralleling LeDoux's (2002: 27–29) description of how self emerges from neural processes, cultural processes render cultural selves that are largely—though not entirely—"implicit," or out of conscious self-awareness. Indeed, the idea of a largely implicit self accords well with psychological anthropologists' understanding of how culture works. One of the most prominent features of cultural knowledge of all kinds is that it is overwhelmingly implicitly transmitted. Whether what is learned remains implicit or becomes explicit depends on how it is learned. Cultural knowledge (much of Western formal schooling being a notable exception) is most often learned by using it, not by rehearsing it in the abstract. The result is that even people who are highly practiced at its enactment may be unable to state it explicitly or reflect on it self-consciously. Cultural models for how to rear children, and hence the lessons children learn in the course of being reared according to such a model, and the cultural selves that these lessons impart, as I will show, are no exception.

CULTURAL MODELS FOR CHILD REARING

What psychological anthropologists call cultural models arise from those life experiences that members of some group or class of people share. They are learned through experience, just as other cognitive schemas are (hence the alternative term *cultural schema*), except that these experiences are widespread in a group. One kind of cultural model is a cultural solution to a task that members of a group must routinely perform, and that, once invented, is transmitted from person to person and from generation to generation. Cultural models of this kind evolve because culture and brain together can achieve shared solutions to human tasks that the individual brain alone is ill-suited to perform. Tasks that are likely candidates for such culturally assisted solutions are ones that are too recurrent and too vital for individuals to do without solutions to them, too complex to make it practical for individuals to re-invent their solution independently, and widespread enough in a group to make a common solution attractive (see Rumelhart et al., 1986: 47; Clark, 1997: 194–200).

Paramount among such recurrent, vital, complex, widespread tasks requiring cultural solutions is the universal task of socializing children. Tasks of this kind that are this critical to human survival and community well being are nowhere left to individuals to solve. In every community of child rearers, a cultural solution to this task evolves.[2] Such a cultural model specifies the kind of adult child rearers desire to raise, and a set of practices, sometimes more habitual and routinely enacted, sometimes more deliberate and strategically deployed, thought to most effectively raise a child to be such an adult.[3] The vision of what kind of adult this should be, and local wisdom about how to raise a child to be one, vary, often dramatically, from community to community. At the same time, certain features of child rearing models are imposed by the parameters of their task, and hence are universal.

The ethnographic picture of cultural models of child rearing that emerges from recent cross-cultural child development research is one of a quite specialized task solution. This task solution engineers the child's experience in three ways, to make child rearing effective. These three features of such models appear to be so critical to effective child rearing that they are reinvented in every case. First, such models universally specify practices that maximize the constancy of the child's experience around the learning of important lessons. Second, such models universally include practices that make the child's experience of learning these lessons emotionally arousing. Third, such models universally attach these lessons to more global evaluations of the child's behavior, and the child herself, as good or bad. Child rearing depends upon constancy, emotional arousal, and evaluation because these three features of experience are especially effective in imparting to children what their rearers desire to convey to them, and in making these lessons durable ones. In this, these models rely on neural processes. In this collaboration between culture and the brain, children are not only effectively reared; they are, we will ultimately see, imbued with culturally distinctive selves.

Constancy of experience is meant both in the sense of that experience's being repeated with regularity, and in the sense of its being undiluted by other, possibly contradictory or diverting experiences that might create confusion, uncertainty, or ambiguity. In neural terms, such experiential constancy translates, in the child's brain, into synaptic patterns (or, in another terminology, cognitive schemas) that may be characterized as highly resolved. I am using the term "high resolution" to capture a pattern of synaptic firing in which the synapses involved are strongly connected to one another and not connected, even weakly, to other synapses. That is, when this group of synapses fire, they all fire without fail, and no others are activated.

In both the sense of insuring regular repetition, and the sense of excluding the contradictory or the extraneous, constancy of experience is achieved in the way that child rearing everywhere is characteristically conducted. While children are taught through explicit injunctions, admonitions, lessons, and corrections of a child's behavior, these teachings are also, and much more frequently and continuously, conveyed in implicit, unarticulated messages about appropriate and inappropriate behavior. Because these unspoken messages implicit in look, gesture, and other body language (including, of course, but hardly limited to conventional verbalizations) are highly habituated, they shape what the child experiences—and, equally importantly, what the child does not experience—with enormous regularity. Much more powerfully than could explicit teachings alone, these habitual, embodied practices converge to immerse the child in a cultural world of a certain constant shape, conveying their lessons repeatedly, redundantly, and unmistakably. To be sure, more generally speaking, our environment is profoundly culturally patterned, a patterning that is continuously being reproduced in our behavior and in the artifacts we make. To appreciate the extent of this patterning one has only to think of the way people in any group walk, or the shape of their domestic dwellings. But child rearing is exceptional in this regard, patterning the child's experience deliberately, vigilantly, and persistently. The child's immersion in this world is fuller still because of wide consensus within a larger community of child rearers that these practices should be adhered to, and by the moral force with which the practices are imbued, reinforcing their enactment by members of this community.

Too, to the degree that constancy means constant repetition of given experiences, the stronger and hence more memorable will be the synaptic pattern that results. Another characteristic of child rearing, emotional arousal—by various widespread techniques such as beating, frightening, teasing, shaming, or praising, some of which I will illustrate in this paper—greatly heightens this effect, making the experience accompanied by arousal especially memorable over the long term. This happens for two reasons. Hormones released during emotional arousal actually strengthen synaptic connections, and emotional arousal organizes and coordinates brain activity, crowding all but the emotionally relevant experience out of consciousness (LeDoux, 2002: 200–234). The child subjected to such arousing experiences can be counted on not to forget the lessons so learned and hence to be socialized once and for all. Moreover, these lessons are indelibly associated with the emotional arousal itself, and with whatever motivation that this arousal entails—to act in such as way as to earn praise, for example, or so as to avoid being frightened. Children are highly motivated to enact lessons learned in the context of emotional arousal; they remember these lessons well; and, remembering them in all their arousing, motivating fullness, they keep on re-enacting them.

A third characteristic of child rearing practices everywhere also depends on emotional arousal, working similarly to frightening, praising, and the like to make lessons memorable and motivating—and, may indeed be coupled with these other emotion-arousing techniques, and with repetition, for maximum effect. This method is at once more general and more explicit than other techniques for arousing emotion, associating important lessons to be learned to global evaluations of the child as good or bad.

To begin with, approval and disapproval are intrinsically emotionally arousing. This is because of their implications for care. Attachment theorists tell us that any threat to an infant's attachment to the caretaker is experienced by the infant as a threat to survival and security. Such a threat is emotionally arousing, naturally, especially to the very young, preverbal infant with limited ways of reading the gravity of environmental threats and responding to them. A caretaker's love and approval are reassurances to the infant that attachment to the caretaker is secure and the infant is safe; love withdrawal and disapproval arouse insecurity, signaling the possibility of neglect or even abandonment.

The feelings of being loved or being unloved retain their capacity to arouse strong emotion into later life. And with this emotion, they carry the continuing motivation to seek love and avoid its withdrawal. On this emotionally arousing, motivating base, caretakers build the child's subsequent, more culturally shaped and elaborated, understandings of what behavior is good and will earn adult love and approval, and what is bad and will bring love withdrawal and disapproval. Typically, in this process, what is good and what is bad are labeled, or otherwise clearly demarcated, for the child.

Thus culture, in the form of shared practices that, as part of a larger shared task solution, engineer the child's experience to be constant and arousing, and the brain, in the form of neural responses to that constant and often arousing experience, collaborate in the universal task of raising humans to adulthood.

In the body of this paper, I will illustrate my three claims about child rearing—that it is designed to produce exceptional constancy in the experience of key lessons, to make these lessons emotionally arousing, and to attach them to evaluations of the child as good or bad—with work by anthropologists who study child development cross-culturally, and who have recently begun to provide us with richer pictures than heretofore of child rearing in different communities worldwide. These recent studies are distinguished by what Miller et al. (2001: 160) have characterized as "a concern with meaning." This new concern with meaning owes itself, in part, to the general turn to cultural meaning beginning with mid-century cultural anthropology, and, more specifically, to the thinking about cultural models that entered psychological anthropology beginning in the 1980s (see Harkness, 1992: 115–116). Cross-cultural child development researchers translated this new theoretical concern into "the recognition that socialization cannot be fully understood without taking into account parents' 'folk theories' or 'ethnotheories'" (Miller et al., 2001; see also Harkness, 1992: 116).[4] This new work offers all the more compelling support for the collaboration of culture and brain for which I argue, because it was collected without any such claim in mind.[5] What is relevant to my argument is a previously unrecognized pattern of child rearing across these cases, a pattern that I presume to be universal. It should be understood that the small fraction of material I am able to present here in support of my argument is drawn from, and borne out by, much larger bodies of systematically collected data on child rearing in the communities where these studies have been conducted. While the studies I have to draw upon are as yet small in number, they provide exceptionally full accounts. This evidence, then, should not be mistaken for the merely anecdotal (aside from a couple of anecdotes based on my own personal experience that I will add).

When I have presented this material, I will return, at the very end, to the question of how child rearing and the brain collaboratively shape a culturally distinctive, lifelong self, the answer to which I hope will be, by then, self-evident.

THE CONSTANCY OF THE CHILD'S EXPERIENCE OF BEING REARED

The child's environment is everywhere engineered in such a way that her experience of important child rearing lessons is exceptionally constant. This constancy is heightened because reinforced by the child's experience, not just with a small set of primary caretakers, but with others within a broader community of shared opinion about child rearing, and by the moral force of such opinions, which leads child rearers not only to assiduously enact child-rearing practices themselves, but to monitor and enforce the practices of others.

Constancy Engineered

Several cases, taken from the cross-cultural study of child development, will demonstrate how child-rearing practices are engineered to make the child's experience constant.

First, Catherine Lutz tells the following anecdote about an incident that occurred while she was conducting field research on the Micronesian island of Ifaluk:

> Whereas American approaches to child rearing and emotion elevate happiness
> to an important position, setting it out as an absolute necessity for the good or

healthy child (and adult), the Ifaluk view happiness/excitement [Lutz's gloss of the Ifaluk word *ker*] as something that must be carefully monitored and sometimes halted in children. Taking the former cultural perspective in my approach to Ifaluk children, I watched one day with an amused smile as a five-year-old girl danced and made silly faces for me as I sat outside her house. A woman with me at the time noticed my grin and said, "Don't smile at her—she'll think that you're not *song*" [another emotion term, glossed by Lutz as "justifiable anger"]. The reasoning process behind this woman's statement to me entailed some of the most central tenets of Ifaluk emotion theory...If I looked justifiably angry at the young girl, she would become afraid (*metagu*), lose her happiness/excitement, and then sit properly and quietly. In this case, the woman did not wait for *ker* to produce misbehavior but anticipated it (Lutz 1988: 167).

Lutz elsewhere (1983; 1987) explains the vital role that training in *metagu*—which she glosses as "fear/anxiety"—plays in the socialization of an Ifaluk child, who is constantly reminded to be *metagu*, as the proper response to someone else's *song* and in an array of other situations. Ifaluk Islanders put such stress on the learning of this emotion because their cultural model of child rearing posits that the child who is *metagu* will perceive and avoid ubiquitous environmental dangers such falling off of cliffs or from trees and falling into open wells and lagoons. A *metagu* child will also prefer the company of others and hence be primed to participate in cooperative food-accumulating activities, in the context of limited land and periodic severe food shortages due to typhoons. And such a child will grow up to be an adult who exhibits the personality trait, highly valued on this small, densely populated island, of *malewelu*, or "calmness," a hyperawareness of the consequences of one's own wrong behavior that leads a person to behave non-aggressively and non-disruptively. In particular, *metagu* being the reciprocal of *song* or "justifiable anger," a child who has learned to be *metagu* will anticipate the *song* or "justifiable anger" of others, especially elders, and be vigilant about his own potential for wrongdoing.

Robert LeVine and his coworkers (LeVine et al., 1994: 210–213) provide another striking cross-cultural example of the regularity of experience imposed by child rearing, this one drawn from the study they conducted among the Gusii, an agricultural people of western Kenya. Over a period of months, the researchers videotaped Gusii mothers interacting with their infants in the yards outside their homes, the infant in an American infant seat and the mother sitting or kneeling on the ground in front of her child.[6] Following a laboratory design that had been used with American mothers, these mothers were instructed to "talk to your baby," "play with your baby," "get your baby's attention." Gusii mothers said it was, of course, silly to talk to a baby. They did comply, however, seeming relaxed and comfortable, if restrained:

> Their speech to the infants consisted largely of repeated verbal formulas familiar in routine interaction, for example, "seka, seka, seka" (smile); "kira, kira, kira" (hush), or the making of attention-getting sounds. Though the situation of interacting with mother face-to-face without being held by her may have been

unique in the experience of these babies (in the first session), they responded
with evident pleasure vocally or motorically and sometimes moved their arms
in a way that seemed to indicate the expectation of being picked up.

Some of the infants laughed, with much movement and vocalization. These
peaks in affective display produced a mixed response in mothers: Some giggled
nervously; others turned away, their faces suddenly devoid of expression. The
infants usually responded with milder but still positive displays. The sessions
seemed flat and monotonous to the observer in the field [an American]... but
microanalysis of the videotapes showed that the mothers' sudden gaze aver-
sions were closely linked to the infants' peaks of affective display and as such
were important junctures in the interactions (LeVine et al., 1994: 211).

The Gusii mothers' pattern of gaze aversion, the researchers tell us, is in
the interests of keeping interaction smooth and even.

The mothers' response to these displays of positive affect is thus to dampen,
diffuse, or diminish the affective level of the interaction. Among American
mothers, by contrast, the goal is usually to build upon, amplify, or extend these
infant behaviors; every effort is made to sustain Play and Talk episodes up to
the limits of the infant's capacities (LeVine et al., 1994: 213).

Gaze aversion is a habitual style of maternal interaction with infants, and is
to be understood in terms of several features of the Gusii cultural model for
child rearing. Soothing and calming, rather than engaging and exciting, make
for a quieter, less demanding infant, one easier to care for in combination with
the agricultural tasks of these overworked mothers, and less likely to come to
harm in a dangerous environment. In addition, looking fondly at one's own
child in front of others can invite jealousy and witchcraft. More, maternal gaze
aversion is part of a longer-term design. Traditional Gusii morality dictates un-
questioning obedience to those of higher status, personified by the homestead
head—as exemplified in the obedience of sons to fathers and wives to hus-
bands. This hierarchical moral code is enacted, in part, through restraint,
avoidance, and social distancing, including sexual embarrassment/modesty/
restraint (*ensoni*), in intergenerational and marital relationships (LeVine et al.,
1994:60). It is a code of prescribed conduct for everyday life of which Gusii
are proud, seeing themselves as morally superior to their Nilotic-speaking
neighbors because of it (LeVine et al., 1994: 60). LeVine and his co-authors
explain the role of gaze aversion in this model for behavior:

Adults rarely converse in the *en face* position but tend to speak side by side,
back to back or at a 90-degree angle, in which one looks at the ground while
the other speaks. Mutual gaze usually occurs at the moment of greeting and is
avoided during the interaction that follows. Excessive eye contact is interpreted
as disrespectful familiarity or improper intrusiveness with sexual or aggressive
intent (LeVine et al., 1994: 222).

Mothers' gaze aversion, thus, anticipates and habituates proper adult social
interaction, which "entails the avoidance of eye contact, particularly between

those of unequal status, including parents and children" (LeVine et al., 1994: 222). As well, gaze aversion is a first step in rearing a compliant subordinate in this highly hierarchical household, a docile toddler who will acquire respect and obedience easily and naturally. LeVine et al. (1994: 254) report on another, more direct, feature of this training: "Deliberate training in respect and obedience can be traced back into the first year of life, in the prevalence of maternal commands even at 3 months, or more firmly after 9 months, when positive utterances have declined and negative utterances (largely commands) are rising."

These instances from Micronesia and Kenya illustrate key features of child rearing everywhere. In each instance, it happens, the child rearer is confronted with a violation of the cultural model, a violation that, it happens, is introduced by an American field researcher. In each instance, the child rearer's reaction is to insist on, or persist in, enacting her own cultural model. The enactment—an Ifaluk woman unsmilingly regarding a child's antics, withholding any sign of approval; a Gusii mother averting her gaze from her infant— is a highly embodied one. That is to say, the culturally significant message, in both cases, is conveyed implicitly in body language, as a matter of practiced habit, rather than being deliberately taught by explicit precept. The Ifaluk woman has occasion to explain to Lutz, the novice child rearer, why she, too, should not smile, but the woman does not tell the little girl why she should not dance and make faces. She merely conveys her lack of approval. Finally, it is easy to imagine both these embodied practices repeated multiple times daily, in their respective communities, along with the multiple daily enactment of other, coordinate practices equally embodied and habitual. Similarly, how many times a day does the American middle-class mother of a toddler reward her child's little accomplishments with praise? It is this implicit, habitual nature of parenting that leads LeVine et al. (1994: 255) to refer to "the absolutism of conventional practice" with which cultural models of infant care are imbued. It is practice that creates considerable constancy of the child's learning experience—as both the Ifaluk and the Gusii cases illustrate well, constancy as much in what it deletes from this experience as in what it structures into it.

Here I cannot resist adding an illustration that comes from a recent visit of mine to Hamburg, Germany. In a class I teach at my home university, a student who had studied abroad in Berlin, had related a story intended to illustrate the unusual rule-following proclivity of Germans. She told how Berliners would stand and wait for red lights to turn green, even when there were no cars coming or, indeed, anywhere in sight. In Hamburg, riding in a car with two of my German hosts, I could not resist asking about this practice. The two Germans agreed unhesitatingly that, yes, they did that, one explaining to me that they did it to set a good example for children. The other German then told about the following interaction she had had with her boyfriend just a few days ago: When he started to cross against a light, she stopped him from doing so. Walking with him later the same day, however, *she* crossed against a light, and, bemused, he asked her how she could be so inconsistent. She explained to him that on the first occasion there had been a child nearby, and she didn't want the child to see him violate the rule.[7] This story brings home, once again, the attention and effort that adults put into the constancy with which children experience the lessons they are being taught.[8]

An Early Start

Part of constancy is continuity over time. Lessons learned in infancy establish a pattern of experience that makes child rearing all the more effective when these are continuous with lessons learned later. Patterns established early are likely the first to be laid down. They are especially unambiguous because they are less likely than later learning to be contradicted or otherwise complicated by other, possibly competing, experience. In addition, these patterns of experience are stronger because ultimately continued over a longer period of time, and because earliest experience, associated as it is with the infant's felt vulnerability with regard to security and survival, is likely to be emotionally arousing. Cultural models of child rearing take advantage of early training, beginning in infancy, to provide constancy and strength of experience. This point is illustrated in the Gusii example and, even more sharply, in this next example, provided by LeVine and Norman (2001), from Karin Norman's study of child rearing in a small south German town outside of Frankfurt.[9] The example is taken from Norman's field notes, which describe a vignette that happens while 2-year-old Karl is being cared for by his maternal uncle and his wife while his parents are off on a 2-week ski holiday. The aunt and uncle are visiting friends for coffee and cake, and spend most of the visit talking about and interacting with Karl. At one point,

> The aunt tells of how early he wakes up in the morning, at six o'clock, "but I'm not to take him out of bed, Sigrid [Karl's mother] said, he's to stay there until nine or he'll just get used to it and she won't have it; she's done that from when he was a baby." So Karl is kept in bed, he stays quiet, she doesn't know what he does, hears him move about in his bed, babbling to himself. Renate, her friend, thought it was expecting a bit too much of him, keeping him in bed that long: "an hour maybe, but three—that's too long" (LeVine & Norman, 2001: 93).

Karl's mother, say the authors (LeVine & Norman 2001:93) "apparently trained her son as an infant to comfort himself in his room alone. She considers herself entitled to have a child who is self-reliant at an early age so as not to interfere with her other activities." More generally, the authors go on to explain, the infant's toleration of isolation and ability to self-comfort are not just for the mother's convenience, but represent the first step toward the important developmental goal of self-reliance.

The discussion about this absent mother's practice also illustrates that variation exists even within a community of child rearers. Practices begun in infancy, as is this one, are especially likely to come under scrutiny and to engender disagreement among members of such a community, just because they demand such perceived precocity on the part of the child. However, even in questioning the extremity of the mother's practice, the aunt's German friend Renate affirms the cultural principle behind it (as do north German parents I had an opportunity to quiz casually about this). What is in question is not *that* this mother leaves her child alone in his bed, but *how long* she does so. Moreover, this morning regime is only one of an array of practices designed to teach infants and small children to stay alone and comfort themselves.[10] Such practices, dictated by the local cultural model of child rearing, seem entirely natural to its subscribers, even as they may seem counter-intuitive, even harmful, to outsiders.

The Community of Child Rearers

The pattern of child rearing to which a child is exposed is even more regular because it extends beyond the primary caretakers and beyond the household to a larger community of child rearers, all of whom share, to a great extent, a common child-rearing model and strategies for its implementation. Within this community, the rearing that children are receiving from their mothers is also being received from their teachers at school, from their aunties, big sisters, and other relatives, and from neighbors and baby sitters.[11] Addressing an academic audience, I have to emphasize the extent to which each of us, as parent or surrogate parent, abides by the cultural model of child rearing shared in our community. Representing, as academics do, a highly educated, elite class, we tend to read, talk and think obsessively about child rearing during our parenting years, debating the pros and cons of different methods of rearing with relish. Also, living as we do in a highly complex society, we think of everything, including child rearing, as diverse (and, for Americans, as a matter of individual choice). Moreover, it is not easy to apprehend a model for child rearing to be able to appreciate how shared it is. Our child-rearing model does not come to us articulated as an entire, explicit credo. Instead, like much cultural knowledge, it is largely tacit in our minds and often only implicit in our actions. As a result, we may not recognize how deeply ingrained, indeed embodied, in us this model of child rearing is. Even the child-rearing manuals middle-class American mothers are so fond of consulting focus on specific effective strategies for bringing up children (such as how to deal with a tantrum), or discuss aspects of child rearing that have become controversial (such as the pros and cons of daycare), leaving unstated and unexamined the most fundamental tenets of the shared cultural model that shapes and motivates these narrower concerns.

But Americans of the professional class do represent a child rearing community, albeit a dispersed one. We have been brought up, ourselves, to value similar traits and qualities in people. When we become parents, we read the same, the latest, child-rearing manuals. We send our children to the same kinds of preschools and schools, whether private ones or high-end public schools in the professional middle-class towns and neighborhoods in which we reside. I will try to bring home the extent to which we share implicit assumptions about bringing up children, with one small but, I hope, telling example. The middle-class Americans I know are unlikely to question the practice, common in middle-class American preschools, of keeping portfolios containing samples of each child's artwork, a record of the child's chosen classroom activities, and written examples of things the child has said—often commentary on pieces of artwork that have been elicited by the teacher. I know I myself leaf through my granddaughters' portfolios with delight when these are brought home at the end of the year. Portfolios express the uniqueness of the child's self, a value to which we subscribe unthinkingly.

As part of a fascinating study of individualism in three New York City communities differing by class, Adrie Kusserow (1996) tells the story of the Board of Education's attempt to introduce upper-middle class teaching methods, including portfolios, into a lower-working class preschool where she was conducting research. Asked about his child's artwork, one father, a prison guard and construction worker, described to Kusserow how

> I went over there they have a class, a school meeting and Miss Tarlin is telling me well we drew these pictures with finger paints, what do you see in them, I said I see a mess, what do you see I mean don't try to read into it, I mean don't even give me all this hogwash, I really don't want to hear it, this is a four-year-old kid, don't tell—I mean they have stacks of paper on a four-year-old kid.

Kusserow then asks him to tell her about his child's portfolio.

> Portfolio it's how they get along, they put their pictures and try to analyze them, what do you see after this child paints a picture, what is it, how do you see your father here or where do you see the flower in this and then they'll try to explain it to you.

She asks him, "Psychoanalysis?" and he becomes more emphatic:

> Psychoanalysis, yeah, I mean you're psychoanalyzing a four-year-old kid that is standing there with their hand in paint, if you ask them draw a picture or a flower and they drew a weed, maybe you could figure something out there, but I don't think you're gonna figure out hand paintin', so I told her it was jut a little too much, and I said you're getting' a little too serious with four-year-olds, she said well this is the Board of Education's rules now so we have to do it, we have to explain it, and I said well I don't want to hear it, this is bullshit, you know what I mean—I'm not—there are people I know in Manhattan who—I know people who have a two-year-old and the two-year-old says instead of da da, says ta ta and they fuckin' analyze it and I mean shit! It's unbelievable, you're better lettin' em go into a pile of mud and put it on the wall, it's the same shit....(Kusserow, 1996: 200–201).

This father's heated resistance to a new school practice reflects a clash of child-rearing models along the fault-line of class. The model on which this working class man draws is very different from the one shared by middle-class Americans. Even though they may share the same national "culture," people of different classes still differ culturally in important respects (Strauss & Quinn, 1997: 7–8). Cultural models of child rearing are one likely locus of difference across class because these models engage profoundly important values, and values are one important way in which a class is defined for its members. In the case Kusserow (1996) describes, what is at stake are two different versions of individualism. For Americans like this working-class father, individualism means the value of toughening up your child in the ultimate interests of self-reliance; for Kusserow's upper-middle-class American parents, it means the value of encouraging the child's self-expression in the ultimate interests of self-actualization. We who share the middle-class child-rearing model within which portfolios make sense, find them, at the least, unobjectionable, and we are surprised at this working class dad's resistance to them. Of course it's good, we think, to encourage the child to express herself.

The Moral Force of Child-Rearing Practices

LeVine and his colleagues have drawn attention to the degree to which cultural models of child rearing are everywhere invested with "moral direction" or "moral rectitude" (LeVine et al., 1994: 248/255). The moral dimension to beliefs and practices surrounding child rearing should not be surprising, given that this task engages adults in the active consideration and reproduction of their dearest-held values. It is this moral force that is reflected in the proclivity, noted by LeVine et al. (1994: 255–256), and others (see Tobin, Wu & Davidson, 1989:188-221; Miller et al., 2001:167–168), and exemplified in the reaction of the working class preschool father interviewed by Kusserow, to be deeply critical of, and resistant to, other child-rearing regimes than one's own. At the same time, this moral force makes child rearers insistent about their own child-rearing goals and practices, and hence persistent and consistent in enacting them. Adults may, for example, feel morally justified in imposing practices earlier in the child's life than they otherwise might (LeVine & Norman, 2001: 84; Strauss & Quinn, 1997: 106). The German mother of our example is likely to be more willing to leave her infant son alone in his bed from the earliest age, and more assiduous in doing so, because she believes she is doing so not just for her convenience, but in the interests of his development into a self-reliant person.

In the examples I have given, maintaining a constant experience for children is the moral thing to do. The child is being taught to be a good person— *metagu* and eventually *malewelu* in the Ifaluk case, or undemanding and ultimately obedient in the Gusii case, or self-comforting and self-reliant in the south German case. In my north German anecdote about not crossing against the light, the broad moral implication was not so self-evident. The matter is a moral one to Germans, we might surmise, because it is perceived as crucial to children's safety. The practice may partake, though, of an even deeper, more distinctive moral value that Germans tend to place on rule-following more generally—as LeVine and Norman (2001: 91–92) put it, the German virtue of "*Ordnugsliebe*, 'love of order,'" which means both self-control and learning to comply with the demands of existing regimes of schedule and discipline." Not crossing against the light seems to have become something of a symbol, to Germans, of such compliance. The Germans who explained this practice to me justified it with certitude and, it seemed to me, pride.

People are not only regular in their own enactment of child-rearing practices; like the German woman who stopped her boyfriend from crossing the street, they are willing to monitor and enforce other people's observance of these practices. Indeed, individuals enforce other's observance of child-rearing practices even, as in the case of the Ifaluk woman sitting beside Lutz, in foreigners and even, as in the case of Karl's mother, in their own absence. This assiduousness not just in enacting given child-rearing practices oneself, but in monitoring and enforcing others' enactment of them, has the effect of reinforcing and extending the constancy in the child's experience of those child-rearing practices deemed to carry morally important lessons.

The moral force with which adults imbue their child rearing is conveyed, along with the lessons infused with this morality, to the children they rear, making these lessons emotionally arousing to these learners because of the approval and disapproval that are inevitably attached to moral judgments. I have already suggested how approval and disapproval work effectively as very general-purpose techniques to recruit emotional arousal in the service of culture-specific child-rearing lessons. As will emerge later in this paper, approval and disapproval are not mere side effects of the morality with which adults infuse the lessons they teach children, but are harnessed much more deliberately to the teaching of these lessons.

THE EMOTIONAL AROUSAL THAT ATTENDS
CHILD REARING

First, consider other, more specific, techniques for arousing emotion, with one or another of which cultural models of child rearing everywhere come equipped. Since arousal of emotion is highly effective in motivating the child learner to behave in desired ways, and in making this learning memorable, and since these are results that socializers seek, it is not surprising that these techniques are relied upon again and again cross-culturally, being adapted to achieve very different child-rearing goals in different communities. As in the examples I give below, these emotion-arousing techniques are often a good bit more contrived than the habitual, embodied practices already discussed. Nevertheless, they may, like other practices, have highly habitual, embodied components, and they are likely to be, like other practices, repeated with frequency, by many different adults in the child's world, beginning early in the child's life—so that they contribute to the constancy of the child's experience at the same time that they make that experience arousing. For one example, Jean Briggs (1998: 6) tells of the playful questioning that is such a big part of the teasing to which Inuit adults submit young children, and that will be introduced at the end of in this section, that it began "in infancy, long before the baby understood speech."

One of the more obvious and common strategies for teaching an emotion-arousing lesson to transgressive children is the practice of frightening them with attack by spirits and other animate beings, natural or supernatural.[12] A good description of frightening as a conventional child-rearing practice comes, once again, from Lutz's Ifaluk material:

> The most striking way in which *metagu* is socialized is through the use of a special type of ghost (*tarita*) which is said to kidnap and eat children. This ghost is impersonated by one of the women of the child's household, who covers and disguises herself with cloths. The ghost, which normally resides in the wooded interior of the island, is called by parents to come take the child if she or he misbehaves. The ghost is most frequently called if the child has aggressed against a peer, or if the child begins to wander away from the house. Appearing menacingly at the edge of the house compound, the ghost causes young children to leap into the arms of any nearby adult. The label *metagu* is used in profusion to describe the child's reaction, and the ghost is then told by one of the adults present that "the child will no longer misbehave" and that it should therefore go away (Lutz 1983:255).

This practice, of frightening children with adults dressed up as apparitions, is common worldwide, but the same effect is often also obtained without benefit of such elaborate staging. Ghanaian adults, for example, seem willing to exploit any potentially frightening being—supernatural, human, or animal—that happens to be at hand. A Ghanaian woman told me that she had a lifelong fear of chickens because, when she transgressed as a small child, her mother used to threaten her that the courtyard chickens (which must have been fully half her height when she was two or three) were going to attack and eat her. Working in a Mfantse fishing community on the central coast of Ghana, West Africa, in the 1960s and 1970s, I found myself unwittingly serving as an impromptu apparition. My costume was my white skin, my European features, and my strange, light, blow-away hair. When I entered a courtyard, some woman would typically shout to the toddlers playing there, "Here comes the foreigner (*bronyi*), she's going to take you away." The children would run screaming from the sight of me. Pretty soon, no admonition was necessary: They saw me, they ran. I imagine that mothers were lining me up as a bogey-man in anticipation of their children's future bad behavior. Then, even when

I wasn't around, they could scare children into obedience by threatening to send them away with me.

Another emotion-arousing technique is shaming. Heidi Fung, Peggy Miller, and their colleagues (Fung, 1999; Fung & Chen, 2001; Miller, Fung & Mintz, 1996; Miller et al., 1997; Miller et al., 2001) have provided a series of analyses of shaming as a Chinese socialization practice, in the context of a comparative study of stories co-narrated to the researcher, in two middle-class communities—one in Chicago and the other in Taipei. A co-narrated story is one in which an adult incorporates the child into the telling. The children in this case were 2-year-olds. In both the Taiwanese and the American communities, mothers regularly co-narrate stories with their children of events in which the child has taken part. However, the Taiwanese and American stories differ sharply.

Here is a typical Taiwanese story co-narrated with a 2-year-old boy, Didi:

Mother: [Looks at child] Eh, eh, you that day with Mama, with younger sister [pats sister's back], with older sister went to the music class. Was that fun?

Child: It was fun.

Mother: What didn't the teacher give you?

Child: Didn't, didn't give me a sticker.

Mother: Didn't give you a sticker. Then you, then what did you do?

Child: I think cried.

Sister: Cried loudly, "Waah! Waah! Waah!"

Mother: Oh, you then cried? Yeah, you constantly went, "Waah, didn't [gestures wiping eyes, makes staccato gesture of fists away from body], why didn't you give me a sticker? [whines] Why didn't you give me a sticker? [whines]," didn't you?

[Child looks up from book, gazes at mother, smiles, and looks down at book again.]

Sister: [To mother] Yes, "Why didn't you give me a sticker?" [claps hand]

Mother: [To child] Sticker. [sighs] Ai, you made Mama lose face [*hao mei-you mianzi*]. That, that, I wanted to dig my head into the ground. Right? [smiles, shakes head, smiles again]

[Child points to picture book and says something unintelligible.]

Sister: Almost wanted to faint [*hun-dao*]. Mommy almost began to faint [*hun-dao*] (Miller, Fung & Mintz, 1996: 251).

The Taiwanese stories are not infrequently organized, as this one is, around the child's past transgressions. Sometimes, as in this story, the loss of face that a transgression has precipitated is referred to explicitly. Sometimes story-telling is an occasion for reasoning with the child about his wrong-doing. Frequently, a confession is extracted from him, or the story ends with a didactic coda that summarizes its moral—e.g., "Now I don't cry at all"; or, "Saying dirty words is not good"—or a tag question that demands concurrence from the child—e.g., "right or not right?" or "understand or not understand?" Outsiders present, including the researcher, are invited by the caregiver to evaluate, criticize, and judge the child, and the imputed negative opinion of absent others is invoked—in one especially amusing example, of future boyfriends who, it is said, would not marry the child after watching her tape-recorded misdeeds (Fung & Chen, 2001:430).

Committed to a moral ideology in which shame is positively valued, the parents felt that they would be remiss as parents if they did not raise their children to know shame and to abide by the rules of appropriate conduct. The larger goal of the cultural model of child rearing that subsidizes this practice is to produce an adult who is sensitive to shame and hence to other people's opinions, evaluations, and judgments (Fung, 1999: 183–184). Only such a person will be upright in conduct, following the right path in life (Miller et al., 2001:172). These researchers (Miller, Fung & Mintz 1996: 266) report that personal storytelling "is a major means by which the socialization of shame is accomplished." The Taiwanese parents viewed the co-narration of transgression stories as an enactment of the indigenous concept of "opportunity education" (*jihui jiaoyu*; Fung, 1999), a cultural task solution the twin principles of which are "that it is more effective to situate a moral lesson in the child's concrete experience than to preach in the abstract and that parents should take every opportunity to provide such concrete lessons" (Miller et al., 2001:167). The immediate moment of transgression itself is the ideal opportunity for education through shaming. However, co-narratives also allow parents to "create an opportunity where none existed" (Fung, 1999: 201), most frequently by piggybacking recollections of previous transgressions on accounts of present ones (Fung & Chen, 2001: 428). "Thus, the child may hear particular misdeeds narrated, and may confess to those misdeeds, again and again. Being able to face one's own misdeeds honestly, and repeatedly if necessary is crucial to this proactive self-corrective process" (Miller et al. 2001: 167).

Shaming of this kind is undoubtedly emotionally arousing.[13] Miller and her co-authors (Miller et al., 2001: 167) are concerned that Chinese shaming tactics will seem unduly harsh to American readers. They point out, "The very fact that children's misdeeds are narrated so often may serve to normalize them. That is, these Taipei parents seem to take for granted, and perhaps their children come to take for granted, that it is natural for young children to make mistakes." A child is expected to be able to bear and handle a reasonable amount of shame (Fung, 1999:191). In the particular co-narration I reproduced, and in most others, we learn, shaming is mitigated by smiles, laughter, and the mother's playful tone of voice. On the other hand, Fung (1999: 201) tells us, children labeled as "recidivists" (rather than "first offenders"), because they have either repeatedly violated a specific rule, or have exhibited a more general pattern of not paying attention to what they are told, are treated to more serious shaming. Fung (1999: 190) reports that most of the Taiwanese parents in her study said that it was important that children *feel* ashamed when they transgressed, and, to this end, socializers' efforts were directed, not just to putting an end to the transgression, but to eliciting these feelings of shame from the child (Fung, 1999:192). Thus, even when the transgressing child complied with the adult's demands, "[i]n more than 80% of those instances, the shaming still proceeded after the compliance" (Fung, 1999:194). In the co-narrative about Didi's disruption of the music class, the public (for the benefit of the researcher in this case) and graphic retelling of Didi's babyish, disruptive behavior and how it made the mother lose face must have been somewhat arousing for the child. Throughout this retelling, he seems to be trying to ignore the situation by burying himself in his picture book, possible evidence of his discomfort. Suggestively, also, we learn from Fung (1999: 196) that later in the same episode, the boy "appropriated, exaggerated, and played with his mother's metaphor, 'faint,' by pointing to his cheek, indicating that it was he who fainted, and by throwing his head and body back against the sofa."

By contrast, the American parents in this study rarely told stories about the child's past transgressions; when they did so, they were careful to portray the child in a positive light despite the misdeed, and often framed these misdeeds as humorous. This pattern seems to be part of wider set of practices that these and other American middle-class caregivers "use to protect their children's self-esteem—handling discipline in the here and now without dwelling on the child's past misdeeds, conducting serious disciplining in private, putting the best face on a child's shortcomings, or even recasting shortcomings as strengths" (Miller et al., 1996: 266–267). The Taiwanese parents would view these practices as educational opportunities squandered.

For a final illustration of emotion-arousing child-rearing techniques, Jean Briggs (1998) has given us a gorgeous study, unparalleled for its fine-grained focus, of the Baffin Island Inuit practice of teasing children. Briggs demonstrates in full how Inuit teasing, like Chinese shaming, quite deliberately arouses emotion in its toddler targets. She followed the socialization of a 3-year-old girl, Chubby Maata, for a number of months. During this time Briggs recorded numerous episodes in which Chubby Maata was badgered and questioned in a characteristic teasing manner. Briggs's analysis of these dramas is much closer and richer than can be conveyed here.

One common topic of teasing, reflected in the following segment of a recorded episode, is the threat of taking the child away. As in this episode, people outside their immediate family circle routinely ask children, "Want to come live with me?" (Briggs, 1998: 94):

> Maata [a teenaged relative paying an evening visit] began to suggest to Chubby Maata that she and Papi [Chubby Maata's puppy] come to live in their house. Her voice was soft, persuasive, seductive—a voice that was often used by adults in speaking to small children when they wanted a child to do something. Chubby Maata consistently wrinkled her nose: "No." After a while, Maata called

Papi to her, petted him, picked him up, and turned toward the door, with Papi in her arms. Chubby Maata let out a cry, rushed to the puppy, grabbed him around his neck with such force that I feared she would choke him, and pulled him strenuously away from Maata. She was half-laughing, but the laugh sounded anxious, too, and she exerted a great deal of energy.

This drama was repeated several times during the first part of the visit, each time initiated by Maata. Once, Chubby Maata, tugging at Papi, trying hard to separate him from Maata, protested, "He's all shitty!" Maata ignored this argument; she didn't let go of Papi—but she didn't take him out of the house, either.

The last time Maata asked Chubby Maata if she and Papi would like to come and live with them, Chubby Maata said something that I didn't hear before she said no; then, after refusing, she commented, as if cheerfully surprised at herself, "Ih! I almost agreed!" Maata's ear was quick. She exclaimed, "Oh, you agree!" And this time she picked up Chubby Maata instead of Papi and started toward the door. Chubby Maata struggled and cried out in protest, and after a few minutes, Maata put her down. Chubby Maata ran first to her mother, who ignored her, and then to Juupi [a visiting uncle], who picked her up and set her on his lap. From that protected position, she looked over her shoulder, laughing with a triumphant gleam at Maata (Briggs 1998: 91).

But Juupi, too, began to tease Chubby Maata, hitting her bottom lightly, then pretending that someone else, the anthropologist, had done the hitting, and then shortly joining Maata in a new game, on another common theme, of "Who do you like?" "Do you like me?" asked Juupi. "Yes." "Just me alone, yes?" he asked in a soft, confidential voice. This time Chubby Maata avoided answering, returning instead to a game she had been playing by herself (Briggs, 1998: 92).

Briggs thinks that Maata is testing the limits of Chubby Maata's attachments, testing "whether she knows what is hers and how determined she is to keep those possessions. And, in testing, she may create or heighten Chubby Maata's emotional awareness that she has a home and wants to stay there and that she has a puppy and wants to keep him" (Briggs, 1998:95). It is, says Briggs, "a highly charged moment, a moment when loving and being loved by one object, Maata, has become associated with the possibility of losing other loved objects: home, mother, puppy" (Briggs, 1998: 110). Briggs interprets this segment as being about attachment—"To whom does she belong? To whom does she want to belong? Who are her friends and allies? Whom does she like? And whom should she like? Whom can she trust? And closely related to these questions: What does she own? And can she keep her possessions?" (Briggs 1998: 108). "In the long run," concludes Briggs (1998: 114), "one of the lessons of dramas like this will be that the two extremes of attachment are both inappropriate. It is dangerous to respond indiscriminately to offers of affection. Such a response might cause one to lose the most important and legitimate source of love and nurturance: one's home." On the other hand, such dramas teach that exclusive relationships can be dangerous too, as

Juupi illustrates by hitting Chubby Maata and later trying to coax her into agreeing that she likes only him.

In other episodes, other themes carry other lessons, adding considerable complexity to Chubby Maata's upbringing. Occasionally the teasing escalates quite far. In another episode Chubby Maata is told repeatedly by Arnaqjuak, her grandmother, "Your father is VERY BAAAD (*piungngitTUUQ*)! Your mother is VERY BAAAD!..." and then asked, "You are bad, aren't you? Your father is bad, isn't that so?" and so on and on in a stream of words that the anthropologist describes as "unremitting and inexorable" (Briggs, 1998: 127). The episode climaxes in "Your genitals are bad. Aaq! They stink! [poking a finger between the little girl's legs] Are you aware of your horrid little (-*ruluk*) genitals? THERE they are! [pretending to pull down Chubby Maata's trousers from behind]."

From earliest infancy, Chubby Maata has been treated as, and encouraged to think of herself as, an adorable little baby (*babykuluk*). Briggs (1998: 134) interprets dramas like this one as teaching her that she is not so perfect ("It's dangerous to think you're perfectly good," one Inuit woman tells Briggs 1998: 256, fn. 16) and that, in her imperfection, she is vulnerable to the sometimes dangerously critical gaze and the sanctions of others. Another, more complex, lesson, though, of this drama is the necessity of protecting others as a means of protecting oneself. Her grandmother's attacks on her parents "will make Chubby Maata feel the absolute *necessity* of protective, loving nurturance, *nallik-*, the highest Inuit value" (Briggs, 1998: 141). Adults teach moral behavior not simply by modeling it, then, but "by pretending to attack it and by creating, in the dramatization of both values and antivalues, appropriate and compelling emotions to support the approved behavior" (Briggs, 1998: 141).

During these familiar rounds of teasing, the child often refuses to answer the provocative questions, sometimes tries to hide her face, or blatantly ignores the teasing. In the episode with the puppy, for example, she initiates a game of running between the door and Juupi, chanting a refrain of nonsense words instead of responding to the adult's questions—reminiscent of the way Didi, the Taiwanese child, tries to weather his mother's shaming by keeping his eyes on his picture book. Sometimes, as when her grandmother teases her about her genitals and pretends to pull down her trousers, or when, another time, her great-great grandfather prevents her from approaching her father by swatting in her direction, Chubby Maata bursts briefly into tears. More often, as she does during the BAAAD drama, she becomes wide-eyed, motionless, and watchful. Briggs (1998: 131) interprets these episodes of teasing as being partly about making Chubby Maata educable and open to sanction. The wide-eyed, motionless, watchful pose suggests to her rearers, as do signs of shyness such as acting subdued and talking in a whisper (Briggs 1998: 59), that she is feeling *ilira-*. This is a feeling that motivates proper behavior, "a mixture of respect and the fear of being scolded or treated unkindly. A person who does not feel *ilira-* is not, and cannot be, social-ized," Briggs (1998: 119) tells us. Inuit *ilira-* thus works not dissimilarly to Ifaluk *metagu*.

The adults smile with their eyes when they tease, and use characteristic dramatic voices, speaking softly and confidentially or chanting emphatically and rhythmically, alternating a seductive, "saccharine-persuasive tone" (Briggs, 1998: 181) with one of mock-hostility, a "throaty timbre used to dra-matize mild threat when speaking to a child" (Briggs, 1998: 121). Some-times, when they do not seem to be getting a rise out of Chubby Maata, adults escalate their teasing, as Maata does when she grabs the child and pretends to take her out the door, and the grandmother does when she tells her that her genitals stink. Other times, when they appear to have gone too far, they de-escalate or desist, and sometimes seem to console. Until the drama has been played out, however, the adults present insist that she pay attention, staring at her intently, ordering her to "Look at me!," removing her hands from her face, persisting with their questions. Tellingly, Briggs (1998: 133) observes about the BAAAD episode that the mother and grandmother "present a united front and won't countenance withdrawal or distraction until the drama has caused pain—a sign that some message has been received with emotional force." This emotional arousal is heightened further by the emotionally dangerous nature of the issues typically raised, and by the way in which they are present-ed, Briggs (1998: 206) says, "in exaggerated and personally relevant form by blowing up the alternatives monstrously—not 'Would you like to come visit me?' but 'Would you like to come live with me?'; not 'Look, Saali's wearing the shirt you gave him' but 'He's stolen your shirt!'; not merely 'Your moth-er's hurt her finger' but 'She's going to die!'; not [in an episode of teasing di-rected at another little child, a boy] 'May I admire your penis?' but 'Shall the puppy bite it off?'"

Briggs attests to the durability and continued motivational force of lessons taught by such an emotionally arousing technique. She sees Inuit culture, she says (Briggs 1998:208), "as a mosaic of dilemmas which echo, cross-cut, confirm, and negate one another; dilemmas that are never totally resolved but have to be juggled and rearranged time after time. The fact that the Inuit adults I know are continually watchful, constantly testing the responses of others, argues that a habit of living with dilemmas—continually constructed and reconstructed as experience changes—carries over into adulthood and lasts a lifetime."

While these techniques of teasing, shaming, and frightening with supernat-urals and other beings are certainly widespread, they are used selectively across communities. Not all techniques fit equally into the overall plan of a given cultural model of child rearing. As LeVine et al. (1994: 254) tell us, the technique of choice for middle-class American parents—praise—is rarely used by Gusii parents. Within the context of a model of child rearing that stresses obedience and respect training, Gusii adults reject praise because it would encourage conceit and make even a good child rude and disobedient. Chinese parents, too, would be wary of too much praising, lest it undermine the moral reflectiveness that they strive to cultivate in their children. Inuit socializers, on the other hand, would never frighten, shame, or beat their children. As Briggs (1998: 142) explains, they accomplish in teasing "play" what they cannot do by means of punishment because Inuit strongly disapprove of scolding or punishing in serious mode, as they strongly disapprove of all shows of aggression.

In turn, contemporary middle-class Americans might be surprised to learn how common the use of these various techniques of frightening, shaming, and teasing is elsewhere. Judging them overly and perhaps unnaturally harsh, we are led to underestimate their typicality. We would be wrong to assume, however, that these methods are abusive. Both Briggs (1998:131) and the Taiwanese research team (Fung 1999:203) are careful to emphasize that Inuit teasing and Chinese shaming, respectively, occur within a context in which the child is well-loved and secure in that love, and are modulated so that they are always kept within reasonable limits. One Taiwanese aunt pointed out to Fung (1999: 190) that "too much shame would only risk harming the child's self-esteem, excluding them from interaction, and making them escape from their own responsibilities to amend and improve." Indeed, apart from the universal impulse to treat children lovingly and compassionately, emotional arousal must be modulated if it is to be effective in making the lessons being taught memorable ones. As LeDoux (2002: 222) summarizes, "As long as the degree of emotional arousal is moderate during memory formation, memory is strengthened. But if the arousal is strong, especially if it is highly stressful, memory is often impaired."

Nevertheless, most contemporary American middle-class parents and teachers could not imagine frightening children with a bogeyman (although that term derives from a Euro-American past), for fear of cultivating children's timidity and squelching their highly desired assertiveness. For similar reasons, they would be critical of the shaming that Taiwanese and other Chinese adults routinely heap on their children, as well as the teasing to which Inuit adults routinely subject theirs. As Miller et al. (2001: 167) point out, the American parents would be concerned that such shaming would damage children's self-esteem and sense of efficacy, qualities that, with assertiveness, we deem essential to self-actualization and, ultimately, success in life. So, it happens, our American middle-class child-rearing model precludes the use of some of the most tried and true techniques for emotion arousal. Perhaps we ourselves use praise so lavishly and unstintingly just because we are denied these other methods. And perhaps part of the unruliness (by world standards) of our children is due to the unwillingness of American middle-class parents to resort to some of the most highly effective techniques of child rearing available because, in our eyes, they are potentially damaging to the child.

THE EVALUATION OF CHILDREN AS GOOD OR BAD

Because of how child-rearing lessons are taught and learned, the knowledge of themselves that children gain from exposure to child rearing practices is largely implicit knowledge. We have seen, for instance, how these lessons are so often embodied in the disapproving glance or the habitual aversion of gaze, or remain tacit in repeated practices such as leaving an infant alone in his bed in the morning, or teasing a child about her relatives. So far in this paper I have been intent on making a case for the prevalence of such practices, which, by their daily repetition, lend such extreme constancy to the child's experience. However, as central as such practices are to cultural models of child rearing everywhere, they are augmented with practices of another sort. Child rearers also do have occasion to label children's behavior for them, or otherwise call attention to it, explicitly.

What rearers are most likely to call children's attention to explicitly is their good and, even more commonly, their bad behavior. This is because, as I have noted, rearers everywhere exploit the child's desire for love and approval in the interests of their own agendas for molding the child into a culturally desirable adult. The most effective way child rearers have to discourage what is culturally defined as bad behavior, and encourage what is culturally defined as good behavior, is to couple their approval or disapproval of given behaviors with labeling or other markers of that which is approved or disapproved. Recall, for one good example, Lutz's (1983: 255) description of how "the label *metagu* is used in profusion to describe the child's reaction" to the ghost who has been called to frighten an especially recalcitrant child, until the lesson has been learned to the adults' satisfaction, and "the ghost is then told by one of the adults present that 'the child will no longer misbehave' and that it should therefore go away." Closer to home, we need only think of the exaggeratedly happy cry of "Good girl!" or "Good boy!" that rings out in middle-class American households, said in a special praise-giving voice and accompanied by an exaggerated expression of delight and often by a little clap, to mark parents' extravagant praise for the toddler's every new accomplishment, such as going to the potty without prompting, or learning to tie her own shoes. In these examples, the emotional arousal of being frightened or praised is coupled, for good measure, with explicit labeling of the approved behavior.

Such explicit acknowledgement of good or bad behavior often relies on language, the behavior at issue either being associated with a specific label, as in the Ifaluk example above, or being evaluated as good or bad in more general terms, as in the American one. The acknowledgement often also includes paralinguistic cues, notably a characteristic tone of voice, like the special dramatic voices in which Inuit adults tease their toddlers, or the voice in which middle-class American parents praise theirs. But evaluation markers need not be linguistic. Other likely components of these explicit teaching episodes are facial expressions (think of the Ifaluk woman's unsmiling face and the Inuit adults' smiling eyes) or gesture (think of the American middle-class parents' clapping or the Gusii mothers' gaze aversion).

The study of Taiwanese opportunity education offers an especially full and detailed example of how child rearers signal to the child that his or her behavior is, in this case, disapproved. The shaming that accompanies a transgression, or stories about the transgression, Fung (1999: 192) explains, is marked in highly variable ways, ranging from referring directly to the child as disobedient (e.g., *bu guai de xiaohaizi*) or his misbehavior as shameful (e.g., *xiuxiu lian*, meaning "shame on you"); or indicating with either a conventional gesture (e.g., striking the index finger on the cheek) or an idiomatic expression (recall the mother's comments about losing face, and wanting to bury her head in the ground); through a wonderfully inventive array of more subtle linguistic, paralinguistic, or bodily cues, including sighing, turning away, a more extended silent treatment, name-calling (e.g., "ugly monster"), withdrawal of love (e.g., "We don't want you"), and sarcastic comments like "How come I have such a child?" or "No spanking for a few days, your skin has become itchy." (One of my favorites is "By the time he's five, I bet I'll have to move into a mental institution"; Fung & Chen, 2001: 425.) The Taiwanese child encounters ample instances of shame clearly demarcated, and becomes adept, in addition, at reading this message across the full array of more subtle, embodied or paralinguistic markers.

But shaming itself is only a means to the end of teaching the child right from wrong (Fung, 1999:190). The exact nature of the shameful wrongdoing itself must also be specified, and this is accomplished in the reasoning about the child's behavior that often accompanies Taiwanese transgression stories, or in the coda that sometimes closes these stories and summarizes what the child has done wrong or, perhaps most effectively, in the practice of making the child confess to his own transgression (Fung, 1999: 202). Remember how the mother of our example pressed her son, "Then you, then what did you do?" and the boy replied, "I think cried."

The whole idea of Chinese opportunity education is to use the infraction as an opportunity for the education, making the child's association between infraction and shamefulness as immediate and unmistakable as possible. Even when this practice seems to dwell exceedingly upon current and past transgressions, it does so in the interests of self-correction, so that the children will learn from their misdeeds and will do better in the future (Miller et al., 2001: 167). Inuit teasing takes a quite different tack. Rather than exploiting a child's infractions as these occur, teasing games intentionally provoke or seduce the child into missteps—for example, wanting what she can't have, expressing antisocial feelings toward people, thinking of herself as perfect, acting babyish—so that these missteps can then serve as object lessons. By stark contrast to the Taiwanese case, too, these lessons themselves are often indirect and ambiguous, and deliberately so. Briggs (1998: 64) tells us, "clarity for the children is not an immediate aim of the adult players." Indeed, a meta-

message of the play is about the uncertainty inherent in social relationships—
that "no communication can ever be trusted to be what it seems to be"
(Briggs, 1998: 67). The pedagogic tenet of this cultural model of child rearing
is *isummaksaiyuq*, or "causing someone to think" (Briggs, 1998: 5/66) about
the possible consequences of a hypothetical dilemma.

Yet, in the course of these lessons, the Inuit child, too, receives dramatically clear signals of adult approval or disapproval. Remember how Chubby
Maata's grandmother tells her that her "horrid little genitals" stink, as a
means of getting across to her that she is not the perfect little child that she
may have thought she was—the darling little baby (*babykuluk)* that, up until
now, she has been encouraged to think of herself as. Oblique as this met-
onymic lesson may be, as puzzled as it may leave Chubby Maata as to why
she is suddenly and unexpectedly being disapproved, it is powerfully disapproving. Other lessons are phrased as tests—comments, questions, or requests that, depending on the child's response, may lead to criticism (Briggs,
1998: 76). For example, one common test of the child's ability to be even-
handedly pro-social—along with protective, loving nurturance, another important Inuit value—is the recurrent game of "Who do you like (*piugi-*; literally, consider good)?" We saw her uncle Juupi initiate this game with Chubby
Maata. On another occasion,

> Arnaqjuaq [Chubby Maata's grandmother] bent down and said to Chubby Maa-
> ta, "Do you like (*puigi-*) her [referring to the anthropologist]?" Chubby Maata
> wrinkled her nose: "No." Arnaqjuaq double-checked: "Do you dislike her?"
> Chubby Maata raised her brows, confirming that she did. Arnaqjuak persisted,
> "Do you dislike *me*?" Chubby Maata wrinkled her nose, and Arnaqjuaq
> laughed: "How little understanding she has (she is *silait-*)! Do you dislike Aita
> [Chubby Maata's infant sister, also present]? Chubby Maata wrinkled her nose.
> Arnaqjuaq laughed again and repeated, "Silait-!"

> I asked Chubby Maata, "Am I the only one (you don't like)?" I didn't see her
> answer, but Arnaqjuaq said to me, "She's silait- (she has no understanding).
> Sometimes she likes (*piusaq-*) and sometimes she can't at all (Briggs, 1998: 124).

Another gambit, the daily, "Because you're a baby," "Are you a baby?" and
"Say '*ungaa*'" (make the cry of a baby), plays with the two sides of baby-
hood, teaching the child that, as much as she is loved and celebrated for her
adorable babyish charm, she is increasingly disapproved for mindless babyish lack of understanding (and approved for ways in which she demonstrates
she has outgrown this babyishness). This criticism, like others, may be explicitly labeled, as when Chubby Maata is called a "foolish little baby" (*si-
lait-*)—usually ambiguously, though, because spoken in the same tender tone
as she is other times called a "darling little baby" (-*kuluk*). Or, the criticism
may be unlabeled, but just as clearly marked—as when, tested by a game her
mother instigates to see whether she can be seduced into serious aggression,
Chubby Maata is made to look foolish and laughed at when she does aggress

against her sister (Briggs, 1998: 70). As different as the Inuit style of teaching children is from the Chinese, both exhibit the universal strategy of recruiting adult approval and disapproval to the task of making children's lessons motivating and memorable.

THE RESULT: CULTURAL SELVES

Thus, across these various ethnographic examples—American, Chinese, German, Gusii, Ifaluk, Inuit—we begin to see how cultural models of child rearing, so variable in the substance of what they teach, are all equally designed to make the child's experience of those important lessons constant, to link those lessons to emotional arousal, and to connect them to evaluations of the child's goodness and badness. My argument has been that these three universal practices are all adaptations to the specialized task of child rearing. And that their effectiveness in accomplishing this task owes itself to neural processes. Constancy of experience alters synaptic connections to accord the pattern of their firing especially highly resolution, so that the lessons to be learned are unmistakable ones. Accompanied by emotional arousal, these lessons are especially motivating and especially unforgettable. Brought home with evaluations of the learner's goodness and badness, these lessons are even more motivating and even more unforgettable. Child rearing must insure that children get the point of the lesson, enact it once they get it, remember it, and continue to be motivated to enact it. Cultural models of child rearing have evolved to suit this task. These models exploit the neural capacities of the children so reared, to achieve a result, human adulthood, that could not have been accomplished by human brain power alone.

At long last I am in a position to address the matter of cultural selves. I hope that these anthropologists' findings about child rearing will have pointed, already, to the intrinsic cultural-ness of selfhood. What results, as a side effect of the experiential constancy and emotional arousal and evaluative messages that characterize the way children are everywhere reared, is a lifelong, culturally distinctive self, one shared with others who have been raised according to the same cultural model. Not only are you your synapses, as LeDoux (2002: 324) puts it, but you are the cultural shape of these synaptic connections. Most profoundly, you are who your synaptic connections have been engineered to be, from infancy onward.

The cultural selves that emerge from exposure to these practices have two sides. To the degree, and it is a substantial degree, that cultural practices engineer the child's learning of important lessons while leaving these lessons unmarked, the culturally patterned selves that result do not become the objects of conscious self-reflection. They are, rather, what LeDoux (2002: 27–29) has called "implicit" selves. (It often takes foreigners to notice, and celebrate—or, more often, disparage—these culturally distinctive selves, so invisible are they to those who so unthinkingly and effortlessly enact them.) Even one's enduring sense of oneself as a good or a bad person, emerging from cumulative unmarked experiences of being loved or unloved, approved or disapproved, need not be well-articulated or readily accessible for examination.

Yet, we also do come to have explicit ideas about who we are—selves that are based, in part at least, on conscious self-reflection. It should now be obvious how this explicit cultural self arises. It arises because rearers do tend to mark approved and disapproved behaviors for didactic purposes. Labeling and otherwise explicitly marking the goodness or badness of one's acts, and—generalized as character traits or simply repeated over and over again— of oneself as an actor, have the effect of crystallizing a conscious, self-reflective sense of oneself. The actual process by which this explicit knowledge of oneself as a moral actor is internalized is nowhere better captured than in a brief episode in Chubby Maata's 3-year-old life. The little girl, having just been mildly scolded by her mother,

> … began to chant, over and over again in a happy-sounding singsong, "Because I'm not gooood; I'm not gooood."

> Liila [her mother] cooed at her little daughter, tenderly, "Because you're not a baby?" Chubby Maata raised her brows, agreeing that she was not a baby, but her mother nevertheless snuffed her warmly and in the same tender voice assured her, "You're a darling little good one."

> Chubby Maata began to chant again, "I am gooood, I am not gooood, I am gooood, I am not gooood." (Briggs, 1998: 143).

Similarly, other children elsewhere must rehearse to themselves, I have (or have not) been appropriately fearful (*metagu*); I was (or was not) a disobedient child (*bu guai de xiaohaizi*); I was a good girl (or a bad girl) today. To be sure, it is hard to imagine any better window into this learning by rehearsal, than that opened by the Inuit adults' penchant for making moral lessons ambiguous, Inuit children's habit of chanting these ambiguous moral lessons aloud, and Briggs's close description of both.

These explicit ideas about ourselves lay the basis for what becomes, over time and repeated experience of the same kind, a more or less stable, more or less coherent, more or less context-independent element of one's identity: the knowledge that I am this or that kind of person. Because of the way it is learned, through approval and disapproval, this identity is infused with evaluative meaning. We not only grow up to be the kind of adult that our rearers want us to be, and so assiduously raise us to be; we ourselves come to desire to be those kinds of people. We may always crave others' praise, or fear ghosts or chickens, or feel acutely uncomfortable under another's direct gaze. Much more generally, we come to want to be self-actualizing, successful Americans; self-contained, self-reliant Germans; Gusii who are morally superior because emotionally restrained; Chinese who, knowing shame, follow the path of right conduct; Ifaluk Islanders who, hyper-aware of their own potential for wrongdoing, are calm and nonagressive; and watchful, vigilant Inuit who take care to be lovingly nurturant to everyone.

NOTES

1. To appreciate the critical role of experience in shaping self, we can imagine what it would be like if experience were random. A self emerging from the brain's processes of plasticity, synthesis, connection, communication, and integration would be pure noise. Of course, this is ridiculous, for neural plasticity evolved for precisely the purpose of processing the patterns that do arise in experience. Life experiences are far from random.

2. To a considerable degree, cultural models for child rearing evolve to match given political-economic contexts. Children in foraging communities are raised to be self-reliant; children in farming and herding communities are raised to be responsible. Boys in communities that formerly practiced endemic warfare were raised to be hyper-masculine and aggressive. Children brought up by peoples living on small, densely populated islands are raised to be peaceable. Where joint labor is necessary for household, clan, or community survival children will be raised to be cooperative. Children in societies where hierarchy is stressed are raised to be respectful and obedient. Where the environment children confront is dangerous, they will be raised restrictively. And so forth. At the same time, there is room for much cultural elaboration of child rearing, and cultural ideas about the kind of adults that child rearers hope to raise come to have a force of their own.

3. While I am arguing that child rearing achieves constancy by the pervasiveness and persistence of habitual means, there can be a more deliberate dimension to the creation of constancy that deserves mention. Child rearers sometimes contrive to focus attention, directing and motivating the learner to think about what is being taught and isolating the learner from distraction, so that what is being taught will in fact be attended to and hence experienced. An example of such attention focusing is provided later in this paper by the case of Inuit adults who, teasing a child, stare at her intently, remove her hands from her face, and repeat their questions multiple times until she gives evidence of having received their message. In this instance, the child is actively trying to resist the lesson; in other cases there may be surrounding distractions that compete for the child's attention. Schools, Western and non-Western, represent perhaps the most formally elaborated of techniques for focusing attention. Relatedly, socializers often lead a child in repeated practice of what they are being taught, intervening to guide and correct this practice when deemed necessary. Practicing is likely to be used when tasks require children to learn new skills or put knowledge together in newly complex ways. A different form of practicing, rehearsal, is used when the child's task is to commit a reasonably large body of knowledge to memory. (See Strauss, 1984: 209–216, for a useful discussion of attention focusing and rehearsal as educational strategies cross-culturally.) Incidentally to their main purposes, attention-

focusing, practicing, and rehearsal all contribute to the constancy of the child's experience. In this paper I stress child-rearing practices that are much more pervasive, and hence contribute much more massively to the constancy of the child's experience, and hence have much more influence on the resulting cultural self.

4. Once, in the middle of the last century, a theoretical school called personality and culture dominated American psychological anthropology. Its practitioners entertained the proposition that the child-training practices of a group shaped adult personality. By the 1960s the school was on the wane. Under continued attack for its functionalist, determinist, and over-simple formulation of the relation between culture, personality, and social structure, and eclipsed by one of the inevitable swings of fashion that have characterized cultural anthropology then and since, the field retreated. Influenced during the same period by behaviorism in psychology and by behavioral primatology, practitioners turned away from grand theory to meticulous descriptive research. The cross-cultural study of child development entered a period characterized by careful, systematic, methodologically sophisticated description of children's lives and, especially, social behavior. As Harkness (1992: 109) has observed, culture was relegated "to a residual category of background variables, and divested of its function as an analytic construct." Even studies beginning to explore "parental ethnotheories" at first focused on discrete practices, such as sleeping or eating routines, level of infant arousal, or children's domestic chores. Gradually, now, interest is expanding to encompass the extent to which human development is enmeshed in larger cultural meaning. It is interesting to note how many of those anthropologists producing the new, meaning-oriented, studies of child development cross-culturally, including those on whose work I have drawn in this paper, are direct or indirect first- or second-generation heirs to the culture and personality tradition.

5. Of those on which I will draw, Lutz's (1988) study is intent on highlighting the cultural constructedness of emotion, and, in particular, showing that Ifaluk Islanders' ethnotheory of the person does not separate the emotional, as does our American ethnotheory, from the cognitive, moral, and social dimensions of personhood. LeVine and his colleagues (1994) use the Gusii case to argue that each system of child rearing must be understood and valued in its own terms, and in terms of the socioeconomic circumstances to which it is adapted—the Gusii model being a "pediatric" one in contrast to our own American "pedagogic" model. Miller and her colleagues (Miller et al., 1996; Fung, 1999; Miller et al., 2001) aim to show, in their work, how Taiwanese middle-class parents' shaming of their children, in co-narrated stories of the children's misbehavior, must be understood in the context of a larger theory of child rearing as "opportunity education," and in contrast to co-narrations by middle-class Chicagoans, whose different concern is to protect their children's self-esteem. Brigg's (1998) study shows how one child is taught, and internalizes, subtle but emotionally powerful interpersonal lessons distinctive to Inuit culture. LeVine and Norman (2001) draw on Norman's south German fieldwork to critique attachment theory—once again interpreting and valuing south German child-rearing practices in their own terms, and resisting their definition in terms of insecure attachment. Finally, Kusserow's (1996) study

demonstrates that there are decidedly different, class-based versions of American "individualism," and shows how these are reproduced within the family and the neighborhood preschool. Of course, these sentence-long descriptions do not begin to do justice to this body of work.

6. The infant seat was used, apparently, to make this experiment comparable to one done with American mothers in Boston. But it must have felt as strange to the Gusii mothers as the experimental instructions that followed, since Gusii mothers carry their babies against their bodies, rather than, as do middle-class American parents, putting them in devices specially designed for infant containment.

7. The traffic light stories continued to be a topic of conversation and, the next day, another German contributed the following true story that had happened to a friend of hers a few days earlier. Biking across the street against the light, he heard a shout behind him. He turned and went back, to be berated by an older gentleman with a dog. "Can't you see," said the man, "that I'm trying to teach my dog to wait for the light."

8. It also suggests that one good way to get adults to follow a rule is to make them think they are doing so to set a good example for their children.

9. To say that the child rearing imposes temporal constancy on a child's experience is emphatically not to say that this experience is seamless and uninterrupted. While some child-rearing goals and strategies are continuous over long periods of time, experienced even into adolescence and adulthood, others, especially surrounding separation and socialization into adulthood, can be quite discontinuous. One has only to think of the transition, in many societies, between being a "lap child" and being a "yard child," that comes with the birth of the next sibling. I could see the trauma of that transition in the blank eyes and listless movements of toddlers wandering Mfantse courtyards. The point is rather, that, experience on either side of such a transition is highly regular—the way an infant is carried, nursed, otherwise attended to, responded to when he cries, spoken to, incorporated into the social scene, played with, ignored, and so forth; and the different way a toddler is fed, otherwise attended to, responded to, spoken to, incorporated into the social scene, ignored, taught, and so forth.

10. Sitting at an outdoor café in Hamburg, my American colleague and I were fascinated to watch three young women chatting through a leisurely lunch while the babies of two of them lay in baby carriages beside their table. We found it odd that the babies were faced away from the women, and in such a position that, for the longest time, we could not tell who were the respective mothers. The baby facing us, just visible over the end of the carriage, was awake, her eyes open but inwardly focused, and rocking herself vigorously enough so that the whole carriage swayed forward and backward. Finally, after fifteen or twenty minutes—long after our American-calibrated clocks began telling the two Americans at the next table that it was time to pay some attention to the baby—the mother got up to briefly check on her child, gave the carriage a peremptory rock, entertained the child with a few shakes of a piece of clothing, and returned to her lunch companions. Of course, Americans follow Germans in valuing and teaching self-reliance. Middle-class Americans do tend to put their infants to sleep in separate rooms, for instance, for the stated rea-

son of teaching them independence (Morelli et al., 1992). But the middle-class goal of raising self-expressive children seems to have made inroads into the goal of raising self-reliant ones, dictating an active cultivation of engagement with the child that, as I and my colleague concluded from our lunchtime observations, is surely extreme, by cross-cultural standards, in its frequency and intensity. LeVine and Norman (2001: 98–101) provide a brief history of how American child rearing has moved away, since the 1950s, from an emphasis on babies playing alone and controlling themselves.

11. Difficulties may surround the employment of nannies from a different class, or *au pairs* from other countries, just because these surrogate caretakers do not share the parents' child-rearing values and strategies.

12. Ethnographies of horticultural societies are full of accounts of male initiation rites, which serve to reverse boy's early feminine identification and establish their masculinity. These rites, which typically occur around early adolescence, are notable for their fear-inducing practices, such as circumcision, isolation, and tests of bravery. Presumably, the arousal of fear reinforces the reversal of gender identity.

13. Daniel Fessler (1999) has argued that the emotion shame has its primitive roots in the quest for rank in hominid and early human societies, and was later recruited for social control, to enforce conformity to group expectations.

REFERENCES

BRIGGS, J.L. (1998). *Inuit morality play: The emotional education of a three-year-old.* New Haven: Yale University Press.

CLARK, A. (1997). *Being there: Putting brain, body, and world together again.* Cambridge, MA: MIT Press.

FESSLER, D. (1999). Toward an understanding of the universality of second-order emotions. In A. Hinton (Ed.), *Biocultural approaches to the emotions* (pp. 75–116). Cambridge, England: Cambridge University Press.

FUNG, H. (1999). Becoming a moral child: the socialization of shame among young Chinese children. *Ethos, 27(2),* 180–209.

FUNG, H. & E.C-H. CHEN (2001). Across time and beyond skin: self and transgression in the everyday socialization of shame among Taiwanese preschool children. *Social Development, 10(3),* 420–437.

HARKNESS, S. (1992). Human development in psychological anthropology. In T. Schwartz, G.M. White & C. A. Lutz, (Eds.), *New directions in psychological anthropology* (pp. 102–122). Cambridge, England: Cambridge University Press.

KUSSEROW, A. (1996). *Reconsidering American individualism: Culture, class and the social construction of the self.* Ph.D. dissertation, Harvard University, Cambridge, MA.

LEDOUX, J. (2002). *Synaptic self: How our brains become who we are.* New York: Viking.

LEVINE, R.A., S. DIXON, S. LEVINE, A. RICHMAN, P.H. LEIDERMAN, C.H. KEEFER, & T.B. BRAZELTON (1994). *Child care and culture: Lessons from Africa.* Cambridge, England: Cambridge University Press.

LEVINE, R.A. & K. NORMAN (2001). The infant's acquisition of culture: early attachment reexamined in anthropological perspective. In C.C. Moore and H.

F. Mathews (Eds.), *The psychology of cultural experience* (pp. 83–104). Cambridge, England: Cambridge University Press.

LUTZ, C.A. (1983). Parental goals, ethnopsychology, and the development of emotional meaning. *Ethos, 11(4),* 246–262.

LUTZ, C.A. (1987). Goals, events and understanding in Ifaluk emotion theory. In D. Holland & N. Quinn (Eds.), *Cultural models in language and thought* (pp. 290–312). Cambridge, England: Cambridge University Press.

LUTZ, C.A. (1988). *Unnatural emotions: Everyday sentiments on a Micronesian atoll and their challenge to Western theory.* Chicago: University of Chicago Press.

MILLER, P.J., H. FUNG & J. MINTZ (1996). Self-construction through narrative practices: a Chinese and American comparison of early socialization. *Ethos, 24(2),* 237–280.

MILLER, P. J., T. L. SANDEL, C-H. LIANG, & H. FUNG (2001). Narrating transgressions in Longwood. *Ethos, 29(2),* 159–186.

MILLER, P.J., A.R. WILEY, H. FUNG & C-H. LIANG (1997). Personal storytelling as a medium of socialization in Chinese and American families. *Child Development, 68(3),* 557–568.

MORELLI, G.A., B. ROGOFF, D. OPPENHEIM & D. GOLDSMITH (1992). Cultural variation in infants' sleeping arrangements: questions of independence. *Developmental Psychology, 28,* 604–613.

RUMELHART, D.E., P. SMOLENSKY, J.L. MCCLELLAND & G.E. HINTON (1986). Schemata and sequential thought processes in PDP models. In J. L. McClelland, D. E. Rumelhart & the PDP Research Group (Eds.), *Parallel distributed processing: Explorations in the microstructure of cognition, Vol. 2: Psychological and biological models* (pp. 7–57). Cambridge, MA: MIT Press.

STRAUSS, C. (1984). Beyond "formal" versus "informal" education: uses of psychological theory in anthropological research. *Ethos 12(3),* 195–222.

STRAUSS, C. & N. QUINN (1997). *A cognitive theory of cultural meaning.* Cambridge, England: Cambridge University Press.

TOBIN, J. L., D. Y. H. WU, & D. H. DAVIDSON (1989). *Preschool in three cultures: Japan, China, and the United States.* New Haven, CT: Yale University Press.

Implicit Self and Identity

THIERRY DEVOS[a] AND MAHZARIN R. BANAJI[b]

[a]Department of Psychology, San Diego State University,
San Diego, California 92182, USA

[b]Department of Psychology, Harvard University,
Cambridge, Massachusetts 02138, USA

ABSTRACT: Recent advances in research on implicit social cognition offer an opportunity to challenge common assumptions about self and identity. In the present article, we critically review a burgeoning line of research on self-related processes known to occur outside conscious awareness or conscious control. Our discussion focuses on these implicit self-related processes as they unfold in the context of social group memberships. That is, we show that group memberships can shape thoughts, preferences, motives, goals, or behaviors without the actor's being aware of such an influence or having control over such expressions. As such, this research brings to the fore facets of the self that often contrast with experiences of reflexive consciousness and introspection. Far from being rigid or monolithic, these processes are highly flexible, context-sensitive, and deeply rooted in socio-structural realities. As such, work on implicit self and identity renew thinking about the interplay between the individual and the collective.

KEYWORDS: self; identity; social cognition; implicit; unconscious; automatic; intergroup; bias; social groups; self-esteem; self-evaluation

When William James (1890) wrote about the unique problem of studying self and identity, he immediately noted the peculiar blurring of the otherwise clear demarcation between the *knower* and the *known*. The object of scrutiny, the self, was also the agent doing the scrutinizing. This illicit merger of the knower and the known has created an epistemological unease that philosophers have worried about and psychologists have either ignored or turned into

This article was first published in 2003 in the *Handbook of Self and Identity* (pp. 153–175), edited by M.R. Leary and J.P. Tangney, and published by the Guilford Press, by whose permission it is reprinted here.

Address for correspondence: Mahzarin R. Banaji, Department of Psychology, Harvard University, Cambridge, MA 02138. Voice: 617-384-9203; fax: 617-495-3728.

banaji@fas.harvard.edu

Ann. N.Y. Acad. Sci. 1001: 177–211 (2003). © 2003 New York Academy of Sciences.
doi: 10.1196/annals.1279.009

an assumption of their theorizing. The human ability for self-awareness and self-reflection is so unique that tapping it as a vital source of information about mind and social behavior has come at the expense of confronting the severe problems of the knower also being the known and of using introspection as the primary path to discovery. In this article, we argue that at least one circumstance can disentangle the knower from the known in the study of self: when self-as-knower does not have full introspective access to self-as-known. When knowledge about oneself resides in a form that is inaccessible to consciousness but can indeed be tapped indirectly, the self-as-knower and the self-as-known can be dissociated in a manner that is epistemologically more pleasing. In this article, we focus on states of unconscious thought and feeling—those marked by a lack of conscious awareness, control, intention, and self-reflection.

Over the past two decades, the study of implicit social cognition has created new paradigms for studying several traditional fields (for reviews, see Banaji, Lemm & Carpenter, 2001; Greenwald & Banaji, 1995; Wegner & Bargh, 1998). At first sight, this trend, it would seem, has little to say about the topic of self and identity. Indeed, it is a common assumption that the studies of self centrally involve experiences of reflexive consciousness (Baumeister, 1998). Individuals reflect on their experiences, self-consciously evaluate the contents of consciousness, and introspect about the causes and meaning of things. In addition, the self is often viewed as playing a consciously active role in making meaning, implementing choices, pursuing goals, and initiating action. Studies that focus on unconscious modes of thinking and feeling, when applied to self and identity processes, question these assumptions, and they do so based on the discovery of mental acts that are fully meaningful and lawful, but that appear to arise without introspective access or deliberative thought.

In this article, we provide an overview of research on the implicit social cognition of self and identity. No attempt is made to exhaustively review the literature at hand. Rather, we focus on reflections of self and identity in a particular social context—the context in which thoughts and feelings about oneself are shaped by membership in a larger collective and in which such thoughts and feelings go beyond the self as target to represent and shape a view of the collective (Banaji & Prentice, 1994; Walsh & Banaji, 1997). Such a focus places us in the respectable company of others who also assume or demonstrate that the individual self is meaningfully considered in reference to social entities that transcend the individual self (Cooley, 1902; Mead, 1934; Turner, Oakes, Haslam & McGarty, 1994). Our unique position limits the coverage to aspects of the self that emerge when (1) viewed in the context of social group memberships and (2) measured via unconscious expressions of thought and feeling. We begin with research paradigms that link the study of self with social group and proceed to specific analyses of basic preference for the ingroup and other attributes associated with the self. We then include analyses of implicit self and identity processes as viewed in research on self-evaluation, performance and behavior, and goal pursuit. In the next major section we attend to the top-down influence of societal and cultural influences on the construction of implicit self and identity. Together, the research we review reveals the plasticity of the self as it develops and exists in close response to the demands of social group and culture.

The term "implicit" is used to refer to processes that occur outside conscious awareness. Evaluations of one's self, for example, may be influenced by group membership, even though the individual is not aware of such an influence. An Asian woman may come to view herself as excelling in math when her ethnic identity is implicitly brought to the foreground but as weak in math skills when her gender is highlighted (see Shih, Pittinsky & Ambady, 1999, for a demonstration of such group membership effects on math performance). There are multiple ways in which one may be unaware of the source of influence on thoughts, feelings, and behavior. For example, one may be unaware of the existence of the source of influence, whereas in other circumstances one may consciously and accurately perceive the source of influence while being unaware of its causative role in self-evaluation. The term "implicit" is also applied to those processes that occur without conscious control. Here, the circumstances are such that one may be perfectly aware of the contingencies that connect a particular stimulus to a response but be unable to change or reverse the direction of the thought, feeling, or action. A person may have a view of herself as egalitarian but find herself unable to control prejudicial thoughts about members of a group, perhaps including groups of which she is herself a member. Although empirical investigations focus on one or another of these aspects of unconscious social cognition, as well as on those that select intention and self-reflection, we use the term "implicit" here to encompass both processes that occur without conscious awareness and those that occur without conscious control.

SELF AND SOCIAL GROUP

Since at least the 1970s, self-concept has been profitably studied by representing it as an information structure with empirically tractable cognitive and affective features (for reviews, see Greenwald & Pratkanis, 1984; Kihlstrom & Cantor, 1984; Kihlstrom et al., 1988). From such a theoretical vantage point came the idea that the self concept, like other representations, could be viewed as possibly operating in automatic mode and that aspects of self may be hidden from introspective awareness (e.g., Bargh, 1982; Bargh & Tota, 1988; Higgins, Van Hook & Dorfman, 1988; Markus, 1971; Rogers, Kuiper & Kirker, 1977; Strauman & Higgins, 1987).

Although strongly social in focus, research in the American social cognition tradition, focused on the interpersonal aspects of self and identity, whereas another tradition with European roots emphasized the association between self and social group, resulting in an intergroup emphasis. The latter's most articulate and encompassing formulation, labeled self-categorization theory (Turner 1985; Turner, Hogg, Oakes, Reicher & Wetherell, 1987), holds that, under particular conditions, group members perceive themselves as exemplars of the group rather than as unique individuals. In this mode, they highlight the similarities between themselves and other ingroup members, and they apply characteristics typical of the ingroup to the self (self-stereotyping). In other words, the representations of self and ingroup become inextricably linked. Until recently tests of this hypothesis mainly involved self-report measures (Biernat, Vescio & Green, 1996; Hogg & Turner; 1987; Simon & Hamilton, 1994; Simon, Pantaleo & Mummendey, 1995). However, several empirical investigations have revealed that the process by which the ingroup may be said to become part and parcel of the self can operate at an implicit level.

Adapting a paradigm developed by Aron, Aron, Tudor, and Nelson (1991), Smith and Henry (1996) examined people's psychological ties to significant ingroups. Participants were asked to rate themselves, their ingroup, and an outgroup on a list of traits. Next, they indicated, as quickly and accurately as possible whether each trait was self-descriptive or not. Self-descriptiveness judgments were faster for traits on which participants matched their ingroup than for traits on which they mismatched. On the contrary, no such facilitation was observed for traits rated as matching or mismatching the outgroup. This finding has been taken to illustrate that the ingroup becomes part of the representation of self, and a follow-up study (Smith, Coats & Walling, 1999) demonstrated that the reverse was also true. Characteristics of the self influenced evaluations of the ingroup. Using a similar procedure, Smith and colleagues (1999) found that participants were faster to make ingroup descriptiveness judgments for traits that matched their self-perceptions. As another example, fraternity or sorority members are faster to make liking judgments for attitude objects (e.g., parties, tattoos, science, beer) on which they match the ingroup rather than on those on which there is a mismatch with the ingroup (Coats, Smith, Claypool & Banner, 2000). Together, these results support the idea of a mental fusion of the self and social group.

The Implicit Association Test (IAT; Greenwald, McGhee & Schwartz, 1998) is a technique developed to assess the strength of implicit associations between concepts (e.g., self, group) and attributes (e.g., evaluation of good–bad, specific traits). The assumption underlying the technique is that the more closely related a concept and an attribute are (e.g., ingroup and good, outgroup and bad), the more quickly information representing the concept and the attribute should be paired. For purposes of obtaining a baseline with which such pairings can be compared, the task includes a measure of response time to contrasting pairs that are made simultaneously (ingroup and bad, outgroup and good).[c]

Recent experiments have used this technique and variations of it to investigate the strength of self + group association, referring to this pairing as a measure of automatic identity with the social group. For example, Devos and Banaji (2003) used this procedure to capture the strength of implicit national identity among citizens of the United States. Participants were asked to categorize as quickly as possible, stimuli presented on a computer screen. Some stimuli were pictures of American or foreign symbols (e.g., flags, coins, maps, monuments), whereas other stimuli were pronouns frequently used to designate ingroups (e.g., "we," "ourselves") or outgroups (e.g., "they," "other"). Participants completed this task twice. In one case, American symbols were paired with words representing the ingroup (e.g., "we," "ourselves"), and foreign symbols were combined with words representing the outgroup (e.g., "they," "other"). In another case, American symbols were combined with outgroup words, and foreign symbols were paired with ingroup words. Results indicated that participants performed the categorization task more quickly when American symbols and ingroup words shared the same response key. In other words, it was easier to associate American symbols with items such as "we" or "ourselves" rather than with "they" or "other." American symbols may be seen here as automatically evoking belonging and implying that at least when unable to control their responses, this sample of Americans strongly identified with their national group.

Using the same technique, other empirical investigations have demonstrated strong implicit associations between self and attributes, roles, or domains stereotypical of gender categories. For instance, female participants could more easily associate idiographic information (e.g., their names, their hometowns) or pronouns such as "me" or "mine" with feminine traits (e.g., gentle, warm, tender) rather than with masculine attributes (e.g., competitive, independent, strong), whereas the opposite was true for male participants (Greenwald & Farnham, 2000; Lemm & Banaji, 1998). Similarly, strong automatic associations between self and the concept "math" for men, and the concept "arts" for women have been obtained repeatedly (Nosek, Banaji & Greenwald, 2002b). In addition, Lane, Mitchell, and Banaji (2001) have shown that implicit identification with a new ingroup could occur early on and without extensive contact with the group. As predicted, Yale students showed stronger implicit identity with Yale as an institution (rather than with Harvard), but strength of identity was equally strong among those who had been on campus for a few days and those who were starting their fourth and final year. Theories of implicit social cognition that assume slow learning (through long-term experience) need to explain the presence of such fast-to-form and fast-to-stabilize implicit identities.

---

[c]For a sample of such tasks, readers may visit implicit.harvard.edu/implicit or www.tolerance.org

The previous examples indicate that group membership comes to be automatically associated with self and that people automatically endorse attributes stereotypic of their group as also being self-descriptive. Recently von Hippel, Hawkins, and Schooler (2001) identified circumstances under which the opposite is true: Counterstereotypic attributes become strongly associated to the self. For example, African Americans were more likely to endorse the trait "intelligent" rapidly (i.e., to be schematic for this attribute) than white Americans if they performed well academically, and white Americans were more likely than African Americans to be schematic for "athletic" if they performed well in that domain. These findings are consistent with the idea that characteristics or features that make one distinctive from others are particularly likely to be represented in the self-concept (McGuire & McGuire, 1988). Both sets of seemingly opposing results may be explained by theories that emphasize the strong association between self and social group. In both cases one's knowledge or understanding of the association between group + attribute comes to influence implicit self-perception.

A PREFERENCE FOR INGROUPS

The links between self and ingroup are not only visible in implicit knowledge and thought, but also present in measures of attitude or evaluation. Tajfel (1974) emphasized this point when he defined "social identity as that part of an individual's self-concept which derives from his knowledge of his membership of a social group (or groups) together with the emotional significance attached to that membership" (p. 69). A growing body of research shows that people evaluate ingroup members more favorably than outgroup members (Brewer, 1979; Mullen, Brown & Smith, 1992), and we examine those studies that used measure of implicit attitude or evaluation. The literature on implicit attitudes clearly suggests that groups unconsciously or automatically trigger more positive affective reactions when they are associated to self. Assessments of ethnic attitudes without perceivers' awareness or control consistently reveal that white Americans have more positive feelings toward white Americans than toward African Americans (Dasgupta, McGhee, Greenwald & Banaji, 2000; Fazio, Jackson, Dunton & Williams, 1995; Greenwald et al., 1998; Wittenbrink, Judd & Park, 1997). Likewise, members of other groups also show implicit preference for the ingroup (Japanese Americans vs. Korean Americans; Greenwald et al., 1998), and findings such as these are expected to be obtained with a wide variety of groups (affiliations with nation, state, and city, with school and sports team, with family and friends). Some studies indicate that implicit intergroup biases in the realm of ethnic relations include both ingroup favoritism (positivity toward white Americans) and outgroup derogation (negativity toward black

Americans) (Dovidio, Evans & Tyler, 1986; Nosek & Banaji, 2001), whereas others suggest that individuals no longer differentially ascribe negative characteristics to ethnic groups but continue to associate positive attributes to a greater extent to whites than to blacks (Gaertner & McLaughlin, 1983). Research also shows that undergraduate students hold a more favorable attitude toward the category "young" than toward the category "old" (Nosek, Banaji & Greenwald, 2002; Perdue & Gurtman, 1990; Rudman, Greenwald, Mellott & Schwartz, 1999). Strong implicit preferences for American symbols have been revealed in several studies (Ashburn-Nardo, Voils & Monteith, 2001; Devos & Banaji, 2003; Rudman et al., 1999). To this list of implicit ingroup preference we add findings that show implicit positive attitudes toward groups based on sexual orientation (Lemm & Banaji, 2000) or social class (Cunningham, Nezlek & Banaji, 2001). In fact, Cunningham and colleagues (2001) have shown implicit positive associations to the category white (rather than black), rich (rather than poor), American (rather than foreign), straight (rather than gay), and Christian (rather than Jewish) among students known to be white, American, and Christian, a majority of whom were assumed to be high on the social class dimension and to be heterosexual. Cunningham and colleagues have taken the extra step of claiming that these implicit preferences do not develop in isolation and that an individual difference marks the pattern: Those who show higher preference for one ingroup also show higher preference for all other ingroups, which is evidence for an implicit ethnocentrism dimension.

In most of the research described, researchers have assessed the implicit attitudes of only people belonging to one particular group. That is, white participants have been shown to have greater implicit liking for whites over blacks, but equivalent data from black participants have not always been available. Of the few studies that do measure both sides, symmetry has been found under some circumstances. Greenwald and colleagues (1998) reported data from both Japanese Americans and Korean Americans, each of whom showed a more positive implicit attitude toward their own ethnic group. The level of immersion in Asian culture moderated this pattern of implicit preferences. More precisely, participants who were immersed in their particular Asian culture (i.e., had a high proportion of family members and acquaintances who were from that culture and were familiar with the language) showed greater ingroup preference. Depending on their religious affiliation, individuals exhibit an implicit preference for Christian or Jewish people (Rudman et al., 1999). The relations between Bavarians and North Germans have also shown strong implicit ingroup bias (Neumann et al., 1998).

Using linguistic patterns to indicate intergroup bias, Maass, Salvi, Arcuri, and Semin (1989) revealed another interesting form of implicit ingroup favoritism. They show that individuals usually described positive behaviors in more abstract language terms ("X is helpful") when performed by an ingroup member than when performed by an outgroup member ("X gave them directions to go to the station"). The opposite held for negative behaviors (see also Karpinski & von Hippel, 1996; von Hippel, Sekaquaptewa & Vargas, 1997). This linguistic bias does not appear to be under volitional control (Franco & Maas, 1996). Recent research indicates that participants from Belgium and Spain automatically attributed secondary emotions, such as affection, pride, and remorse, more to ingroups than to outgroups (Leyens et al., 2000). Given that such secondary emotions are also seen to be uniquely human characteristics, this finding is consistent with the idea that ingroups are viewed as being more human than outgroups.

The tendency to favor the ingroup attitudinally (e.g., along a good–bad dimension) sometimes underlies implicit stereotyping (e.g., the assignment of specific qualities that may also vary in evaluation). For example, both men and women hold similar implicit gender stereotypes, but they are exhibited to a stronger extent when they reflect favorably on their own group (Rudman, Greenwald & McGhee, 2001). Male participants are more likely to differentiate men and women with respect to an attribute such as "power," whereas female participants are more likely to do so on a trait such as "warmth." In other words, each group emphasizes stereotypes in an ingroup-favorable direction. These findings parallel observations based on self-report measures as well (Lindeman & Sundvik, 1995; Peabody, 1968).

Using measures of consciously accessible cognition, the ingroup bias has been shown to emerge under minimal conditions: The mere categorization of individuals into two distinct groups elicits a preference for the ingroup (Diehl, 1990; Tajfel, Billig, Bundy & Flament, 1971). There is now evidence that a minimal social categorization is sufficient to automatically or unconsciously activate positive attitudes toward self-related groups and negative or neutral attitudes toward non-self-related groups. For example, Perdue, Dovidio, Gurtman, and Tyler (1990) found that participants responded faster to pleasant words when primed with ingroup pronouns (such as "we" or "us") rather than with outgroup pronouns (such as "they" or "them"), even though they were unaware of the group-designating primes. Thus the use of words referring to ingroups or outgroups might unconsciously perpetuate intergroup biases. More recently, Otten and Wentura (1999) showed that neutral words automatically acquired an affective connotation simply by introducing them as group labels and by relating one of them to participants' self-concepts. The self-related group label functioned equivalently to *a priori* positive primes, whereas the other label functioned similarly to *a priori* negative primes. In other words, as soon as a word designated an ingroup, it acquired a positive connotation, whereas words referring to an outgroup immediately conveyed a negative valence. Using a different procedure, Otten and Moskowitz (2000) also found evidence for implicit activation of positive affect toward novel ingroups. A minimal intergroup setting was combined with a well-established procedure measuring spontaneous trait inferences (Uleman, Hon, Roman & Moskowitz, 1996). Results showed that when behaviors implied a positive trait about the ingroup, they were more likely to be categorized in a manner consistent with the implied trait than when the behaviors were performed by an outgroup member or when the traits implied were negative. These experiments suggest that the ingroup bias occurs automatically or unconsciously under minimal conditions (see also Ashburn-Nardo et al., 2001).

PREFERENCES FOR SELF EXTEND TO ATTRIBUTES ASSOCIATED WITH SELF

These findings are reminiscent of research showing that the mere ownership of an object or its association to the self is a condition sufficient enough to enhance its attractiveness. Nuttin (1985) found that when individuals were asked to choose a preferred letter from each of several pairs consisting of one alphabetical letter from their names and one not, they tended reliably to prefer alphabets that constitute their names. This finding, known as the "name letter effect" (NLE), has been replicated in many countries (Nuttin, 1987) and with samples from very different cultures (Hoorens, Nuttin, Herman & Pavakanun, 1990; Kitayama & Karasawa, 1997). In addition, the preference for name letters has been shown to be stable over a 4-week period (Koble, Dijksterhuis & van Knippenberg, 2001).

In order to test whether the preference for name letters depended on a conscious decision, Nuttin (1985) invited participants to search for a meaningful pattern in the pairs of letters presented. Despite the fact that no time limit was imposed and that a monetary award was promised to anyone who could correctly identify the prearranged pattern of letters, not a single participant could come up with the solution. This finding supports the idea that the NLE does not stem from a conscious recognition of the connection between the attribute and one's self. Several alternative interpretations of the effect have been ruled out. For instance, the NLE does not seem to be a remainder of the positive mastery affect most people experienced when they first succeeded in reading or writing their own names (Hoorens & Todorova, 1988; Hoorens et al., 1990). In addition, the NLE does not appear to be due to an enhanced subjective frequency of own name letters as compared with non-name letters (Hoorens & Nuttin, 1993). The most convincing interpretation of this effect at present is that preference for letters in one's name reflects an unconscious preference for self, and its generality is shown through research on preference for other similar self-related information, such as birthdates over other numbers (Kitayama & Karasawa, 1997; Koole et al., 2001). Finch and Cialdini (1989) showed that this effect extended to greater liking for otherwise undesirable characters (e.g., Rasputin), and Prentice and Miller (1992) showed that sharing a birthday with another person led participants to be more cooperative in a competitive situation. Recently, Pelham, Mirenberg, and Jones (2002) have shown that the extent of implicit positive evaluation of self influences where people choose to live and what people choose to do for a living. Across a dozen studies, they found that people are more likely to live in cities or states and to choose careers whose names share letters with their own first or last names. For example, a person named Louis is disproportionately likely to live in St. Louis, and individuals named Dennis or Denise are overrepresented among dentists. If corroborated with continued evidence of such relationships, these findings suggest that personal choices may be constrained by linkage to self that is not noticed, not consciously sought, and even surprising. Interesting as such research is in suggesting automatic attitude preference for self, the studies are quasi-experimental in that name letters and birth dates are not manipulated variables. Feys (1991) has provided experimental evidence for the idea that mere ownership of an object is a sufficient condition to enhance its attractiveness. Participants first learned to discriminate four computer-displayed graphic icons (which represented the participant in a computerized game) from four others that represented the participant's opponent (the computer). When participants subsequently judged all eight patterns for aesthetic attractiveness, the self-associated patterns received higher ratings. Thus individuals evaluated an object more favorably simply from the act of owning it (see also Beggan, 1992). Objects attached to the self are immediately endowed with increased value. These findings, along with the classic attitude-similarity effect, were interpretable as implicit self-esteem effects (Greenwald & Banaji, 1995); they reveal introspectively unidentified (or inaccurately identified) effects of the self attitude on evaluations of associated objects.

BALANCING SELF AND SOCIAL GROUP

Work reviewed so far highlights the cognitive and affective ties between self and group memberships and stresses the fact that individuals are not necessarily fully aware of these bounds on their thinking or that they are aware but unable to control their operation. Now we turn to the relationships between the cognitive and affective components that make up the self system. Several theories predict some consistency between constructs that represent self and social group. For example, social identity theory (Tajfel, 1974; Tajfel & Turner, 1986) assumes some interrelations between self-esteem, group identification, and ingroup bias. According to the theory, social identification serves as a source of self-esteem. Generally speaking, individuals strive to maintain or increase their self-esteem. They can derive a sense of self-worth through favorable intergroup comparisons: Group membership contributes to positive self-esteem if the ingroup can be positively differentiated from outgroups. Thus self-esteem should be enhanced by membership in a valued group, and strong identification with the group should go hand in hand with positive evaluation of the ingroup. Evidence for the role of self-esteem in intergroup comparisons is mixed (Abrams & Hogg, 1988; Brown, 2000; Hogg & Abrams, 1990; Rubin & Hewstone, 1998). Moreover, support for the idea that there should be a positive correlation between group identification and ingroup favoritism is not overwhelming (Brown, 2000; Hinkle & Brown. 1990); this relationship is obtained only under specific circumstances (Brown et al., 1992). The absence of expected relationships has led to examinations of these constructs using implicit measures. For example, Knowles, Peng, and Levy (2001) found that the strength of the automatic association between self and whites (ingroup identification) was positively correlated with the intensity of the pro-white implicit attitude (ingroup favoritism) and also accounted for the extent to which individuals possessed a restrictive representation of their ethnic group (ingroup exclusiveness).

Recently, Greenwald and colleagues (2002; see also Greenwald et al., 2000) proposed a unified theory of social cognition that predicts patterns of interrelations between group identification, self-esteem, and ingroup attitude. Their approach draws its inspiration from theories of affective–cognitive consistency that dominated social psychology in the 1960s (Abelson et al., 1968) and allows them to integrate a range of otherwise isolated findings obtained with the IAT (Greenwald et al., 1998). This approach is based on the assumption that social knowledge (including knowledge about the self) can be represented as an associative structure. From this point of view, the structure of the self is a network of associations: The self is linked to traits, groups, concepts, or evaluations. A core principle of the theory is that attitudes toward self and concepts closely associated with self (i.e., components of self-concept or identity) should tend to be of similar valence. In other words, according to the *balance-congruity* principle, if someone holds a positive attitude toward the self and considers that a particular concept (e.g., a group, an attribute, or a domain) is part of his or her self-concept, this person should also hold a positive attitude toward that particular concept.

A study on women's gender identity illustrates this principle more concretely. For women, one would typically expect an association between self and the concept "female" (gender identity or self + female) and a positive association toward the self (positive self-esteem or self + good). Based on the balance-congruity principle, these two links should also be accompanied by a third link: a positive association toward the concept "female" (liking for female or female + good). More precisely, the strength of the positive attitude toward "female" should be a joint (or interactive) function of the strength of the associations between self and positive and between self and female. Data supported this prediction: As gender identity increased, so did the positive relation between self-esteem and liking for women (see also Farnham, Greenwald & Banaji, 1999). Further support for similar hypotheses was found in studies on race and age identities. Interestingly, the balance-congruity principle always received stronger support when tested with implicit than with explicit measuring tools.

Another key principle of the theory, the *imbalance–dissonance* principle, is that the network resists forming new links that would result in a component's being tied to pairs of bipolar-opposed constructs. A study on self-concept and gender stereotypes about mathematics demonstrates the heuristic value of this principle (Nosek et al., 2002b). Relative gender stereotypes link the concept "math" with "male" and the concept "arts" with "female." Both men and women displayed automatic associations fitting these stereotypes. Given that women also associate the self to the concept "female," the imbalance–dissonance principle leads to the prediction that women should therefore not associate themselves with "math." Using a variety of social groups and differing clusters of attributes that measure attitude, stereotype, and self-esteem, Greenwald and colleagues (2002) show evidence for balanced identities: The stronger the connection between self and social group, the more likely are the preferences and beliefs to follow in stereotypic fashion. Moreover, such effects were primarily obtained when implicit measures of self and group identity were used and appeared in weaker form on measures of conscious affect and cognition.

SELF-EVALUATION

Having shown the presence of self and social group connections on attitude and beliefs, we turn to research that demonstrates shifts in self-evaluation that also occur without conscious intention. For example, the unconscious activation of significant others has implications for self-evaluation. Baldwin (1992) proposed that the internalization of relationships involves the development of *relational schemas;* these cognitive structures represent regularities in patterns of interpersonal interactions. Often, the sense of self can be derived from such well-learned scripts of interpersonal evaluations. In other words, activated relational schemas shape self-evaluative reactions, even when these schemas are primed below the level of awareness. Indeed, subliminal exposure to the name of a critical versus an accepting significant other led participants to report more negative versus positive self-evaluations (Baldwin, 1994). Similarly, undergraduate students evaluated their own research ideas less favorably after being subliminally exposed to the disapproving face of their department chair rather than the approving face of another person (Baldwin, Carrell & Lopez, 1990). These effects occurred only when the prime was a significant other. For instance, Catholic participants rated themselves more negatively after exposure to the disapproving face of the Pope, but not after exposure to the disapproving face of an unfamiliar person. In addition, if the Pope did not serve as a figure of authority, self-evaluation remained unaffected by the priming manipulation.

Mitchell, Nosek, and Banaji (2003) have shown that subtly varying the race and gender composition of the context in which a particular social group is evaluated strongly affected implicit attitudes. For example, they found that white women expressed a more negative attitude toward black females when race (rather than gender) was the distinctive categorization criterion. On the other hand, highlighting gender elicited a relatively negative attitude toward white males, whereas making race salient triggered a more positive attitude. Although these studies do not speak directly to the issue of self and identity, they lend support to the idea that intergroup biases vary as a function of the frame through which a given situation is filtered.

Unobtrusively making a social identity salient can also influence self-evaluation. S. Sinclair, Hardin, and Lowery (2001) asked participants to indicate how others and they themselves evaluated their verbal and math ability. Before they made these judgments, participants reported either their gender or ethnic identity. This subtle manipulation affected impressions attributed to others. For example, when their gender identity was salient, Asian American women reported that others evaluated them higher in verbal ability than math ability, but when their ethnic identity was salient, they stated that others evaluated them higher in math ability than verbal ability. This social identity manipulation not only affected perceived evaluations of others, but also translated into self-stereotyping effects: Changes in self-evaluations paralleled changes in evaluations of the self by others. In other words, individuals were more likely to endorse the stereotype associated with their group when their membership in that particular group was subtly implied. It is quite unlikely that participants were aware of the impact of the manipulation on their self-evaluations, and the results may be taken as evidence of implicit self-stereotyping. Internalized expectations about one's social group can shape self-evaluations, though perhaps only or especially when they are unobtrusively activated.

Research on implicit self-esteem also indicates that contextual variations can produce an effect on unconscious or automatic preferences. For example, Bylsma, Tomaka, Luhtanen, Crocker, and Major (1992) demonstrated that self-descriptive judgments were faster for positive adjectives after positive than after negative feedback. Using the name-letter test described earlier, a recent study shows that such an effect did not occur after participants had received failure feedback on an alleged IQ test, but that it reemerged once participants were given the opportunity to affirm a personally important value (Koole, Smeets, van Knippenberg & Dijksterhuis, 1999). Thus it appears that a failure on an alleged intelligence test increases the accessibility of failure-related cognitions and reduces, at least temporarily, participants' implicit self-esteem. Affirming an important aspect of one's self-concept permits counteracting the negative consequences of the feedback. Such work illustrates the dynamic nature of self-related processes (Markus & Wurf, 1987). It is a fact of modern life that people belong to a range of social groups, both chosen and given. As societies become more heterogeneous, the opportunity for comparing and contrasting oneself to others will only increase. Across time and situations, varying identities may come forward or recede from consciousness. Effects that appear to be unsystematic and unpredictable may be quite lawful when unconscious social influences on self-evaluations are considered. Routine use of measures of implicit social cognition will need to be considered in a wide range of research topics, rather than relegating them to a subset of research on particular topics, as appears to be the case at present.

PERFORMANCE AND BEHAVIOR

If thoughts and feelings are transformed by the activation of social group membership, it is expected that behavior should be influenced as well. Yet, because cognition and affect are much better understood systems than is behavior, studies of the latter have been less frequently reported. Perhaps for this reason, and because behavior is the gold standard in this science, studies that show the influence of social group on self-relevant behavior are attention-getting. This is certainly true of work on *stereotype threat,* or situations in which the presence of a negative stereotype about one's group can handicap the test performance of members of the group (Steele, 1997; Steele & Aronson, 1995). According to the proponents of this theoretical framework, when African American students perform a scholastic or intellectual task, they face the threat of confirming a negative stereotype about their group's intellectual ability. This threat, it is speculated, interferes with intellectual functioning and can lead to a detrimental impact on performance. Support for this argument has now been obtained in many experiments showing the influence of subtle activation of race/ethnicity, gender, class, and age distinctions on performance on standardized tests. For example, Steele and Aronson (1995) found that stereotype threat can affect the performance of African American college students, who performed significantly worse than white Americans on a standardized test when the test was presented as diagnostic of their intellectual abilities. This effect did not occur when the test was presented as non-diagnostic of their ability. Other studies have demonstrated that women underperform on tests of mathematical ability when the stereotype associated with their group was made salient (Spencer, Steele & Quinn, 1999). Shih and colleagues (1999) showed that activating gender identity or ethnic identity among Asian women shifted performances to be respectively inferior or superior on a math test. Students of low socioeconomic status (SES) performed worse than students of high SES only when a test was presented as diagnostic of their intellectual abilities (Croizet & Claire, 1998). The manipulations producing these effects are often rather subtle. In some cases, it is sufficient to ask participants to indicate their group membership just prior to assessing their performance (Steele & Aronson, 1995). Using age as the social category, Levy (1996) showed that subliminally activated negative stereotypes about the elderly produced decrements in the memory performance of elderly participants. In contrast, the activation of positive stereotypes of the elderly improved their memory performance. Interestingly, the same manipulations did not affect the performance of young individuals, who should not be susceptible to the threat posed by the negative stereotype about elderly individuals.

There is now considerable evidence that the activation of trait constructs or stereotypes can automatically or unconsciously influence social behavior. When trait constructs or stereotypes are primed in the course of an unrelated task, individuals subsequently are more likely to act in line with the content of the primed trait construct or stereotype (Bargh, Chen & Burrows, 1996). For instance, if participants were exposed to words related to rudeness, they were more likely to interrupt an ongoing conversation. If, instead, they were primed with words related to politeness, chances were higher that they would respond in a polite fashion, waiting for the conversation to end without interruption. Priming the stereotype of the elderly caused participants to walk more slowly down the hallway after leaving the experiment. Not only did the subliminal presentation of African American faces lead participants to behave with greater hostility, it also increased the hostility of the person they were interacting with (Chen & Bargh, 1997). Thus the effect is not restricted to commonly accepted social groups, such as gender, class, or race/ethnicity, but works through the meaningful activation of information (as in the polite–rude study). Yet social groups tend to be among the dimensions of social life that provide clear and consensual stereotypes and may be particularly effective at producing a connection to oneself.

For instance, studies showed that priming a stereotype of professors or the trait "intelligent" enhanced performance on a general knowledge task (similar to Trivial Pursuit) and that priming the stereotype of soccer hooligans or the trait "stupid" decreased performance on the test (Dijksterhuis & van Knippenberg, 1998). More important, recent findings suggest that these effects are mediated by passive perceptual activity and are direct consequences of environmental events (priming manipulations). Indeed, manipulations or factors known to produce changes in perception also affected behaviors. For example, priming stereotypes of social categories produced assimilation effects like the ones we just described, whereas activating specific exemplars of the same categories led to contrast effects (Dijksterhuis et al., 1998). More precisely, if participants were primed with the category "professors" (rather than "supermodels"), their own intellectual performance was enhanced (assimilation effect), but if they were primed with the exemplar "Albert Einstein" (rather than "Claudia Schiffer"), a decrement in their performance resulted (contrast effect). The strength of stereotypic associations also mediates the impact of experience on behavior (Dijksterhuis, Aarts, Bargh & van Knippenberg, 2000). Those who report having high contact with the elderly showed a stronger association between the category "elderly" and the attribute "forgetful" than people who had less contact with the elderly. We speculate that such an effect of greater stereotyping that relies on direct experience can exist in the presence of a positive attitude toward the group. Those with a positive attitude toward the elderly but with experience that strengthens a stereotype (perceiving them to be forgetful) may have no recourse but to show the negative stereotype, even in the face of a consciously positive attitude.

Other studies have demonstrated that individuals can fail to detect changes in their actions when those actions were induced implicitly. For example, people can be unaware that their behaviors shift in accordance with the behaviors of others. Chartrand and Bargh (1999) coined the term "chameleon effect" to describe the tendency to mimic unconsciously the postures, mannerisms, or facial expressions of one's interaction partners. They showed that the mere perception of another's behavior automatically increased the likelihood of engaging in that behavior oneself. Individuals were more likely to rub their faces or shake their feet if they interacted with someone who was performing that behavior. Such an effect is assumed to serve an adaptive function by facilitating smooth social interaction through increases in liking between individuals involved in the interactions.

Vorauer and Miller (1997) also observed that people engaged in behavior matching and that they were unaware of doing so. Individuals who read another's positive self-description conveyed more positive impressions of their own satisfaction with academic achievements and university experiences compared with those who first read another's negative self-description. Participants' own sense of the impression they had conveyed was not affected by this manipulation. Thus people failed to detect the extent to which they were induced to present a particular impression of their feelings and experiences. The extensive information that individuals possess about their general personal qualities, as well as about their feelings in the moment, may make it difficult to perceive social influence on their actions. In each of these cases, the irony is that, of all the special domains of knowledge, self-knowledge is assumed to be well known and well defended against intrusion. Such discoveries both highlight the pervasiveness of social influences on the self and point to the inadequacy of introspection as the only tool for obtaining self-knowledge. Indirect measures reveal the subtle but important ways in which the social construction of self unfolds and the lack of conscious access to the process.

SELF-MOTIVES AND GOAL PURSUITS

In recent years, research on self and identity has put a greater emphasis on the motivational mechanisms that propel social behavior. In particular, the role of self-enhancement has been the focus (Baumeister, 1998; Kunda, 1990; Sedikides, 1993; Swann 1990), with investigations of a desire for positive feedback about the self and self-protective reactions unleashed by threatening experiences. Several lines of research suggest that unconscious or automatic processes are triggered when the self or the ingroup is threatened. Spencer, Fein, Wolfe, Fong, and Dunn (1998) showed that threat to self-image can automatically activate stereotypes of social groups even under conditions that otherwise do not produce such activation (i.e., under cognitive load; see Gilbert & Hixon, 1991). Following negative feedback, participants were more likely to view others in stereotypic ways, and this reaction has been taken to suggest a dynamic process of restoring a positive self-image (Fein & Spencer, 1997). Recently, L. Sinclair and Kunda (1999) demonstrated that a self-enhancement motive not only prompted stereotype activation but also led to an inhibition of applicable stereotypes. Participants motivated to disparage a black doctor (because of his criticism of them) inhibited the stereotype of doctors and used a race stereotype, whereas participants motivated to esteem the same target (because of his praise of them) inhibited the race stereotype and relied on the doctor stereotype. In these examples, the threat was directed toward the self, but similar reactions might also be at stake when the ingroup is threatened. Maass, Ceccarelli, and Rudin (1996) showed that the linguistic intergroup bias (the propensity to describe in more abstract ways behaviors depicting the ingroup favorably) was intensified when an outgroup was seen to threaten the ingroup, supporting the idea that this bias is a result of a motivation to protect the ingroup. Pratto and Shih (2000) investigated the links between implicit intergroup biases and the personality variable captured by social dominance orientation (SDO), the degree to which people endorse ideologies that justify hierarchical relationships among groups in society (Pratto, Sidanius, Stallworth & Malle, 1994). Using a priming technique, they found that individuals high in SDO exhibited stronger implicit intergroup biases than people who generally support group equality, but this difference occurred only following a threat to participants' social identity.

Individuals do not merely seek to preserve or establish a positive self-image; they also feel the need to be similar to others (need for *assimilation)* and to maintain their uniqueness (need for *differentiation).* According to the optimal distinctiveness model (Brewer, 1991), identity stems from a tension between these two needs. Individual security and well-being are threatened when one of these needs is not met: Excessive depersonalization no longer offers a basis for self-definition, and excessive individualization renders one vulnerable to isolation and stigmatization. These motives affect people's identification even at the implicit level. Using a measure of speed of response adapted by Smith and Henry (1996), Brewer and Pickett (1999) found that the need for assimilation increased students' implicit identification with their university, whereas the need for differentiation decreased their group identification.

Work based on Bargh's (1990) automotive model is centrally relevant to this discussion, beginning with the idea that pursuit of goals can occur automatically and nonconsciously. Goals activated outside of awareness, control, or intention are pursued similarly to goals chosen through deliberate or conscious means. For example, Chartrand and Bargh (1996) demonstrated that information-processing goals, such as impression formation or memorization, can be automatically activated and pursued. Gardner, Bargh, Shellman, and Bessenhoff (2000) observed that the same brain region reacts whether an evaluation goal is consciously or unconsciously activated. Individuals primed nonconsciously with an achievement goal performed better on an achievement task and were more likely to persist at the task than individuals who were not primed with such a goal (Bargh, Gollwitzer, Lee-Chai, Barndollar & Trotschel, 2001). In addition, Chartrand (2000) found that success or failure at a nonconsciously activated goal led to the same consequences that resulted from success or failure at conscious goal pursuit. Specifically, succeeding at a nonconscious goal improved people's mood, and failure depressed it, paralleling shifts in mood usually occurring in the presence of consciously activated goals.

This research highlights the similarities between conscious and nonconscious self-motives or goals. Other researchers have examined the extent to which implicit and explicit motives differ. McClelland, Koestner, and Weinberger (1989) investigated the differences between self-reported motives (explicit) and motives identified in associative thoughts (implicit). Among other things, they make the case that implicit motives predict spontaneous behavioral trends over time, whereas self-attributed motives predict immediate responses to specific situations. They also report evidence suggesting that implicit motives represent a more primitive motivational system derived from affective experiences, whereas self-attributed motives are based largely on more cognitively elaborated constructs. This finding is consistent with research by Woike (1995) on the relationship between implicit or explicit motives and most-memorable experiences. Implicit motives were associated with affective experiences about the implicit motive, whereas explicit motives were related to routine experiences corresponding to self-descriptions.

Levesque and Pelletier (in press) argued that automatic processes could regulate *intrinsic* and *extrinsic* motivations and that these processes were functionally distinct from their explicit counterparts. *Intrinsic* motivation involves doing activities for the pleasure and satisfaction inherent in doing them, whereas *extrinsic* motivation refers to behaviors that are performed for instrumental reasons, that is, in order to attain a goal or an outcome. These authors found that cognitive structures relevant to intrinsic and extrinsic motivations could temporarily be made accessible through priming of associated constructs and that they influenced self-reported motivation. In addition, explicit and implicit motivations predicted different outcomes: Self-reported intrinsic motivation predicted immediate intentions about long-term behavior, whereas chronically accessible intrinsic motivation predicted the actual long-term behavior.

Research on self and identity has documented the pervasiveness of self-presentational concerns (Baumeister, 1982; Leary, 1995), and a common claim is that techniques assessing implicit attitudes or beliefs are usually free of self-presentational concerns. However, such an argument assumes that when people try to make a good impression, they are fully aware of doing so. Research on implicit self-motives and goals raises the possibility that such motives or goals may operate unconsciously and that self-presentation itself is a complex process that could include components that are strategic but inaccessible to conscious awareness and control.

SOCIETAL AND CULTURAL FOUNDATIONS

We now turn our attention to the influence of societal and cultural realities on implicit identities. We have indicated already that stereotypes about social groups have a profound impact on the implicit self. Automatic associations involving the self often reflect an internalization of cultural stereotypes. Other lines of research bring to the fore the societal roots of implicit processes. We begin with the premise that more often than not, relations between groups are hierarchically organized (Sidanius & Pratto, 1999). In other words, social groups rarely occupy interchangeable positions, and groups that enjoy greater social favors usually remain in that position for extended periods, whatever may be the criteria that characterize the hierarchy (e.g., numerical status, social status, or power; Sachdev & Bourhis, 1991). What is the impact of these factors on social identities? To what extent do members of dominant and subordinate groups exhibit a preference for their own group? On this issue, contrasting predictions can be formulated. On one hand, one would expect that members of subordinate groups engage in more ingroup bias than members of dominant groups. This would be consistent with the idea that the former have a stronger need to achieve a positive social identity, which should be satisfied by increasing favorable intergroup distinctions. On the other hand, we might hypothesize that members of subordinate groups are less likely than members of dominant groups to display a preference for their group because social conditions consistently impose a less favorable evaluation of the subordinate group. At least in the case of natural groups, the evidence at hand seemed to support the first alternative. A meta-analysis conducted by Mullen and colleagues (1992) indicated that members of low-status groups had a tendency to exhibit a stronger ingroup bias than members of high-status groups. In the case of ethnic comparisons in the United States, African Americans often display more ethnocentric intergroup perceptions than do white Americans (Judd, Park, Ryan, Brauer & Kraus, 1995).

However, a different pattern of findings has emerged with some regularity when implicit social identity has been examined. Data from a demonstration Web site, *implicit.harvard.edu/implicit,* provide some insights on this issue (Nosek et al., 2002) that support those from more traditional laboratories (Greenwald et al., 2002). Web data show that on a measure of conscious feeling, white respondents report a preference for the group "white" over the group "black," and black respondents report an opposite and even stronger preference for their own group. This strong explicit liking reported by black respondents stands in sharp contrast to performances on the implicit measure. Unlike white respondents, who continue to show a strong preference for white over black on the implicit measure of liking, black respondents show no such preference. This pattern of results mimics laboratory data obtained with college students (Banaji, Greenwald & Rosier, 1997): Black students exhibited strong explicit liking and identification with their own ethnic group (compared with white students), whereas a reverse pattern was observed on implicit measures (with white students showing stronger implicit ingroup preference). In addition, Jost, Pelham, and Carvallo (2002) found that students from high- and low-status universities both implicitly associated academic characteristics with the higher status group and extracurricular activities with the lower status group. Moreover, students from the high-status university exhibited significant ingroup favoritism on an implicit measure, whereas students from the low-status university did not.

These findings illustrate that the expected ingroup preference effect is moderated by sociocultural evaluations of social groups. On explicit measures, disadvantaged group members exert effort to report positive attitudes, but the lower social standing of their group is internalized sufficiently so as to be detected in their failure to show an implicit preference for their own group. On the other hand, advantaged group members' preferences show the combined benefit of both ingroup liking and the sociocultural advantage assigned to their group. Such results are consistent with the notion of *system justification* (Jost & Banaji, 1994), or the idea that beyond ego justification and group justification lies the more insidious tendency to justify the system or status quo, even when it reflects poorly on one's self or group. Members of dominant groups share thoughts, feelings, and behaviors that reinforce and legitimize existing social systems, which is in their interest, but, surprisingly, so do members of less dominant groups. Examples reviewed in this section indicate that ideological bolstering can occur outside conscious awareness, and this prevents perceivers and even targets of prejudice from questioning the legitimacy of social arrangements.

It would be erroneous to claim that members of subordinate groups cannot display strong implicit preference for their group. It depends on the comparison group. Devos and Banaji (2003) found that Asian American and African American students showed only a slight implicit preference for their ethnic group when it was compared with white Americans. However, when their group was compared with another minority group, ingroup favoritism was more pronounced: Asians displayed strong preference for Asian Americans relative to African Americans, whereas African Americans showed the opposite effect. This finding is consistent with the idea that members of minorities seek to maintain a positive social identity through downward social comparisons (Tajfel & Turner, 1986; Wills, 1981). In addition, we should stress that members of ethnic minorities often display strong implicit preferences for the self relative to others (Banaji et al., 1997; Nosek, Banaji & Greenwald, 2002a), suggesting that members of disadvantaged groups (who show low group esteem) do not show lower self-esteem; they are able to avail themselves of opportunities to protect self-esteem (Crocker & Major, 1989). Thus, to the degree that members of subordinate groups are influenced by cultural evaluations of their group, they may develop a negative social identity, but it may not necessarily translate into a negative view of self (Pelham & Hetts, 1999).

Very little research has analyzed the relationship between self and identities that may be in conflict. We have chosen to study these by viewing connections between national and ethnic identity (Devos & Banaji, 2003). The United States is a perfect testing ground, being, as it is, a pluralist society composed of identifiable ethnic groups that vary in length of association, immersion into mainstream culture, and conditions of immigration. We investigated the extent to which ethnic groups are implicitly conceived as being part of America in a culture that explicitly holds that all groups be treated equally. We assumed that the hierarchy present in American society would structure implicit beliefs about the links between ethnicity and American identity. More precisely, we hypothesized that white Americans are unconsciously viewed as being more essentially American and as exemplifying the nation, whereas ethnic minorities are placed psychologically at the margins (Sidanius, Feshbach, Levin & Pratto, 1997; Sidanius & Petrocik, 2001).

Using techniques developed to assess implicit attitudes or beliefs (Greenwald et al., 1998; Nosek & Banaji, 2001), we examined the extent to which various ethnic groups (white, Asian, and African Americans) were associated with the category "American" (relative to "foreign"). For example, we asked participants to pair, as quickly as possible, American or foreign symbols (e.g., flags, maps, coins, monuments) with faces that varied in ethnicity (white, Asian, and African Americans), but were clearly understood to be American.[d] Although participants were aware that all individuals were Amer-

---

[d]A sample task is available at www.tolerance.org or may be obtained by writing to the authors.

ican, irrespective of ethnicity, consistently the data indicated that African and Asian Americans were less strongly associated with the category "American" than were white Americans. Participants categorized items faster when American symbols were paired with white American faces than with Asian or African American faces. These findings did not merely reflect the fact that members of ethnic minorities were viewed as more foreign; using the appropriate technique (Nosek & Banaji, 2001), we showed that they are excluded from the category "American." Such implicit associations are sometimes consistent with people's explicit beliefs. For example, Asian Americans are viewed as less American than white Americans at both explicit and implicit levels of responding. Indeed, people stated explicitly that they did not consider Asian and white Americans to be equally American even when both held citizenship; they also considered Asian Americans to have weaker ties to American culture than whites.

In other cases, we found strong discrepancies between explicit, and implicit beliefs (Devos & Banaji, 2003). For instance, at the explicit level, African and white Americans were not differentiated. In particular, both groups were perceived to be strongly and equally tied to American culture. However, in sharp contrast to the parity expressed at the explicit level, African Americans were viewed unconsciously as less American than were white Americans. These implicit associations were revealed even when explicit beliefs or knowledge showed the contrary. For example, on explicit measures, in a domain such as track and field sports, in which black Americans dominate, we found that black athletes were more strongly associated with the category "American" than were white athletes. Participants explicitly endorsed the statement that black athletes represent to a greater extent than white athletes "what America is all about" or that they contribute to a greater extent "to the glory of the American nation." However, at the implicit level, black athletes were less strongly associated with the category "American" than were white athletes. In an attempt to find a condition that would surely remove this bias, we tested the association between ethnic and national category by blatantly selecting exemplars who are known Asian Americans and known white foreigners. We still could not shake off the strong implicit association between white and American: Participants were able to associate "American" with known white foreigners (e.g., Gérard Depardieu, Katarina Witt, Hugh Grant) more swiftly than with known Asian Americans (e.g., Connie Chung, Kristi Yamaguchi, Michael Chang). In other words, even though people were fully aware that someone like Gérard Depardieu is not American and that Connie Chung is, it remained easier to make the white + American connection. We conclude from these studies that the national identity of being American is associated with the ethnic identity of being white—and sufficiently intimately so as to be irremovable even when it is consciously rejected.

In the previous studies, participants were all white Americans. In separate data collections (Devos & Banaji, 2003) we examined the role of group membership and found that Asian American participants displayed very similar implicit associations. Among other things, they viewed their own group as being less American than the group "white," showing an internalization that is detrimental to their personal and group interests. Indeed, such implicit association potentially hurts their national identity. African Americans, on the other hand, did not display the same pattern of associations. Although viewed by white participants to be less American, they themselves perceived their own group to be as American as the group "white" and more American than the group "Asian American." Implicit associations are rooted in experiences, they bear the mark of cultural socialization, and they reflect differences between ethnic groups at these levels. African Americans, perhaps because of the presence of other minorities who may be seen as less American, do not internalize the belief that resides in the minds of the advantaged majority, whereas Asian Americans do.

In sum, despite declarations of equality before the law, under a variety of circumstances, white Americans are unconsciously conceived of as being more American than Asian Americans or African Americans. Such implicit beliefs both reflect the hierarchy between ethnic groups within American society and contribute to the preservation of existing social arrangements (Jost & Banaji, 1994).

Research on culture and self-concept shows that members of different cultures often define and evaluate the self in different ways. A major distinction in cross-cultural psychology is the opposition between *collectivist* and *individualist* societies (Triandis, Bontempo, Villareal, Asai & Lucca, 1988; Triandis, McCusker & Hui, 1990). In *collectivist* cultures, people define themselves as members of groups, subordinate their personal goals to group goals, and show strong emotional attachment to the group. In *individualist* cultures, people place a strong emphasis on self-reliance, individual achievement, and personal goals. In their work on the self-concept, Markus and Kitayama (1991, 1994) argued that the self is defined in terms of interdependence in Asian cultures. In other words, the self is inherently collective in these cultures. In contrast, the typically Western conception of self is one in which individuals see themselves as distinct and independent from others. Hetts, Sakuma, and Pelham (1999; see also Pelham & Hetts, 1999) used this distinction to compare the implicit and explicit self-concepts of people who varied in their exposure to individualistic cultures but who were currently living in the *same* culture. More precisely, they examined to what extent explicit and implicit self-evaluations of recent Asian immigrants differed from those of European Americans and Asian Americans reared in the United States. At the explicit level, they found little difference between these groups. In particular, Easterners emigrating to a Western culture seemed to endorse the kind of self-concept promoted in individualistic societies. However, a different picture emerged at the implicit level. Using response latency and word-completion techniques, Hetts and colleagues found strong differences between groups in terms of personal versus group regard. For people reared in an individualistic culture, ideas that were automatically associated with the individual and collective identities were relatively positive. For people socialized in a collectivist culture, the group or collective identity automatically elicited positive thoughts, but ideas tied to individual identity were neutral, ambivalent, or even negative. Such discoveries are consistent with the idea that the need for positive regard is expressed through social or collective identities in some cultures and in individualistic ways in others.

In sum, the cultural context can overshadow differences in cultural experiences when measured through explicit self-evaluations, but implicit self-evaluations continue to reveal the mark of cultural socialization. These results could be taken as evidence that implicit self-evaluations are less influenced by normative demands than their explicit counterparts. More fundamentally, they also suggest that implicit self-evaluations are slower to change. Because they are overlearned associations rooted in experiences, it may take substantial or highly salient contradictory experiences to shift them. Consistent with this argument, Hetts and colleagues (1999) report that implicit self-evaluations of recent immigrants to the United States become increasingly individualistic over time.

IMPLICIT AND EXPLICIT SELF-CONCEPT

So far, we have placed the emphasis on research demonstrating that self-related processes do occur unconsciously or automatically. On several occasions, we pointed out that findings at the implicit level were convergent with observations based on self-report measures. In other cases, we stressed the fact that investigations of unconscious or automatic processes revealed a different picture from what we knew based on assessments of explicit self-concepts or identities. In this section, we examine more carefully how implicit and explicit self-related processes might be intertwined.

This issue has been addressed mostly in the domain of self-esteem or self-evaluation. For example, Bosson, Swann, and Pennebaker (2000) examined systematically the correlations between various measures of implicit and explicit self-esteem. Although some implicit measures correlated significantly with explicit measures, the magnitude of the observed correlations was relatively small (all $rs < .27$). Using confirmatory factor analysis, Greenwald and Farnham (2000) demonstrated that implicit self-esteem and explicit self-esteem were distinct constructs (positively, but weakly, correlated). Research by Hetts and colleagues (1999) on the influence of culture on the self-concept also indicated that measures of implicit self-regard or group-regard were generally uncorrelated with explicit measures of self-concept. Spalding and Hardin (1999) found a correlation of $-.05$ between the Rosenberg Self-Esteem Scale (Rosenberg, 1965) and a priming technique designed to assess implicit self-esteem. In addition, they showed that implicit self-esteem predicted some behavioral consequences, whereas explicit self-esteem did not. In their study, participants took part in either a self-relevant or a self-irrelevant interview and were then rated by the interviewer on their anxiety. When the interview was self-relevant, participants low in implicit self-esteem appeared more anxious than participants high in implicit self-esteem. Explicit self-esteem did not predict participant's apparent anxiety. Interestingly, individuals' own ratings of anxiety were linked to explicit self-esteem but not to implicit self-esteem.

Several studies support the idea that, under some circumstances, self-descriptions may switch from a controlled mode to an automatic mode. One would expect automatic self-evaluations to be much more positive than controlled self-evaluations because people have a lifetime of practice describing themselves mostly in positive terms. Paulhus and Levitt (1987) demonstrated that a shift in self-description occurred when people were emotionally aroused. Participants were asked to indicate the self-descriptiveness of a set of traits. These traits were presented on a computer screen, along with emotional or nonemotional distractors. The presence of emotional distractors induced participants to claim more of the positive and fewer of the negative traits than they did in the presence of nonemotional distractors. A similar positivity effect was found when participants' attentional capacity was reduced (Paulhus, Graf & Van Selst, 1989).

Koole and colleagues (2001) demonstrated that encouraging participants to rely on their feelings clearly led to implicit self-esteem effects (positivity biases for name letters and birthdate numbers). In contrast, these forms of implicit self-esteem were no longer apparent when participants were encouraged to find reasons why they felt the way they did. Thus deliberative forms of processing can overrule automatic self-evaluations. In addition, Koole and colleagues found that the ability to engage in conscious self-reflection affected the degree of congruence between implicit self-esteem and self-reported evaluations of the self. For example, slow self-evaluations were less congruent with implicit self-evaluation than fast self-evaluations. Similarly, when participants' cognitive resources were deprived (high cognitive load), implicit self-evaluations predicted self-reported evaluations, but that was not the case when cognitive resources were available (low cognitive load). These findings support the idea that when the capacity or the motivation to engage in conscious self-reflection is lacking, implicit self-evaluations will be the prevailing influence on phenomenological experience. In sum, the evidence at hand suggests that implicit and explicit self-concepts are distinct constructs, although, at least under some circumstances, connection may also be detected.

CONCLUSIONS

The question of how we know ourselves and what we know about ourselves is of fundamental interest to understanding how personal knowledge is represented, the degree to which such knowledge is constructed in social context, and its implications for health and well-being. Yet the epistemological quagmire inherent in the empirical assessment of knowledge about oneself has always posed a problem, as noted at the start of this article. We recommended that analyses of unconscious self-processes may assist in this regard, and we focused on the social aspect of self and identity, restricting our attention to a particular aspect of the self—one that emerges in the context of social group membership. From the initial research using implicit or indirect measures of self and identity, we already have evidence about the visible role of social group membership in creating a sense of self and self-worth.

The work reviewed in this article raises several possible issues that need to be incorporated into an understanding of self. Processes that capture group identity can operate without introspective access or deliberative thought. Such group identity and even knowledge about social groups (that is automatically learned even if consciously denied) can have indirect influence on assessments of the self. An unspoken assumption has been that implicit attitudes, beliefs, and motives about oneself are hard to change given that they are overlearned associations about a well-known object. Several findings reported in this article would suggest, to the contrary, that implicit associations are not rigid and that shifts in self-definitions or self-evaluations can occur without conscious awareness or intention. Situational or contextual manipulations reveal the plasticity of self-related implicit social cognition.

Finally, several lines of research reported in this article show the subtle but crucial ways in which sociocultural realities shape self-related mental processes. In many instances, the impact of sociostructural influences on psychological processes becomes more obvious when research is focused on the nitty-gritty of mental processes that are not consciously accessible but may nevertheless be found using indirect measures. In that regard, work on implicit processes offers the promise to renew thinking about the obvious interplay between the psychological and the social, the individual and the collective.

ACKNOWLEDGMENTS

Preparation of this article was supported by grants from the National Institute of Mental Health (No. MH-57672) and from the National Science Foundation (No. SBR9709924) to Mahzarin R. Banaji and by a Swiss National Science Foundation Fellowship (No. 8210-056562) to Thierry Devos.

REFERENCES

ABELSON, R.P., ARONSON, E., MCGUIRE, W.J., NEWCOMB, T.M., ROSENBERG, M.J. & TANNENBAUM, P. (Eds.). (1968). *Theories of cognitive consistency: A sourcebook.* Chicago: Rand-McNally.

ABRAMS, D. & HOGG, M.A. (1988). Comments on the motivational status of self-esteem in social identity and intergroup discrimination. *European Journal of Social Psychology, 18,* 317–334.

ARON, A., ARON, E.N. TUDOR, M. & NELSON, G. (1991). Close relationships as including other in the self. *Journal of Personality and Social Psychology, 60,* 241–253.

ASHBURN-NARDO, L., VOILA, C.I. & MONTEITH, M. J. (2001). Implicit associations as the seeds of intergroup bias: How easily do they take root? *Journal of Personality and Social Psychology, 81,* 789–799.

BALDWIN, M.W. (1992). Relational schemas and the processing of social information. *Psychological Bulletin, 111,* 461–484.

BALDWIN, M.W. (1994). Primed relational schemas as a source of self-evaluative reactions. *Journal of Social and Clinical Psychiatry, 13,* 380–403.

BALDWIN, M.W., CARRELL, S.E. & LOPEZ, D.F. (1990). Priming relationship schemas: My advisor and the Pope are watching me from the back of my mind. *Journal of Experimental Social Psychology, 26,* 435–454.

BANAJI, M.R., GREENWALD, A.G. & ROSIER, M.R. (1997, October). *Implicit esteem: When collectives shape individuals.* Paper presented at the Second Annual SESP Preconference on the Self. Toronto, Ontario, Canada.

BANAJI, M.R., LEMM, K.M. & CARPENTER, S.J. (2001). The social unconscious. In A. Tesser & N. Schwartz (Eds.), *Blackwell handbook of social psychology: Intraindividual processes* (pp. 138–158). Oxford, UK: Blackwell.

BANAJI, M.R., & PRENTICE, D.A. (1994). The self in social contexts. *Annual Review of Psychology, 45,* 297–232.

BARGH, J.A. (1982). Attention and automaticity in the processing of self-relevant information. *Journal of Personality and Social Psychology, 43,* 425–436.

BARGH, J.A. (1990). Auto-motives: Preconscious determinants of social interaction. In E.T. Higgins & R.M. Sorrentino (Eds.), *Handbook of motivation and cognition* (Vol. 2, pp. 93–130). New York: Guilford Press.

BARGH, J.A., CHEN, M. & BURROWS, L. (1996). Automaticity of social behavior: Direct effect of trait construct and stereotype activation on action. *Journal of Personality and Social Psychology, 71,* 230– 244.

BARGH, J.A., GOLLWITZER, P.M., LEE-CHAI, A., BARNDOLLAR, K. & TROTSCHEL, R. (2001). The automated will: Nonconscious activation and pursuit of behavioral goals. *Journal of Personality and Social Psychology, 81,* 1014–1027.

BARGH, J.A. & TOTA, M.E. (1988). Context-dependent automatic processing in depression: Accessibility of negative constructs with regard to self but not others. *Journal of Personality and Social Psychology, 54,* 925–939.

BAUMEISTER, R.F. (1982). A self-presentational view of social phenomena. *Psychological Bulletin, 91,* 3–26.

BAUMEISTER, R.F. (1998). The self. In D.T. Gilbert, S.T. Fiske & G. Lindzey (Eds.), *The handbook of social psychology* (Vol. l, pp. 680–740). Boston: McGraw-Hill.

BEGGAN, J.K. (1992). On the social nature of nonsocial perception: The mere ownership effect. *Journal of Personality and Social Psychology, 62,* 229–237,

BIERNAT, M., VESCIO, TK. & GREEN, M.L. (1996). Selective self-stereotyping. *Journal of Personality and Social Psychology, 71,* 1194–1209.

BOSSON, J.K,. SWANN, W.B,. JR. & PENNEBAKER, J.W. (2000). Stalking the perfect measure of implicit self-esteem: The blind men and the elephant revisited. *Journal of Personality and Social Psychology, 79,* 631–643.

BREWER, M.B. (1979). Ingroup bias in the minimal intergroup situation: A cognitive-motivational analysis. *Psychological Bulletin, 86,* 307–324,

BREWER, M.B. (1991). The social self: On being the same and different at the same time. *Personality and Social Psychology Bulletin, 17,* 475–482.

BREWER, M.B. & PICKETT, C.L. (1999). Distinctiveness motives as a source of the social self. In T.R. Tyler & R.M. Kramer (Eds.). *The psychology of the social self* (pp. 71–87). Mahwah, NJ: Erlbaum.

BROWN, R. (2000). Social identity theory: Past achievements, current problems and future challenges. *European Journal of Social Psychology, 30,* 745–778.

BROWN. R., HINKLE, S., ELY, P.G., FOX-CARDAMONE, L., MARAS, P. & TAYLOR, L.A. (1992). Recognizing group diversity: Individualist–collectivist and autonomous–relational social orientations and their implications for intergroup processes. *British Journal of Social Psychology, 31,* 327–342.

BYLSMA, W.H., TOMAKA, J. LUHTANEN, R., CROCKER, J. & MAJOR, B. (1992). Response latency as an index of temporary self-evaluation. *Personality and Social Psychology Bulletin, 18,* 60–67.

CHARTRAND, T.L. (2000). *Mystery moods and perplexing performance: Consequences of succeeding or failing at a nonconscious goal.* Manuscript submitted for publication.

CHARTRAND, T.L. & BARGH, J.A. (1996). Automatic activation of impression formation and memorization goals: Nonconscious goal priming reproduces effects of explicit task instructions. *Journal of Personality and Social Psychology, 71,* 464–478.

CHARTRAND, T.L. & BARGH, J.A. (1999). The chameleon effect: The perception–behavior link and social interaction. *Journal of Personality and Social Psychology, 76,* 893–910,

CHEN, M. & BARGH, J.A, (1997). Nonconscious behavioral confirmation processes: The self-fulfilling consequences of automatic stereotype activation. *Journal of Experimental Social Psychology, 11,* 541–560.

COATS, S., SMITH, E.R., CLAYPOOL, H.M. & BANNER, M.J. (2000). Overlapping mental representations of self and ingroup: Reaction time evidence and its relationship with explicit measures of group identification. *Journal of Experimental Social Psychology, 36,* 304–315.

COOLEY, C.H. (1902). *Human nature and social order.* New York: Scribner's.

CROCKER, J. &. MAJOR, B. (1989). Social stigma and self-esteem: The self-protective properties of stigma. *Psychological Review, 96,* 608–630.

CROIZET, J.-C. & CLAIRE, T. (1998). Extending the concept of stereotype threat to social class: The intellectual underperformance of students from low socioeconomic backgrounds. *Personality and Social Psychology Bulletin, 24,* 588–594.

CUNNINGHAM, W.A., NEZLEK, J.B. & BANAJI, M.R. (2001). *Conscious and unconscious ethnocentrism: Revisiting the ideologies of prejudice.* Manuscript submitted for publication.

DASGUPTA, N., MCGHEE, D.E., GREENWALD, A.G. & BANAJI, M.R. (2000). Automatic preference for White Americans: Eliminating the familiarity explanation. *Journal of Experimental Social Psychology, 36,* 316–328.

DEVOS, T. & BANAJI, M.R. (2003). *American = White?* Manuscript submitted for publication.

DIEHL, M. (1990). The minimal group paradigm: Theoretical explanations and empirical findings. In W. Stroebe & M. Hewstone (Eds.), *European review of social psychology* (Vol. 1, pp. 263–292). Chichester, UK: Wiley.

DIJKSTERHUIS, A., AARTS, H., BARGH, J.A. & VAN KNIPPENBERG, A. (2000). On the relation between associative strength and automatic behavior. *Journal of Experimental Social Psychology, 36,* 531–544.

DIJKSTERHUIS, A., SPEARS, R., POSTMES, T., STAPEL, D., KOOMEN, W., VAN KNIP- PENBERG. A. & SCHEEPERS, D. (1998). Seeing one thing and doing another: Contrast effects in automatic behavior. *Journal of Personality and Social Psychology, 75,* 862–871.

DIJKSTERHUIS, A. & VAN KNIPPENBERG, A. (1998). The relation between perception and behavior, or how to win a game of Trivial Pursuit. *Journal of Personality and Social Psychology, 74,* 865–877.

DOVIDIO, J.F., EVANS, N. & TYLER, R.B. (1986). Racial stereotypes: The contents of their cognitive representations. *Journal of Experimental Social Psychology, 22,* 22–37.

FARNHAM, S.D., GREENWALD, A.G. & BANAJI, M R. (1999). Implicit self-esteem. In D. Abrams & M.A. Hogg (Eds.). *Social identity and social cognition* (pp. 230–243). Malden, MA: Blackwell.

FAZIO, R.H., JACKSON, J.R., DUNTON, B.C. & WILLIAMS, C.J. (1995). Variability in automatic activation as an unobtrusive measure of racial attitudes: A bona fide pipeline? *Journal of Personality and Social Psychology, 69,* 1013–1027.

FEIN, S. & SPENCER, S.J. (1997). Prejudice as self-image maintenance: Affirming the self through derogating others. *Journal of Personality and Social Psychology, 75,* 31–44.

FEYS, J. (1991). Briefly induced belongingness to self and preference. *Journal of Personality and Social Psychology, 21,* 547–552.

FINCH, J.F & CIALDINI, R.B. (1989). Another indirect tactic of (self-) image man- agement: Boosting. *Personality and Social Psychology Bulletin, 5,* 222–232.

FRANCO, F.M. & MAASS, A. (1996). Implicit versus explicit strategies of outgroup discrimination: The role of intentional control in biased language use and reward allocation. *Journal of Language and Social Psychology, 15,* 335–359.

GAERTNER, S.L. & MCLAUGHLIN, J.P. (1983). Racial stereotypes: Associations and ascriptions of positive and negative characteristics. *Social Psychology Quar- terly, 46,* 23–30.

GARDNER, W., BARGH, J.A., SHEL1MAN, A. & BESSENHOFF, G. (2000). *This is your brain on primes: Lateralized brain activity is the same for nonconscious and conscious evaluative processing.* Manuscript submitted for publication.

GILBERT, D.T. & HIXON, J.G. (1991). The trouble of thinking: Activation and appli- cation of stereotypic beliefs. *Journal of Personality and Social Psychology, 60,* 509–517.

GREENWALD, A.G. & BANAJI, M.R. (1995). Implicit social cognition: Attitudes, self-esteem, and stereotypes. *Psychological Review, 102,* 4–27.

GREENWALD, A.G., BANAJI, M.R., RUDMAN, L.A, FARNHAM, S.D., NOSEK. B.A. & MELLOT, D.S. (2002). Unified theory of implicit attitudes, stereotypes, self- esteem, and self-concept. *Psychological Review, 109,* 3–25.

GREENWALD, A.G., BANAJI, M.R., RUDMAN, L.A., FARNHAM, S.D., NOSEK, B.A. & ROSIER, M. (2002). Prologue to a unified theory of attitudes, stereotypes, and self-concept. In J.P. Forgas (Ed.), *Feeling and thinking: The role of affect in social cognition* (pp. 308–330). New York: Cambridge University Press.

GREENWALD. A.G. & FARNHAM, S.D. (2000). Using the implicit association test to measure self-esteem and self-concept. *Journal of Personality and Social Psychology, 79,* 1022–1038.

GREENWALD, A.G., MCGHEE, D.E. & SCHWARTZ, J.L.K. (1998). Measuring individual differences in implicit cognition: The implicit association test. *Journal of Personality and Social Psychology, 74,* 1464–1480.

GREENWALD, A.G. & PRATKANIS, A.R. (1984). The self. In R.S. Wyer & T.K. Srull (Eds.), *Handbook of social cognition* (pp. 129–178). Hillsdale, NJ: Erlbaum.

HETTS, J.J., SAKUMA, M. & PELHAM, B.W. (1999). Two roads to positive regard: Implicit and explicit self-evaluation and culture. *Journal of Experimental Social Psychology, 35,* 512–559.

HIGGINS, E.T., VAN HOOK, E. & DORFMAN, D. (1988). Do self-attributes form a cognitive structure? *Social Cognition, 6,* 177–206.

HINKLE, S. & BROWN, R. (1990). Intergroup comparisons and social identity. Some links and lacunae. In D. Abrams & M.A. Hogg (Eds.), *Social identity theory: Constructive and critical advances* (pp. 48–70). New York: Harvester Wheatsheaf.

HOGG, M.A. & ABRAMS, D. (1990). Social motivation, self-esteem, and social identity. In D. Abrams & M.A. Hogg (Eds.), *Social identity theory: Constructive and critical advances* (pp. 28–47). New York: Harvester Wheatsheaf.

HOGG, M.A. & TURNER, J.C. (1987). Intergroup behaviour, self-stereotyping and the salience of social categories. *British Journal of Social Psychology, 26,* 325–340.

HOORENS, V. & NUTTIN, J.M. (1993). Overvaluation of own attributes: Mere ownership or subjective frequency? *Social Cognition, 11,* 177–200.

HOORENS, V., NUTTIN, J.M., HERMAN, I.E. & PAVAKANUN, U. (1990). Mastery pleasure versus mere ownership: A quasi-experimental cross-cultural and cross-alphabetical test of the name letter effect. *European Journal of Social Psychology, 20,* 18–205.

HOORENS, V. & TODOROVA, E. (1988). The name letter effect: Attachment to self or primacy of own name writing? *European Journal of Social Psychology, 18,* 365–368.

JAMES, W. (1890). *The principles of psychology.* New York: Holt.

JOST, J.T. & BANAJI, M.R. (1994). The role of stereotyping in system-justification and the production of false consciousness. *British Journal of Social Psychology, 33,* 1–27.

JOST, J.T., PELHAM, D.W. & CARVALLO, M.R. (2002). Nonconscious forms of system justification: Cognitive, affective, and behavioral preferences for higher status groups. *Journal of Experimental Social Psychology, 38,* 586–602.

JUDD, C.M., PARK, B., RYAN, C.S., BRAUER, M. & KRAUS, S. (1995). Stereotypes and ethnocentrism: Diverging interethnic perceptions of African American and white American youth. *Journal of Personality and Social Psychology, 69,* 460–481.

KARPINSKI, A. & VON HIPPEL, W. (1996). The role of the linguistic intergroup bias in expectancy maintenance. *Social Cognition, 14,* 141–163.

KIHLSTROM, J.F. & CANTOR, N. (1984). Mental representation of the self. In L. Berkowitz (Ed.). *Advances in experimental social psychology* (Vol. 17, pp. 1–47). Orlando, FL; Academic Press.

KIHLSTROM, J.F., CANTOR, N., ALBRIGHT, J.S., CHEW, B.R.. KLEIN, S. B. & NIEDENTHAL, P. M. (1988). Information processing and the study of the self. In L. Berkowitz: (Ed.), *Advances in experimental social psychology* (Vol. 21, pp. 145–178). San Diego, CA: Academic Press.

KITAYAMA, S. & KARASAWA, M. (1997). Implicit self-esteem in Japan: Name letters and birthday numbers. *Personality and Social Psychology Bulletin, 23,* 736–742.

KNOWLES, E.D., PENG, K. & LEVY, T.H. (2001). *Ingroup overexclusion and identity protection in the categorization of sex and race.* Unpublished manuscript.

KOOLE, S.L, DIJKSTERHUIS, A. & VAN KNIPPENBERG, A. (2001). What's in a name: Implicit self-esteem and the automatic self. *Journal of Personality and Social Psychology, 80,* 669–685.

KOOLE, S.L., SMEETS, K., VAN KNIPPENBERG, A. &. DIJKSTERHUIS, A. (1999). The cessation of rumination through self-affirmation, *Journal of Personality and Social Psychology, 77,* 111–125.

KUNDA, Z. (1990). The case for motivated reasoning. *Psychological Bulletin, 108,* 480–498.

LANE, K., MITCHELL, J.P. &. BANAJI, M.R. (2001, February). Formation of implicit attitudes: Direct experience not required. Poster presented at the annual meeting of the Society for Personality and Social Psychology, San Antonio, TX.

LEARY, M.R. (1995). *Self-presentation: Impression management and interpersonal behavior.* Madison, WI: Brown & Benchmark.

LEMM, K.M. &. BANAJI, M.R. (1998, April). *Implicit and explicit gender identity and attitudes toward gender.* Paper presented at the annual meeting of the Midwestern Psychological Association, Chicago, IL.

LEMM. K.M. & BANAJI, M.R. (2000, February). *Motivation to control moderates the relationship between implicit and explicit prejudice.* Poster presented at the annual meeting of the Society for Personality and Social Psychology, Nashville, TN.

LEVESQUE, C. & PELLETIER, L.G. (in press). On the investigation of primed and chronic autonomous and heteronomous motivational orientations. *Personality and Social Psychology Bulletin.*

LEVY, B. (1996). Improving memory in old age through implicit self-stereotyping. *Journal of Personality and Social Psychology, 71,* 1092–1107.

LEYENS, J.-P., PALADINO, P.M., RODRIGUEZ-TORRES, R., VAES, J., DEMOULIN, S., RODRIGUEZ-PEREZ, A. & GAUNT, R. (2000). The emotional side of prejudice: The attribution of secondary emotions to ingroups and outgroups. *Personality and Social Psychology Review, 4,* 186–197.

LINDEMAN, M. & SUNDVIK, L. (1995). Evaluative bias and self-enhancement among gender groups. *European Journal of Social Psychology, 25,* 269–280.

MAASS, A., CECCARELLI, R. & RUDIN, S. (1996). Linguistic intergroup bias: Evidence for ingroup-protective motivation. *Journal of Personality and Social Psychology, 71,* 512–526.

MAASS, A., SALVI, D., ARCURI, L. & SEMIN, G.R. (1989). Language use in intergroup contexts: The linguistic intergroup bias. *Journal of Personality and Social Psychology, 57,* 981–993.

MARKUS, H. (1977). Self-schemata and processing information about the self. *Journal of Personality and Social Psychology, 35,* 63–78.

MARKUS, H. & WURF, E. (1987). The dynamic self-concept: A social psychological perspective. *Annual Review of Psychology, 38,* 299–337.

MARKUS, H.R. & KITAYAMA, S. (1991). Culture and the self: Implications for cognition, emotion, and motivation. *Psychological Review, 98,* 224–253.

MARKUS, H. & KITAYAMA, S. (1994). The cultural construction of self and emotion: Implications for social behavior. In S. Kitayama & H.R. Markus (Eds.), *Emotion and culture: Empirical studies of mutual influence* (pp. 89–130). Washington, DC: American Psychological Association.

MCCLELLAND, D.C., KOESTNER, R. & WEINBERGER, J. (1989). How do self-attributed and implicit motives differ? *Psychological Review, 96,* 690–702.

MCGUIRE, W.J. & MCGUIRE, C.V. (1988). Context and process in the experience of self. In L. Berkowitz (Ed.), *Advances in experimental social psychology* (Vol. 21, pp. 97–144). San Diego: Academic Press.

MEAD, G.H. (1934). *Mind, self, and society.* Chicago: University of Chicago Press.

MITCHELL, J.P., NOSEK, B.A. & BANAJI, M.R. (2003). Contextual variations in implicit evaluation. *Journal of Experimental Psychology: General, 132,* 455–469.

MULLEN, B., BROWN, R. & SMITH, C. (1992) Ingroup bias as a function of salience, relevance, and status: An integration. *European Journal of Social Psychology, 21,* 103–122.

NEUMANN, R., EBERT, M., GABEL, B., GUELSDORTFF, J., KRANNICH, H., LAUTERBACH, C. & WIEDL, K. (1998). Vorurteile zwischen Bayern und Norddeutschen: Die Anwendung einer neuen Methode zur Erfassung evaluativer Assoziationem in Vorurteilen [Prejudice between Bavarians and North Germans: Applying a new method for assessing evaluative association within prejudice]. *Zeitschrift Fur Experimentelle Psychologie, 45,* 99–108.

NOSEK, B. & BANAJI, M.R. (2001). Measuring implicit social cognition: The go/no-go association task. *Social Cognition, 19,* 625–666.

NOSEK, B., BANAJI, M.R. & GREENWALD, A.G. (2002a). Harvesting implicit group attitudes and beliefs from a demonstration website. *Group Dynamics, 6,* 101–115.

NOSEK, B.A., BANAJI, M.R. & GREENWALD, A.G. (2002b). Math = male, me = female, therefore math ≠ me. *Journal of Personality and Social Psychology, 83,* 44–59.

NUTTIN, J.M. (1985). Narcissism beyond Gestalt and awareness: The name letter effect. *European Journal of Social Psychology, 15,* 353–361.

NUTTIN, J.M. (1987). Affective consequences of mere ownership: The name letter effect in twelve European languages. *European Journal of Social Psychology, 17,* 381–402.

OTTEN, S. & MOSKOWITZ, G.B. (2000). Evidence for implicit evaluative ingroup bias: Affect-biased spontaneous trait inference in a minimal group paradigm. *Journal of Experimental Social Psychology, 36,* 77–89.

OTTEN, S. & WENTURA, D. (1999). About the impact of automaticity in the Minimal Group Paradigm: Evidence from affective priming tasks. *European Journal of Social Psychology, 19,* 1049–1071.

PAULHUS, D.L., GRAF, P. & VAN SELST, M. (1989). Attentional load increases the positivity of self-presentation. *Social Cognition, 7,* 389–400.

PAULHUS, D.L. & LEVITT, K. (1987). Desirable responding triggered by affect: Automatic egotism? *Journal of Personality and Social Psychology, 51,* 245–259.

PEABODY, D. (1968). Group judgments in the Philippines: Evaluative and descriptive aspects. *Journal of Personality and Social Psychology, 10,* 290–300.

PELHAM, B.W. & HETTS, J.J. (1999). Implicit and explicit personal and social iden- tity: Toward a more complete understanding of the social self. In T.R. Tyler & R. Kramer (Eds.), *The psychology of the social self* (pp. 115–143). Mahwah, NJ: Erlbaum.

PELHAM, B.W., MIRENBERG, M.C. & JONES, J.K. (2002). Why Susie sells seashells by the seashore: Implicit egotism and major life decisions. *Journal of Person- ality and Social Psychology, 81,* 469–487.

PERDUE, C.W., DOVIDIO, J.F., GUTMAN, M.B. &. TYLER, R.B. (1990). Us and them: Social categorization and the process of intergroup bias. *Journal of Personal- ity and Social Psychology, 59,* 475–486.

PERDUE, C.W. & GUTMAN, M.B. (1990). Evidence for the automaticity of ageism. *Journal of Experimental Social Psychology, 16,* 199–216.

PRATTO, F. & SHIH, M. (2000). Social dominance orientation and group context in implicit group prejudice. *Psychological Science, 11,* 515–518.

PRATTO, F., SIDANIUS, J., STALLWORTH. L.M. & MALLE, B.F. (1994). Social domi- nance orientation: A personality variable predicting social and political atti- tudes. *Journal of Personality and Social Psychology, 67,* 741–763.

PRENTICE, D. & MILLER, D.T. (1992). *The psychology of ingroup attachment.* Paper presented at the Conference on the Self and the Collective, Princeton, NJ.

ROGERS, T.B., KUIPER. N.A. & KIRKER, W.S. (1977). Self-reference and the encod- ing of personal information. *Journal of Personality and Social Psychology, 35,* 677– 688.

ROSENBERG, M. (1965). *Society and the adolescent self-image.* Princeton, NJ: Prin- ceton University Press.

RUBIN, M. & HEWSTONE, M. (1998). Social identity theory's self-esteem hypothe- sis: A review and some suggestions for clarification. *Personality and Social Psychology Review, 2,* 40–62.

RUDMAN, L.A., GREENWALD, A.G. & MCGHEE, D.E. (2001). Implicit self-concept and evaluative implicit gender stereotypes: Self and ingroup share desirable traits. *Personality and Social Psychology Bulletin, 27,* 1164–1178.

RUDMAN, L.A., GREENWALD, A.G., MELLOT, D.S. & SCHWARTZ, J.L.K. (1999). Measuring the automatic components of prejudice: Flexibility and generality of the Implicit Association Test. *Social Cognition, 17,* 437–465.

SACHDEV, I. & BOURHIS, R.Y. (1991). Power and status differentials in minority and majority group relations. *European Journal of Social Psychology, 21,* 1–24.

SEDIKIDES, C. (1993). Assessment, enhancement, and verification determinants of the self-evaluation process. *Journal of Personality and Social Psychology, 65,* 317–338.

SHIH, M., PITTINSKY, T.L. & AMBADY, N. (1999). Stereotype susceptibility: Identity salience and shifts in quantitative performance. *Psychological Science, 10,* 80–83.

SIDANIUS, J., FESHBACH, S., LEVIN, S. & PRATTO, F. (1997). The interface between ethnic and national attachment: Ethnic pluralism or ethnic dominance? *Public Opinion Quarterly, 61,* 102–133.

SIDANIUS, J. & PETROCIK, J.R. (2001). Communal and national identity in a multi- ethnic state: A comparison of three perspectives. In R.D. Ashmore, L. Jussim, & D. Wilder (Eds.), *Social identity, intergroup conflict, and conflict resolu- tion.* New York: Oxford University Press.

SIDANIUS, J. & PRATTO, F. (1999). *Social dominance: An intergroup theory of social hierarchy and oppression.* New York: Cambridge University Press.

SIMON, B. & HAMILTON, D.L. (1994). Self-stereotyping and social context: The effects of relative ingroup size and ingroup status. *Journal of Personality and Social Psychology, 66,* 699–711.

SIMON, B., PANTALEO, G., & MUMMENDEY, A. (1995). Unique individual or interchangeable group member? The accentuation of intragroup differences versus similarities as an indicator of the individual self versus the collective self. *Journal of Personality and Social Psychology, 69,* 106–119.

SINCLAIR, L. & KUNDA, Z. (1999). Reactions to a Black professional: Motivated inhibition and activation of conflicting stereotypes. *Journal of Personality and Social Psychology, 77,* 885–904.

SINCLAIR, S., HARDIN, C.D. & LOWERY, B. (2001). *Self-stereotyping in the context of multiple social identities.* Manuscript submitted for publication.

SMITH, E.R., COATS, S. & WALLING, D. (1999). Overlapping mental representations of self, ingroup, and partner: Further response time evidence and a connectionist model. *Personality and Social Psychology Bulletin, 25,* 873–882.

SMITH, E.R. & HENRY, S. (1996). An ingroup becomes part of the self: Response time evidence. *Personality and Social Psychology Bulletin, 22,* 635–642.

SPALDING, L.R.. & HARDIN, C.D. (1999). Unconscious unease and self-handicapping: Behavioral consequences of individual differences in implicit and explicit self-esteem. *Psychological Science, 10,* 535–539.

SPENCER, S.J., FEIN, S., WOLFE, C.T., FONG. C. & DUNN, M.A. (1998). Automatic activation of stereotypes: The role of self-image threat. *Personality and Social Psychology Bulletin, 24,* 1139–1152.

SPENCER, S.J., STEELE, C.M. & QUINN, D.M. (1999). Stereotype threat and women's math performance. *Journal of Experimental Social Psychology, 35,* 4–28.

STEELE, C.M. (1997). A threat in the air: How stereotypes shape intellectual identity and performance. *American Psychologist, 52,* 613–629.

STEELE, C.M., & ARONSON, J. (1995). Stereotype threat and the intellectual test performance of African Americans. *Journal of Personality and Social Psychology, 69,* 797–811.

STRAUMAN, T.J. & HIGGINS, E.T. (1987). Automatic activation of self-discrepancies and emotional syndromes: When cognitive structures influence affect. *Journal of Personality and Social Psychology, 53,* 1004–1014.

SWANN, W.B., Jr. (1990). To be adored or to be known? The interplay of self-enhacement and self-verification. In E.T. Higgins & R. M. Sorrentino (Eds.), *Handbook of motivation and cognition* (Vol. 2, pp. 408–448). New York: Guilford Press.

TAJFEL, H. (1974). Social identity and intergroup behaviour. *Social Science Information, 13,* 65–93.

TAJFEL, H., BILLIG, M.G., BUNDY, R.P. & FLAMENT, C. (1971). Social categorization and intergroup behaviour. *European Journal of Social Psychology, 1,* 149–178.

TAJFEL, H. & TURNER, J.C.(1986). The social identity theory of intergroup behavior. In S. Worchel & W.G. Austin (Eds.), *Psychology of intergroup relations* (pp. 7–24). Chicago: Nelson-Hall.

TRIANDIS, H.C., BONTEMPO, R., VILLAREAL, M.J., ASAI, M. & LUCCA, N. (1988). Individualism and collectivism: Cross-cultural perspectives on self-ingroup relationships. *Journal of Personality and Social Psychology, 54,* 323–338.

TRIANDIS, H.C., MCCUSKER, C. & HUI, C.H. (1990). Multi-method probes of indi-
vidualism and collectivism. *Journal of Personality and Social Psychology, 59,*
1006–1020.
TURNER, J.C. (1985). Social categorization and the self-concept: A social cognitive
theory of group behaviour. In E.J. Lawler (Ed.), *Advances in group processes:
Theory and research* (Vol. 2, pp. 77–122). Greenwich, CT: JAI Press.
TURNER, J.C., HOGG. M.A., OAKES, P.J., REICHER, S.D. & WETHERELL, M. (1987).
Rediscovering the social group: A self-categorization theory. Oxford, UK:
Blackwell.
TURNER, J.C., OAKES, P.J., HASLAM, S.A. & MCGARTY, C. (1994). Self and collec-
tive: Cognition and social context. *Personality and Social Psychology Bulle-
tin, 20,* 454–463.
ULEMAN. J.S., HON, A., ROMAN, R.J. & MOSKOWITZ, G.B. (1996). On-line evi-
dence for spontaneous trait inferences at encoding. *Personality and Social
Psychology Bulletin, 22,* 377–394.
VON HIPPEL, W,. HAWKINS, C. & SCHOOLER, J.W. (2001). Stereotype distinctive-
ness: How counter-stereotypic behavior shapes the self-concept. *Journal of
Personality and Social Psychology, 81,* 193–205.
VON HIPPEL, W., SEKAQUAPTEWA, D. & VARGAS, P. (1997). The linguistic inter-
group bias as an implicit indicator of prejudice. *Journal of Experimental
Social Psychology, 33,* 490–509.
VORAUER, J.D. & MILLER, D.T. (1997). Failure to recognize the effect of implicit
social influence on the presentation of self. *Journal of Personality and Social
Psychology, 73,* 281–295.
WALSH, W.A. & BANAJI, M. (1997). The collective self. In J.G. Snodgrass & R. L.
Thompson (Eds.), *The self across psychology: Self-recognition, self-aware-
ness and the self concept.* (pp. 193–214). New York: New York Academy of
Sciences.
WEGNER, D.M. & BARGH, J.A. (1998). Control and automaticity in social life. In
D.T. Gilbert, S.T. Fiske & G. Lindzey (Eds.), *The handbook of social psychol-
ogy* (Vol. 2, pp. 446–496). Boston: McGraw-Hill.
WILLS, T.A. (1981). Downward comparison principles in social psychology. *Psy-
chological Bulletin, 90,* 245–271.
WITTENBRINK, B., JUDD, C. M. & PARK, B. (1997). Evidence for racial prejudice at
the implicit level and its relationship with questionnaire measures. *Journal of
Personality and Social Psychology, 72,* 262–274.
WOIKE, B.A. (1995). Most-memorable experiences: Evidence for a link between
implicit and explicit motives and social cognitive processes in everyday life.
Journal of Personality and Social Psychology, 68, 1081–1091.

The Mind's Self-Portrait

DANIEL M. WEGNER

Department of Psychology, Harvard University,
Cambridge, Massachusetts 02138, USA

ABSTRACT: Scientific psychology and neuroscience are taking increasingly precise and comprehensive pictures of the human mind, both in its physical architecture and its functional processes. Meanwhile, each human mind has an abbreviated view of itself, a self-portrait that captures how it *thinks* it operates, and that therefore has been remarkably influential. The mind's self-portrait has as a central feature the idea that thoughts cause actions, and that the self is thus an origin of the body's actions. This self-portrait is reached through a process of inference of *apparent mental causation*, and it gives rise to the experience that we are consciously willing what we do. Evidence from several sources suggests that this self-portrait may often be a humble and misleading caricature of the mind's operation—but one that underlies the feeling of authorship and the acceptance of responsibility for action.

KEYWORDS: consciousness; mental causation; self-insight; volition

Minds are marvelous to look at from the inside. In addition to all the things we can see that seem to be *out there*—all the sights and sounds and feels and the like—our minds also afford us views of *themselves*. Gilbert Ryle (1949) described minds as seeming almost *self-luminous*, as though they light themselves up from the inside. The view of their workings that we gain through our minds moment-to-moment provides a series of ideas that seems to lay out their operation in full detail. In a sense, our minds present us with their own theory of psychology—or perhaps something more akin to a set of laws. The mind's self-portrait appears as a complete picture of its own operation, something so simple and clear that we can't help but believe it. And the major feature of this self-portrait is the idea that we cause ourselves to behave.

Consider the classic case of lifting a finger. You think of lifting it and it goes up. You think of putting it down and it goes down. Up, Down, Up,

Address for correspondence: Daniel M. Wegner, Ph.D., Department of Psychology, Harvard University, 1470 William James Hall, 33 Kirkland Street, Cambridge, MA 02138.
wegner@wjh.harvard.edu

Ann. N.Y. Acad. Sci. 1001: 212–225 (2003). © 2003 New York Academy of Sciences.
doi: 10.1196/annals.1279.011

Down. This regularity is striking. Your thought seems to cause your action, and you get a distinct sense of authorship with each movement. The mind depicts to itself no other part of the process whereby the finger moves. The thought pops into consciousness, and the action too is consciously observed, and that's *it*. All the machinery in the mind's basement that might be creating this conscious show—*the rest of the mind and brain*—remains unobserved. The mind's eye view of the causation of action creates a caricature, then, a simple conscious snapshot of what may be an immensely complicated set of processes involving multiple sites of brain activation and a welter of unconscious cognitive processes—a mechanism that could only be discovered in full detail with an infinite supply of government grant money. The mind simplifies itself.

As a rule, these are fighting words, pointed barbs against free will in the perennial battle between free-willers and determinists. Free-willers are students of mind who are entirely taken by the mind's self-portrait, and who have championed ideas of free will, self-determination, human agency, and rational choice to say that thoughts regularly do cause actions. The mind's self-portrait is accepted at face value, and other accounts of human action are accepted only to the degree that they can be fit with this fundamental canon. By this view, there really is a self, an author of our actions who creates them by consciously willing them. On the other hand, there are also students of mind who say the mind's self-portrait is bad art, no more than a misleading "folk theory" whose main feature is an impossible homunculus. This is the refrain of classically deterministic psychological theorists such as Freud and Skinner, of course, and more recently it is the assumption embraced by most sciences of the mind. The theme comes up often enough nowadays that Tom Wolfe titled an article on contemporary neuroscience "Sorry, but Your Soul Just Died."

The absurdity of all this, of course, is that the soul cannot die. As long as we have minds that keep presenting their self-portrait to us with every passing moment, we will continue to be convinced of the importance of our conscious will and will continue to feel we have selves no matter how much science piles up evidence for selfless mechanisms underlying our actions. Because the idea that minds are mechanisms will always suffer by comparison to the mind's self-portrait, it could be deeply useful to study how this portrait arises. How do we come to think that we have conscious will? How exactly does this portrait get painted every few moments every day of our waking lives? The challenge suggested by this analysis is to understand the mechanisms of mind responsible for the way mind appears to itself.

This paper begins with a précis of the theory of *apparent mental causation,* a set of ideas designed to account for the human experience of conscious will. The central notion is that people experience conscious will to the degree they can infer that their thought caused their action. Because this theory is detailed elsewhere (Wegner, 2002; Wegner & Wheatley, 1999), this paper only begins with it, and then goes on to comment on the mind's self-portrait as it relates to the problem of self-insight. Why, in particular, would the mind's self-portrait be so limited? The first problem of insight is why we don't see the big picture. The second problem of self-insight is why the mind's self-portrait takes this particular form: Why is it useful for us to think that we have selves that cause our actions? In what follows, then, we consider how the mind reaches the intuition that it is an author, and then the implications of this system for understanding human self-insight more generally.

APPARENT MENTAL CAUSATION

The basic idea of the theory of apparent mental causation is that conscious intention and action are caused by unperceived forces: You think of lifting that finger and then lift that finger—not because conscious thinking causes doing, but because other forces of mind and brain (that are not consciously perceived) cause both the thinking and the doing. On the basis of your conscious perceptions of your thoughts and actions, after all, it is impossible to tell in any given case whether your thought was causing your action, or something else was causing both of them. The deep intuition we all have about the power of our conscious will arises because thought and act are the only recognizable objects in our mind's self-portrait. We experience consciously willing our actions, then, when our minds lead us to make a further brushstroke on the canvas: We *infer* that our thought causes our action.

How do we go about drawing this causal inference? Imagine, for instance, the action of taking a drink from a glass. This is something that sometimes can feel quite willful, and at other times can feel absent-mindedly automatic. If you have just thought about drinking and then do so, it may feel more willful—whereas if you have been thinking about having a cookie and then suddenly find yourself drinking instead, it is likely to feel less willed. Furthermore, the thought of drinking must occur just prior to the action to maximize the experience of will, as thoughts that occur far beforehand (and that then are forgotten until the action), or thoughts of the drink that only appear after you've had the drink, do not seem to prompt a sense of willed drinking. And if someone else puts the glass in your hand and pushes it toward your mouth, you may discount the causal role of any prior thought and again feel the act is unwilled. These simple observations point to three key sources of the experience of conscious will–the *consistency, priority,* and *exclusivity* of the thought about the action. For the perception of apparent mental causation, the thought should be consistent with the action, occur just before the action, and not be accompanied by other potential causes.

Studies of how people perceive external physical events (Michotte, 1963) indicate that the perception of causality is highly dependent on these features of the relationship between the potential cause and potential effect. The candidate for the role of cause must yield movement that is consistent with its own movement, must come first or at least at the same time as the effect, and must be unaccompanied by rival causal events. The absence of any of these conditions undermines the perception that causation has occurred (Einhorn & Hogarth, 1986; Kelley, 1972, 1980; McClure, 1998).

Consistency

Consider the consistency principle first. The idea here is that for a thought occurring before action to be perceived as the cause of the action (and so prompt an experience of conscious will), the thought must be semantically linked to the action. A thought about changing the TV channel followed by the press of a button on the remote, for instance, will feel willed, whereas a thought about world peace followed by sitting down on the remote and having the channel change will not yield the same experience. The role of consistency is evident in Penfield's (1975) study of movements induced through electrical stimulation of the motor cortex. Conscious patients were prompted by stimulation of the exposed brain to produce movements that were not simple reflexes and instead appeared complex, multi-staged, and voluntary. Their actions looked nothing like simple shock-induced spasms, but like actions done on purpose. Yet, their common report of the experience was that they did not "do" the action, and instead felt that Penfield had "pulled it out" of them. Without thoughts consistent with the action, they experienced the action as an unwilled occurrence.

As another example of consistency, consider what happens when people with schizophrenia experience "hearing voices." Although there is good evidence that these voices are self-produced, the typical response to such auditory hallucinations is the report that the voice belongs to someone else. The inconsistency of the utterance with the person's prior thoughts leads to the inference that the utterance was not consciously willed—and so to the delusion that there are others' voices speaking "in one's head" (Daprati et al., 1997; Frith & Done, 1989; Graham & Stephens, 1994; Hoffmann, 1986). Ordinarily, we know our actions and verbalizations in advance of their performance, at least in rough form, and we experience the authorship of action because of the consistency of this preview with the action.

A laboratory test of the consistency principle examined whether people will accept authorship of actions merely because they have had thoughts consistent with those actions (Gibson & Wegner, 2003). For this study, participants were asked to type letters randomly at a computer keyboard without seeing the screen. They were told that the experiment was designed to examine "automatic typing" and that their random responses would be analyzed. Just before this task, participants were exposed 5 times to the prime word *deer* in what they were told was an unrelated computer task. Then the "automatic typing" began and participants typed for 5 minutes. The experimenter ostensibly ran a program on the typed text to extract the words that had been typed, and then asked participants to rate each of a series of words to indicate the degree to which they felt they had authored that word. None of the words rated were actually produced. Participants reported higher authorship ratings for the word they had seen in the prior computer task (*deer*) relative to other words, and also reported relatively higher ratings that they had authored an associated word, *doe*. These findings suggest that people can experience will for an action that was never performed, merely when they have prior thoughts consistent with the action.

Priority

The priority principle influences apparent mental causation when consistent thoughts appear at varying times around the action. Priority supports inferences of conscious will when the thought appears in a timely way just before the action, and departures from immediate priority lead to experiences of involuntariness. In a study of this principle, Wegner and Wheatley (1999) presented people with thoughts (e.g., a tape-recorded mention of the word *swan*) relevant to their action (moving an onscreen cursor to select a picture of a swan). The movement the participants performed was actually not their own, as they shared the computer mouse with an experimental confederate who gently forced the action without the participants' knowledge. Nevertheless, when the relevant thought was provided either 1 s or 5 s before the action, participants reported feeling that they acted intentionally in making the movement. The operation of the priority principle in this case was clear because on other trials, thoughts of the swan prompted 30 s before the forced action or 1 s afterward did not yield an inflated experience of will. It is worth noting, too, that on trials for which action was not forced, thoughts about actions that were provided to participants did not lead them actually to move toward the mentioned items. So, even when the action is forced and thought of the action is baldly prompted by an outside stimulus—appearing in this case over headphones—the timely occurrence of thought before action leads to an erroneous experience of apparent mental causation.

Exclusivity

The exclusivity principle suggests that apparent mental causation is affected by the perception of alternative causes of action. When events other than one's own thoughts or agents other than oneself become known in the context of an action, their presence leads to the discounting of own thoughts as a cause, and thus undermines the experience of will. So, for example, hypnosis leads people to perform actions that they attribute strongly to the hypnotist, and these actions are experienced as involuntary. Similarly, people who are not hypnotized but are merely obeying the instructions of another person may discount the influence of their own thoughts on the action and experience a lack of conscious will. Milgram (1974) commented on this phenomenon in his famous shock experiments, noting the occurrence of an "agentic shift" in which self loses the sense of authorship of the obedient actions.

Now as a rule, experiences of will are not undermined when alternative causes of action remain unperceived. If you don't know what is causing your action, you continue to move along merrily thinking that you are driving the bus. So, for instance, people in one study were asked to choose to move one or the other index finger whenever they heard a click (Brasil-Neto, Pascual-Leone, Valls-Sol, Cohen, & Hallett, 1992). Transcranial magnetic stimulation (TMS) was applied alternately to the left or right motor strip to influence the movement. This stimulation led participants to have a marked preference to move the finger contralateral to the site stimulated, particularly at short response times. However, respondents reported consciously willing the movements during the TMS influence, indicating a lack of insight into the alternative causal mechanism producing their actions. The experience of conscious will in this study was not measured with precision, so it remains possible that slight adjustments to the experience occurred as a result of the unperceived stimulation.

Subconscious exposure to knowledge of outside sources of action does seem to influence conscious will in studies of the subliminal priming of agents (Dijksterhuis, Wegner, Aarts & Preston, 2003). Participants in these experiments were asked to react to letter strings on a computer screen by judging them to be words or not—and to do this as quickly as possible in a race with the computer. On each trial in this lexical decision task, the screen showing the letters went blank either when the person pressed the response button, or automatically at a short interval (about 400–650 ms) after the presentation. This made it unclear whether the person had answered correctly and turned off the display or whether the computer did it, and on each trial the person was asked to guess who did it. In addition, however, and without participants' prior knowledge, the word "I" or "me" or some other word was very briefly presented on each trial. This presentation lasted only 17 ms, and was both preceded and followed by random letter masks—such that participants reported no awareness of these presentations.

The subliminal presentations influenced judgments of authorship. On trials with the subliminal priming of a first-person singular pronoun, participants more often judged that they had beaten the computer. They were influenced by the unconscious priming of self to attribute an ambiguous action to their own will. In another study, subliminal priming of the word "computer" reduced judgments of own agency. And in a third study, participants were subliminally primed on some trials with the thought of an agent that was not the self—God. Among those participants who professed a personal belief in God, this prime reduced the causal attribution of the action to self. Apparently, the decision of whether self is the cause of an action is influenced by the unconscious accessibility of self versus nonself agents. This suggests that the exclusivity of conscious thought as a cause of action can be influenced even by the unconscious accessibility of possible agents outside the self.

Normally, the influence of outside forces on one's experience of will for an action occurs because of conscious belief in the presence of those forces. This occurs, for example, in the intriguing phenomenon of "facilitated communication" or FC. FC was introduced as a technique for helping autistic and other communication-impaired individuals to communicate without speaking. A "facilitator" would hold the client's finger above a letter board or keyboard, ostensibly to brace and support the client's pointing or key-pressing movements, but not to produce them. Clients who had never spoken in their lives were sometimes found to produce lengthy typed expressions this way, at a level of detail and grammatical precision that was miraculous. Studies of FC soon discovered, however, that when separate questions were addressed (over headphones) to the facilitator and the client, those heard only by the facilitator were the ones being answered. Facilitators commonly expressed no sense at all that they were producing the communications, and instead attributed the messages to their clients. Their strong belief that FC would work, along with the conviction that the client was indeed a competent agent whose communications merely needed to be facilitated, led to a breakdown in their experience of conscious will for their own actions (Wegner, Fuller & Sparrow, 2003). Without a perception that one's own thought is the exclusive cause of one's action, it is possible to lose authorship entirely and attribute it even to an unlikely outside agent.

The principles of consistency, priority, and exclusivity appear to govern the inferences people make about the mind's influence on action. Their operation can push the perception of authorship around quite independent of any actual causal relationship between thought and action. The self-portrait that the mind presents to us can sometimes be a very poor likeness, in other words—a portrayal built on information that happens to be accessible, and on some causal guesswork about what that information means. Although the experimental study of apparent mental causation is only in its inception, there exists a wide array of anomalous phenomena whose interpretation is rendered more tractable by the logic of apparent mental causation (Wegner, 2002).

SELF-INSIGHT

Of all the different forms that the mind's self-portrait might take, why does it take this one? Imagine for a minute that we are building a robot and want it to know itself (McCarthy, 1995). Would we start immediately to build a robot that would think it is *causing itself to behave?* In giving it this rather abbreviated and conceited view of itself, would we also then leave out the vast amounts of process information it might conceivably be wired up to access? Such a robot would not know the contents of most of its memory registers, the signals sent to its motor units, the status of its logic circuits, or most other things about its own operation—but it would know that it had moved its finger (presuming, of course, that it had a finger). Why would we want a robot, or for that matter a person, with such an understanding of its own mind?

Capacity Limitations

One possibility is that this is simply all we can get. Perhaps self-insight takes mental resources that are normally devoted to other things. Whatever self-insight might arise from contemplating one's navel, after all, has never been highly compatible with effective action (unless that action specifically involves the navel) and contemplating the mental operations underlying thought and action may similarly not be the best use of the limited resource of mind. The greatest difficulty of achieving self-insight is, of course, doing this in any reasonable way *in parallel* with effective cognitive operations of other kinds (Ericsson & Simon, 1984; Nisbett & Wilson, 1977; Wilson, 2002). Thinking about the mind's operations may be difficult during the mind's operations because thinking about them is a secondary task that interferes with the operations themselves. As Ryle so keenly observed, the mind is far from self-luminous. It seems to require considerable focused candlepower merely to light up the main hall leading to its labyrinthine depths.

The problem of capacity limitation is not, by itself, insurmountable. Conceivably, if attempts at self-insight were undertaken often enough and the mental task requiring insight were simple enough, one might begin to assemble a more complete picture of the mind's operation (Ericsson & Simon, 1984). But there could still be a problem inherent in the simultaneity of these tasks that presents a further complication. Minsky (1968) and McDermott (2002) have pointed out that in simple artificially intelligent systems, there could be a logical limitation to self-knowledge. If a system is operating and has not yet finished its job, perfect self-knowledge of its operation (the relevant inputs, the processes operating on them, the resultant outputs) also contains information indicating what the system's operation will be. Self-insight into a mental operation, in other words, presumes that the mental operation is complete and is completely specified. Any mental operation that is to remain open to change cannot be open to full insight as it is ongoing. Self-insight seems to limit the flexibility of the mind's operations because it presumes their completion.

Self-insight may be limited to the experience of willing our own actions because we don't have the mental resources to see more than this, or because the pursuit of insight is precluded by the unfinished nature of our mental activities. These ideas suggest that in building a robot mind or designing a human one, we may need to accept a shorthand version of self-insight. Rather than expecting to collect large amounts of information, we might better plan on getting only a relatively focused set of insights. The mind's self-portrait will have to be less a mural and more a doodle. Still, why would the doodle look the way it does? Why does it portray the self as an author?

Mind Perception

Self-insight may also be shaped by processes involved in figuring out minds in general—not just our own. The perception of minds seems to require a set of special skills that go beyond the skills involved in perceiving the world of objects and events. Minds require an appreciation of goal-directedness, for example, which seems far less important for the perception of other things. Knowing what a mind believes is also helpful, as is knowing where a mind is attending, what it can remember, how it feels, and so on. A range of abilities may be required for appreciating that minds are even possible, let alone for apprehending the qualities of minds that might be relevant to their operation. Psychologists and philosophers of many stripes have contributed to the idea that people have "theories of mind" that are involved in the tasks of mind perception, and without the ability to use these theories such perception might be cumbersome or unattainable (Astington, 1993; Baron-Cohen, 1994; Dennett, 1987; Flavell, 1999; Hauser & Carey, 1998; Heider, 1958; Wellman, 1992).

The special skills that support the perception of other minds serve to constrain the range of causal forces we can perceive in our own minds. Because the general process of mind perception involves looking for the mind's goals and processing observed behavior in terms of those goals (Heider & Simmel, 1944), the application of this strategy in perceiving own mind tends to focus our attention on our own goals. The general tendency in mind perception to perceive behavior as resulting from prior mental states (such as desires or thoughts) likewise prompts us to apply this same causal template to the conscious evidences we perceive in our own minds. Perhaps the most general property of mind perception, however, is the tendency to perceive minds as origins of behavior. We see gods or spirits or people or animals behind many events in the world, ascribing these events to them as authors and often ending the analysis at that point (Guthrie, 1993). Without insisting on further insight into mechanism, we assign authorship to minds. It seems, then, that our proclivity for believing that we are agents who cause our actions is not a private conceit but an application of a general principle. We find origins of our actions in ourselves just as we find origins in faces in the clouds. The insight offered by the mind's self-portrait is, in this sense, largely a matter of perceiving oneself as the origin of one's actions.

It may even be that perceiving our own minds *as* minds cuts short any further analysis we might normally apply to systems we do not perceive as having minds. The assumption that a rock *wants* to fall, for example, might obviate any examination of the forces of gravity, friction, and the like that could aid in understanding its physically determined trajectory. The perception of our minds as minds brings in one set of tools of understanding, but suggests we entirely discard others (Carey, 1996). Our minds' self-portraits will not entertain them as objects, as cascades of events, or as mechanisms, even though they might appear to be just such items in the eyes of an outsider wearing a white coat.

Conscious Previews

The logic we have examined to this point suggests that we might view our minds in a limited way, using a template we use for the perception of minds in general. We see ourselves as origins of our actions because this is a shorthand view that we often use to understand minds of all kinds. However, there is an important feature of the mind's inner world that dramatically enhances our inclination to understand our minds in this way: We are often the beneficiaries of a mental system that delivers previews of action to consciousness before the action occurs. Thinking about a finger movement just before the finger movement may not be the cause of the movement—but it is certainly an attention-getting attractor for any causal inferences the mind might be inclined to make. Intentions are private previews of action that invite the mind's standard self-portrait. Of course we are agents who cause our actions—we know them in advance!

Let us stop for a moment and reconnoiter. The theory of apparent mental causation turns the everyday notion of intention on its head, and it is useful to review what things look like from this new perspective. The theory says that people perceive that they are intending and understand behavior as intended or unintended—but that they do not really intend. Instead, conscious thoughts coming to mind prior to action are described in the theory as *previews* of action, ideas that surface into consciousness as the result of unconscious processes like those that create the action itself. The theory is mute on whether these thoughts actually cause action, as it treats only the perception of the thought/action relationship, not the true relationship. Conscious previews of action are fundamentally involved in how the mind portrays its operation to itself, however, and thus they deserve careful analysis. Previews pretty much nail shut the case for the mind's self-portrayer, as they seem to indicate that some part of the mind knew about the action all along, before it happened.

Why would previews of action come to mind so regularly before action if *not* to cause action? If conscious will is indeed the construction that the theory of apparent mental causation suggests, we must wonder why thoughts that look and feel like intentions might have evolved in humans when they may not have the function of causing action. What good are epiphenomena? One way to account for previews is to suggest that they are deeply adaptive for people, both in a simple sense and in a more profound sense.

Previews are adaptive in a simple sense because they create a social signaling system—akin to turn signals on motor vehicles. Telling others which way we are going is not only useful in traffic, but can be lifesaving in a variety of circumstances. Reporting previews to others allows us to keep others out of our way, it often helps us to excuse our behavior, and it can invite others to join with us as well. These functions would be unavailable to a person who could not discern what he or she might do next, or to someone who was unable to report these self-predictions to others. In this simple sense, conscious previews could have evolved merely to allow us the luxury of bending our social world to our mind's imagined futures.

The more profound evolutionary story for conscious previews draws upon their usefulness in establishing personal experiences of will—and so in creating a deep sense of authorship. Conscious previews of action create feelings of conscious will when we find ourselves doing the actions we premeditated. These feelings would seem unlikely to arise if we did not experience previews of action. The experience of conscious will is valuable as a marker, a quasi-emotional experience that highlights the actions that feel as though they are our own, and this marker function is sufficiently important for human social life that it could well motivate the processes that produce previews.

Conscious will serves as a personal guide to authorship of action—an *authorship emotion*. The person who feels will for an action typically then feels responsibility for that action, and so will also be susceptible to moral emotions such as pride or guilt depending on the action's effects. Just as emotions of sadness or anxiety serve as "somatic markers" and draw the person's sustained attention toward evolutionarily relevant behaviors (Damasio, 1994), experiences of conscious will serve as feelings that anchor self-perceptions of authorship. Although a thought that previews an action may not have caused the action, the person's *perception* of a causal link is enough to activate the entire system of perceived personal causation that anchors the moral evaluation of self. Moral actions, in other words, need not to be traceable to a mind for the owner of that mind to experience moral emotions. All that is needed is the occurrence of previews, and the subsequent self-attribution of authorship that results when the person perceives them as causes of action. The mind's self-portrait leads the person to think of the self as an author of action—a certain *kind* of author, one who does good or bad things. This, in turn, creates opportunities for subsequent behavior. Thoughts and feelings about the self derive from memories of what one has done, and the determination of authorship is the basis for these memories.

CONCLUSION

According to the theory of apparent mental causation, the feeling that we consciously will our actions is traceable to an inference we make from the match between our conscious thoughts and observed action. When a thought appears in consciousness just prior to an action, is consistent with the action, and is not accompanied by salient alternative causes of the action, we experience conscious will and ascribe authorship to ourselves for the action.

The mind's self-portrait thus features the sense of authorship. By arranging for a limited view of itself, by portraying itself as an agent that causes action, and by developing the capacity to preview actions in support of this system, the mind comes to discern its own actions and accumulate a sense of self. This sense of self accrues from estimates of the role of own thoughts in action, and is produced by the system that infers apparent mental causation. Far from a simple homunculus that "does things," then, the self can be understood as a system that arises from the experience of authorship, and is developed over time. We become selves by experiencing what we do, and this experience then informs the processes that determine what we will do next. The self, in this view, is not an agent, an origin of action—but instead is an accumulated structure of knowledge about *what this particular mind can do*.

REFERENCES

ASTINGTON, J.W. (1993). *The child's discovery of mind.* Cambridge, MA: Harvard University Press.

BARON-COHEN, S. (1994). How to build a baby that can read minds: Cognitive mechanisms in mindreading. *Cahiers de Psychologie Cognitive, 13*(5), 513–552.

BRASIL-NETO, J.P., PASCUAL-LEONE, A., VALLS-SOL, J., COHEN, L.G., & HALLETT, M. (1992). Focal transcranial magnetic stimulation and response bias in a forced-choice task. *Journal of Neurology, Neurosurgery, and Psychiatry, 55*, 964–966.

CAREY, S. (1996). Cognitive domains as modes of thought. In D.R. Olson & N. Torrance (Eds.), *Modes of thought: Explorations in culture and cognition* (pp. 187–215). New York: Cambridge University Press.

DAMASIO, A.R. (1994). *Descartes' error: Emotion, reason, and the human brain.* New York: Avon.

DAPRATI, E., FRANCK, N., GEORGIEFF, N., PROUST, J., PACHERIE, E., DALERY, J. & JEANNEROD, M. (1997). Looking for the agent: An investigation into consciousness of action and self-consciousness in schizophrenic patients. *Cognition,, 65*, 71–86.

DENNETT, D.C. (1987). *The intentional stance.* Cambridge, MA: Bradford Books/ The MIT Press.

DIJKSTERHUIS, A., WEGNER, D. M., AARTS, H. & PRESTON, J. (2003). Unconscious priming of conscious will. Manuscript submitted for publication.

EINHORN, H.J. & HOGARTH, R.M. (1986). Judging probable cause. *Psychological Bulletin, 99*, 3–19.

ERICSSON, K.A. & SIMON, H.A. (1984). *Protocol analysis: Verbal reports as data.* Cambridge, MA: MIT Press.

FLAVELL, J.H. (1999). Cognitive development: Children's knowledge of the mind. *Annual Review of Psychology, 50*, 21–45.

FRITH, C.D. & DONE, D.J. (1989). Experiences of alien control in schizophrenia reflect a disorder in the central monitoring of action. *Psychological Medicine 19*, 359–363.

GIBSON, L. & WEGNER, D.M. (2003). *Believing we've done what we were thinking: An illusion of authorship.* Paper presented at the Society for Personality and Social Psychology, Los Angeles, CA.

GRAHAM, G. & STEPHENS, G.L. (1994). Mind and mine. In G. Graham & G.L. Stephens (Eds.), *Philosophical psychology* (pp. 91–109). Cambridge, MA: The MIT Press.

GUTHRIE, S.E. (1993). *Faces in the clouds: A new theory of religion.* New York: Oxford University Press.

HAUSER, M. & CAREY, S. (1998). Building a cognitive creature from a set of primitives: Evolutionary and developmental insights. In D.D. Cummins & C. Allen (Eds.), *The evolution of mind* (pp. 51–106). New York: Oxford University Press.

HEIDER, F. (1958). *The psychology of interpersonal relations.* New York: Wiley.

HEIDER, F. & SIMMEL, M. (1944). An experimental study of apparent behavior. *American Journal of Psychology, 57*, 243–259.

HOFFMANN, R.E. (1986). Verbal hallucinations and language production processes in schizophrenia. *Behavioral and Brain Sciences, 9*, 503–548.

KELLEY, H.H. (1972). Causal schemata and the attribution process. In E. E. Jones, D.E. Kanouse, H.H. Kelley, R.E. Nisbett, S. Valins & B. Weiner (Eds.), *Attribution: Perceiving the causes of behavior* (pp. 151–174). Morristown, NJ: General Learning Press.

KELLEY, H.H. (1980). Magic tricks: The management of causal attributions. In D. Gurlitz (Ed.), *Perspectives on attribution research and theory: The Bielefeld Symposium* (pp. 19–35). Cambridge, MA: Ballinger.

MCCARTHY, J. (1995, July 15, 2002). *Making robots conscious of their mental states.* Retrieved September 22, 2002, from the World Wide Web: http://www-formal.stanford.edu/jmc/consciousness/consciousness.html

MCCLURE, J. (1998). Discounting causes of behavior: Are two reasons better than one? *Journal of Personality & Social Psychology, 74*(1), 7–20.

MCDERMOTT, D.V. (2002). *Mind and mechanism.* Cambridge, MA: MIT Press.

MICHOTTE, A. (1963). *The perception of causality* (T. R. Miles & E. Miles, Trans.). New York: Basic Books.

MILGRAM, S. (1974). *Obedience to authority.* New York: Harper & Row.

MINSKY, M. (1968). Matter, mind, and models. In M. Minsky (Ed.), *Semantic information processing* (pp. 425–431). Cambridge, MA: MIT Press.

NISBETT, R. E. & WILSON, T. D. (1977). Telling more than we can know: Verbal reports on mental processes. *Psychological Review, 84*, 231–259.

PENFIELD, W. (1975). *The mystery of mind.* Princeton, NJ: Princeton University Press.

WEGNER, D. M. (2002). *The illusion of conscious will.* Cambridge, MA: MIT Press.

WEGNER, D.M., FULLER, V.A. & SPARROW, B. (2003). Clever hands: Uncontrolled intelligence in facilitated communication. *Journal of Personality and Social Psychology, 85,* 5–19.

WEGNER, D.M. & WHEATLEY, T.P. (1999). Apparent mental causation: Sources of the experience of will. *American Psychologist, 54,* 480–492.

WELLMAN, H.M. (1992). *The child's theory of mind.* Cambridge, MA: MIT Press.

WILSON, T.D. (2002). *Strangers to ourselves: Discovering the adaptive unconscious.* Cambridge, MA: Harvard University Press.

The Seven Sins of Memory

Implications for Self

DANIEL L. SCHACTER, JOAN Y. CHIAO, AND JASON P. MITCHELL

Department of Psychology, Harvard University,
Cambridge, Massachusetts 02138, USA

ABSTRACT: We examine the relation between memory and self by considering errors of memory. We draw on the idea that memory's imperfections
can be classified into seven basic categories or "sins." Three of the sins concern different types of forgetting (*transience, absent-mindedness*, and
blocking), three concern different types of distortion (*misattribution, suggestibility*, and *bias*), and one concerns intrusive memories (*persistence*).
We focus in particular on two of the distortion-related sins, misattribution
and bias. By describing cognitive, neuropsychological, and neuroimaging
studies that illuminate these memory sins, we consider how they might
bear on the relation between memory and self.

KEYWORDS: memory; self; forgetting; distortion; misattribution; bias

Scientists and philosophers have long recognized an intimate connection between memory and the self. Ideas about the nature of this relationship can
be found as early as 1829 when James Mill underscored not only the strong
interdependence between self and memory, but went so far as to suggest that
the two are actually one and the same:

> The phenomenon of Self and that of Memory are merely two sides of the same
> fact, or two different modes of viewing the same fact ... This succession of feel-
> ings, which I call my memory of the past, is that by which I distinguish my Self
> (Mill, [1829/1982], p. 175).

The strong relation between memory and self has not escaped the attention
of modern theorists, either. Indeed, in his recent book *Synaptic Self*, Joseph
LeDoux (2002) has made the case for the close interplay between memory
and self by contending that in the absence of learning and memory processes,

Address for correspondence: Daniel L. Schacter, Department of Psychology, Harvard University, 33 Kirkland St., Cambridge, MA 02138. Voice: 617-495-3855; fax: 617-496-3122.
dls @wwjh.harvard.edu

Ann. N.Y. Acad. Sci. 1001: 226–239 (2003). © 2003 New York Academy of Sciences.
doi: 10.1196/annals.1279.012

the self would only be "an empty, impoverished expression of our genetic constitution" (p.9). From a different perspective, Greenwald (1980) argued for a similarly tight link between memory and self, claiming that the past is remembered "as if it were a drama in which the self is the leading player" (p. 604). Thus, not only is our sense of self based on memories of past experiences, as Mill contended, but our retrieval, recollection, and reconstruction of the past is, reciprocally, influenced by the self. Given these links between memory and self, it seems that we cannot make much progress in thinking about the self without first trying to understand memory and how it contributes to the online narrative that comprises one's sense of self.

In its attempt to contribute to such an understanding, this paper takes a somewhat counterintuitive tack. Rather than trying to tackle memory head-on by examining the ways in which it typically blends into the fabric of our everyday lives, we try to gain insight into the self by instead looking at the imperfections, foibles, and quirks of memory. If memory and self are related, it follows that an understanding of the self will benefit from, or even depend on, a better understanding of memory's imperfections and failures. To this end, we describe memory failures within the context of recent proposals by Schacter (1999, 2001) that memory's imperfections can be organized into seven basic categories or "sins" (by analogy to the seven deadly sins). We first briefly summarize the seven sins of memory and then focus on a pair of the sins that, we believe, have direct and important implications for the self.

THE SEVEN SINS OF MEMORY: A BRIEF OVERVIEW

In the ancient world, and later as part of Catholic theology, the seven deadly sins were those transgressions fatal to spiritual progress. When applied to memory, the seven sins describe those ways in which the normal, everyday operations of our mind may occasionally produce suboptimal or flawed memory experiences. TABLE 1 outlines these seven sins of memory. The first three of the seven memory imperfections can be thought of as sins of omission, that is, different types of forgetting. *Transience* refers to the decreasing accessibility of memory over time. This fundamental feature of memory was first documented in the laboratory by Ebbinghaus (1885/1964) over a century ago, but examples of transience are also plentiful in everyday experience; try, for example, to recall where you were this time exactly one year ago. To the extent that our sense of self is built, at least in part, on these kinds of recollections about what has happened to us, transience will have important implications for self. Indeed, which aspects of our experience remain available to us and which, in contrast, fade away over time will contribute importantly to how we think of ourselves. The second sin, *absent-mindedness*, refers to lapses of attention that result in forgetting to do things. We all experience this kind of irritating, everyday forgetfulness when we cannot recall where we

TABLE 1. The seven sins of memory

Sin	Description	Example
Transience	Decreasing accessibilty of memory over time	Simple forgetting of long-past events
Absent-mindedness	Lapses of attention that result in forgetting	Forgetting location of car keys
Blocking	Information is present but temporarily accessible	Tip-of-the-tongue
Misattribution	Memories are attributed to an incorrect source	Confusing a dream for a memory
Suggestibility	Implanted memories about things that never occurred	Leading questions produce false memories
Bias	Current knowledge and beliefs distort our memories of the past	Recalling past attitudes in line with current attitudes
Persistence	Unwanted recollections that we can never forget	Traumatic war memories

placed our eyeglasses or when we temporarily lose our car in a crowded parking lot. However, this sin does not appear to be strongly related to the self. The third sin, *blocking,* refers to cases in which information has not faded out of memory but is temporarily inaccessible for a variety of reasons. The most common example of blocking is probably the "tip of the tongue" experience, where we temporarily cannot retrieve a name or word that, nevertheless, we are certain that we know (e.g., Schwartz, 1999; Maril, Wagner & Schacter, 2001). Examples of blocking of more direct relevance to the self can be found in rare, but fascinating, cases of amnesia in which people are unable to recall large aspects of their past and even their own identities (Kihlstrom & Schacter, 2000; Klein, Rozendal & Cosmides, 2002).

In contrast, the next three sins can be thought of as sins of commission: instances in which memory is present but wrong. *Misattribution* occurs when we remember that something happened to us, but attribute the memory to an incorrect source. We might recall, for example, that we heard a fact on the radio, when it was instead told to us by a friend. Or, we might have only imagined doing something but then mistakenly come to believe that we've actually done it, sometimes resulting in a phenomenon called false recognition. The second sin in this group, *suggestibility,* refers to implanted memories, often generated by leading questions or suggestions that lead us to believe things about ourselves, sometimes entire events, that never actually occurred. Dramatic examples of suggestibility have been documented, such as the bizarre story of Paul Ingram. Ingram, a Washington State sheriff's deputy, came to believe that he had sexually abused his daughters as part of his participation in a satanic cult (Wright, 1994). Although all indications are that the incidents in question never happened and that his beliefs were formed largely in response to suggestive questioning, Ingram came to a radically different view of his past—and self—than was warranted by actual events. Ingram eventually came to reject his suggested memories, but such examples of suggestibility (for review, see Loftus & Ketcham, 1994; Pendergrast, 1995; Schacter, 1996, 2001) illustrate the wide-ranging implications of memory distortion for the sense of self. The third of the distortion-related sins, *bias*, refers to the ways in which our current knowledge and beliefs can distort our memories for the past. Indeed, what we know and believe about ourselves in the present can be a powerful lens through which we view the past (Ross & Wilson, 2000).

Finally, *persistence*, the seventh sin, refers to unwanted recollections that people cannot forget. These tend to be traumatic experiences that haunt our memories and that cannot be expunged from our mind. Persisting memories can, in extreme cases, become self-defining recollections that permanently color how we view the present, past, and future, such as the intrusive memories sometimes experienced by war veterans or survivors of sexual assault (Applebaum, Uyehara & Elin, 1998; Holman & Silver, 1998).

This brief overview suggests a number of intriguing points of contact between self and the memory sins. As mentioned above, the connection between memory and self is most obviously apparent for two of the memory sins—misattribution and bias—and we now turn to highlighting the implications of these two sins for an understanding of the self. Our laboratory has begun to examine both of these sins using a combination of cognitive, neuroimaging, and neuropsychological approaches, and we briefly describe some of this work in the context of related observations made by others.

MEMORY SINS: MISATTRIBUTION

As he did about most topics of psychological inquiry, William James had something interesting to say both about memory distortion in general as well as about how inaccurate memories are related to the self. In his classic *Principles of Psychology*, James (1890) made an explicit link between memory errors and the self:

> Alterations of memory are either losses or false recollections. In either case the me is changed. False memories are by no means rare occurrences in most of us, and, whenever they occur, they distort the consciousness of the me. Most people, probably, are in doubt about certain matters ascribed to their past. They may have seen them, may have said them, done them, or they may only have dreamed or imagined they did so. (James, [1890/1950], p. 373)

According to James, then, errors in remembering not only produce memory distortions but also result in self-distortions. Knowing whether we actually did something—or only dreamed or imagined it—clearly has significance for how we understand both our autobiographical history and our general sense of self. When we mistake a dream or a fantasy for an actual event in the past, we are committing a classic misattribution error with the potential to change how we view ourselves and our relationships with others (Jacoby, Kelley & Dywan 1989; Johnson, Hashtroudi & Lindsay, 1993; Schacter, 2001).

One striking illustration of how a distorted memory can result in a distorted —or even false—self comes from an extreme case of misattribution following brain damage. Moscovitch (1989) described the interesting case of H.W., who sustained damage to the ventromedial aspects of the frontal lobes (the basal forebrain area) as a result of a burst aneurysm. The location of the brain damage caused H.W. to be amnesic for previous events, rendering him unable to recall his past experiences. More interestingly, however, H.W. filled in the gaps in his memory by confabulating. This fabrication of a new past that makes sense of the self can be seen in the following excerpt (Moscovitch, 1989, pp. 135–137):

MOSCOVITCH: Can you just tell me a little bit about yourself? How old are you?
H.W.: I'm 40, 42. Pardon me, 62. [the latter is correct]
MOSCOVITCH: Are you married or single?
H.W.: Married.
MOSCOVITCH: How long have you been married?
H.W.: Oh, about 4 months.
MOSCOVITCH: What's your wife's name?
H.W.: Martha. [correct]
MOSCOVITCH: How many children do you have?
H.W.: Four [he laughs]. Not bad for four months.

H.W. goes on to talk a little bit about his children, accurately naming all of them, and then Moscovitch asks the patient if everything he had been saying sounds a little strange. Laughing, H.W. said he did think it a little strange. But then the depth of H.W.'s conviction becomes clear:

MOSCOVITCH: I think when I looked at your record it said that you've been married for over 30 years. Does that sound more reasonable to you if I told you that?
H.W.: No.
MOSCOVITCH: Do you really believe that you have been married for four months?
H.W.: Yes.
MOSCOVITCH: You have been married for a long time to the same woman, for over 30 years. Do you find that strange?
H.W.: Very strange.

Although H.W. has manufactured what appears to be a false self, he still has the general sense of his past right. He knows that he has been married and the names of his four children, but he is wrong on one critical dimension, the temporal context of his past. He lacks appropriate information regarding the relative timing of life events, and therefore misattributes some key experiences that have occurred over the past thirty years to the past four years. In addition, he also seems to have a defective ability to monitor the appropriateness of this information.

Clearly, H.W. represents an extreme case of misattribution (for other cases in which damage to frontal regions is associated with heightened misattribution, see Parkin, Ward, Binschaedler, Squires & Powell, 1999; Schacter, Curran, Galluccio, Milberg & Bates, 1996). Recently, we have been examining more prosaic forms of misattribution in the laboratory, to help explain both the extreme cases like H.W., as well as how misattribution may be relevant to understanding's one's own past—and hence, self—more generally.

One method recently developed by psychologists to study misattribution and its neural bases is known as the Deese–Roediger–McDermott (or DRM) paradigm (Roediger & McDermott, 1995). In the DRM paradigm, participants study a set of associated words that all converge on a non-presented theme word, which is never seen or heard during study list presentation. For example, participants might hear the following list of words: *candy, sour, sugar, bitter, good, taste, tooth, nice, honey, soda, chocolate, heart, cake, eat,* and *pie*. Later, participants perform a recognition test consisting of words from the study list, such as *taste*, along with completely unrelated words that were not presented earlier, such as *point*. Critically, the recognition test also includes a nonstudied theme word on which all the studied associates converge, such as *sweet*. Numerous studies using the DRM procedure show that, after having studied lists like the one above, participants exhibit extremely high levels of false alarms to the theme word—sometimes indistinguishable from hit rates to studied words—and that these false alarms are often accompanied by extremely high confidence. Even in this straightforward experimental paradigm, then, people can feel certain that they recently experienced an event—hearing the word *sweet* on the study list—that, in fact, had never occurred (e.g., Gallo & Roediger, 2002; Norman & Schacter, 1997; Payne, Elie, Blackwell & Neuschatz, 1996; Roediger & McDermott, 1995).

One way to think about this misattribution error is that it represents memory for the general sense, or gist, of what was presented. Indeed, these misattributed memories are "accurate" at the semantic or gist level (cf., Brainerd & Reyna, 1998; Payne et al., 1996; Schacter, Verfaellie & Pradere, 1996), since participants in these types of experiments heard words that referred to just about everything to do with sweetness, except the word *sweet* itself. Thus, false recognition in the DRM procedure may be one way of getting a handle on memory for general or gist-like information and its contributions to misattribution more generally.

To understand the brain basis for these kinds of misattribution errors, we have taken several complementary approaches, including the study of amnesic patients. Such patients typically have experienced damage to the hippocampus and related structures in the medial temporal lobe or to regions of the diencephalon. As a result, these patients are unable to remember their recent experiences explicitly, despite otherwise normal cognitive functions (for review, see Kopelman, 2002; Squire, 1992). The studies in our laboratory included a mixed group of amnesics that included cases of Korsakoff's disease, as well as patients with damage to the medial temporal lobe as a result of anoxia, encephalitis, and stroke. Using the DRM procedure, these studies (Schacter, Verfaellie & Pradere, 1996; Schacter, Verfaellie & Anes, 1997; Schacter, Verfaellie, Anes & Racine, 1998; Verfaellie, Schacter & Cook, 2002) have consistently shown that amnesic patients are less susceptible to this form of misattribution error than are healthy controls (for similar findings from related procedures, see Koutstaal, Schacter, Verfaellie, Brenner & Jackson, 1999; Koutstaal, Schacter & Verfaellie, 2001). This finding is reliably observed despite the fact that amnesics tend to false alarm *more* often than controls to unrelated words that had no associative links to words presented earlier.

One way of framing these results is to suggest that the medial temporal lobe and diencephalic structures damaged in amnesic patients play a critical role in remembering the general sense or gist of what has recently taken place. We know that such regions are, of course, critical for remembering the particular words on a study list or the specifics of past events, and these results would suggest that the same regions may also contribute importantly to gist memory. In other words, because of damage to medial temporal lobe and diencephalic regions, amnesics may lose out on both specific memory as well as gist memory.

This framework is supported by neuroimaging studies in which we scanned participants during the recognition component of the DRM procedure, after having studied a series of associate lists. Our initial studies revealed activation in the vicinity of the medial temporal lobes during both true recognition and false recognition as compared to a low-level fixation baseline (Schacter, Reiman, et al., 1996; Schacter, Buckner, et al., 1997). Interestingly, there were no differences in the medial temporal regions during true recognition and false recognition, highlighting the strength of participants' false memory for the critical lures.

In a more recent study (Cabeza, Rao, Wagner, Mayer & Schacter, 2001), we again presented DRM lists (along with similar categorized lists) during study. Lists were presented on videotape by either a male or female source, and participants were instructed to try to remember both the words and by whom they were presented. This slightly different experimental design was used to increase the amount of visual/perceptual processing in which participants engaged during study list presentation: previous behavioral research has indicated that when participants focus on perceptual information during study of DRM lists, false recognition is reduced relative to true recognition (e.g., Schacter, Israel & Racine, 1999). Following our "perceptual" study conditions, fMRI was used to scan participants during a recognition test. Replicating and extending previous results, we found that the hippocampus showed activation during both true and false recognition compared with a control condition in which subjects responded to new words that were unrelated to previously studied words; there were no differences in hippocampal activation during true and false recognition. In contrast, a different structure within the medial temporal lobe, the parahippocampal gyrus, showed greater activation during true recognition than during false recognition, perhaps reflecting memory for perceptual aspects of the study context. This idea is consistent with several lines of evidence implicating the parahippocampal gyrus in visual processing and memory (for discussion, see Cabeza et al., 2001).

Together, the neuropsychological and neuroimaging data suggest that the hippocampus may be involved in making semantic or associative information available to support memory for the general gist of previously studied items. Although the studies we considered used word lists in laboratory settings, it is nonetheless interesting to think about the potential role of the hippocampus for the larger issue of memory and self. Clearly, a brain region that plays a role in memory for the gist of the past should contribute importantly to the maintenance of a sense of a consistent self over time. However, because neuroimaging investigations of the self have only recently begun, we can only speculate at the present time about the critical role played by the hippocampus in maintaining a sense of self.

MEMORY SINS: BIAS

As mentioned above, bias can be defined as retrospective distortions produced by current knowledge and beliefs. Schacter (2001) delineated five different types of memory biases (consistency, change, egocentric, hindsight, and stereotypic biases). The bias most directly relevant to the present discussion is *egocentric bias,* a pervasive tendency to remember the past in a self-enhancing manner. The existence of such a bias is, of course, no surprise: one need only look to the quintessential "fish tale," in which the incredible size of an earlier year's catch is extolled. The existence of such egocentric biases has also been demonstrated empirically in elegant studies conducted by Michael Ross and his colleagues (see, for example, Ross & Wilson, 2000), who have demonstrated a variety of ways in which people distort past recollections in order to enhance the present self (see also Taylor's [1988, 1991] work on positive illusions).

Egocentric bias reflects, in part, the strong role played by the self in the encoding and retrieval of episodic memories. Beginning with the work of Rogers and colleagues (Rogers, Kuiper & Kirker, 1977), and since replicated and extended by many others (for review, see Symons & Johnson, 1997), it has been shown that when information is encoded in relation to ourselves, it is usually better remembered than other types of semantic information. These findings, often referred to collectively as the "self-reference effect," suggest that the self serves as a potent knowledge structure with a powerful influence on what we retain and later recall from our everyday experiences.

Recently, Kelley et al. (2002; see also Craik et al., 1999) have used fMRI to elucidate some of the brain regions that play a role in the self-reference effect. In this study, participants were scanned while they either decided whether a series of trait adjectives (e.g., *honest, friendly*) described themselves or decided whether they described a familiar other person (in this case, George Bush). The first condition has been used extensively to engage processing in relation to the self, while the latter condition is assumed to involve semantic, but not self-referent, encoding. These conditions were compared to a nonsemantic encoding condition in which participants judged whether words appeared in upper or lower case. Semantic, but non-self, encoding (compared with the nonsemantic control condition) was associated with activation in the left inferior prefrontal cortex, an area implicated in semantic encoding by a number of earlier fMRI studies (e.g., Wagner et al., 1998). In contrast, self-referent encoding was associated with activation in a distinct frontal region, the medial prefrontal cortex. These findings therefore suggest a link between the medial prefrontal region and encoding of information relevant to the self, although the nature of that link is not well understood. However, because self-referent encoding did not simply produce more activation in the same brain regions as semantic, non-self encoding, these data strongly suggest that self-referent encoding is not merely a stronger form of semantic encoding. Rather, self-referent and semantic encoding engaged distinct brain regions, suggesting a qualitative difference between the two types of memory encoding.

Likewise, a form of bias closely related to egocentric bias, called *consistency bias*, also bears on our understanding of the self. Consistency bias refers to our tendency to reshape the past to make it consistent with present knowledge and beliefs. The work of Ross and colleagues (Ross & Wilson, 2000) indicates that this kind of bias is often used to help preserve self-stability, allowing us to remember the past in a way that supports our current self. A classic study by Marcus (1986) on political attitudes illustrates the point. Individuals were asked to rate their attitudes towards various political issues in 1973 and then again in 1982. In the 1982 session, they were also asked to recall what their attitudes had been back in 1973. Critically, people demonstrated a systematic tendency to misjudge their past attitudes in a particular direction; specifically, people tended to misremember their past attitudes in line with the attitudes they currently held. For instance, if a person had expressed liberal views on drug use in 1973 but had grown more conservative over the intervening decade, they were likely to recall their earlier stance as more conservative than it had actually been. According to Ross and others, this type of consistency bias allows us to present ourselves as being stable and consistent over time, even though, in fact, we have changed.

Consistency bias is also related an to interesting phenomenon with clear relevance to the understanding of the self, namely *cognitive dissonance*, which has been studied extensively by social psychologists. Cognitive dissonance refers to the psychological discomfort that results from conflicting thoughts and feelings. For example, an unhappily married person who believes that her marriage should be successful may try to distort the past to make the present seem more palatable. A man who purchases an expensive car, but then reads a negative review asserting that the car has serious problems, might try to belittle the reviewer as a misinformed or ignorant amateur who should not be writing about cars.

Social psychologists have traditionally assumed that the experience of cognitive dissonance requires the ability to recall the behavior that produced conflict in the first place. If the man who bought the car does not remember making the purchase, the bad magazine review should not bother him and he should not experience dissonance. This rationale assumes that the past can influence the present only through conscious or explicit recollection of past happenings. However, more than two decades worth of research on implicit memory (Schacter, 1987) has demonstrated that past experiences can influence subsequent experience and behavior despite an absence of conscious or explicit recollection. This effect is revealed most clearly in studies of amnesic patients, who often exhibit intact implicit memory for recent experiences despite reduced or completely absent explicit memory (for reviews, see Schacter & Curran, 2000; Squire, 1992; Verfaellie & Keane, 2002).

Can cognitive dissonance occur in the absence of explicit memory? If so, then amnesic patients should be susceptible to the effect, just like healthy participants in earlier studies. Lieberman, Ochsner, Gilbert & Schacter (2001) have provided relevant data. This study was based on earlier work in which consistency bias and dissonance were created by asking participants to choose one of two art prints that they had previously rated as equally desirable. After making this somewhat difficult choice, people later claim to like the chosen print more and the rejected print less than they had indicated earlier. Presumably, people act to reduce the dissonance that arises from choosing one print over the other by indicating that they had liked the preferred print better all along. The question that Lieberman et al. (2001) asked is whether this type of bias require explicit recall of which print was chosen.

To address this question, amnesic patients and control participants first ranked art prints according to how much they liked them. Both groups of participants then made a choice between two prints, indicating which one they would prefer to hang in their homes. Later, they ranked all the prints a second time according to how much they liked them. Finally, all participants were given an explicit memory test in which they were asked to indicate which prints they had chosen earlier. As one would expect, amnesic patients showed no explicit memory for which prints they had chosen earlier, whereas controls remembered their choices well. Nevertheless, both groups of participants inflated how much they liked the chosen print relative to the print they had passed over. That is, amnesic patients—just like control participants—ranked the chosen print higher and the rejected print lower during the second ranking compared with the first ranking; in contrast, there was no change in the rankings of control prints about which subjects made no choice. These results suggest that amnesic patients were trying to reduce the dissonance created by choosing between the two prints even though they lacked conscious memory for making the choice that produced dissonance in the first place.

To the extent that the type of cognitive dissonance examined in this paradigm is related to a consistency bias that people use to maintain stability between current and past selves, the results suggest that considering implicit forms of memory is critical for understanding the relation between memory and self. Indeed, this is a key point made by LeDoux (2002) in *Synaptic Self*, where he argues that much of what we call "self" is the product of implicit learning and memory processes that occur without awareness. We concur with this assessment and suggest that future research on memory and self explore this link more fully.

CONCLUDING COMMENTS

We have considered a variety of ways in which imperfections of memory, especially misattribution and bias, may relate to the self. Although still in its infancy, existing cognitive, neuropsychological, and neuroimaging research on the self has already begun to illuminate relevant issues. Against the backdrop of these recent attempts to understand the link between memory and self, we are impressed by the prescience and cogency of Williams James' observation that false memories "distort the consciousness of the me." Since it is never a bad idea to refer back to James when speculating about broad psychological topics, we conclude by offering one of his general reflections about the relation between memory and self as food for thought:

> If a man wakes up some fine day unable to recall any his past experiences, so that he has to learn his biography afresh, or if he only recalls the facts of it in a cold abstract way, as things that he is sure once happened, or if, without this loss of memory, his bodily and spiritual habits all change during the night, each organ giving a different tone, and the act of thought becoming aware of itself in a different way, he feels and he says that he is a changed person (James, [1890/1950], p. 336).

ACKNOWLEDGMENTS

Preparation of this paper was supported by Grants NIA AG08441 and NIMH MH57505 to D.L.S. J.P.M. was supported by a predoctoral National Research Service Award fellowship. J.Y.C. was supported by a National Science Foundation predoctoral fellowship.

REFERENCES

APPLEBAUM, P.S., UYEHARA, L.A. & ELIN, M.R. (1998). *Trauma and memory: Clinical and legal controversies.* London, U.K.: Oxford University Press.

BRAINERD, C.J. & REYNA, V.F. (1998). When things that were never experienced are easier to "remember" than things that were. *Psychological Science, 9,* 484–489

CABEZA, R., RAO, S.M.,WAGNER, A.D., MAYER, A. & SCHACTER, D.L. (2001). Can medial temporal lobe regions distinguish true from false? An event-related functional MRI study of veridical and illusory recognition memory. *Proceedings of the National Academy of Sciences USA 98(8),* 4805–4810.

CRAIK, F.I.M., MOROZ, T.M., MOSCOVITCH, M., STUSS, D.T., WINOCUR, G., TULVING, E. & KAPUR, S. (1999). In search of the self: A PET investigation of self-referential information. *Psychological Science, 10,* 26–34.

EBBINGHAUS, H. (1885/1964). *Memory: A contribution to experimental psychology.* New York: Columbia University, Teacher's College.

GALLO, D.A. & ROEDIGER, H.L., III. (2002). Variability among word lists in evoking memory illusions: Evidence for associative activation and monitoring. *Journal of Memory and Language, 47,* 469–497.

GREENWALD, A.G. (1980). The totalitarian ego: Fabrication and revision of personal history. *American Psychologist, 35,* 603–618.

HOLMAN, E.A. & SILVER, R.C. (1998). Getting "stuck" in the past: Temporal orientation and coping with trauma. *Journal of Personality and Social Psychology, 74,* 1146–1163.

JACOBY, L.L., KELLEY, C.M., & DYWAN, J. (1989). Memory attributions. In H.L. Roediger & F.I.M. Craik (Eds.), *Varieties of memory and consciousness: Essays in honour of Endel Tulving* (pp. 391–422). Hillsdale, NJ: Erlbaum.

JAMES, W. (1890). *Principles of psychology.* New York: Holt.

JOHNSON, M., HASHTROUDI, S. & LINDSAY, D. (1993). Source monitoring. *Psychological Bulletin, 114,* 3–28.

KELLEY, W.M.,MACRAE C.N., WYLAND C.L., CAGLAR, S., INATI, S., HEATHERTON, T.F. (2002). Finding the self? An event-related fMRI study. *Journal of Cognitive Neuroscience, 14(5),* 785–794.

KIHLSTROM, J.F. & SCHACTER, D.L. (2000). Functional amnesia. In F. Boller & J. Grafman (Eds.), *Handbook of neuropsychology,* 2nd ed. (Vol. 2: *Memory and its disorders,* ed. by L.S. Cermak, pp. 409–427). Amsterdam: Elsevier Science.

KLEIN, S.B., ROZENDAL, K. & COSMIDES, L. (2002). A social-cognitive neuroscience analysis of the self. *Social Cognition, 20(2),* 105–135.

KOPELMAN, M D. (2002). Disorders of memory. *Brain, 125(10),* 2152–2190.

KOUTSTAAL, W., SCHACTER, D.L., VERFAELLIE, M., BRENNER, C. & JACKSON, E.M. (1999). Perceptually based false recognition of novel objects in amnesia: Effects of category size and similarity to category prototypes. *Cognitive Neuropsychology, 16,* 317–341.

KOUTSTAAL, W., VERFAELLIE, M. & SCHACTER, D.L. (2001). Recognizing identical versus similar categorically related common objects: Further evidence for degraded gist-representation in amnesia. *Neuropsychology, 15,* 268–289.

LEDOUX, J. (2002). *Synaptic self: how our brains become who we are.* New York: Viking Penguin.

LIEBERMAN, M.D., OCHSNER, K.., GILBERT, D.T. & SCHACTER, D.L. (2001). Do amnesics exhibit cognitive dissonance reduction? The role of explicit memory and attention in attitude change. *Psychological Science, 12(2),* 135–140

LOFTUS, E. & KETCHAM, K. (1994). *The myth of repressed memory: false memories and allegations of sexual abuse.* New York: St. Martin's Press.

MARCUS, G.B. (1986). Stability and change in political attitudes: Observe, recall, and "explain." *Political Behavior, 8,* 21–44.

MARIL, A., WAGNER, A. & SCHACTER, D.L. (2001). On the tip of the tongue: An event-related fMRI study of semantic retrieval failure and cognitive conflict. *Neuron, 31(4),* 653–660.

MILL, J.S. (1829/1982). *Analysis of the phenomena of the human mind.* London, UK: Longmans, Green, Reader, and Dyer.

MOSCOVITCH, M. (1989). Confabulation and the frontal system: Strategic vs. associative retrieval in neuropsychological theories of memory. In H. L. Roediger III & F. I. M. Craik (Eds.), *Varieties of memory and consciousness: Essays in honour of Endel Tulving* (pp. 133–160). Hillsdale, NJ: Erlbaum.

NORMAN, K.A. & SCHACTER, D.L. (1997). False recognition in young and older adults: Exploring the characteristics of illusory memories. *Memory and Cognition, 25,* 838–848.

PARKIN, A.J., WARD, J., BINSCHAEDLER, C., POWELL, G. & SQUIRES, E.J. (1999). False recognition following frontal lobe damage: The role of encoding factors. *Cognitive Neuropsychology, 16,* 243–266.

PAYNE, D.G., ELIE, C.J., BLACKWELL, J.M. & NEUSCHATZ, J.S. (1996). Memory illusions: recalling, recognizing and recollecting events that never occurred. *Journal of Memory and Language, 35,* 261–285.

PENDERGRAST, M. (1995). *Victims of memory: Incest accusations and shattered lives.* London, UK: Harper Collins.

ROEDIGER, H.L., & MCDERMOTT, K.B. (1995). Creating false memories: Remembering words not presented in lists. *Journal of Experimental Psychology: Learning, Memory and Cognition, 22(3),* 814–816.

ROGERS, T.B., KUIPER, N.A., & KIRKER, W.S. (1977). Self-reference and the encoding of personal information. *Journal of Personality and Social Psychology,* 35, 677–688.

ROSS, M. & WILSON, A.E. (2000). Constructing and appraising past selves. In D.L. Schacter & E. Scarry (Eds.), *Memory, Brain and Belief.* (pp. 231–258). Cambridge, MA: Harvard University Press.

SCHACTER, D.L. (1996). *Searching for memory: The brain, the mind, the past.* New York: Basic Books.

SCHACTER, D.L. (1999). The seven sins of memory: Insights from psychology and cognitive neuroscience. *American Psychologist, 54,* 182–203.

SCHACTER, D.L. (2001). *The seven sins of memory: How the mind forgets and remembers.* Boston, MA: Houghton Mifflin.

SCHACTER, D.L., BUCKNER, R.L., KOUTSTAAL, W., DALE, A. & ROSEN, B. (1997). Late onset of anterior prefrontal activity during true and false recognition: An event-related fMRI study. *NeuroImage, 6,* 259–269.

SCHACTER, D.L. & CURRAN, T. (2000). Memory without remembering and remembering without memory: Implicit and false memories. In M.S. Gazzaniga (Ed.) *The cognitive neurosciences.* (2nd ed.). Cambridge, MA: MIT Press.

SCHACTER, D.L., CURRAN, T., GALLUCCIO, L., MILBERG, W. & BATES, J. (1996). False recognition and the right frontal lobe: A case study. *Neuropsychologia, 34,* 793–808.

SCHACTER, D.L., ISRAEL, L. & RACINE, C. (1999). Suppressing false recognition in younger and older adults: The distinctiveness heuristic. *Journal of Memory and Language, 40*, 1–24.

SCHACTER, D.L., REIMAN, E., CURRAN, T., SHENG YUN, L., BANDY, D., McDERMOTT, K.B. & ROEDIGER, H.L. (1996). Neuroanatomical correlates of veridical and illusory recognition memory: Evidence from positron emission tomography. *Neuron, 17,* 1–20.

SCHACTER, D.L., VERFAELLIE, M. & PRADERE, D. (1996). The neuropsychology of memory illusions: False recall and recognition in amnesic patients. *Journal of Memory and Language, 35*, 319–334.

SCHACTER, D.L., VERFAELLIE, M. & ANES, M.D. (1997). Illusory memories in amnesic patients: Conceptual and perceptual false recognition. *Neuropsychology, 11*, 331–342.

SCHACTER, D.L., VERFAELLIE, M., ANES, M. & RACINE, C. (1998). When true recognition suppresses false recognition: Evidence from amnesic patients. *Journal of Cognitive Neuroscience, 10*, 668–679.

SCHWARTZ, B.L. (1999). Sparkling at the end of the tongue: The etiology of tip-of-the-tongue phenomenology. *Psychonomic Bulletin Review, 6(3),* 379–93.

SQUIRE, L.R. (1992). Memory and the hippocampus: A synthesis from findings with rats, monkeys, and humans. *Psychological Review, 99*, 195–231.

SYMONS, C.S., & JOHNSON, B.T. (1997). The self-reference effect in memory: A meta-analysis. *Psychological Bulletin, 121,* 371–394.

TAYLOR, S.E. (1989). *Positive illusions: Creative self-deception and the healthy mind.* New York: Basic Books.

VERFAELLIE, M., SCHACTER, D.L. & COOK, S.P. (2002). The effect of retrieval instructions on false recognition: exploring the nature of the gist memory impairment in amnesia. *Neuropsychologia, 40(13)*, 2360–2368.

VERFAELLIE, M. & KEANE, M. M. (2002). Impaired and preserved memory processes in amnesia. In Squire, L.R. & Schacter, D.L. (Eds.). *Neuropsychology of memory (3rd ed.)*, pp. 35–46 . New York: Guilford Press, pp. 35–46.

WAGNER, A.D., DESMOND, J.E., GLOVER, G.H., & GABRIELI, J.D.E. (1998). Prefrontal cortex and recognition memory: fMRI evidence for context-dependent retrieval processes. *Brain,121,* 1985–2002.

WRIGHT, L. (1994). *Remembering satan.* New York: Knopf.

Renovating the House of Being

Genomes, Souls, and Selves

ALEX MAURON

Bioethics Research and Teaching Unit, Faculty of Medicine, University of Geneva, Switzerland

ABSTRACT: In recent years, the views of the German philosopher Peter Sloterdijk about humanism and the biological self-engineering of mankind caused much turmoil in European intellectual circles. However, this is just one episode in a more general current controversy about the ethics of self-manipulation, a debate that often centers around the recent progress in genomics and the possibility of shaping human genetic structure. The complete sequencing of the human genome has reinforced this focus. Making the human genome the object of a highly visible world-wide research effort has reinforced popular notions stressing the centrality of the genome in defining individuality and humanity. As a result, proponents and opponents of the self-engineering of human nature have often concentrated on technologies related to the genome. However, if one compares "genome-based" and "brain-based" explanations of Self and behavior, it turns out that neural aspects of human nature are more directly relevant. Many philosophical and ethical questions traditionally raised about genetics and genomics acquire more relevance and urgency when re-examined in the context of neuroscience.

KEYWORDS: genome; genetic essentialism; bioethics; neuroethics; Sloterdijk

A PHILOSOPHICAL SKIRMISH

"Who could overlook the fact that the house of being is disappearing under scaffolding—and nobody knows what it will look like after the renovations." This quotation is from the well-known German philosopher Peter Sloterdijk, who gave a presentation at the Los Angeles Goethe Institute a few years ago under the title "The Operable Man" (Sloterdijk, 2000a). Sloterdijk had

Address for correspondence: Alexandre Mauron, Ph.D., Bioethics Research and Teaching Unit, University of Geneva Medical School, CH1211, Geneve 4, Switzerland. Voice: +41-22 702 5790; fax: +41-22 702 5792.

alexandre.mauron@medecine.unige.ch

Ann. N.Y. Acad. Sci. 1001: 240–252 (2003). © 2003 New York Academy of Sciences.
doi: 10.1196/annals.1279.013

become famous in central Europe because of a rather fierce public controversy. In 1999, he gave a lecture on Heidegger's *Letter on Humanism* at Elmau in Bavaria. In this talk, he supposedly advocated a program of genetic revision of the human species by large-scale genetic engineering. This caused a public outcry among German academic philosophers as well as in the highbrow press, who accused Peter Sloterdijk of wanting to revive a program of Nazi-like eugenics and selective breeding of future human generations. (Graumann [2000] provides a useful account of the debate and its implications as regards the standing of philosophical expertise in public discourse.) The title of Sloterdijk's text (2000b), "Rules for the Human Park," and its zoological metaphor were provocative and seemed to lend themselves to this interpretation. Nevertheless, a more accurate study of Sloterdijk's views shows that these accusations represent a fairly crude misreading of his statements. This does not mean that Sloterdijk's views are bland and uncontroversial; quite to the contrary. However, his claim is rather that traditional humanistic education is already a form of "human domestication," and as such perhaps not so different in principle from future biological interventions into human nature. In other words, the misunderstanding between Sloterdijk and his critics was based on their belief that Sloterdijk's program is one of replacing the noble ideas of humanistic education by a biotechnological dystopia of human breeding, selection and brutal manipulation. In reality, far from advocating such a eugenic program, Sloterdijk maintains a critical distance both from classical humanism and from the self-shaping character of modern "anthropotechniques," as he calls them. In fact, this new word is used in the Sloterdijkian vocabulary as a common concept for traditional education and domestication and biotechnologically based autopoietic interventions by humans on humans, along the lines of the motto *homo faber sui ipsius* ["man, maker of himself"]. Sloterdijk then calls for a common code to regulate all anthropotechniques, whether they are traditional or biologically based.

These views result from Sloterdijk's persistent engagement with philosophical anthropology in the Continental sense, as well as with the thought of Heidegger and Nietzsche. In his "Rules for the Human Park" (2000b), Sloterdijk traces the genealogy of contemporary humanistic thinking from the "telecommunication" of the learned elites, both by direct correspondence in letter writing and by the dialogue of learned minds through great books crossing the centuries (this is a *topos* that pervades humanistic culture: It is "ce tintamarre de tant de cervelles philosophiques"—the din of so many philosophical brains—that Montaigne imagines hearing while sitting quietly in his library [Montaigne, 1595]). Sloterdijk shows how this form of humanism evolved into bourgeois humanism, from the French Revolution onwards all the way to the end of World War II, acquiring more and more authoritarian overtones as its claims to universal validity become more and more self-assured: "The absolute power of imposing the classics to youth and to assert the universal validity of national readings" (Sloterdijk, 2000c). Finally, the last half century has seen the demise of modern humanism as a tool of social control and as a means for taming the beast in man and controlling social violence. This does not mean that humanism has disappeared. In the words of a French commentator of Sloterdijk, Yves Michaud, "literature has not disappeared for all that: it has merely become one subculture among others. Such is the crisis of humanism, with the overwhelming savagery and bestiality of the 20th century" (Michaud, 2002). Actually, Sloterdijk's critique of humanism can be seen as rather ambiguous. Is it humanism's failure at efficient domestication of man's bestiality which is at issue, or is this domestication itself called into question, in a Nietzschean vein? This ambivalence is reflected in his assessment of biological anthropotechniques and explains why his work has been variously interpreted as an enthusiastic clarion call for the biotechnological reform of mankind, or as a critical or nostalgic negative commentary on this technological enterprise. Whatever the case may be, what is radically taken to task in Sloterdijk's writings is the conventional moral divide between traditional humanistic education (good) and biotechnological influence of human nature (bad). Roughly speaking, both are thought to be ethically ambivalent.

What made Sloterdijk's recent works controversial, and even inflammatory for some, is his revival of the theme of *homo faber sui ipsius* without condemning it out of hand. This topic fuels contemporary imagination in many ways and also creates a great deal of controversy in contemporary cultures, although it is basically a very old *topos* of Western civilization. One should mention the Platonic myth of Prometheus and Epimetheus, which already contrasts the animal's determined capabilities and fixed fate with man's destiny, the latter being indeterminately open towards shaping and self-shaping, because humans are endowed with the open-ended gifts of fire and *technai* (the arts). Sloterdijk's previous work had been concerned with the way humans creates "spheres", that is, controlled environments which isolate them from the randomness of nature and basically consist of extensions of their own nature, which retroactively influences itself. In his recent work (2000c) *The Domestication of Being* this theme is taken up again. Since humans are masters of *technai*—but, of course, even more so now that technique includes biotechnology—humans have been constructing bubbles which insulate them from selective pressure. In these novel, artificialized environments, the nurturing capacities of nature and culture are increasingly indistinguishable. Not for nothing does Sloterdijk call these bubbles "utero-technical environments."

CO-CREATOR OR DEMIURGE?

But let us go back to the theme of *homo faber sui ipsius*. It is not only immemorial as a *topos*, but its moral ambivalence is old as well. An important

strand in classical and Christian culture views this faculty of man quite positively. One of the best-known statements of this view comes from the Renaissance writer, Giovanni Pico della Mirandola, who writes in his "On the
Dignity of Man" (1486):

> God chose to have man as a creature that does not have any distinctive image;
> He placed him in the middle of the world and spoke to him: "We did not give
> you any specific home nor an specific face nor any other special gift, oh Adam,
> so that you may have and possess any home, any face and any gift that you sure-
> ly wish for yourself according to your wish and own opinion. (p. 18)"

More recently, a strand of theological thinking intitiated by the German
theologian Karl Rahner has extolled man's status as a co-creator, a collaborator of the Creator God, including to some extent a co-creator of human nature (reviewed by Cole-Turner [1987]). On the other hand, there is a strand of
contemporary thinking, discernible, for instance, in the writing of the more
conservative bioethicists, which sees autopoietic ambitions of humans as the
ultimate *hubris*, especially in debates on gene technology, cloning, embryo
research, and the like. The idea of humans taking charge of their own biological nature is seen as a further step towards the usurpation of divine powers
by man. Although reducing this conservative critique to the oft-mentioned
cry against "playing God" tends to make a straw man of ethical opinions that
are often more subtle, it is nevertheless the case that various forms of rever-
ence for human nature as a given reality outside of human control lie at the
heart of much conservative thinking in bioethics today. This is particularly
clear in the work of several appointees from the humanities and the social sciences to the new President's Council on Bioethics (2002).

One contemporary discussion in which this theme figures prominently is
the debate about reproductive cloning. The bioethicist Dan Brock (2002) remarks that part of the theological disapproval of cloning comes from the idea
that, through reproductive cloning, man is manufactured rather than begotten
by sexual reproduction. On the other hand, everybody agrees that it would be
absurd to ascribe less dignity and worth to a human being that resulted from
cloning than to one that has been born in the traditional way. In the words of
Dan Brock, "[I]t is the nature of the being, not how it is created, that is the
source of its value and makes it worthy of respect: Children created by assisted reproductive technologies do not have less moral value." This statement is uncontroversial, and yet it seems to conflict with a conventional
wisdom that is deep-rooted in Christian culture. According to the Nicean
Creed, Jesus Christ is *"genitum non factum"* ["begotten not made"], and so
is man, since many christological reflections that try to make sense of the human nature of Christ have close connections with traditional Western understandings of the human person, its origin, and its specific dignity and status
in divine and human law. In contemporary culture, "begotten not made" can
be easily naturalized into "begotten by normal sex, not made by biotechnol-

ogy." It appears that such "scientistic" translations of traditional theological and moral views operate in much conservative bioethical thinking on both sides of the Atlantic.

At this point, we have gathered one important insight. Within the general theme of man's shaping of human nature, the sub-theme that links reproduction and self-manufacturing is especially important. Conventional wisdom burdens it with a specific kind of moral disapproval. It is supposed to be especially wrong to manufacture humans rather than to beget them, the latter concept implying an accepting stance towards a gift of nature and God (to express the idea of "having a child," the German language uses the expression *ein Kind bekommen*, literally *to receive a child*). This attitude is also understandable from a historical perspective, because in the European bioethical discussion, the autopoietic *hubris* of man is often summarized under the term "eugenics." But strictly speaking, eugenics only refers to the intentional direction of heritable human nature, which uses procreation as a tool or vehicle of directed change. Furthermore, eugenics basically involves selection within a naturally given diversity of genomes. Historically, eugenic programs always involved the selective breeding of the "good" traits and the weeding out of the "bad," rather than the *de novo* enhancement of human nature. In that sense, the debate on eugenics is necessarily more narrow than the broader issues raised by the program of *homo faber sui ipsius*, the self-engineering of man. Nevertheless, it seems that whenever the issue of technological change of human nature is broached, the notion of eugenics comes to the fore.[a] The broader, and in some sense more interesting, question of whether it is legitimate for mankind to reshape its own nature tends to be reduced to a narrower, genome-centered question, namely whether one should or not allow intentional genomic changes. This illustrates an important strand of current conventional wisdom: that the human genome is increasingly thought of as the "essence" of the human person and that if there is to be a self-shaping of human nature, the genome will necessarily be the principal substrate of this autopoietic endeavour.[b]

---

[a]Another reason is the rhetorical firepower of the word "eugenics." It comes with such historical baggage that it often functions in public discourse as an operator of moral disapproval, rather than as a descriptive term with a precise historical and/or conceptual reference.

[b]When speaking of an autopoietic program, or of *homo faber sui ipsius*, we refer primarily to anthropotechniques that have collective implications, not just individual ones. An example would be germ-line engineering, which affects not just particular individuals, but potentially an indeterminate number of future people. In contrast, purely personal self-modifying practices that would only be sporadically used (say enhancement psychosurgery, to mention a more or less futuristic example) would be less relevant. Still, it may be difficult to trace a clear-cut boundary between the two. For instance, practices that start as purely individual actions but that gain wide currency later thus become social realities. In addition, even if one considered purely individual self-shaping practices, there would remain moral ambiguities. For instance, American culture highly values the "self-made man," but that conventional approval would presumably not extend automatically to self-improvement by purely biological means,that is, without implying traditional moral qualities such as willpower, self-reliance and the like.

SHAPING THE GENOME, SHAPING THE SELF

What does it mean for mankind to shape "it-Self"? As this symposium shows, there are many dimensions to this question. One interpretation of the Self is predominant in such debates for good and for less good reasons. In previous work which I will now summarize, my starting point has been the following question: according to a widely received view, educating, taming, shaping the minds of human beings by traditional means is okay, but intervening in the human genome is not okay. Therefore, why is neuronal manipulation ethical and genomic manipulation unethical? (Mauron, 2000). Part of the answer lays, I believe, in a social representation of the genome as the ontological core of an organism, determining both its individuality and its species identity (Mauron 2001). In the words of Jim Watson, the human genome is, at least in part, "what makes us *us*." Expanding this definition, one could say that the human genome is what makes us human, and my genome is what makes me *me* and you *you*. From this point of view, it becomes easy to see how intervening on the phenotypes of humans will be thought of as superficial, whereas intervening on the genotype will be seen as essential and intimate. Thus it becomes apparent how the metaphor that pits the genome against "all the rest" mobilizes highly suggestive conceptual couples such as "inner–outer" or "core–surface." If we add to this the common idea that genomic modifications are permanent, whereas phenotypic changes are possibly transient, it becomes understandable how, as a substrate of directed human change, the genome becomes more controversial. This genomic essentialism has become a permanent component of popular culture, especially in media reports of the results of behavioral genetics. These are rife with discoveries of the violence gene, the homosexuality gene, the alcoholism gene or even the language gene, presented as exciting findings that are both intellectually alluring and socially dangerous. However, contrary to what many critics of behavioral genetics have asserted, the wrongness of such popularizations does not usually come from any basic mistakes of the research that lies behind them, but from the essentialist metaphysics through which these findings are filtered. In this essentialist view, the genome becomes a bag of essential properties and dispositions that make up the typical human as well as its individual variations.

The problem is that this "genomic metaphysics" is flawed. One of the most interesting ways in which the genome-based concept of individuality can be shown to be deficient is when considering the beginnings of personal individuality as they are discussed in controversies on the standing of the human embryo. The traditional conservative position says that the embryo is a fully fledged human individual ever since fertilization. In actuality, the Catholic church says that the early *embryo should be treated* like a person ever since fertilization, without actually asserting that it *is* a person. This reservation is due to the keen awareness of several Catholic theologians of the fragility of specifically metaphysical assertions surrounding the standing of the early embryo (Ford, 1991).

Although moral condemnation of abortion is very ancient in Christian culture, modern times have seen a change in the reasoning on which this condemnation is based. This is not so much due to knowledge of scientific facts on fertilization and development, but rather to the peculiar way these facts are integrated in a traditional essentialist metaphysical framework. For many theologians subscribing to a conservative position on abortion, embryo research and the like, the old Aristotelian and Scholastic framework of hylomorphism is still valid, although in a revised form that takes on board what many assume to be the results of modern science. Therefore, within that tradition, it is thought that the question of the standing of the early embryo can be resolved straightforwardly by introducing into the classical ontological framework the data of modern biology. The idea is that a novel individual is formed as soon as a new diploid genome is formed at fertilization. In other words, the genome is thought to become the material manifestation of the individual soul. This is yet another example of how conservative bioethical positions often result from a scientistic reinterpretation of classical philosophical or theological positions. The genetic program is made to play the role of the Aristotelian *eidos* or the Scholastic *forma*, which shapes and forms living matter into a specifically human essence. I have examined elsewhere why this conflation of the modern genome concepts with classical ontological categories appears so compelling to individuals steeped in the Scholastic tradition and pointed out the fact that this intellectual familiarity between Aristotelian thought and the informational metaphor of molecular biology was discovered early on in the history of molecular biology (Mauron, 2002). I have also discussed the major failure of genomic accounts on individuality to explain personal identity and this argument is briefly restated here.

The most basic and minimalistic account of the person is contained in the notion of numerical identity. To be a person implies that one is the same person throughout one's biography, that is, that one persists as one and the same individual through time, independently of contingent changes that occur throughout one's life. At first sight, it might be thought that having a genome of a certain kind is a material expression of this numerical identity. This is because a new diploid genome is indeed created at fertilization. This genome is novel in the sense that it results from the contingent reunion of two genealogies, of two independent causal chains that converge onto the new diploid genome. Furthermore, this genome will largely remain the same throughout the possible future individual's life. Nevertheless, the formation of a new genome cannot be equated with the beginning of a new numerical identity and this can be easily shown when considering the case of identical twins. In this case, one genomic individual, namely the zygote, produces two distinctive persons. Because of the principle of temporal continuity mentioned above, asserting that the zygote is a person is equivalent to saying that it is numerically identical to the person or persons it will eventually become. However, in the case of twins, this is a self-contradictory statement. Indeed, the zygote would have to be numerically identical to each of the two born twins, but because of the transitivity of identity, this would imply that the born twins are numerically identical to each other, which is manifestly not the case. This proves that the "zygote-as-person" thesis is untenable, already on purely logical grounds. One should note that the lack of congruence between genomic identity and personal identity is basically a logical problem and does not depend on the common assertion that "genes are not everything; there is also the environment." The latter statement is largely true, of course, but invoking the issues of gene versus environment, or nature versus nurture, is not necessary in order to conclude that cloning can never produce "the same" individual again. The real reason is that genomic identity does not have the required logical properties to provide the basis for personal identity.

FROM GENOME TO BRAIN

If we consider that a proper account of numerical identity is a *sine qua non* for a materialist interpretation of the Self, we see that brain-based accounts of identity have much more relevance. Having a particular brain is much more congruent with having a stable identity through time than having a particular genome. Unlike the genome, the brain changes, and yet remains "the same" in the sense of belonging to the same person, that is, in defining to a large extent one and the same person's identity. The combination of stability and change that characterizes the brain is much like the combination of stability and change for persons. In addition, most of the ethical perplexities raised by genomics are transposable, perhaps with an even higher degree of urgency, to the field of neurosciences and the recent birth of "neuroethics" is a telling sign of that (Roskies, 2002).

If we think of the genome and the brain as two instantiations of the Self and try to summarize their similarities and differences, we come up with the lists in TABLE 1. On any quantitative measure of complexity, the brain far surpasses the genome (Table 1, line *a*). Since the publication of the first working sequence of the human genome, it has become commonplace to point to the modest number of human genes (not much more than 30,000 [Claverie, 2001]) as a kind of narcissistic disappointment for the human species. In fact, no popular presentation of the Human Genome Project is complete without philosophical musings on the fact that we have less than three times as many genes as the fruit-fly, and other such melancholy comparisons. Furthermore, the nature of complexity is relatively easily conceptualized in the case of the genome, as compared to the brain (TABLE 1, lines *b,c*). The informational content of a genetic sequence comes about by a simple combination of 4 nu-

TABLE 1. A comparison of the genome and brain according to complexity and link to the Self

	Genome	Brain
a	Relatively modest complexity	Extremely high complexity
b	Inherent metric of complexity through rules of genetic code	Highly multidimensional complexity
c	Complexity comes about through relatively simple combinatorial rules	Presumably many levels of complex combinatorial rules
d	Genomic identity has no direct link with numerical identity	Some form of brain-based identity has relatively direct links with numerical identity
e	Genomic identity has no direct link with biographical identity	Some form of brain-based identity has relatively direct links with biographical identity
f	Deterministic explanations of complex behavior are structurally incomplete	Deterministic explanations of complex behavior can be complete

cleotide bases and can be given a quantitative expression in terms of information theory. In turn, the DNA sequence is given "meaning" through the simple and explicit rules of the genetic code. This view is actually an oversimplification, since alternative splicing, unknown functions of non-coding sequences, and others processes may provide additional "layers" of complexity to the genome. Nevertheless, as compared to the genome, the brain's complexity resides in many more aspects of its structure and functions. Brain cell types, types of synapses, the wiring of neuronal circuits, and above all the plastic nature of its structure make the brain a developmentally dynamic reality that has many levels of complexity, none of them easily reducible to simple and obvious combinatorial rules. A continuous interplay of "brain events" and "world events" shapes every brain into a unique and irreproducible entity. There lies the fundamental difference with the genome. What I call "my genome" is actually instantiated in every cell of my body by a concrete set of DNA molecules. These are near-perfect tokens of a given type: the genome that was put together at fertilization. In addition, that genome could just as well be someone else's, namely if I had a monozygotic twin. Genomes are inherently replicable. Their structure is ideally suited for self-copying and living cells come with all the biochemical hardware designed to do just that. Brains are precisely the opposite. Because their structure does not come about by merely "unwrapping" some preexisting genetic program, but by the constant interplay of internal developmental processes and external contingent stimuli, they are inherently unique and irreproducible. Except in science-fiction fantasies on teleportation, brains cannot be copied into a second

Self. This is why the brain provides a much better material home for the numerical and biographical identity of persons that the genome does (TABLE 1, lines *d,e*). Every brain necessarily has a history of its own and thus much more resembles the human self "itself," as it were, than the static database represented by the genome.

All this does not imply that genomic explanations have nothing to do with the Self—far from it. On the contrary, behavioral genetics may well have even more intriguing philosophical and ethical implications, once a brain-based perspective is taken on board. For one thing, the neurosciences are increasingly involved directly in expanding and explaining results from behavioral genetics (Hamer, 2002). In addition, this link-up of genetics with the brain may shed a new light on some old controversies. Let us take just one example, the issue of free will and responsibility. Current behavioral genetics is increasingly assertive in proposing explanations of complex behavior that involves moral agency. For instance, recent data about violent behavior towards children in families where child abuse is prevalent suggest an interesting genetic effect (Caspi, McClay, Moffit et al., 2002). It is not that abusive behavior is genetically determined, but rather that in specific families, a genetic factor seems to be predictive of whether an abused child will eventually go on to display some form of abusive and antisocial behavior. In this case, a gene is not thought to cause a behavior all by itself, but partially specifies how an individual will react to a particular set of environmental and biographical circumstances. Without being reductionistic in a naïve sense, this and similar findings do affect received understandings of free will, moral deliberation, and agency. This is beginning to be recognized in the bioethics community. A recent report by the London-based Nuffield Council of Bioethics (2002) reviews the ethical implications of behavioral genetics. Of interest, it suggests that genetic variations that influence antisocial behaviour do not exculpate offenders, but should nevertheless be taken into account by judges, on a par with "environmental factors, such as poverty or an abusive childhood."

The truly "shocking" implications of the recent findings of behavior genetics only appear when their implications are worked out at the neural level. Let us ask how this particular finding about genetic determinism and child abuse looks from a "brain-based" perspective: First, note that the genetic polymorphism identified by Caspi et al. explicitly points towards a neurobiological explanation because it affects MAOA (monoamine oxidase A), an enzyme that metabolizes several catecholamine neurotransmitters. Thus the complete explanation of this particular instance of genetic determinism requires an understanding of the biochemical and neurophysiological mechanisms underpinning mood and emotions. Now, for a bearer of the variant MAOA gene to display antisocial behavior certainly requires other psychological dispositions, as well as specific external inputs from that person's experiences and social environment. But it is none other than the brain that provides the locus of integration of the affective dispositions that are influenced by this particular gene with personality, character, and other cognitive and motivational idiosyncrasies of the individual in question, as well as with the perceptive and experiential determinants resulting from this person's biography and environment. The genetic influences on affective states and tendencies are necessarily mediated through the brain. So are any other psychological features of the individual. So too are all experiences and environmental influences upon that person's subjective states and behavior. There is no other place than the brain in which all contributing causes to a person's behavior can act in a causally efficient manner. Unlike "genetic determinism," brain determinism cannot be refuted by pointing to some additional exogenous element of reality that participates causally to the behavior to be explained. Faced with a genetic explanation of moral agency, one can always answer: "ah! but there is the environment!"; but if the explanation is in terms of brain function, there is nowhere else to turn to (TABLE, line *f*). Thus brain-based explanations of behavior have the potential of being complete in a sense in which genomic explanations must forever remain partial.

When looked at the gene level, what looks like "soft" determinism ssmay be equivalent to "hard" determinism when taking the brain on board. The arguments traditionally used to defuse the "shocking" aspects of genetic determinism, such as the importance of the environment and incomplete penetrance of genetic factors, no longer seem to work when one looks at "brain determinism." Unlike genetic determinism, the philosophical merits of brain determinism seem largely identical to those of philosophical determinism itself, and that is a much harder nut to crack.

Genetics and genomics have provided a fertile ground for many ethical speculations on the autopoietic powers that accrue to mankind through its increasing mastery of the biosciences. This has been a powerful influence in making specific topics such as eugenics and genetic control central issues in such debates. On the other hand, the link between genes and personal identity is rather indirect, unlike the link between the brain and the Self. This suggests that many of these controversies are actually more pressing and closer to present and future realities when recast in the terms of neuroscience. As compared to genomics, recent discoveries in neuroscience are more likely to bring turbulence to such classical philosophical concepts in ethics as free will, intention, moral deliberation, and ascription of responsibility. Furthermore, once the ontological privilege wrongly attributed to the genome is toned down, the prophetic *gravitas* that accompanies many public debates on genetic engineering may soften up to some extent. For although genetic manipulation is especially striking to public opinion on account of its permanent and irreversible effects, these characteristics actually apply to brain-based manipulation as well. Changing the brain is changing destiny, and if that involves new social practices, this amounts to changing human destiny just as surely as changing human genes. Indeed, more attention could be devoted to the troubling implications of willfully shaping the human brain. At that point, we may find ourselves in a predicament similar to Sloterdijk's: hunting for the hard-to-find moral difference between the technological fine-tuning of brain states (for instance, by a new generation of psychopharmacological agents) and the more traditional brain-shaping tools wielded by educators, prophets, and politicians. And we may well conclude that moral ambivalence is to be found everywhere.

REFERENCES

BROCK, D.W. (2002). Human cloning and our sense of self. *Science 296,* 314–316.

CASPI, A., MCCLAY, J., MOFFITT, T.E., et al. (2002). Role of genotype in the cycle of violence in maltreated children [see comments.]. *Science, 297,* 851–854.

CLAVERIE, J.M. 2001. Gene number. What if there are only 30,000 human genes? *Science, 291,* 1255–1257.

COLE-TURNEr, R.S. (1987). Is genetic engineering co-creation? *Theology Today, 44(3),* 338–349.

FORD, N.M. 1991. When did I begin? In *Conception of the human individual in history, philosophy and science.* Cambridge: Cambridge University Press.

GRAUMANN, S. (2000). Experts on philosophical reflection in public discourse—the German Sloterdijk debate as an example. *Biomedical Ethics Newsletter, 5(1),* 27–33. Accessible on the Web: http://www.izew.uni-tuebingen.de/texte/ pub_gr_1.pdf (accessed on October 22, 2002).

HAMER, D. (2002). Genetics. Rethinking behavior genetics. *Science, 298:* 71–72.

MAURON, A. (2000). The Question of Purpose. In G. Stock and J. Campbell (Eds.), *Engineering the human germline: an exploration of the science and ethics of altering the genes we pass to our children.* New York: Oxford University Press.

MAURON, A. (2001). Essays on science and society. Is the genome the secular equivalent of the soul? *Science 291,* 831–832.

MAURON, A. (2002). Genomic metaphysics. *Journal of Molecular Biology, 319(4),* 957–962.

MICHAUD, Y. (2002). *Humain, inhumain, trop humain. Réflexions philosophiques sur les biotechnologies, la vie et la conservation de soi à partir de l'oeuvre de Peter Sloterdijk.* Castelnau Le Lez: Climats.

MIRANDOLA, PICO DELLA. 1486. *Oratio de hominis dignitate.* Accessible on the Web: http://www.gmu.edu/departments/fld/CLASSICS/mirandola.oratio.html (accessed on October 22, 2002)

MONTAIGNE, M. DE. 1595. *Essais,* vol. 2, chap. 12 *Apologie de Raimond de Sebonde.*

NUFFIELD COUNCIL ON BIOETHICS. (2002). *Report: Genetics and human behaviour.* London: Nuffield Council on Bioethics.

ROSKIES, A. (2002). Neuroethics for the new millenium. *Neuron, 35(1),* 21–23.

SLOTERDIJK, P. (2000a). The operable man: on the ethical state of gene technology. Enhancing the human: genomics, science fiction, and ethics collide. Goethe Institute, Los Angeles. Published on the Web: www.goethe.de/uk/los/symp/ enindex.htm (accessed on October 22, 2002).

SLOTERDIJK, P. (2000b). Règles pour le parc humain: Une lettre en réponse à la Lettre sur l'humanisme de Heidegger (French translation from German by O. Mannoni). Paris: Mille et une nuits.

SLOTERDIJK, P. (2000c). *La Domestication de l'Etre* (French translation from German by O. Mannoni). Paris: Mille et une Nuits.

UNITED STATES PRESIDENT'S COUNCIL ON BIOETHICS. Membership list posted on the Web: http://www.bioethics.gov/cloningreport/members.html (accessed on October 22, 2002).

Feelings of Emotion and the Self

ANTONIO DAMASIO

*Department of Neurology, University of Iowa College of Medicine,
Iowa City, Iowa 52242, USA*

ABSTRACT: The self is a critical component of consciousness. The neural correlates of self have proven elusive, but it is reasonable to suggest that, in its simplest form, the self process requires a composite representation of the ongoing state of the organism as reflected in subcortical and cortical somatic maps within the central nervous system. The basis for these maps is a wealth of signals originating in different sectors of the body-proper. Some of these signals portray the actual state of the body as modified by emotions in response to interactions with the environment; but other signals are the result of internal simulations controlled from other regions of the central nervous system.

KEYWORDS: self; conciousness; body; feeling.

There are different perspectives on the self, different possible definitions, and with each perspective and definition, naturally, comes a different explanation. Yet it is likely that something like an essence of self can be uncovered behind the multiplicity of views. In this article I suggest that a neurobiological account can help us find such an essence. The title of this article includes the words "feelings" and "self" because I believe the neural basis of feelings and of self have a shared neurobiological stem.

When we use the word *self* we think of something that bespeaks individuality. The word self often stands for an individual—a mind or a body, or both as a unity. In addition, we think of something that denotes stability and continuity over time, as well as singularity. In fact, singularity is so strongly associated with the notion of self that the finding of multiple selves is regarded as pathological. The notion of self is a synonym of personhood, and,

Address for correspondence: Dr. Antonio Damasio, Department of Neurology, University of Iowa College of Medicine, 200 Hawkins Drive, Iowa City, IA 52242-1053. Voice: 319-356-4296; fax: 319-353-6277.

Antonio-damasio@uiowa.edu

NOTE: This text is based on the transcript of an audiotaped presentation.

Ann. N.Y. Acad. Sci. 1001: 253–261 (2003). © 2003 New York Academy of Sciences.
doi: 10.1196/annals.1279.014

connected to whatever meaning, self always implies a *reference*, for example, to an organism, to its behavior, or to its mind.

To speak of self is also, of necessity, to speak of consciousness. If I tell you that I have a headache, I must dig below the level of language and the referent pronoun "I" to the level of self in my consciousness. If I were not conscious of the headache, that is, if I did not have a mind, awareness, and a self, I would still have the headache, but I would not know it was me having the headache. The self is the key reference in the process of consciousness. The self endows us with a subjective perspective.

The minimal level of self necessary for consciousness to occur is implemented as a mental representation. This does not mean, incidentally, that the self is some sort of mental homunculus. There has been a well-justified rejection of the notion of the homunculus, and an effective demonstration that in searching for the self we should not be looking for an all-knowing entity that thinks on its own and gives us the knowledge of who we are. Also we should not be looking for some sort of special brain center where the self would reside. To a first approximation, the self is a stable representation of individual continuity which serves as a mental reference for the organism within the conscious mind. (This first approximation corresponds to my notion of core self. To denote the notion of self which corresponds to identity and personhood, I refer to *autobiographic self* or *extended self.* The autobiographic self is physiologically based on the simpler, core self, but its discussion is beyond the scope of this brief title. See Damasio [1999] for a treatment of these different concepts.)

TOWARD A NEURAL CORRELATE OF THE SELF PROCESS

As is the case with consciousness in general, I believe the self is based on a neurobiological process. I also believe that the key to the self is the representation of the continuity of the organism. As I have suggested elsewhere (Damasio, 1999; Damasio, 2003a), a likely support for the representation of organismic continuity is the neural system responsible for the representation of our own bodies. At this point we should consider this an intuition. However, it is a plausible intuition, one which can inform valuable hypotheses, and it is not mine alone. There is a venerable tradition of seeing the self as connected to a representation of the body. One finds the notion in the philosophers Spinoza, Nietzsche, William James, Husserl, Heidegger, and Merleau-Ponty, and one can find it even in the high priesthood of neuroscience, as in the early thinking of the neurophysiologist Charles Sherrington.

This point of view can be illuminated by a simple experiment that the reader can perform by looking away from this book, toward a wall, for a few seconds, and then returning to view the book again. The visual representations of the book page, with which the reader started, were realized in the visual cortices; but as the reader looked at the wall the representation gave way entirely, in those same cortices, to the representation of the wall; then it gave way again to the representation of the book page. While all those changes were happening, however, we know for certain about something that did not change: the representations of the body remained in continuous operation within the somatic-related cortices. There was no change of the *kind* of content available in those structures.

This disparity highlights a curious situation. We have some senses that are at the mercy of the movements of the body. The images we form on the basis of these senses are determined by what happens to come into our sensory fields, especially the telereceptive fields. Yet other senses are condemned, so to speak, to look continuously at precisely the same content, that is, the organism as a whole. It is this continuous representation of the organism, of the body, for short, that I consider to be the backbone of the self as we know it. It is an ongoing, composite representation of a host of body activities, which occurs in a host of brain structures, as many as a dozen, and it is based upon signals coming from the body to the brain, some purely chemical, and some neural, that is, neurochemical. There is a sameness to this representation, a stability, which contrasts with the variety and discontinuity of external sensory representations.

The content remains the same, stable and continuous, but it is important to note that the representations of the organism also vary. Yet, this variance is within a very narrow range, as mandated by survival; if the variance is excessive, one dies or gets sick. The minimal variance occurs as part of the constant adjustments and balancing needed for homeostasis, that is, for life itself. The variations operate within strict limits and contrast sharply with the infinite variability of external sensations, or the variability of our flow of memories.

The foregoing provides a context for an idea of the possible neural correlates of the self. This is not enough, however. We still need to understand what the somato-sensing system actually looks like, a task which has eluded us for a long time. One reason why we have not fully understood this system is that we have looked at the somatosensory system in far too narrow a way. For some, the notion of somatosensory simply conjures up the musculoskeletal system; for others, as was the case with William James, it conjures up mostly the visceral system. These views are most incomplete. We can grasp the system only if we understand its full scope and depth.

The first step toward the desired understanding is to overcome the tendency to limit our senses to the traditional five: sight, hearing, touch, taste, and olfaction. Such a limitation ignores kinesthesia (the sense of movement derived from proprioception via the musculoskeletal system); it ignores the vestibular sense; no less importantly, it ignores the sensing of the viscera and the internal milieu. Interestingly, if one goes back to the 19th century, one can find thinkers such as Weber, who spoke of a *Gemeingefuhl*, an overall sense of our bodies which included signals from the internal milieu; or Sherrington, toward the end of the 19th century, who spoke of "interoception," the sense of the material "me," or the physical self. Curiously, in later editions of his famous textbook, Sherrington no longer talked this way. Interoception, which is very much the process I regard as most critical for the self, was dropped (see Damasio [2003b] and Craig [2002] for review).

I look at the roster of "senses" differently. As noted, there are, of course, the exteroceptive senses: vision, smell, hearing, taste, and mechanical contact; but there is also a separate and most interesting grouping of interoceptive neural senses that include the proprioceptive and vestibular senses; the visceral sense; and the sense of the internal milieu which can be taken together with that of pain and temperature. Also, we must remember that, evolutionarily, before the arrival of these neural senses, the entire organism was a chemo-sensor, having an ability whose remnants are still present in humans and other complex species. Chemo-sensing occurs in the form of signals that contact "open" areas of the nervous system—areas devoid of the blood–brain barrier, such as the area postrema or the subfornical organs—where chemical molecules can influence directly the state of neural tissue and produce cascades of events within the central nervous system. Thus it is important to realize that nerve fibers are not indispensable to sense that there are changes occurring within the body. Those changes can also be sensed through chemical action on nervous tissue.

Along with this chemoreceptive system there is another major component of the neural self, the C and A delta fiber system, made up of nerve endings that are free and located in literally every nook and cranny of our bodies, in every type of tissue. They appear also in the more specific system of the vagal nerve. This system is very different from that made up by A alpha and A beta fibers. The C and A delta system is evolutionarily older, made of thin and mostly unmyelinated fibers that conduct signals at a slow velocity, between 1and 2 meters per second. By contrast, the A alpha and A beta fibers transmit signals as fast as 60 meters per second. This faster system is well adapted to the sensing of the external world. The older, slower system is equally well adapted for sensing the internal environment of the organism.

The range of sensitivity of the C and A delta fiber system is wide. It responds to local pH, partial pressure of oxygen and CO_2, glucose levels, levels of lactic acid, glutamate, histamine, serotonin, and so on. It further includes the local assessment of temperature and mechanical stress, and registers processes such as the flush of the skin, itches, tickles, sensuous touch, and genital arousal. I suspect the grounding for the perception of our own being, at any given moment, is conveyed by this general system originating in sensors that are located throughout the structure of our bodies. The system can register activities as gross as mechanical stress, but also as subtle as a moment of genetically programmed cell death, or apoptosis. When a cell is injured through, say, ischemia, the system responds. These fibers signal continuous-

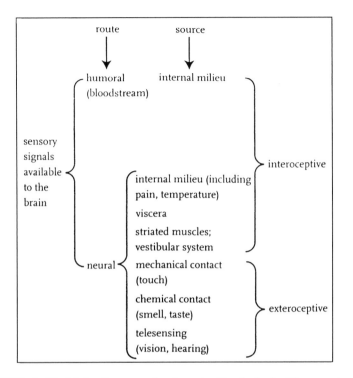

FIGURE 1. The kinds of sensory signal received by the brain. There are two routes of transmission: humoral (in which chemical molecules conveyed by the bloodstream directly activate neural sensors in the hypothalamus or in circumventricular organs such as the area postrema); and neural (in which electrochemical signals are transmitted in neural pathways). There are two sources for all these signals: the external world (exteroceptive signals), and the inner world of the body (interoceptive signals). The main source of the latter is the viscera and the internal milieu, but signals related to the state of the musculoskeletal and vestibular systems participate as well.

ly, whether we want them to or not; no control is possible on our part (FIG. 1).

A DEDICATED SYSTEM

Within the central nervous system all these signals are transmitted by a dedicated set of pathways and nuclei. In the spinal cord the system recruits lamina I of the posterior horn, the region where the C and A delta fibers terminate. These fibers do not go into the other posterior horn laminae and do not enter the white matter either. They go only to this particular region. Above the level of the spinal cord, in the brainstem, they go to the trigeminal nucleus, specifically to the segment known as the pars caudalis, which is the direct equivalent of lamina I in the spinal cord. These brainstem fibers carry signals from the body structures of the head, the oral cavity, the skin, of face and scalp, and the facial muscles of emotion and jaw movement.

Other interesting aspects of this system reflect its specialization. In the posterior horn of the spinal cord we see that the neurons arising from these fibers traverse from one side of the spinal cord to the other, within the gray matter, and then ascend toward the telencephalon, via the brainstem. Neurons carrying signals from muscles and from outside the body take quite a different route: they enter the white matter, rather than the gray matter of the posterior horn, and then ascend into the telencephalon without making any synapses until they reach the brainstem. The C and A delta fiber pathway, the system that gives us the overall sense of the body's interior, allows for intervention from top-down control which arises in nuclei of the periaqueductal gray and of the hypothalamus, the periventricular nucleus in particular. These regions can influence the signals coming from the body's interior.

How does this system participate in making the maps of the body state that I regard as the key correlate for the sense of self? The answer is that the signals that enter the spinal cord and trigeminal nucleus eventually ascend to an equally dedicated nucleus of the thalamus, the VMpo nucleus (ventromedial nucleus, posterior part). Until recently it had been thought that the signals projected to the VP nuclei of the thalamus (ventroposterior), but the work of A.D. Craig (Craig, 2002) has shown that the VMpo constitutes the terminal region for these signals. From the VMpo, projections continue to the dorsal and anterior insula.

The insular regions receive other important body signals along the way, namely those that travel in projections from the parabrachial nucleus in the brainstem, and also from the nucleus tractus solitarius, which picks up on information from the viscera through the vagus nerve. Also, there is a further convergence of information from the circumventricular organs, which pick up information directly through sensing the chemical environment in the brain. All of these other structures use another relay nucleus in the thalamus, the VMb nucleus (ventromedial, basal part), which then projects to the dorsal insula. This means that signals from the body's interior ultimately come together, continuously, in the insula. The organization of the insula even appears to be graded, across subregions, in a manner similar to that of visual regions within the visual cortices. The body's interior is mapped neurally from back to front. It is even possible that the highest level of this representation is integrated mostly in the right anterior insula, as has been suggested by Craig. Signals from the insula are then made available to the anterior cingulate and orbitofrontal cortices (FIG. 2).

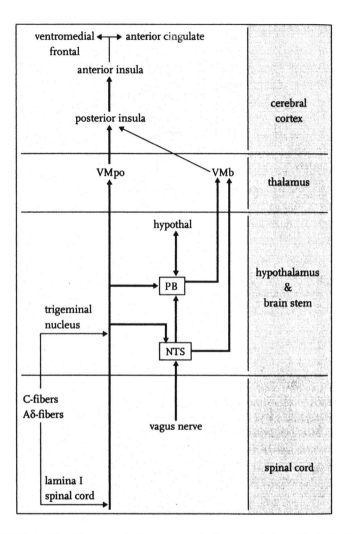

FIGURE 2. Signaling from body to brain. A diagram of the critical structures involved in conveying internal milieu and visceral signals to the brain. A substantial part of the critical signaling is conveyed by pathways from the spinal cord and the brainstem's trigeminal nucleus. At every level of the spinal cord, in a region known as "lamina I" (in the posterior horn of the spinal cord's gray matter, and in the caudal part of the trigeminal nucleus), the information conveyed by peripheral nerve fibers of the C and Aδ types (thin, unmyelinated, and slow-conducting) is brought to the central nervous system. This information hails from literally everywhere in our entire body and relates to parameters as diverse as the state of contraction of smooth muscles in arteries, the amount of local blood flow, local temperature, the presence of chemicals signifying injury to local tissue, the level of pH, O_2 and CO_2. All of this information is further conveyed to a dedicated nucleus of the thalamus (VMpo) and then on to neural maps in the posterior and anterior insula. Subsequently the insula can signal to regions such as the ventromedial prefrontal

[over]

BODY REPRESENTATION, FEELINGS, AND SELF

It is intriguing to learn that these same parts of the insula are involved systematically in the feelings of emotion. As shown in functional imaging studies, feeling emotions such as happiness, anger, fear, and sadness is accompanied by different patterns of activity in structures of the insula, along with other regions of the central nervous system in the brainstem and diencephalon (Damasio et al., 2000). Feelings of coolness and heat, pain of various sorts, sensations related to respiration and exercise, itch, disgust, sexual arousal, the highs associated with drugs such as ecstasy and morphine, and even the feelings of craving associated with these drugs, all of these engage the insular cortices, emphasizing the point that this region thoroughly relates to bodily state (see Craig [2002] and Damasio [2003b] for review).

Parts of this robust system are found in non-human species. The basic system, through the brain stem and hypothalamus, can be seen in most mammals. However, the final leg of the system, from the VMpo to the insula, appears to be present only in primates. This suggests that while many species can have a continuous representation of the body capable of supporting feelings of emotion and a sense of self, only primates might, through the addition of structures that facilitate high-level convergence, generate the sort of higher-order mappings that would make the sense of self become most encompassing.

The notion that the right insula would provide the highest level of integration is in keeping with this possible evolutionary progression. We got a preliminary inkling of this possibility while looking at data arrived at through the study of lesions in humans. Lesions which compromise the ability to experience emotional feelings and to sense the body are often located on the right side of the somatosensory complex, including and in particular to the right insula cortex. The patients so affected have a compromised sense of self as well.

---

cortex and the anterior cingulate cortex. On the way to the thalamus, this information is also made available to the nucleus tractus solitarius (NTS), which receives signals from the vagus nerve (a major path for information from the viscera that bypasses the spinal cord); to the parabrachial nucleus (PB); and to the hypothalamus (hypothal). In addition to being important recipients and processor of this information (it is conceivable that some sense of self might actually emerge from activity at this level), the PB and the NTS also convey signals to the insula via yet another thalamic nucleus (VMb). Intriguingly, the pathways related to the movement of the body and to its position in space use an entirely different chain of transmission. The peripheral nerve fibers convey those different chains of transmission. The peripheral nerve fibers that convey those signals (Aβ) are thick and conduct at fast speeds. The parts of the spinal cord and trigeminal nerve nucleus used for body movement signaling are also different, and so are the thalamic relay nuclei and the ultimate cortical target (the somatosensory cortex I).

We begin, then, with a multi-level coalescence of signals from a vast array of sources: the chemically based circumventricular organs and the hypothalamus, the C and A delta fiber system, and the vagal system. These signals are conveyed through special thalamic lines into the insula. Other regions of the somatosensory system, namely, the cortices of SI and SII (somatosensory cortex I and somatosensory cortex II) in both hemispheres along with their attending association cortices, incorporate signals arising in the musculoskeletal system and the vestibular system. These cortices are richly interconnected with those of the insula. The ensuing cross-signaling provides a composite and continuous map of the body state. The composite brings together the internal milieu and viscera—which narrowly change in their constant search for homeostasis—along with the invariant aspects of the musculoskeletal system. As I see it, this composite is the neural foundation for the self, the grounding of the material "me" (Damasio, 2003a). This is only the beginning of the self process, of course. To build the kind of self we associate with personhood it takes abundant personal memory and to generate a sense of identity and autobiography with the complexity we find in humans it takes language as well.

REFERENCES

CRAIG, A.D. (2002) How do you feel? Interoception: the sense of the physiological condition of the body. *Nature Reviews Neuroscience, 3*, 655–666.

DAMASIO, A.R. (1999, 2000). *The feeling of what happens: Body and emotion in the making of consciousness*. New York: Harcourt.

DAMASIO, A.R. (2003a).The person within. *Nature, 423,227*.

DAMASIO, A.R. (2003b). *Looking for Spinoza: Joy, sorrow and the feeling brain*, New York: Harcourt.

DAMASIO, A.R., GRABOWSKI, T.J., BECHARA, A., DAMASIO, H., PONTO, L.L.B., PARVIZI, J. & HICHWA, R.D. (2000). Subcortical and cortical brain activity during the feeling of self-generated emotions. *Nature Neuroscience, 3*, 1049–1056.

The Computational Self

TERRENCE SEJNOWSKI

Howard Hughes Medical Institute, Salk Institute for Biological Studies, La Jolla, California 92037, USA

Division of Biological Sciences, University of California at San Diego, La Jolla, California 92093, USA

ABSTRACT: Your brain is never at rest. Shifting patterns of activity course through your brain at night as you review the events of the day and plan the next day before falling asleep. Rumination is a reflection of the Self that is not directly driven by sensory stimuli. When we record from single neurons in the brain, we discover that even in the absence of sensory stimulation, neurons are continuously active. This is called maintained, or spontaneous, activity, and although it is well documented, it has not been as well studied. Most experiments are designed to look for signals that are elicited by sensory stimuli above the background, without mentioning whether the background has changed too, as it often does. New methods have been developed recently that allow us to study the brain's spontaneous activity and to explore how it might provide clues to the origin and nature of the Self.

KEYWORDS: independent component analysis; electroencephalogram (EEG); event-related potentials (ERPs); spontaneous activity; computer models

There are many different levels of investigation in neuroscience, and FIGURE 1 illustrates these levels ranging from molecules to the entire brain over 10 orders of magnitude of spatial scale. At meetings of the Society for Neuroscience, attended by more than 25,000 neuroscientists working at all of these levels, one can be overwhelmed by the sheer amount of knowledge we have uncovered about the brain, more in the last 10 years than in all previous history. Integrating between levels can help to unify this knowledge and allow us ultimately to understand how complex brain states that give rise to the Self arise from molecular, synaptic, cellular, network, and systems mechanisms.

Address for correspondence: Terrence J. Sejnowski, Salk Institute, 10010 N. Torrey Pines Road, La Jolla CA 92037. Voice: 858-587-0423; fax: 858-587-0417.
terry@salk.edu

Ann. N.Y. Acad. Sci. 1001: 262–271 (2003). © 2003 New York Academy of Sciences.
doi: 10.1196/annals.1279.015

Levels of Investigation

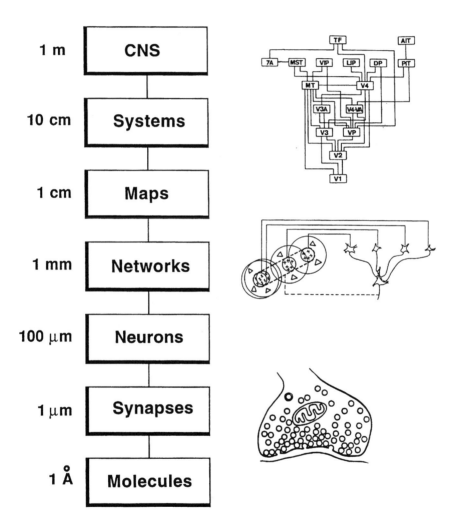

FIGURE 1. Levels of investigation of the brain organized according to spatial scale. Behavior is a property at the highest level involving the entire central nervous system. At the lowest level we can study the individual molecules of the brain such as neurotransmitters and receptors. There are many intermediate levels between these two that could contribute to the origin and nature of Self.

We are now faced with a "Humpty Dumpty" project: We've taken apart the brain and we know almost all of its pieces, but we are like the child who has taken apart his father's watch and is trying to put it back together again. How are we going to do that with as complex and dynamic a structure as the brain?

At the Computational Neurobiology Laboratory at the Salk Institute, we approach the problem of integration by developing new techniques for analyzing brain recordings, new computer models for simulating brain activity, and mathematical theory for understanding the activity. Computer models allow us to study how the many components of the brain interact together. Such models can give us insight into how these interactions give rise to percepts and thoughts. Once a model has been confirmed experimentally it can be mathematically analyzed to extract general principles.

FORESTS AND TREES: UNDERSTANDING NEURONS IN POPULATIONS

Over the last 50 years, there has been an especially strong focus on single neurons, spurred by the seminal development of the microelectrode, a thin piece of wire with a very sharp tip. If you put it into the brain and get lucky, you can record from a single neuron. The advantage of isolating a single neuron is that one can listen to what it is saying and find out in great detail its specific preferences. In the visual system, for example, we can determine which properties of the visual world each neuron responds to best. The trouble is that there are 100 billion neurons. Recording from all of them would not only take a very long time, but in the end, we would have only a huge catalog.

The real problem is that we know too much. We see all the trees, but we don't see the forest. In *The Computational Brain,* Patricia Churchland and I (1992) predicted that 100 years from now, when the history of our period in neuroscience is written, this period will be said to be based on the "theory of the microelectrode"; that we were so focused on the tip of that recording device that we were blinded to the obvious fact that neurons interact in complex patterns. In the brief summary I will present here, I will describe what brain activity looks like at a high level, looking at the forest. At the end we will return to the Self and describe a research program for how to find it in large populations of neurons.

FIGURE 2 summarizes a popular model that dominates our current view of how the brain computes. The figure shows how the brain of a monkey responds to a visual stimulus. First, neurons in the retina are activated and then 30 milliseconds later, following some processing in the retina, the signal arrives in the lateral geniculate nucleus, a visual relay nucleus in the thalamus. Shortly thereafter, it arrives in the primary visual cortex, where perception

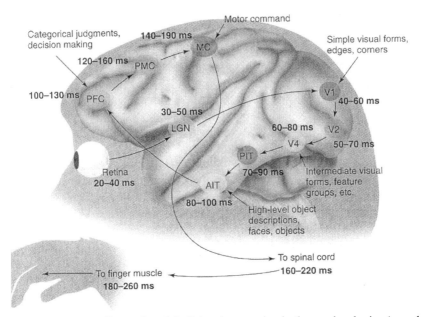

FIGURE 2. Feedforward model of signal processing in the monkey brain. According to this model, there is a feedforward flow of information from the stimulus through a hierarchy of areas in the visual system, where it is recognized and then sent to the frontal cortex, where an action plan is formulated and finally to motor cortex, where motor commands are issued to subcortical structures. This model ignores the spontaneous activity found throughout the cortex and the extensive feedback projections that accompany each feedforward connection. (Adapted from Thorpe and Fabre-Thorpe [2001].)

begins. The signal then goes from the area V1 to V2, and from V2 to V4. From V4 it then travels to the inferotemporal cortex, taking about 90 milliseconds. The visual information then travels to the front of the brain, the prefrontal cortex, where other neurons may go through another sequence, finally arriving at the motor cortex where activation occurs to produce an action.

This is a purely "feed-forward" architecture, a chain of events that occurs in linear fashion leading from sensory stimulus to motor act. It dominates the way most experiments in cognitive neuroscience are designed, especially those on awake and behaving monkeys: A monkey is restrained in a chair, given a complex sensory stimulus, and then trained to respond in particular ways while neurons are recorded from different parts of the brain. On the basis of these experiments we know about how neurons respond during reflexive tasks. The neurons in each area represent something about the task: sensory neurons represent features of the world; motor neurons represent actions, including which muscles are going to be activated; neurons in prefrontal cortex represent what is being planned, and activity may be maintained even in the absence of a sensory stimulus. The goal of this approach is to understand what the brain represents at each stage of processing. The three questions being asked are: representation, representation, and representation.

There are, however, other types of questions that can be asked. An entirely different class of questions concerns interneuronal communication, and can be illustrated with an analogy. Imagine that we could scale up the brain so that a person would be about the size of a neuron. The brain would be about 20 miles across, about the size of New York City. Now imagine that one such neuron sitting, say, at a conference in Manhattan, has a very important message. It is representing some important fact about the world and wants to communicate it to a particular motor neuron over in the Bronx. With no direct connection, how is it going to get the message there? A single neuron is only connected to about ten thousand others, but there are many others that might need to receive its message. This is a communication problem. The brain's communication problem is even more daunting than this analogy allows since there are only about 10 million people in the New York metropolitan area, but there are 100 billion neurons in a brain.

To continue with the analogy, we'd have to pack the conference room cheek to jowl and stack people 20 miles high to mirror the 3-D structure of the brain. Imagine what it's like to be a neuron in the brain. One would be sitting in sea of people, trying to make sense of signals coming in, making decisions about what to signal out. How can we understand neurons and the brain from the perspective of the forest rather than the trees?

A window into the large-scale electrical activity in the brain has been available for nearly 100 years. Scalp recordings, called the electroencephalogram (EEG), report the summed activity from thousands of millions of synapses. Such averages can indicate whether someone is awake or asleep and can detect epileptic seizures, which typically generate very large spike and wave discharges. Although EEG recordings are helpful to clinical physicians trying to diagnose and assess brain damage, they have taught us little about how neurons represent the world. It's like a Martian trying to understand something about human beings by placing a microphone over a football stadium and recording crowd noises. The Martian might learn about touchdowns and crowd waves but not too much about human beings and the mechanisms through which they interact. It has not been able to disentangle the sources of the gross signals provided by the EEG. We believe our laboratory has solved this problem. Surprisingly, although EEG has not taught us anything about representation in the brain it may have much to teach us about the global communication network (Laughlin and Sejnowski, 2003).

PATTERNS IN THE NOISE

To describe this new methodology let's start with the "cocktail party problem." Imagine oneself at a cocktail party with other people around talking and perhaps a band playing in the background. If the problem is to pick out one strong signal from this cacophony we might be able to do it. But if we imagine trying to pick up one weak signal from hundreds of other signals in the surrounding environment, the problem becomes significantly more difficult. It might seem that this is not possible without first knowing something about the nature of the signals. For example, suppose the signals are all white noise sources. Mixtures of noise also sound like noise. This problem in blind source separation is now solvable because of recent advances in signal processing called independent component analysis (ICA) (Makeig, Westerfield, Jung, et al., 2002). We have used a computational algorithm for ICA that was developed in my laboratory to dissect out the independent sources of signals from the brain just as we are able to isolate each of the sources of sound in the cocktail party. To solve the brain cocktail party problem, we need to record the EEG from hundreds of locations, and sort out the hundreds of sources that contribute to the EEG.

If we take all raw EEG data from individual trials and apply ICA, we obtain several dozen independent sources, as shown in FIGURE 3. Each source contains two parts, a scalp map, which is a static picture of the "weighting" of each electrode, and the time course by which the scalp map is modulated. Some sources of electrical signals in the EEG come not from the brain itself, but from eye movements, which produce EEG artifacts that are much larger than brain signals, as shown in FIGURE 3 (top left). Other artifacts involve muscle noise such as that generated by temporal muscles when gritting teeth. All of these artifacts are separated by ICA into different output channels, giving us some confidence that the technique can at least help us eliminate artifacts from EEG.

Even in the absence of a sensory stimulus, there are ongoing sources of brain rhythms, including prominent sources that oscillate at 10 Hz, called alpha rhythms. There are several sources of occipital alpha. There are others, centered over the motor cortex in the hand area, called mu rhythms, which precipitously quench after a motor act, like pressing a button, as shown in FIGURE 3 (bottom right). With ICA it is now possible to discriminate among the various alpha rhythms and pick out their unique properties and roles. For example, we have discovered that these sources and several others not in the figure do not change their amplitude in response to sensory stimuli, but rather their phase (Jung, Makieg, McKeowan, et al., 2001), as shown in FIGURE 3 (bottom middle). When a sensory stimulus is presented to a human, the ongoing rhythms become phase-shifted so that within 100 ms they are reset. When 100 single trials are averaged, the resulting average "event-related potential" (ERP) has a sequence of peaks and troughs that arise from this phase resetting of multiple sources. The traditional way of interpreting the ERP is as a sequence of overlapping activations in different brain regions. With new analysis techniques we can look at individual trials and see a different picture. When the stimulus first appears, it interacts with the ongoing background

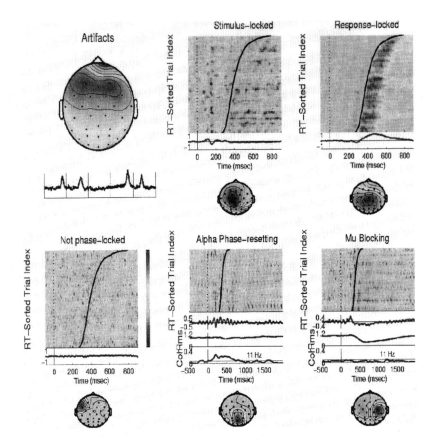

FIGURE 3. Classes of independent components derived from an ICA analysis of single event-related potential (ERP) trials from a visual reaction task. The component in the *upper left* corner is an artifact caused by an eye blink (strong localization to the front of the scalp shown above and with a large-amplitude, slow time course shown below). Each of the other panels shows the ERP image (Jung et al., 2001), formed by sorting each trial by response time (black line) and illustrating positive values of the ERP as black, zero as gray, and negative values as white. The line beneath the ERP image is the average of the ERPs. Some components are time-aligned with the sensory stimulus (*top middle*), some are aligned with the motor response (*top right*), while others are oscillatory (*bottom*). The component shown on the *bottom middle* has an ongoing 10-Hz frequency that is phase-shifted by the stimulus without changing in amplitude (trace below the average ERP). There is a systematic phase shift that increases the coherence between trials (*bottom trace*). The component on the *bottom right,* which is centered over the motor cortex, also has a 10-Hz oscillation, but this decreases in amplitude after the motor response. Some oscillatory components (*bottom left*) are not affected by the stimulus. (Adapted from Jung et al. [2001].)

EEG generators, shifting the phase, and it is the phase shifting itself that gives rise to the peaks. This tells us that we really should think of ERPs as being not separate from, but rather a property of, the ongoing background EEG, the continuous, spontaneous activity.

ATTENTION

The modulation of the EEG with state of arousal and attention suggests that it might reflect more dynamic aspects of cortical processing. Further insights into these elusive signals arise from directly recording the local field potentials (LFPs) from the cortex. The same microelectrodes that are used to record from single neurons also carry low-frequency information about population synaptic activity within a restricted region of a cortical column. Normally the LFP is filtered out with a high-pass filter, but there are further clues about how the brain regulates the flow of activity from an analysis of the LFP during an attention task in a monkey.

Fries and colleagues (2001) investigated the synchrony of neurons in area V4 that respond to visual stimuli. Monkeys were trained to fixate on a central spot and to attend to either of two stimuli presented simultaneously and at the same eccentricity. One of the stimuli fell inside the receptive field of a neuron whose activity was recorded. Thus the responses to the same stimulus could be compared in two conditions, with visual attention inside or outside the neuron's receptive field. At the same time, the local LFP was recorded from a nearby electrode. The correlations between single neurons and the neighboring population became more synchronized at high frequencies (30–70 Hz) and less so at low frequencies (0–17 Hz) when attention was directed into the receptive field of the neuron.

How can changes in the degree of correlation be linked to attention? We have shown that the observed changes in synchrony in V4 could have a significant impact on the responses of downstream neurons (Salinas and Sejnowski (2001). Compared to the firing rate of a neuron in response to independent synaptic inputs impinging randomly, even a small amount of correlation in the impinging spike trains produce more output spikes. This occurs in neurons in which the total excitatory and inhibitory inputs are roughly balanced, and as a consequence they are sensitive to the fluctuations in the membrane potential. Correlations in the inhibitory inputs, which are concentrated near the soma of cortical pyramidal neurons, are particularly effective in enhancing the firing rate of a neuron and could also serve as a mechanism for synchronizing thousands of cells in a cortical column. These experimental and modeling studies suggest that top-down spatial attention can regulate the flow of information between populations of neurons in cortical areas through correlations in their spike trains: Signals carried by neurons are boosted by increasing their degree of synchrony.

The EEG is a global measure of correlations among distant regions of the brain. Neurons that are firing spikes that are uncorrelated will result in incoherent electrical signals that will cancel at the level of the scalp. Only those populations of neurons that have a significant degree of synchrony will contribute to the EEG. This suggests that the EEG may provide valuable insights into the global regulation of information flow between the parts of the brain when the brain is engaged in a task. This may explain why the EEG has not been helpful in uncovering how information is represented in the brain—the coherent signals reflect a complex communication network that can be dynamically reconfigured by top-down planning, expectation, and attention rather than the content itself.

COMPUTATIONAL SELF

Going back to the diagram of the pathways shown in FIGURE 2, we now have a different way of understanding what might be happening in the brain during a typical stimulus–response task. First, even before the stimulus appears, there is spontaneous background activity, which is a reflection of the expectation of a stimulus. When the visual stimulus appears, it resets ongoing activity and sets off a chain of events that, under some circumstances, sets up coherent patterns and oscillations that open communication channels, allowing different parts of the brain to talk to each other. This may be how the brain solves the "Manhattan to the Bronx" problem. The key is to examine coherent activity in large populations of neurons, which can be monitored locally through the LFP and globally through the EEG.

Where is the Self in these correlated patterns of activity? It should be possible to explore this question with the techniques that have introduced here. The key will be to devise tasks that are less time-locked to external stimuli, but instead are self-generated. For example, in the block-copy task (Ballard, Hayhoe, Li, and Whitehead, (1992), the subject is shown a pattern of multicolored blocks and instructed to construct a copy of the pattern from a set of spare blocks. The subject is free to determine the order in which the blocks are picked up. How are the communications patterns between brain areas modulated during the conscious choices made during this task? Coordinated eye and hand movements are involved that go beyond simple lever presses. How is the flow of information between sensory and motor regions regulated? These issues and even more complex tasks can be explored, including ones that involve human communication. A trace of the Self should emerge from these studies.

Although we might be able to devise computational theories for the Self based on the coherent responses of neurons in different parts of the brain, will this lead us to a theory of consciousness? There may be some aspects of consciousness that can be explained with these theories, such as visual awareness (Crick and Koch, 2003), but there may be others, such as the subjective aspects of consciousness, that may elude computational accounts. Ultimately the Self may be found by looking more closely at the brain's spontaneous activity, a part of the background that we have ignored for too long. During sleep the background in the cortex becomes more globally coherent than during states of alertness (Destexhe and Sejnowski, 2001). What changes during sleep states is the pattern of activity, and it is in these patterns that traces of the Self may be found.

REFERENCES

CHURCHLAND, P.S. & SEJNOWSKI, T.J. (1992). *The computational brain.* Cambridge, MA: MIT Press.

BALLARD. D.H., HAYHOE, M.M., LI, F. & WHITEHEAD, S.D. (1992). Hand-eye coordination during sequential tasks. *Philosophical Transactions of the Royal Society of London, Series B Biological Sciences, 337,* 331–338.

CRICK, F. & KOCH, C. (2003). A framework for consciousness. *Nature Neuroscience, 6,* 119–126.

DESTEXHE, A. & SEJNOWSKI, T.J. (2001). *Thalamocortical assemblies: How ion channels, single neurons and large-scale networks organize sleep oscillations.* Oxford: Oxford University Press.

FRIES, P., REYNOLDS, J.H., RORIE, A.E. & DESIMONE, R. (2001). Modulation of oscillatory neuronal synchronization by selective visual attention. *Science, 291,* 1506–1507.

JUNG, T.-P., MAKEIG, S., MCKEOWN, M.J., BELL, A.J., LEE, T.-W. & SEJNOWSKI, T.J. (2001). Imaging brain dynamics using independent component analysis, *Proceedings of the IEEE, 89,* 1107–1122.

LAUGHLIN, S.B. & SEJNOWSKI, T.J. (September 26, 2003). Communication in neuronal networks. *Science.*

MAKEIG, S., WESTERFIELD, M., JUNG, T.-P., ENGHOFF, S., TOWNSEND, J., COURCHESNE, E. & SEJNOWSKI, T.J. (2002). Dynamic brain sources of visual evoked responses. *Science, 295,* 690–694.

SALINAS, E. & SEJNOWSKI, T.J. (2001). Correlated neuronal activity and the flow of neural information. *Nature Reviews Neuroscience, 2,* 539–550.

THORPE, S.J. & FABRE-THORPE, M. (2001). Seeking categories in the brain. *Science, 291,* 260–263.

A Parallel Between Radical Reductionism in Science and in Art

ERIC R. KANDEL AND SARAH MACK

Howard Hughes Medical Institute, Center for Neurobiology and Behavior, Columbia University College of Physicians & Surgeons, New York, New York 10032, USA

ABSTRACT: Neural science represents an important bridge between the natural sciences concerned with the nature of the physical world and the humanities concerned with the nature of human existence. We try to illustrate this bridging function in two ways. One, we show that many neural scientists study the brain to address humanistically important questions about the mind first raised by classical philosophy. Second, in certain instances the humanities and neural sciences use common methodologies to achieve their respective goals.

KEYWORDS: art; science; reductionism; bridge; methodology; humanism

> *We are closer to attaining cheerful serenity by simplifying thoughts and figures. Simplifying the idea to achieve an expression of joy. That is our only deed.* —HENRI MATISSE

One of the subtexts of this symposium on the Self is to bridge the two cultures delineated by C.P. Snow in his Rede Lectures of 1959, that of the Sciences, concerned with the physical nature of the universe, and that of the Humanities, concerned with the nature of human experience. In this essay, we try to bridge this divide from the perspective of neural science, and we

Address for correspondence: Eric Kandel, M.D., Howard Hughes Medical Institute, Center for Neurobiology and Behavior, Columbia University College of Physicians & Surgeons, 1051 Riverside Drive, New York, New York 10032. Voice: 212-543-5202; fax: 212-543-5474.
Erk5@columbia.edu

Ann. N.Y. Acad. Sci. 1001: 272–294 (2003). © 2003 New York Academy of Sciences.
doi: 10.1196/annals.1279.016

try to do so in two ways. First, we show that many scientists who study the brain see neural science as a way to address, in a direct and compelling fashion, important philosophical questions. Second, we will try to make the less obvious point that beyond common substantive concerns the humanities and the sciences sometimes share common methodologies.

We begin by addressing the use of biology and specifically the biology of learning and memory to address important questions in the humanities. From a humanistic perspective, the study of learning and memory has proven to be an endlessly fascinating investigation because it addresses one of the most remarkable aspects of human behavior: our ability to acquire new ideas from experience. Learning is the mechanism whereby we acquire new knowledge and memory is the mechanism whereby we retain that knowledge over time. Indeed, we are in good measure who we are because of what we have learned and what we remember.

Conversely, many psychological and emotional problems are thought to result, at least in part, from experience, and specific disorders of learning and disturbances of memory haunt the developing infant as well as the mature adult. Down syndrome, Fragile X, the normal weakening of memory with age, and the devastation of Alzheimer's disease are only the more familiar examples of a large number of diseases that affect memory.

For biologists interested in mind, the study of learning has the further appeal that, unlike thought, language, and consciousness, learning is *the* mental process that is most accessible to a molecular analysis. Elementary forms of learning and memory have been well characterized by classical psychology following the discovery by Thorndike and Pavlov of operant and classical conditioning in the first half of the 20th century, and these basic forms of learning represent the most clearly delineated and, for the experimenter, most easily controlled of any mental process.

Yet, despite its discrete nature, learning is appealing because it has broad cultural ramifications. Each of us knows what we know about our world and its civilizations because of what we have learned. In the largest sense, learning goes beyond the individual to the transmission of culture from generation to generation. Learning is a major vehicle for behavioral adaptation and the only vehicle for social progress.

Animals and humans have only two major types of mechanisms available for adapting to their environment: one is biological evolution and the other is learning. Of these, learning is by far the more common, and the more efficient. Biological evolution is slow, often requiring thousands of years in higher organisms. By contrast, learning is rapid and occurs repeatedly within the brief life span of an individual. Moreover, the ability to learn and to remember is a characteristic feature of all moderately evolved animals.

This potential for learning is not fixed throughout the animal kingdom but parallels the complexity of the nervous system and therefore reaches its highest form in human beings. In humans, learning reaches a new level of effectiveness and leads to the establishment of a completely new kind of evolution—cultural evolution—which has now largely supplanted biological evolution as a means of transmitting knowledge and adaptations across generations. The capacity to learn is so remarkably developed in humans that societies change almost exclusively by cultural evolution, that is, by learning, rather than by biological evolution.

In fact, there is no evidence for biological change in size or structures of the brain since *Homo sapiens* appeared in the fossil records some 50,000 years ago. All human accomplishments from antiquity to modern times are the product of cultural evolution, and therefore of memory.

Finally, the biological study of learning raises some of the vital issues that have traditionally confronted Western thought. What aspects of the organization of the mind are innate? How does the mind acquire knowledge of the world?

Serious thinkers of each generation have struggled with these questions. By the end of the 17th century, two opposing views emerged. The British empiricists Locke, Berkeley, and Hume argued that the mind does not possess innate ideas, but that all knowledge derives from sensory experience and is, therefore, learned. By contrast, the continental philosophers Descartes, Leibniz, and particularly Kant argued that the mind is born with *a priori* knowledge—pre-knowledge—that predisposes it to receive and interpret sensory experience in an innately determined, perceptual framework.

During the early part of the 19th century, it gradually became clear that the methods of philosophy—observation, introspection, argument, and speculation—could, by themselves, neither distinguish nor reconcile these conflicting views because the issues they raise revolve around the question of what goes on in the brain when we learn. These questions require a direct examination of the brain. In recent years neural science has done just that and we now have begun to have some preliminary answers to these difficult questions.

Already by the 1950s, it had become clear that the black box of the brain was, in fact, capable of being opened and thereby gradually demystified. The problems of memory storage, once the exclusive concern of psychologists and psychoanalysts, became approachable with the methods of modern biology. As a result, interest in memory shifted from a psychological to a biological approach, an approach that was designed to translate some of the central unresolved questions in the psychology of learning and memory into the empirical language of biology. The question now became: What sort of changes does learning produce in the neural networks of the brain? How is memory stored? And, once stored, how is memory maintained? What are the molecular steps whereby a transient short-term memory is converted to an enduring, self-maintained, long-term memory?

The purpose in attempting this translation was not to replace psychological thinking with the logic of molecular biology, but to contribute to a new synthesis—a new science of the mind—that would do justice to the interplay between the mentalistic psychology of memory storage and the molecular biology of cell signaling (Kandel, 2001).

Some who entered the field of learning and memory with the intention of studying the cell and molecular mechanisms were initially tempted to tackle this problem in its most complex and intriguing form. But it soon became clear that irrespective of the neural systems involved, the molecular mechanisms whereby a memory is stored are likely to have a general solution. If that was so, then one was best off taking a reductionist approach. One needed to study not the most complex but the simplest instance of memory storage, and to study it in animals with the simplest possible nervous system. A number of investigators therefore searched for experimental animals in which a simple behavior, modifiable by learning, was controlled by a very simple neuronal circuit made up of a small number of nerve cells.

After an extensive search, we focused in on the giant marine snail *Aplysia*. As one can tell at a glance (FIG. 1), *Aplysia* is an ideal organism for a radical reductionist analysis of learning (Kandel, 2001; Hawkins et al., 1983). Indeed, the advantages of the snail for a reductionist analysis were appreciated almost a decade earlier by Henri Matisse, who at the end of his career realized, in a brilliant reductionist advance, that he could completely reconstruct the basic elements of a snail with only 12 simple blocks of color, cut out of paper (FIG. 1). The purity of color, which characterizes Matisse's last and perhaps greatest period, has been said by the art historian Olivier Berggruen "to induce in the viewer, a feeling of freedom, of liberation from all that is material" (Berggruen, 2003). The colored surfaces capture both the essential form and movement of the snail. As we will show later, this radical reductionist approach has been used by other artists to explore other boundaries of visual art.

The reason that *Aplysia* is so suitable for a reductionist analysis is that it can generate a variety of different behaviors, yet it controls all of its behavior with a very simple nervous system made up only of a relatively few nerve cells. While our brain has 10^{12} nerve cells, *Aplysia* has only 2×10^4 or 20,000. As a result, simple behaviors may involve only about 100 cells. This enormous simplification in numerical complexity makes possible precise identification of individual cells' contributions to the behavior they help define (FIG. 2).

In this simple animal we delineated the simplest possible behavior: the reflex withdrawal of the animal's respiratory organ in response to stimulation of its siphon. This defensive withdrawal is much like the withdrawal of a hand from a hot object. We found, surprisingly, that even this elemental act, mediated by a very small number of nerve cells, is capable of being modified by a variety of different forms of learning (FIG. 3).

We next defined the neural circuit of this behavior in cellular detail (FIG. 4). The reflex involves 24 sensory neurons that connect to six motor neurons both directly and through interneurons (Kandel, 2001).

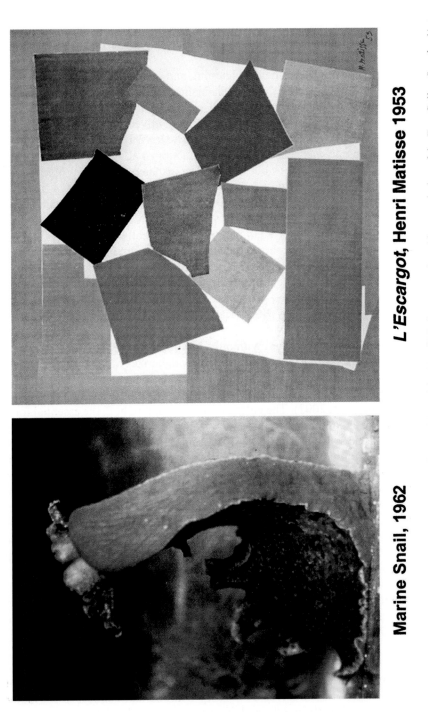

Marine Snail, 1962   *L'Escargot*, Henri Matisse 1953

FIGURE 1. *Left:* Marine snail (*Aplysia*); *right: The Snail* (1953) by Henri Matisse; reproduced by permission of the Tate Galley, London/Art Resource, New York. 2003 succession H. Matisse, Paris. Artists' Rights Society (ARS), New York.

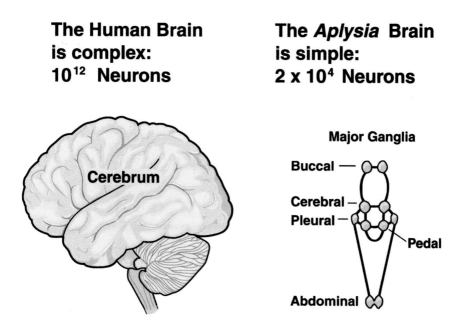

FIGURE 2. Comparison of the human and *Aplysia* brain. The human brain is complex (10^{12} neurons), while the brain of *Aplysia* is simple (2×10^4 neurons).

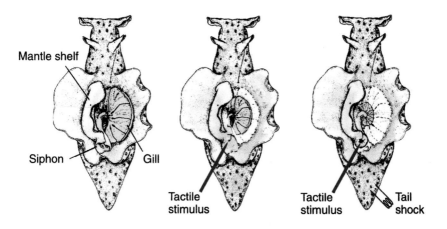

FIGURE 3. Modification of *Aplysia* gill withdrawal reflex by learning.

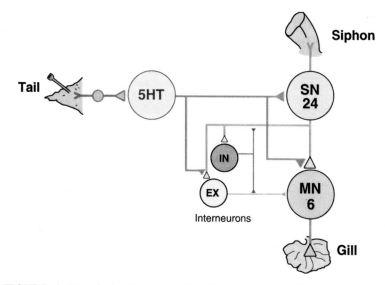

FIGURE 4. Neural circuit of the gill withdrawal reflex. Stimulation of the tail strengthens the circuit's connection through serotonergic modulatory neurons.

In examining the neural circuit, we were struck by a remarkable invariance of behavior. Not only did every animal use the same cells in the reflex circuit, but those cells were interconnected in precisely the same way in every animal we examined. Each sensory cell or interneuron connected to a particular set of target cells and to no others. This invariance has been found for other behaviors and gave us the first insight into a simple example of Kantian *pre-knowledge*. We saw that *built into the brain, under genetic and developmental control, is the very basic architecture of behavior*, in this case the capability for withdrawal.

But this insight raised a deep question in the cell biological study of learning: How can learning occur in such a precisely wired neural circuit? How can one reconcile the invariance of the neural circuit of a behavior with its capability for modification? To address this question, we examined the connections of the neurons that drive the gill withdrawal reflex during actual learning and during various stages of memory storage, and found that the apparent paradox had a rather simple solution. Learning, we found, acts by modulating the *strength* of these precisely interconnected cells (Castellucci et al., 1978; Hawkins et al., 1983). Thus, even though the genetic and developmental program assures that the connections between cells are invariant and correctly specified, it does not specify precisely the absolute strength of the connections. Much as Locke might have predicted, learning plays upon the basic connections of the neural circuit to alter their strength. Moreover, the persistence of this change is the mechanism whereby memory is stored.

Thus, we see here a reconciliation of the Kantian and Lockean points of view in a most elementary and reduced form.

How does learning occur and how is memory maintained in the short term and in the long term? To address this question, we have focused on one form of learning—sensitization—a form of learned fear. If you present an *Aplysia* with a noxious stimulus to the tail it perceives this as a threat and it learns to enhance its reflex response in preparation for escape. Thus the same weak tactile stimulus to the siphon that previously produced only a moderate withdrawal of the gill will now produce a massive withdrawal following a sensitizing stimulus to the tail. Moreover, the memory of the offensive stimulus is a function of training trials. Practice makes perfect even in snails! Following a single tail shock the animal manifests a short-term memory for the event and the reflex is enhanced for a period of minutes. By contrast five or more repeated stimuli will produce a long-term memory that lasts days to weeks. The tail stimuli that produce sensitization strengthen the reflex by activating three sets of modulatory neurons of which the most important is serotonergic. These serotonergic cells act on the sensory neurons, including on their terminals, to enhance the strength of their connections. As is the case with behavior, a single stimulus produces a transient strengthening of these connections

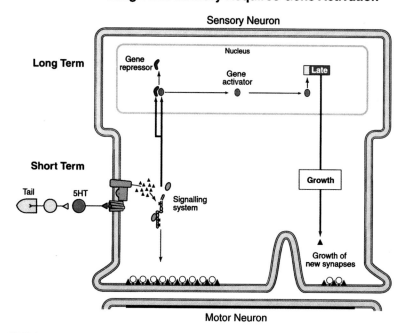

FIGURE 5. Single sensory neuron and its connections. Long-term memory requires gene activation.

lasting minutes. Repeated stimuli produce a persistent strengthening lasting days to weeks.

We can now examine these changes at the molecular level and ask: How is the short-term process set up with one training trial, and how is it converted to the long-term process with five repeated training trials? We illustrate this in FIGURE 5, which is a blow-up of a single sensory neuron and its connections. When a single shock to the tail activates the serotonergic modulatory system, the resulting release of serotonin activates within the sensory neuron an intracellular signaling cascade mediated by the signaling molecule cAMP. cAMP recruits an enzyme, the cAMP-dependent protein kinase (PKA), that acts to strengthen transiently the synaptic connection between the sensory and the motor neuron by enhancing transmitter release from the sensory neuron (FIG. 5). With repeated tail shocks and repeated release of serotonin, the cAMP-dependent protein kinase moves into the nucleus where it removes an inhibitory constraint, cAMP response element binding protein-2 (CREB-2), and activates CREB-1 genes, which lead to the growth of new neuronal connections.

Three features of these results are noteworthy. First, *there are inhibitory constraints on memory.* To switch on the long-term process, not only must one activate memory enhancer genes such as CREB-1, but one must inactivate memory suppressor genes such as CREB-2 (Bartsch et al., 1995, 1998). These inhibitory constraints set a threshold on memory. As a result, not everything one sees and experiences is put into long-term memory (see also Tully et al., 1994; Yin et al., 1994).

Second, once the inhibitory constraint is removed, the switch for long-term memory is triggered and activates a cascade of genes. Thus, repeated exposure through learning gives rise to the *activation of genes* (Dash et al,. 1990; Bartsch et al., 1998). So genes are not simply the determinants of behavior — they are also *servants of the environment.* Genes are responsive to environmental contingencies; they respond to social and environmental influences.

Third, what gives the memory its long-term persistence is that the activation of genes by learning gives rise to the growth of *new synaptic connections* (Bailey and Chen, 1983; Kandel, 2001). So if you remember anything of this essay, it is because you will walk away with a slightly different brain than you had before you started to read it.

This set of mechanisms has proven to be very general. They apply to invertebrate as well as vertebrate, to explicit as well as implicit memory (Squire and Kandel, 2000; Kandel, 2001).

Let us consider the issue of neuronal growth. We ask: How important is growth in determining the functional architecture of the *human* brain? FIGURE 6 depicts the proportional representation of the body's surfaces in the human sensory cortex. Until quite recently it was thought that this representation was fixed. But as a result of the work of Michael Merzenich at UCSF, we now know that this is not so (Merzenich et al., 1988).

FIGURE 6. Somatic-sensory homunculus showing the relative sizes of cortical areas devoted to the skin's surface. Areas of greatest sensitivity are most generously represented in the cortical map.

Merzenich first showed that the cortical maps of an adult monkey are subject to constant modification on the basis of use or activity of the peripheral sensory pathways. Leslie Ungerleider has shown similar modifications in the human map (Ungerleider et al., 2002). Since all of us are brought up in somewhat different environments, are exposed to different combinations of stimuli, and are likely to exercise our motor and perceptual skills in different ways, the architecture of each brain will be modified in a unique way. Every reader of this essay will have a slightly different brain, because they have different life experiences. Even identical twins with identical genes will have different experiences and therefore different brains. This distinctive modification of brain architecture, along with a distinctive genetic makeup, constitutes the biological basis for the expression of individuality.

The degree of modification appears to vary as a function of age (FIG. 7). In one study, Thomas Elbert at the University of Konstanz in Germany and his colleagues imaged the brains of string instrument players and compared them to the brains of non-musicians (Elbert et al., 1995). String players are an interesting group for studies of how experience affects the brain because during performance the second to fifth fingers of the left hand are manipulated individually and are continuously engaged in skillful behavior. In contrast, the fingers of the right hand, which move the bow, do not express as much patterned, differentiated movement. Brain imaging studies of these musicians revealed that their brains were different from the brains of non-musicians. Specifically, the cortical representation of the fingers of the left hand, but not of the right, was larger in the musicians. These results dramatically confirm in humans what animal studies had already revealed in more detail. The representation of body parts in the cortex depends on use. Moreover, these structural changes depend on the particular age of the individual at the time of training. They are more readily achieved in the early years of life. Thus Wolfgang Amadeus Mozart is Mozart not simply because he had the right genes,

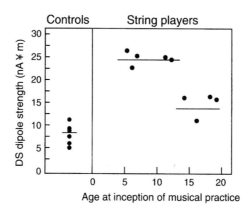

FIGURE 7. Comparison of string players with non-musicians with respect to the size of the cortical representation of the fifth finger of the left hand. Among string players, those who began playing before age 13 have a larger representation than those who began later.

but also because he began practicing his musical skills at a time when his brain was most sensitive to being modified by experience.

This malleability of cortical architecture has profound implications for medicine and for psychoanalytically oriented psychiatry. What can be formed by experience can presumably be undone by experience. We would therefore argue that insofar as psychotherapy works, it does so by creating an environment that permits modification of the brain.

Reductionist approaches of the sort we have outlined here are central to science. Yet there is a concern among certain humanists that a biological reductionist analysis will diminish our fascination with mental activity or will trivialize its deeper issues. We would argue to the contrary that reduction, in this case through cell and molecular biology, in no way denies the richness or complexity of thought. Rather, by focusing on one component of a mental process at a time, reduction can expand our vision, allowing us to perceive previously unanticipated interrelationships between biological and psychological phenomena.

This type of reductionism is not limited to biologists, but is also used implicitly and sometimes explicitly in other humanistic endeavors, such as art. In art, as in science, reductionism does not trivialize our perception—of color, light, and perspective—but allows us to see each of these components in a new way. Indeed artists, particularly modern artists, have intentionally limited the scope and vocabulary of their expression to convey in minimalist form the most essential, even spiritual ideas of their art.

FIGURE 8. *Calais Pier: An English Packet Arriving*, painted in 1803 by J.M.W. Turner; reproduced by permission of the National Gallery, London.

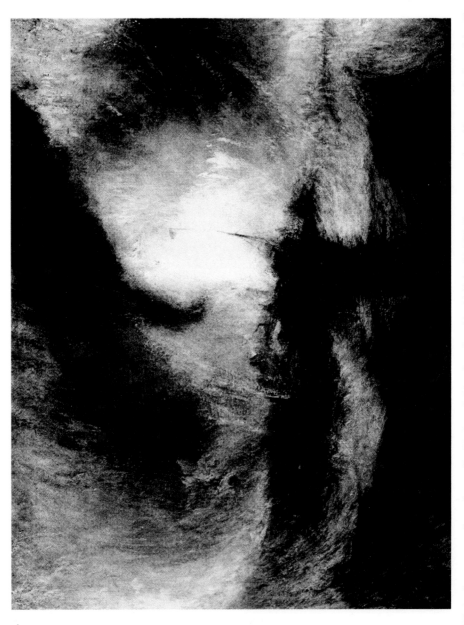

FIGURE 9. *Snowstorm: Steamboat off a Harbour's Mouth*, painted in 1842 by J.M.W. Turner; reproduced by permission of the Clore Collection, Tate Gallery, London/Art Resource, New York.

FIGURE 10. Untitled; painted by Mark Rothko in 1938; © Kate Rothko Prizel and Christopher Rothko/Artists' Rights Society (ARS), New York

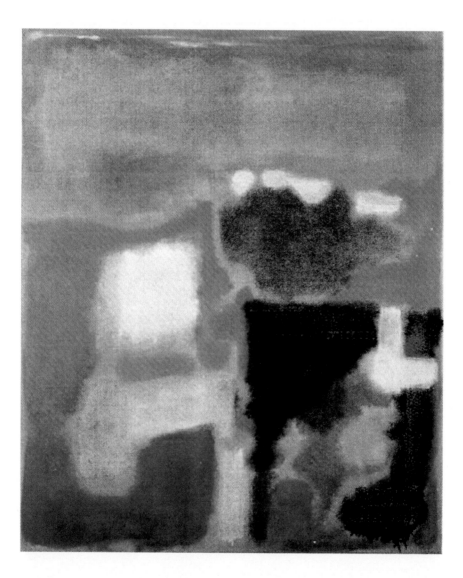

FIGURE 11. No. 1; painted by Mark Rothko in 1948–1949; © Kate Rothko Prizel and Christopher Rothko/Artists' Rights Society(ARS), New York.

FIGURE 12. No. 46; painted by Mark Rothko in 1957; © Kate Rothko Prizel and Christopher Rothko/Artists' Rights Society (ARS), New York.

One artist who uses reductionism primarily of form is J.M.W. Turner. Turner, one of Britain's greatest artists, was a master of seascapes, capable of rendering the effects of nature in a way that is at once epic in scale, yet great in detail. In 1803, early in his career, he painted "Calais Pier." An admirably realistic painting, it depicts several ships on rough seas through dramatic use of light, shadow and perspective, and through careful attention to figurative detail —sails strained by the wind, a white seagull against a dark storm cloud. Waves, clouds, the horizon, boats, sails, and people are all clearly represented (Fig. 8).

Forty years later, in 1842, Turner takes on a similar theme in the painting "Snowstorm," but now he reduces drastically its figurative elements: gone are the clearly delineated clouds, sky, and waves; the ship is merely suggested by the line of its mast. The distinction between sea and sky is so diminished as to be barely perceptible, and yet one senses the upheaving masses of water, the sweep of wind and rain pounding the imagined ship with terrible force. The depiction is remarkably abstract; all is achieved in the absence of clearly defined form. Yet in spite of this reduction the painting conveys overwhelmingly the power and dynamism of the forces of nature (FIG. 9).

An artist who takes this reductionist approach even further is Mark Rothko, a painter whose work is most complex and challenging when it is most apparently simple and reduced. His early work of the 1930s was figurative and fairly unremarkable (Fig. 10). Yet even here, there are premonitions of Rothko's more mature style in the block-like treatment of the figures and in the layering of paint that gives those blocks a surprising luminosity and weightlessness. In places, the forms appear to be lit from within.

As Rothko's work develops he becomes more reductionist, stripping away overt references to recognizable imagery. In FIGURE 11, the colored shapes float and interact with one another to suggest the natural world or even human figures, and yet the *human drama,* which is evident in the painting, now has clearly become detached from the *human form.*

By the 1950s, Rothko has limited the number of forms and colors in his palette even further until he is left with a few colored rectangles stacked on a vertical field of color (FIG. 12). This simplified visual vocabulary and the astounding variety and beauty he creates with it define Rothko's work for the rest of his life. Reductionism was seen by the artist as necessary to expand the possibilities of the work itself. As Rothko said "The familiar identity of things has to be pulverized in order to destroy the finite associations with which our society increasingly enshrouds every aspect of our environment." For Rothko and for many a viewer of Rothko's paintings the stripping away becomes an unveiling of a higher truth.

Within this reduction, Rothko creates a startling sense of space and light on the canvas. Thin layers of paint applied in various degrees of saturation and transparency allow the background to show through intermittently, transforming the top layer into a luminous, translucent veil. There is no perspec-

FIGURE 13. No. 5; painted by Mark Rothko in 1964; © Kate Rothko Prizel and Christopher Rothko/Artists' Rights Society, New York.

tive in any conventional sense, only a suggestion of shallow space that brings the colors forward. In his work we see beautiful examples of how light issues from motionless rectangles.

In the 1960s Rothko takes the reductionist approach to its extreme. His focus shifts from contrasting colors to the *absence* of color—the black canvas (Breslin, 1993). What at first sight appears to be a monochromatic rectangle slowly reveals forms, planes of light delineated by slight shifts in hue or tonality (FIG. 13). These works are more challenging than Rothko's lushly colored canvases, yet they are just as evocative. In spite of the work's radical simplicity, viewers consistently invoke mystical, psychic, religious references to describe Rothko's effects. The culmination of this work is a series of black canvases that form the interior of a space devoted to spiritual reflection—the Rothko Chapel in Houston.

Another artist who deliberately restricts himself to a limited set of tools is Dan Flavin, a Columbia University–trained artist, who focuses not on form or color but on light. His art consists of composing standard fluorescent fix-

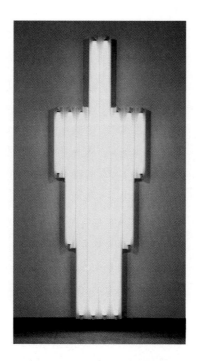

FIGURE 14. *"monument" for V. Tatlin* by Dan Flavin. From the Collection of the Walker Art Center, Minneapolis, gift of the Leo Castelli Gallery; reproduced by permission.© 2003 Estate of Dan Flavin/ Artists' Rights Society (ARS), New York.

tures into glowing installation pieces that form environments of light and color (FIG. 14). Flavin's pieces defy the notion of art as object—his light emanates from the fixtures, pervading the atmosphere and reflecting off walls, floors, and viewer alike. The distinction between viewer and object is no longer clear. The atmosphere created by the work establishes a unique relationship with the viewer: when you are in the presence of one of Flavin's light constructions *you* see *yourself* by its light.

As Flavin and his predecessors illustrate, just as reductionism in science does not take away from the poetry of science, so reductionism in art does not detract from its mystery or beauty but brings emphasis to its components and introduces other complexities. In a larger sense, we hope these arguments suggest that in the decades ahead, the neural science of mind is likely to be in a good position to bridge the sciences concerned with the physical world and the humanities concerned with the nature of human existence.

In the specific instance of art, how do we bring neural science and art together in a meaningful and systematic way? There are two approaches one can envision: one immediate, the other long-term.

The immediate task is concerned with the *cognitive* or *perceptual* analysis of viewing a picture. What is the neural processing for a complex scene? This is a top-down analysis of visual processing such as is evident in the work of Margaret Livingstone (2002) and Semir Zeki (1999).

But the longer-term, more difficult task is concerned with the biology of judgment, taste, aesthetic sensibility. Why is a radically reduced Rothko or a Flavin successful? Does it distill that which is most essential and powerful in art? Why does it suggest to us a sense of spirituality? What are the biological underpinnings of our response to art? These are issues addressed in artistic terms by David Freedberg (1989) and in neurobiological terms by Ramachandran (1999).

At the moment, this second set of questions is a very distant goal, but one that in principle is attainable. In a larger sense, we are here also asking: What is it about art that is so pleasing? So universal? Why is it that no culture has survived without art even though art is not essential for survival? It is not a dietary requirement, yet it clearly satisfies a drive that is essential to human nature. We make a beginning with one suggestion regarding Rothko.

The Rothko is uncluttered. It does not rely on an external framework of knowledge. It is highly ambiguous, as is great poetry, and focuses our attention in a way that is *self-referential*! As a result, we project our own impressions, memories, aspirations and feelings onto the canvas. It is, if you will, like a perfect psychoanalytical transference, or like the repetition of a word or a tone in Buddhist meditation.

Finally, why would we want this bridge between art and science? What would be its benefits, and who would gain from it? It is clear what the gain would be for neural science. From a biological point of view, one of the ultimate challenges is to understand the perceptual processing by the brain of conscious experience and emotion. But it is also conceivable that this bridge might be useful for the artists themselves. A number of artists from Brunelleschi and Masaccio to Richard Serra and Damian Hirst have been interested in science. Much as Leonardo and other Renaissance artists used the revelations of human anatomy to help them depict the human form in a more compelling and accurate manner, so contemporary artists are likely to benefit from insights into brain processes that inform them about the critical features of emotional response. Neurobiology might also provide clues to the nature of creativity itself. Understanding the biology behind artistic insights, inspiration and physical artistry could be valuable to artists seeking to heighten their own creative powers. In the future, as in the past, new insights into the neurobiology of perception and into the even less understood neurobiology of visual reconstruction and of emotional response are likely to influence artists and give rise to new forms of representation.

Indeed some artists who are intrigued by the workings of the mind have attempted this already. One such artist is Jean Magnano-Bollinger, who uses pen and ink drawings on a segment of a scroll to record what is going on in

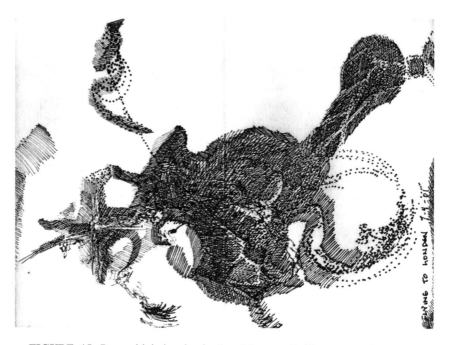

FIGURE 15. Pen and ink drawing by Jean Magnano-Bollinger; reproduced by permission of the artist.

her brain (FIG. 15). She seeks a direct communication between brain and paper, without intervening processes such as feelings, sensations, and aesthetic judgments. She writes:

> The most important note about these scrolls is that they were recorded *with my eyes closed.* They were not *drawn* to create art; they are recordings of my attempts to understand process and movement of mind to focus as deeply as possible on brain.

Here, Magnano-Bollinger relies on introspection to recreate what is going on in her brain. But as we argued at the beginning of this essay, while introspection is helpful and necessary to get one going, by itself it is not sufficient to give one a detailed understanding of the brain and its mental processes. Traditional introspection might now be enhanced by knowing how aspects of the mind work. Thus we would argue that insights into the neurobiology of visual perception and emotional response are not only important goals for the biology of mind; these insights will also prove to be a stimulus for new art forms and new expressions of creativity. While the sciences and the humanities will continue to have their own distinctive concerns, we should, in the decades ahead, come to appreciate more and more how they come to be generated through a common computational device: the human brain.

ACKNOWLEDGMENTS

This paper was originally entitled "Steps Towards a Molecular Biology of Memory: A Parallel Between Radical Reductionism in Science and Art," presented at a symposium entitled Perception, Memory and Art, which formed part of the activities at the inauguration of Lee Bollinger as the 19th president of Columbia University on October 3, 2002. We would like to thank Emma Gibbs for help with an earlier version of this manuscript and Jean Magnano-Bollinger for discussing with us her pen and ink drawing.

REFERENCES

1. BAILEY, C.H. & CHEN, M.C. (1983). Morphological basis of long-term habituation and sensitization in Aplysia. *Science, 220,* 91–93.

2. BARTSCH, D., GHIRARDI, M., SKEHEL, P.A., KARL, K.A., HERDER, S.P., CHEN, M., BAILEY, C.H. & KANDEL, E.R. (1995). *Aplysia* CREB2 represses long-term facilitation: Relief of repression converts transient facilitation into long-term functional and structural change. *Cell, 83,* 979–992.

3. BARTSCH, D., CASADIO, A., KARL, K.A., SERODIO, P. & KANDEL, E.R. (1998). CREB1 encodes a nuclear activator, a repressor, and a cytoplasmic modulator that form a regulatory unit critical for long-term facilitation. *Cell, 95,* 211–223.

4. BERGGRUEN, O. (2003). Resonance and depth in Matisse's paper cut-outs. In O. Berggruen and M. Hollein (Eds.), *Henri Matisse: Drawing with scissors—Masterpieces from the late years. (*pp. 103-127). Munich: Prestel.

5. BRESLIN, JAMES E.B. (1993). *Mark Rothko: A biography.* Chicago: University of Chicago Press.

6. CASTELLUCCI, V.F., CAREW, T.J. & KANDEL, E.R. (1978). Cellular analysis of long-term habituation of the gill-withdrawal reflex in *Aplysia californica. Science, 202,* 1306–1308.

7. DASH, P.K., HOCHNER, B. & KANDEL, E.R. (1990). Injection of cAMP-responsive element into the nucleus of *Aplysia* sensory neurons blocks long-term facilitation. *Nature 345,* 718–721.

8. ELBERT, T., PANTEV, C., WIENBRUCH, C., ROCKSTROH, B. & TAUB, E. (1995). Increased cortical representation of the fingers of the left hand in string players. *Science, 270,* 305–307.

9. FREEDBERG, D. (1989). *The power of images: Studies in the history and theory of response.* Chicago and London: University of Chicago Press.

10. HAWKINS, R.D., ABRAMS, T.W., CAREW. T.J. & KANDEL, E.R. (1983). A cellular mechanism of classical conditioning in *Aplysia*: Activity-dependent amplification of presynaptic facilitation. *Science, 219,* 400–405.

11. KANDEL, E.R. (2001). The molecular biology of memory storage: A dialogue between genes and synapses. *Science, 294,* 1030–1038.
12. LIVINGSTONE, M. (2002). *Vision and art: The biology of seeing.* New York: Harry N. Abrams.
13. MERZENICH, M.M., RECANZONE, E.G., JENKINS, W.M., ALLARD, T.T. & NUDO, R.J. (1988). Cortical representational plasticity. In P. Rakic and W. Singer (Eds.), *Neurobiology of neocortex (*pp. 41–67). New York: Wiley.
14. RAMACHANDRAN, V. S., AND HIRSTEIN, W. (1999). The science of art: A neurological theory of aesthetic experience. *Journal of Consciousness Studies, 6,* 15–51.
15. SNOW, C.P. (1959). *The two cultures and a second look.* Cambridge, MA: Cambridge University Press.
16. SQUIRE, L. & KANDEL, E.R. (2000). *Memory: From mind to molecules.* New York: Scientific American Books.
17. TULLY, T., PREAT, T., BOYNTON, C. & DEL VECCHIO, M. (1994). Genetic dissection of consolidated memory in *Drosophila melanogaster. Cell, 79,* 35–47.
18. UNGERLEIDER, L.G., DOYON, J. & KARNI, A. (2002). Imaging brain plasticity during motor skill learning. *Neurobiology Learning Memory, 78,* 553–564.
19. YIN, J.C.P., WALLACH, J.S., DEL VECCHIO, M., WILDER, E.L., ZHUO, H., QUINN, W.G. & TULLY, T. (1994). Induction of a dominant negative CREB transgene specifically blocks long-term memory in *Drosophila. Cell, 79,* 49–58.
20. ZEKI, S. 1999. Art and the brain. *Journal of Consciousness Studies, 6,* 76–96.

The Self

Clues from the Brain

JOSEPH LeDOUX

Center for Neural Science, New York University,
New York, New York 10003, USA

ABSTRACT: Can we find a way of thinking about the self that is compatible with modern neuroscience? I think we can. First of all, we have to recognize that "the self" is not the same as "the conscious self," since much of who we are as individuals takes place out of conscious awareness. Second, we have to accept that some aspects of the self, especially the unconscious aspects, occur in and can be studied in other species, allowing us to relate these aspects of the self to detailed brain mechanisms. Finally, it also helps to think of the self in terms of memory. Obviously, much of who we are is based on memories learned through personal experience, including both conscious or explicit memories and unconscious or implicit memories. This is particularly important since much progress has been made in relating memory to the cells and synapses of the brain. By viewing the self as a network of memories the effort to relate the self to the brain can build on this progress. Emphasizing memory and experience does not take away from the fact that our genetic history also contributes to who we are. In fact, genes and experience, or nature and nurture, are, in the end, not different things, but different ways of doing the same thing—wiring the synapses of our brain. In many ways, the self is synaptic. This synaptic view of the self is not meant as a challenge to other views, such as spiritual, cultural, or psychological views. It is instead, just a way of understanding how these other aspects of who we are relate, deep down, to the brain.

KEYWORDS: self; personality; consciousness; unconscious; memory; learning; brain; neurons; synapses; genes

Who are you and why are you that way? The answer, of course, lies in your brain. But accepting this statement and understanding it are two different matters. Let's begin with a simple definition of what I mean by "you." I am using "you" to refer to the slightly more formal term, your "self," and more

Address for correspondence: Joseph E. LeDoux, Ph.D., Henry and Lucy Moses Professor of Science, Center for Neural Science, New York University, 4 Washington Place, Room 1108, New York, NY 10003-6621. Voice: 212-9983930 or 3937; fax: 212-995-4704.
  ledoux@cns.nyu.edu

Ann. N.Y. Acad. Sci. 1001: 295–304 (2003). © 2003 New York Academy of Sciences.
doi: 10.1196/annals.1279.017

generally to the even more formal term, "the self." However, this refinement is still not sufficient to allow us to ask questions about the brain because existing concepts about the self are not very compatible with what we know about the workings of the brain.

REFINING THE SELF

In modern psychology the notion of the self is closely tied in with consciousness, in the sense of being self-aware, possessing agency or conscious control, having self-knowledge, a self-concept and self-esteem, of being self-critical, of feeling self-important, and striving towards self-actualization. Carl Rogers, a pioneer self-psychologist, summed up this view early on, defining *the self* as "the organized, consistent conceptual gestalt composed of perceptions of the characteristics of the "I" or "me" (Hall et al., 1998). For Rogers, these perceptions are "available to awareness, though not necessarily in awareness." Many contemporary "self" psychologists have a similar focus on self-consciousness, emphasizing the self as an active agent in the control of mental states and behavior (Markus and Kitayama, 1991; Cantor et al., 1986).

Philosophers, too, have tended to focus on the importance of consciousness in selfhood. Descartes, for example, emphasized the ability to know oneself as the defining feature of human nature. John Locke had also had something like this in mind, arguing that one's self or "personality extends itself beyond present existence to what is past, only by consciousness" (Dennett, 1976). Perhaps the best-known modern philosophical treatment of this topic is an article by Peter Strawson (1959) called "Persons." To define a person, Strawson distinguished between two kinds of statements: those that can obviously be applied to material bodies that exhibit consciousness ("is in pain," "is thinking," "believes in God") and those that can be applied equally to material bodies that are conscious and that are not ("is heavy," "is tall," "is hard"). In the tradition of Descartes, Locke, and Strawson, many contemporary philosophers take the view that personhood is a characteristic of intelligent, conscious creatures, and that consciousness defines personhood. Daniel Dennett, for example, says that, among other things, a being is a person if it is rational, verbal, conscious, in fact, self-conscious."

In spite of the long tradition of emphasis on the self as a conscious entity in philosophy and psychology, there is a growing interest in a broader view of the self (Gallagher, 2000; Sorabji, 2001; Churchland, 2002), one that recognizes the multiplicity of the self (Gallagher, 1996; Rochat, 1995; Bermudez, 1996; Neisser, 1988; Damasio, 1999; James, 1890; Elster, 1985) and emphasizes distinctions between different aspects of the self, especially conscious and non-conscious aspects (Gallagher, 2000). This movement argues that the self that we are aware of and strive to improve, that is, the self that we have a sense of, is too narrow a view of what the self really is. Non-conscious aspects of the self were central to early psychodynamic theories of personality (e.g., Freud, Jung, and the neo-Freudians) and have long been part of the Buddhist attempt to eliminate the conscious self (Kolm, 1985; Epstein, 1995). Particularly relevant is the new wave of research in social psychology showing that many important aspects of human social behavior, including decision making and the way we react to members of racial and ethnic groups, to name but a few examples, are mediated without conscious awareness (Bargh, 1990; Greenwald and Banaji, 1995; Bargh and Chartrand, 1999; Higgins et al., 1985; Wilson et al., 2000; Wilson, 2002).

In sum, it would appear that any discussion of the self and the brain needs to recognize that the self is multifaceted, and especially that it has conscious and unconscious aspects. But so far I've emphasized the self of *people*. Do other creatures also have selves?

THE SELF IN EVOLUTION

Strawson's seminal distinction between things that are conscious (people) and things that are not (rocks and chairs) does not leave much room for other animals. Consciousness, at least the kind of consciousness we have in mind when we talk about our own mental states, was very likely added to the brain recently in evolutionary history. It was layered on top of all the other processes that were already there in our animal ancestors. Nevertheless, although other animals are not conscious in the human sense, they are not simply objects, like rocks or chairs.

Non-human animals are living creatures with nervous systems that represent external events internally and that allow their bodies to interact with and change the material world in ways that rocks and chairs do not. The concept of a conscious person, a conscious self, while useful as a way of evaluating issues related to being human, is less valuable as a general-purpose concept for understanding existence in the context of our animal ancestry—only people can be persons. Because we must pursue many aspects of how the brain works through studies of non-human organisms, we need a conception of who we are that recognizes the evolutionary roots of the human body, including the brain.

Unlike the notion of a person, the notion of the self can be thought of along an evolutionary continuum. While only humans have the unique aspects of the self made possible by the human brain, other animals have the kinds of selves made possible by their brains. To the extent that many of the systems that function non-consciously in the human brain function similarly in the brains of other animals, there is considerable overlap in the non-conscious aspects of the self between species. Obviously, the more similar the brains, the more overlap that will exist. Once we accept that the self of a human can have conscious and non-conscious aspects, it becomes easy to see how other animals can be thought of as having selves, so long as we are careful about which aspects of the self we are ascribing to each species in question.

The existence of a self thus comes with the territory of being an animal. All animals, in other words, have a self, regardless of whether they have the capacity for self-awareness. As a result, the self consists of more than what self-aware organisms are aware of. These differences within organisms (conscious vs. unconscious aspects) and between organisms (creatures with and without consciousness) are not captured by an undifferentiated notion of the self, but can be accounted for by recognizing the self as a multifaceted entity, consisting of both explicit (conscious) and implicit (unconscious) aspects. So how do we get from the multiplicity of self to the brain?

SELF AND MEMORY

Because you are a unique individual, the particular multifaceted aspects of the self that define "you" are present in your brain alone. And in order for you to remain who you are from minute to minute, day to day, and year to year, your brain must somehow retain the essence of who you are over time. In the end, then, the self is essentially a memory, or more accurately, a set of memories.

That one word, "memory," is the key to our ability to begin to understand the self in terms of how the brain works. Few research topics in neuroscience have been more successful than the study of the brain mechanisms of memory, and its companion, learning. If the self is encoded as memories, then we have a way of beginning to understand how the self is established and maintained in the brain.

One of the greatest achievements of modern neuroscience has been the elucidation of the manner in which memories are formed. Across many different kinds of studies, the conclusion has arisen that memories are synaptic in nature (Squire and Kandel, 1999).

Synapses are the tiny spaces, the connections, between neurons, but more important they are the means by which the brain does its business. For example, your memory of a particular experience involves changes in the synaptic connections among the neurons that are engaged by the stimuli that constitute the experience. To the extent that the self is a set of memories, the particular patterns of synaptic connections in an individual's brain and the information encoded by these connections are the keys to who that person is (LeDoux, 2002).

It was once thought that memory was a single capacity mediated by a single brain system. We now know that many different systems in the brain are able to learn during experiences and to store information about different aspects of the experience (Squire and Kandel, 1999; Eichenbaum, 2002; LeDoux, 2002). While some aspects of the experience are stored in a system that makes it possible to consciously recall the experience, most of the learning occurs in systems that function unconsciously or implicitly. When viewed in terms of memory, the multiplicity of the self becomes less mysterious and, in fact, becomes approachable through the brain.

GENES AND THE SELF

But what about genes? Don't they also make important contributions to personality and the self by shaping the brain? Absolutely! All of the capacities that we have as *Homo sapiens,* including our capacities to learn and remember, are made possible by the genetic makeup of our species. What we put in memory systems as individuals is up to experience, but the existence and basic mode of operation of these systems is due to our species' genes. At the same time, we each have a family genetic history that is a variation on the theme of being a human, and a personal set of genes that is a variation on our family's, and these variations also influence who we are.

The most well-articulated view of the role of genes in shaping behavioral and mental characteristics comes from biological trait theories of personality, which propose that one's enduring qualities are due to their genetic background (Hall et al., 1998). Considerable evidence has been amassed to support the view that some traits, such as the extent to which one is extroverted (gregarious) vs. introverted (shy, fearful, withdrawn), are highly influenced by one's genetic history. Nevertheless, genes have been found to account for at most 50% of any particular personality trait (Tellegen et al., 1988). For many traits the influence is far less and often not measurable. Further, life's experiences, in the form of learning and memory, shape how one's genotype gets expressed. There is a relatively new concept known as phenotypic plasticity, which refers to the fact that genes can give rise to different outcomes in different environmental circumstances (Pigliucci, 2001). Even the most ardent proponents of genetic determination of behavior admit that genes and environment interact to shape trait expression. It's a matter of how much, not whether, both are important.

While the fact that both nature and nurture contribute to who we are is widely acknowledged, less recognized is that, from the point of view of how the brain works, nature and nurture are not different things but different ways of doing the same thing: wiring synapses (LeDoux, 2002). That is, both genes and experiences have their effects on our minds and behavioral reactions by shaping the way synapses are formed. Moreover, in many ways, the genetic influence on personality can also be thought of as memory—a memory encoded across generations and species rather than one encoded by individual experience. From this perspective, synapses are the key to both genetic and learned influences on who we are. Without genes, we would have to relearn all the lessons achieved in evolutionary history by our species. Without learning and memory, personality would be an empty, impoverished expression of our genetic constitution. Learning allows us to transcend our genes.

SYNAPTIC SICKNESS

Given the fact that our self is encoded in the synaptic connections of systems that function consciously and unconsciously, will we know what a person is when we figure out how these systems function? Actually, no. Figuring out the synaptic mechanisms underlying each mental process is going to be quite a challenge. But we need to go beyond the mere explanation of how each process works in isolation. We need to understand how the many processes interact, and how the particular interactions that take place inside each of our brains gives rise to and maintains who we are. We are not our perceptions, memories, or emotions, but all of these combined, and synaptic interactions between the systems that underlie the individual processes are key to keeping the self integrated in space (across brain systems) and time (across the days of our lives).

Synaptic connections are also at the core of mental disorders. These were long thought of simply as chemical imbalances. While chemical changes are important, the key is not the chemicals themselves, but the circuits in which the chemicals act. For example, many drugs used to treat mental disorders alter the monoamine class of chemicals in the brain (serotonin, dopamine, norepinphrine, acetylcholine). These chemicals are widely distributed throughout the brain, but the alterations that affect a particular problem, such as schizophrenia, are now believed to be restricted to a select subset of the many circuits that use the chemical in question. And, as with normal brain function, pathological brain function can arise because synaptic circuits are altered by genetic or experiential factors, or some combination of the two.

Treatment of mental illness, whether by drugs or psychotherapy, is a process of changing one's mental states and behaviors. Changing of mental states and behaviors is, by definition, a process of learning and memory, which, as we've seen, are ultimately due to synaptic plasticity. Breakthroughs in understanding the synaptic basis of learning and memory are also relevant to the learning and memory that occurs during therapy. What is particularly interesting is the fact that many of the drugs used to treat depression and anxiety disorders affect the same molecular cascades that have been implicated in learning and memory. This suggests that drug therapy may be a way of placing the brain in a state conducive to learning, enabling patients to alter their behavior in adaptive ways.

THE PARADOX OF PARALLEL PLASTICITY

The fact that so many systems in the brain are able to change during experience raises the paradox of parallel plasticity. How is it that a coherent personality, a self, is ever established and maintained if different systems are able to learn and store information on their own? Why, in other words, don't the systems come to function completely independent of one another?

One reason is that although the different systems have different functions (e.g., seeing and hearing; controlling movements; detecting and responding to food, mates, and predators; and planning and decision making), they experience the same world. Thus, they process information differently, but about the same life events.

Another reason is that brain systems do not exist in synaptic isolation. They are connected with other systems. And just as the inputs to a particular system can serve as the basis for learning and memory within a system, connections between systems can serve as the basis for coordinated learning between systems.

A third factor is the existence of convergence zones, regions that are able to integrate the activity of other regions. Convergence zones tend to engage in so-called higher-order processing since they integrate the activities of areas devoted to specific functions. Not only can convergence areas put information together, but they can also send commands back to the lower-order systems, allowing some high-level control of and coordination across the specific systems.

Then there is the widespread nature of certain chemical systems, such as monoamines. When these systems are turned on, they release their chemicals throughout the brain. These chemicals can then serve as signals that facilitate learning across widely distributed systems.

Monoamine systems tend to be activated during significant experiences, such as ones that are emotionally charged. Indeed, activation of emotion systems is one of the key ways that parallel plasticity is coordinated and the self glued together. The brain has a number of emotion systems, including networks involved in the identification of sexual partners and food sources, as well as detecting and defending against danger. When one of these systems is active, the others tend to be inhibited. For example, other things being equal, animals will hang out in areas where they feel safe. So when it comes time to search for food, their fear of certain places, like wide open spaces, or places where they've encountered a predator before, might have to be overcome, if that's where food is likely to be found. The hungrier the animal is, the more it will tolerate fear and anxiety and take risks to get food. Similarly, both eating and sexual arousal are decreased by activation of systems involved in fear and stress. But once aroused, sexual desire can override many other brain systems—people risk all sorts of adverse consequences for a sexual fling. Not only does the arousal of an emotional state bring many of the brain's cognitive resources to bear on that state, it also shuts down other emotion systems. As a result, during intense emotional arousal, learning is coordinated across systems in a very specific manner, ensuring that the learning that occurs is relevant to the current emotional situation.

Obviously, the broader the range of emotions that a child expresses, the broader will be the emotional range of the self that develops. This is why childhood abuse is so devastating. If a significant proportion of the early emotional experiences one has are due to activation of the fear system rather than positive systems, then the characteristic personality that begins to build up from the parallel learning processes coordinated by the emotional state is one drenched in negativity and hopelessness rather than in affection and optimism.

The wide influence of emotional arousal results in many brain systems being activated at the same time, many more than if you are engaged in quiet cognitive activity. And because more brain systems are typically active during emotional than purely cognitive states, and the intensity of arousal is greater, the opportunity for coordinated learning across brain systems is greater during emotional states. By coordinating parallel synaptic plasticity throughout the brain, emotional states promote the development and unification of the self.

Most of us, most of the time, are able to piece together synaptic connections that hold our self together. Sometimes, though, thoughts, emotions, and motivations come uncoupled. When this happens, the self is likely to begin to disintegrate, and mental health to deteriorate. When thoughts are radically dissociated from emotions and motivations, as in schizophrenia, personality can in fact change drastically. When emotions run wild, as in anxiety disorders or depression, you are no longer the person you once were. And when motivations are captured by drug addiction, the emotional and intellectual aspects of life suffer.

SYNAPTIC AND OTHER SELVES

Given the importance of synaptic transmission in brain function, it's practically a truism to say that the self is synaptic. What else could it be? But not everyone will be happy with this conclusion. Many people will surely counter that the self is psychological, social, or spiritual, rather than neural, in nature. My assertion that synapses are the basis your personality does not assume that your personality is determined by synapses; rather, it's the other way around. Synapses are simply the brain's way of receiving, storing, and retrieving our personalities, as determined by all the psychological, cultural, and other factors, including genetic ones. So as we begin to understand ourselves in neural, especially synaptic, terms, we don't sacrifice the other ways of understanding existence. We don't, in other words, have to think more narrowly about people once we find out that synapses are important. A neural understanding of human nature in fact broadens rather than constricts our sense of who we are (LeDoux, 2002).

REFERENCES

BARGH, J.A. (1990). Auto-motives: Preconscious determinants of social interaction. In T. Higgins & R.M. Sorrentino (Eds.), *Handbook of motivation and cognition* (pp. 93–130). New York: Guilford.

BARGH, J.A. & CHARTRAND, T.L. (1999). The unbearable automaticity of being. *American Psychologist, 54,* 462–479.

BAUMEISTER, R.F. (1998). The *Self.* In D.T. Gilbert, S.T. Fiske & G. Lindzey (Eds.), *The handbook of social psychology.* Boston: McGraw-Hill.

BERMUDEZ, J. (1996). The moral significance of birth. *Ethics, 106,* 378–403.

CANTOR, N., H. MARKUS, P. NIEDENTHAL & P. NURIUS. (1986). On motivation and the self concept. In R.M. Sorrentino & E.T. Higgins (Eds.), *Handbook of motivation and cognition: Foundations of social behavior.* New York: Guilford.

CHURCHLAND, P.S. (2002). Self-representation in nervous systems. *Science 296,* 308–310 [reprinted in this volume. ED.].

DAMASIO, A.R. (1999). *The feeling of what happens: Body and emotion in the making of consciousness.* New York: Harcourt Brace.

DENNETT, D. (1976). On the conditions of personhood. In A.O. Rorty (Ed.), *The identities of persons.* Berkeley: University of California Press.

EICHENBAUM, H. (2002). *The cognitive neuroscience of memory.* New York: Oxford University Press.

ELSTER, J. (1985). *The multiple self.* New York: Cambridge University Press.

EPSTEIN, M. (1995). *Thoughts without a thinker: Psychotherapy from a Buddhist perspective.* New York: Basic Books.

GALLAGHER, S. (1996). The moral significance of primitive self-consciousness. *Ethics, 107,* 129–140.

GALLAGHER, S. (2000). Philosophical conceptions of the self: Implications for cognitive science. *Trends in Cognitive Science, 4,* 14–21.

GREENWALD, A.G. & BANAJI, M.R. (1995). Implicit social cognition: Attitudes, self-esteem, and stereotypes. *Psychology Review, 102,* 4–27.

HALL, C.S., LINDZEY, G. & CAMPBELL, J.B. (1998). *Theories of personality.* New York: John Wiley & Sons.

HIGGINS, E.T., KLEIN, R. & STRAUMAN, T. (1985). Self concept discrepancy theory: A psychological model for distinguishing among different aspects of depression and anxiety. *Social Cognition, 3,* 51–76.

JAMES, W. (1890). *Principles of psychology.* New York: Holt.

KOLM, S.-C., (1985). The Buddhist theory of "no-self." In J. Elster (Ed.), *The multiple self.* New York: Cambridge University Press.

LeDoux, J.E. (2002). *Synaptic self—How our brains become who we are.* New York: Viking.

MARKUS, H.R. & KITAYAMA, S. (1991). Culture and the self: Implications for cognition, emotion, and motivation. *Psychology Review, 98,* 224–253.

NEISSER, U. (1988). Five kinds of self knowledge. *Philosophical Psychology, 1,* 35–39.

PIGLIUCCI, M. (2001). *Phenotypic plasticity: Beyond nature and nurture.* Baltimore: Johns Hopkins University Press.

ROCHAT, P. (1995). *The self in infancy: Theory research.* New York: Elsevier.

SORABJI, P. (2001). *Emotion and peace of mind: From Stoic agitation to Christian temptation.* New York: Cambridge University Press.

SQUIRE, L.R. & KANDEL, E.R. (1999). *Memory: From mind to molecules.* New York: Scientific American Library.

STRAWSON, P. (1959). Persons. In *Individuals: An essay in descriptive metaphysics.* London: Methuen.

TELLEGEN, A., LYKKEN, D.T., BOUCHARD, T.J., JR., WILCOX, K.J., SEGAL, N.L. & RICH, S, (1988), Personality similarity in twins reared apart and together. *Journal of Personality and Social Psychology,* 54, 1031–1039.

WILSON, T.D. (2002.) Strangers to ourselves: Self-insight and the adaptive unconscious. Cambridge, MA: Harvard University Press.

Conclusions: From Self-Knowledge to a Science of the Self

JACEK DEBIEC AND JOSEPH E. LeDOUX

Center for Neural Science, New York University,
New York, New York 10003, USA

ABSTRACT: Traditional accounts of the self represented in religion, literature, philosophy, and other branches of the humanities, are grounded in
the subject's personal introspections. This source of knowledge has had a
profound impact on terminology, concepts, and theories of the self. By
contrast, the scientific method, which uses observational and experimental
data, is aimed at objective analyses. The scientific approach to the self, by
its very nature, is distinct from the approach in the humanities, and therefore reveals a different view of the self, and sparks new debate about what
the self really is. Moreover, different scientific disciplines, spanning the
natural and social sciences, investigate different levels of organization,
leading to a multifaceted scientific picture of the self. This conference and
volume explored areas where some of the different approaches to the self
overlap and will, it is hoped, promote the establishment of a richer, more
coherent image of what the self is.

KEYWORDS: self; science; humanities; brain; first-person account; third-
person account

For Karl Popper, an eminent twentieth-century philosopher who explored relations between the sciences and the humanities, the defining properties of
human nature included the notions of self, and of other selves, the use of ar-
tificial tools, the invention of language, and the awareness of death.[1] Popper's view is relevant to questions about the origins of humanity, as well as
to our current condition and our future—the problem of individuality and
social identity, the use of technology and communication, and the awareness
of natural constrictions are timeless in their relevance to human society. Indeed, many of the ideas central to discussions about the essence of 'the self,"
or in the case of humans, "the person," were formulated long ago and persist

Address for correspondence: Dr. Jacek Debiec, Center for Neural Science,New York University, 4 Washington Place, Room 809, New York, NY 10003-6621. Voice: 212-998-3624; fax:
212-995-4704.
jacek@cns.nyu.edu

Ann. N.Y. Acad. Sci. 1001: 305–316 (2003). © 2003 New York Academy of Sciences.
doi: 10.1196/annals.1279.018

today in folk psychology, culture, and philosophy. These ideas provide a substantial theoretical framework for the functioning of public life and institutions. For instance, many religious traditions are built on the concept of an immortal essence (soul) through which the individual survives physical demise, and existing legal systems are grounded in beliefs about agency and control of action by the individual. In a direct or, more often, indirect way, these popular views influence significant aspects of social life. Thus, discussions about the self do not merely reflect what we know about ourselves, but also determine who we are and how we think, feel, and act towards one another.

Few topics have produced as wide a range of opinions as "the self." This volume and its antecedent meeting, "The Self: From Soul to Brain," reflect an attempt to bridge the gap between some of the diverse perspectives, spanning the humanities on one end, and the empirical sciences on the other.

The long tradition of inquiry into human nature represented in the humanities is embedded in the subjective experience of the individual, whereas the sciences, guided by the scientific method, substitute external observation and controlled experimentation for subjective experience. Although this distinction is not always sharp (one's subjective mind experiences objective reality, and personal biases sometimes enter scientific enquiry), there nevertheless exists a fundamental epistemological gap between the sciences and humanities. Discontinuities also occur within each field. In science, for example, particular disciplines investigate different levels of organization—the self, as studied by social scientists, does not necessarily resemble the self discussed by brain scientists. The result is a multifaceted if not confused picture of the self.

In order to advance discussions on the self, it is essential that the points of both disagreement and overlap between the different perspectives be made explicit. However, traditional notions and assumptions are deeply rooted in the culture of each field. This volume and the earlier meeting have, we hope, helped close some of the gaps, especially between the natural and social sciences, and will hopefully facilitate future attempts to understand the self in a more coherent way.

SELF-KNOWLEDGE

The primary source of knowledge about the self has traditionally been individual experience. With the rise of modern science, the context in which questions about human nature were asked dramatically changed. The subjective point of view was replaced with an approach that aimed at objective analysis. The more recent development of the cognitive and brain sciences has paved the way for new insights into the self. We cannot yet predict all of the implications of these new approaches. Still, from the various lines of research presented in this volume, a cluster of issues that characterize crucial aspects of the current debate on the self emerges.

There is nothing more intimate than the sense of oneself. Grounded in an immediate self-awareness and self-consciousness, our self-knowledge emerges from everyday-life experiences and is expressed in a common language. This unique source of knowledge implies both the content and the persistence of who we think we are. However, even if our subjective mind is a primary source of knowledge that we have about our "selves," it is not the only one. We learn much who we are from others. This perspective is usually referred to as the observer's, or the third-person, account. Although the scientific perspective on the self is a variant of the third-person account, it actually goes far beyond ordinary observation. Is this "self" that emerges from scientific studies still the same self you think about when you say "I"?

Proponents of the introspection-based subjective knowledge approach would probably answer "no." As emphasized by the French philosopher, Paul Ricouer: "A critical point, which at first sight appears to be simply linguistic but which in fact goes far beyond this, is that there is no parallelism between the sentences "I grasp with my hands" and "I think with my brain."[2] On the phenomenal level, humans do not have a direct experience of their brains as they do of their hands. The existing discrepancy between the subjective and the objective understanding of the self is characterized both by the source of knowledge and the language in which this knowledge is expressed. Whereas the first-person account of the self usually refers to experiences available to everyone, it seems more familiar, easier to identify with than a third-person account that is being advanced using highly sophisticated technologies, such as scans of brain activity, to name one, and which is expressed in abstract scientific terms. From the point of view of the subjective self, observational and experimental data cannot replace personal experience, and cannot substitute for anything as evident as the "I." Ricouer is right, "my hands" are mine, are a part of "me." How can I refer to myself in terms of brain, which is not "mine," that does not belong to my "self"?

KNOWLEDGE AND SCIENCE

At Ricoeur's level of analysis, it is difficult to disagree with proponents of the "subjective self" concept. Scientific knowledge cannot replace the subjective sense of the self. However, can we narrow our understanding of the self to this level? In our everyday life, the first-person account has to be complemented by the third-person perspective by what we learn about ourselves from others.

The controversy that occurs between the first-person and the scientific accounts of human nature is not an isolated phenomenon. It should be considered as a part of a broader cluster of problems that arose with the progress of science. Direct observations of regularities in a surrounding environment resulted in a creation and development of the prescientific folk physics, which was then replaced by the science of physics. While folk physics is a product of a common sense,[3] physics requires a rich theoretical and experimental apparatus. There are a number of examples showing how, since its beginnings, science has constantly challenged common sense. The laws of nature are often beyond the comprehension of our basic intuitions. For instance, ideas of space, time, and matter initially grasped by common sense underwent profound changes over the centuries. Concepts like "space-time" in general relativity or "field" in quantum mechanics, although initially rooted in the subject's perception of surrounding reality, require far more than common sense in order to be comprehended. Similarly, the elucidations on consciousness and causation of actions presented in this volume by Daniel Wegner[4] and by Daniel Dennett[5] profoundly differ from popular views on free conscious will. The analogy between folk physics and physics on one side, and folk psychology and psychology on the other seems justifiable. The strangeness of a scientific description of the self apparently corresponds with the unfamiliar scientific picture of the universe. Yet the proponents of the "first-person perspective philosophy" may argue that for the perceiving subject the dimension of reality conceptualized by folk physics and physics is basically the same. Both systems describe something referred to as external to the self. However, can we do more on the basis of the first-person perspective than to state the existence of the cleavage between the subjective "I" and the objective world?

Even if science cannot fill this gap, it is very helpful in understanding its nature.

First, however, one major remark about the nature of scientific methodology has to be made more explicit. While the self-knowledge, rooted in the first-person perspective, is grounded in experiences available almost to everyone, scientists, on the contrary, design experiments that are far from everyday-life experiences—for example, they investigate rare cases of brain lesions or study non-human animals. Despite the fact that these examples of the scientific lines of research do not resemble the original context of an existential experience, they provide insights into basic mechanisms that constitute and underlie this experience. Accordingly, subtle experiments of Daniel Wegner and his colleagues elucidate how the mind attributes the authorship of actions to itself.[4] And Gazzaniga and colleagues, studying split-brain patients, show that the neural representation of self-knowledge is distinct from other representations of knowledge.[6] Studying medical conditions that cause memory impairment, Daniel Schacter and his coworkers elucidate the mechanisms and strengths of the self-relevant information.[7] The bias towards the first-person account has deep biological roots.

Science not only explicates how this self-insightful self is constructed and what its natural limitations are, but it also attempts to explain what this self-aware self is for. Thus general evolutionary theory suggests that the conscious self arises as a function of social communication and responsibility for actions. "Conscious will serves as a personal guide to authorship of action—an authorship emotion. The person who feels will for action typically then feels responsibility for that action, and so will also be susceptible to moral emotions such as pride or guilt depending on the actions effects" argues Daniel Wegner.[4] Interestingly, major traditional ethical and moral systems are based on the "first-person perspective" in philosophy.[8] The self is thus the key reference in the process of recognizing the responsibility for actions. The privileged epistemological status of the subjective self comes from the significance of its function in the human organism.

As Antonio Damasio explicates in his article, neural networks representing our bodies in brain tissue generate the unique sense of our unity and continuity over time.[9] This feeling comes to awareness in a process of child development in the second year of life. Michael Lewis's work describes first steps in the emergence of conscious self and its impact on subsequent progress in emotional, cognitive, and social dimensions.[10] Investigation of pathological conditions, such as autism, studied by Francesca Happé, reveals the relation between the development of self-awareness and psychological and social functioning.[11]

HIDDEN SELVES

Although the sense of self is a product of brain activity, the brain itself remains outside of personal experience. Thus the most fundamental mechanisms of the self, such as representational capacities of the brain,[12] are beyond the grasp of the subjective mind. The persuasive character and historical domination of the first-person perspective in the quest for self have deep biological roots. Transcending natural constrictions, science illuminates implicit mechanisms of the self in the brain, as well as offers a glimpse into the emergence of the conscious "I."

Though long viewed as an oxymoron, the notion that much of the self operates implicitly or unconsciously has recently become popular. Though the unconscious has been an important part of psychology since Freud, the new view of the unconscious mind is somewhat different from that promoted by Freud. The cognitive and emotional unconscious, according to LeDoux,[13] are unconscious not because of repression but simply because these functions are not wired into the circuitry of consciousness. This idea also was emphasized in several of the papers, including those of Quinn, Banaji, Wegner, Schacter, and Gazzaniga, Damasio, and Kandel.

The recognition of implicit or unconscious aspects of the self has opened a new perspective. Since many of these unconscious aspects of the self are organized similarly in humans and other creatures, important aspects of human behavior, emotions and personality, aspects of the self, can be elucidated through animal research. Though consciousness, and thus the conscious self, is notoriously difficult to study in animals, new approaches to the self are made possible by the recognition that much of the self operates unconsciously. Hauser argues that other primates at least have key aspects of explicit self awareness. But even creatures who do not have conscious selves have unconscious aspects of the self that are given to humans by our biological heritage. Animal studies thus reveal basic aspects of the self that humans share with other species, such as learning and memory,[14] emotions,[15] and altruistic behaviors,[3] to give only few examples.

Because implicit aspects of the self exist outside of the organizing and integrating aspects of consciousness, they are less subject to and restricted by whatever unifying properties consciousness confers on "the self." The implicit self is thus perhaps best thought of as a collection of "implicit selves." The conscious self, too, can be manifest in different ways (we are sometimes different persons in different situations). An important topic for future work is the extent to which different conscious personalities are reflections of the unconscious activation of implicit brain systems in different situations.

LOST SOULS?

The dichotomy between the subjective and the objective is not the only dualism inherited from the past. Most of the attempts to reconcile the humanities and their accounts of the self with the scientific approach have been traditionally dominated by the "mind-brain" or the "soul-body" problem. Why then is this issue not central to this volume?

Dualistic views on human nature, often associated with Descartes, rarely gain proponents among brain scientists. The late Nobel Laureate, Sir John Eccles, is one of the last neurobiologists, who actively promoted a dualism where mind and brain interact with one another. According to his view, the self-conscious mind exercises a superior interpretative and controlling role upon the neural events.[16] Eccles applied this interactionist idea in order to explicate the assumed unity of conscious experience. He believed that it was impossible to develop a neurobiological theory which could explain how a diversity of brain events come to be synthesized making a unified conscious experience possible. Whereas neuroscientific methodologies used to study consciousness are still insufficient, the proposed unity of conscious experience is also questionable. For instance, phantom limb syndrome studies reveal the incongruence between the somatosensory and visual systems as the somatosensory experience does not match perceived reality.[17] Moreover, as has been demonstrated in this volume[6] and elsewhere,[18] the unitary sense of self-consciousness may be explained in brain terms. At this time, interactionist dualism seems improbable. As Daniel Dennett argues, "today, materialism has swept dualism and its insoluble mysteries of interaction aside, so this is no longer regarded as a convenient, or even tenable, hypothesis."[5]

Yet, ontological dualism should not be identified with interactionism. Actually, interactionism together with psychosomatic parallelism is considered by some to be a degenerate form of the dualism once deliberated.[19] Although ontological dualism is not currently a popular view among natural scientists, it is perhaps premature to declare its twilight. New effort has been recently made in analytical philosophy to explore dualistic accounts of human nature.[20] These new approaches differ in important ways from Cartesian dualism and are often based on the assumption of the irreducible character of the first-person account.

For ancient Greeks, the ontological plane was the ultimate level of explanation in the analysis of reality. Aristotle, for instance, considered any completely developed or finished individual thing to be composed out of two irreducible entities: *matter* and *form*. Such an ultimate entity, also referred to as a "substance," was to exist in and of itself. The question of whether a human being was made out of one or two substances was thus secondary. In Aristotle's eyes, the soul was nothing but a form of the body, a principle or a set of principles, as we would say in our times. Only much later was the concept of the soul specifically used to account for particular mental phenomena. Nancey Murphy in her overview of the history of the "soul" in the Western culture demonstrates that Judeo-Christian philosophy and theology have a potential to complement scientific advancements, as well as to be in a conflict with them.[21]

Studying neural circuits in the brain is still sometimes referred to as "the scientific search for the soul."[22] Does a "soul" make any sense to the study of the brain, other than as a metaphor? Due to historical circumstances, the notion of the "soul" nowadays seems to be confined to religious discourse. It is plausible to conclude that the future of this concept depends on the interaction between religious traditions and the modern, scientific view of the world. For instance, attempts to reconcile some of the traditional Christian views with the "unity of nature" advanced by the natural sciences resulted in different versions of monism, either dual-aspect or emergentist views.[23] Whereas the emergentist account posits that the new properties and processes that emerge at higher levels of organization of nature, though one in substance, cannot be reduced to the level described by physics alone, dual-aspect monism implies that reality is neither mental nor physical, but it is only perceived in two different ways.

Whereas some contemporary theologians, such as representatives of emergentist monism, refuse to postulate the existence of soul,[24] some other religious authors consider the "soul" to be merely "a capacity for a particular realm of experience rather than a nonphysical essence inhabiting the body."[25] While none of the scientific disciplines explicitly refer to the word "soul," the future of this term is not directly related to the advancement of science. It is rather up to philosophy or theology to make sense of this concept in the modern world. Nevertheless, the compatibility with scientific knowledge would be the ultimate test for such views. On the other side, a reliance on a limited field of study, as well as an ignorance of philosophical issues, may lead to quasi-metaphysical explanations, such as "genomic metaphysics," critically viewed by Alex Mauron in this volume.[26]

It is sometimes said that by postulating the mind-body division, and by excluding consciousness from the domain of a scientific study, Descartes permitted the rest of the science to go forward.[27] The spectacular progress in the scientific study of the mind resulted in an overwhelming criticism of "Descartes' error"[28] and thus in an increased interest in ontology among neuroscientists. Will this interest last when such conceptual collisions no longer exist?

POINTS OF CONVERGENCE

To grasp human nature is a primary goal for a variety of disciplines, each of which uses different theoretical backgrounds and methodologies. This diversity of approaches results in a many-sided image of the self and makes bridge-building between particular perspectives both necessary and difficult. One possible solution is to explore specific domains, where different fields of study converge. Such an analysis can provide a more detailed characterization of the common problems, as well as highlight the interpretative limitations of the specialized areas of research. That is, defining and investigating the existing points of convergence promotes establishment of foundations for a more coherent understanding of what a person is.

A good example of an attempt that blends natural and social sciences approaches to the self, and proposed by several of the authors of this volume, is the study of learning and memory. The fundamental role of memory for human individuality has long been recognized. Augustine of Hippo, whose ideas dominated Western philosophy for centuries, wrote in his *Confessions*: "Great is the power of memory, an awe-inspiring mystery.... And this is mind, and this is I myself."[29] Advances in the study of brain development and neural plasticity have shed new light on the old philosophical insights into relations between memory and individuality. This new perspective calls for reexamination of some of the earlier disputes between natural and social sciences. One of these controversies, often referred to, is the nature-nurture problem.

On the basis of cross-cultural research on child rearing, Naomi Quinn elucidated in her article how learning shapes significant features of human personality in the course of development.[30] The process of cultural patterning involves lessons accompanied by emotional arousal. Most of this learning occurs without introspective access, and in adult life results in unconscious or automatic preferences. Mahzarin Banaji and her colleague Thierry Devos give an overview of how these implicit aspects of the self provide scaffolding for social life and culture.[31] Much progress has been recently made in localizing sites of plasticity for emotional learning in the brain,[15] bringing cultural and brain studies closer to each other. Moreover, increasing evidence demonstrates the involvement of genes in the formation and maintenance of memory by neural circuits.[14] Eric Kandel and Sarah Mack discuss ways how questions originally asked in psychology and social sciences could be translated into the language of molecular biology.[32]

Linking learning to genes is a promising new approach that may help to resolve some of the old controversies, including the nature-nurture problem. Instead of antagonizing different perspectives, as noted by Kandel[32] and LeDoux,[13] genes and experiences, at the level of synapses, contribute to shaping one's individual self.

Ancient intuitions about the existence of "animal soul"[21] are thus seen in a new perspective through modern science. Studies of relatively simple organisms, such as the marine snail *Aplysia* (studied by Kandel), as well as of primates, our closest animal relatives (studied by Hauser), may reveal different levels of organization of the self, especially implicit aspects of the self. Research of primates, as Hauser explains, may also help to explicate neural architecture of the explicit self.[3]

Progress in the study of the self leaves us with the promise that new fields will emerge, where the natural and social sciences converge, and that the current mosaic will be replaced by a more coherent picture of the self. Bridges linking disciplines will help to establish theories balancing between conscious and unconscious aspects of the self, as well as to reconcile some of the traditional controversies, such as the nature-nurture problem.

THE "SELF" ITSELF

The title of this volume, *The Self: From Soul to Brain*, depicts a conceptual continuum and to some extent a conceptual transition—ideas previously expressed in terms of soul have been reexamined in terms of brain. Indeed, the "self" seems to have the status of a transitional term only "borrowed" by science. While for Daniel Dennett, "self" is a metaphor, "which appears to reside in a place in a brain,"[5] Patricia Churchland identifies "self" with "a set of representational capacities of the physical brain."[12] According to Joseph LeDoux "self" accounts for the "characteristic ways you think, feel and act," "the essential features of 'you' that make you a unique individual," and is explained by learned and innate synaptic connections between the neurons in the individual's brain.[13] Gazzaniga and colleagues, on the other hand, define "self" as a "representation of what we know about ourselves."[6] Terry

Sejnowski hopes for formalization of the self as a set of mathematical equations.[33]

A variety of views of the self, or of the "selves," thus emerged from the conference. But defining "self" was not the goal. The hope was more that the concept of self be refined rather than defined. The early Hellenic philosopher, Heraclitus, noted, "The soul is undiscovered, though explored forever to a depth beyond report."[34] The subsequent quest for the self has revealed not one but many depths. The ancient Greeks were aware of the limited character of such an endeavor. Science rearranges these limits.

NOTES AND REFERENCES

1. POPPER, K.R. (1998). Comments on the prehistoric discovery of the self and on the mind-body problem in ancient Greek philosophy. In *The world of Parmenides: Essays on the presocratic enlightenment*, pp. 222–250. London: Routledge.
2. RICOUER, P. (2000). In *What makes us think? A neuroscientist and a philosopher argue about ethics, human nature, and the brain*. J.P. Changeux & P. Ricouer (Eds.), p. 16. Princeton, NJ: Princeton University Press.
3. HAUSER, M.D. (2003). Knowing about knowing: Dissociations between perception and action systems over evolution and during development. *Annals of the New York Academy of Sciences, 1001,* 79–103 [this volume].
4. WEGNER D.M. (2003). The mind's self-portrait. *Annals of the New York Academy of Sciences, 1001,* 212–225 [this volume].
5. DENNETT, D.C. (2003). The self as a responding-and responsible-artifact. *Annals of the New York Academy of Sciences, 1001,* 39–50 [this volume].
6. TURK, D.J., HEATHERTON, T.F., MACRAE, C.N., KELLEY, W.M. & GAZZANIGA, M.S. (2003). Out of contact, out of mind: The distributed nature of the self. *Annals of the New York Academy of Sciences, 1001,* 65–78 [this volume].
7. SCHACTER, D.L., CHIAO, J.Y. & MITCHELL, J.P. "Seven sins of memory: implications for self" *Annals of the New York Academy of Sciences, 1001,* 226–239 [this volume].
8. DILMAN, I. (1999). *Free will: A historical and philosophical introduction*. London: Routledge.
9. DAMASIO, A. (2003). Feeling of emotions and the self. *Annals of the New York Academy of Sciences, 1001,* 253–261 [this volume].
10. LEWIS M. (2003). The emergence of consciousness and its role in human development. *Annals of the New York Academy of Sciences, 1001,* 104–133 [this volume].
11. HAPPÉ, F. (2003). Theory of mind and the self. *Annals of the New York Academy of Sciences, 1001,* 134–144 [this volume].
12. CHURCHLAND, P.S. (2003). Self-representation in nervous system. *Annals of the New York Academy of Sciences, 1001,* 31–38 [this volume].
13. LEDOUX, J.E. (2003). The self: clues from the brain. *Annals of the New York Academy of Sciences, 1001,* 295–304 [this volume].

14. KANDEL, E.R. (2001). The molecular biology of memory storage: a dialogue between genes and synapses. *Science, 294,* 1030–1038.
15. LeDOUX, J.E. (1998). *Emotional brain: The mysterious underpinnings of emotional life. New York:* Simon & Schuster.
16. ECCLES, J. (2000). In *The self and its brain.* K. Popper and J.C. Eccles (Eds.), pp. 355–376. London and New York: Routledge.
17. RAMACHANDRAN, V.S. (1999). Phantom limbs, neglect syndromes, repressed memories, and Freudian psychology. *International Review of Neurobiology, 35,* 291–333.
18. For review see CRICK, F. & KOCH, C. (2003). A framework for consciousness. *Nature Neuroscience, 6,* 119–126.
19. See Ref. 2, p.13.
20. CORCORAN, K. (Ed.) (2001). *Soul, body, and survival. Essays on the metaphysics of human person.* Ithaca and London: Cornell University Press.
21. MURPHY, N. (2003). Whatever happened to the soul? Theological perspectives on neuroscience and the self. *Annals of the New York Academy of Sciences, 1001,* 51–64 [this volume].
22. CRICK, F. (1995). *The Astonishing hypothesis: The scientific search for the soul.* New York: Simon & Schuster.
23. For instance, see CLAYTON, P. (1999). Neuroscience, the person, and God: an emergentist account. In *Neuroscience and the person: Scientific perspectives on divine action,* R.J. Russell et al. (Eds.), pp. 181–214. Vatican Observatory Publications—Center for Theology and the Natural Sciences. Vatican City State—Berkeley, California.
24. See Ref. 23, p. 211.
25. BROWN, W.S. (1998). Conclusion: reconciling scientific and biblical portraits of human nature. In *Whatever happened to the soul?,* p. 221. W.S. Brown et al. (Eds.) Minneapolis, MN: Fortress Press.
26. MAURON, A. (2003). Renovating the house of being: genomes, souls and selves. *Annals of the New York Academy of Sciences, 1001,* 240–252 [this volume].
27. CHURCHLAND, P.S. (2002). *Brain–wise: Studies in neurophilosophy,* p. 62. Cambridge MA: The MIT Press.
28. DAMASIO, A. (1994). *Descartes' error: Emotion, reason, and the human brain,* New York: Avon Books.
29. AUGUSTINE, SAINT. *Confessions.* Oxford: Oxford University Press [1991].
30. QUINN, N. (2003). Cultural selves. *Annals of the New York Academy of Sciences, 1001,* 145–176 [this volume].
31. DEVOS, T. & BANAJI, M.R. (2003). Implicit self and identity. *Annals of the New York Academy of Sciences, 1001,* 177–211 [this volume].
32. KANDEL, E.R. & MACK, S. (2003). A parallel between radical reductionism in science and in art. *Annals of the New York Academy of Sciences, 1001,* 272–294 [this volume].
33. SEJNOWSKI, T. (2003). The computational self. *Annals of the New York Academy of Sciences, 1001,* 262–271 [this volume].
34. HERACLITUS. (2001). *Fragments: the Collected Wisdom of Heraclitus,* translated by Brooks Haxton (Trans.), p. 45. New York: Viking.

Index of Contributors